The Historical Research Group of Si

CW00456854

The Historical Research Group of Sittingbourne (HRGS) is a no
up in 2004, by a group of local historians. Its purpose is to promote and help preserve the
history and heritage of our local area. HRGS is spearheading local groups and individuals
who wish to work together to research those named on our local war memorials.

Aims of the project:

To investigate all those commemorated on the Swale war memorials within Sittingbourne
and local parishes, and those who lived or were loved in this area. We are also working with
Faversham and Sheppey researchers.

Please contact us: The Historical Research Group of Sittingbourne would like to know if
you have information, or relatives who died in the First or Second World War who were
local to Sittingbourne and the surrounding areas. Please help us to tell their stories by
contacting HRGS at:

The Heritage Hub, The Forum, Sittingbourne, ME10 3DL

Open Tuesday to Saturday 10am to 4pm.

Email us at research@hrgs.co.uk or visit www.hrgs.co.uk

The story of those who fought or gave their lives during both World Wars can be found via
a Digital Roll of Honour at the above address, please encourage others to pay us a visit, and
help us tell their story. Our research is ongoing. Proceeds from this book will help keep open
our exhibition.

First published in 2023 by Historical Research Group of Sittingbourne
Copyright © 2023 The Historical Research Group of Sittingbourne

The right of Stephen Palmer, a volunteer of HRGS, to be identified as the author of this work has been
asserted in accordance with the Copyright, Designs and Patents Act 1988.
All reasonable efforts have been made to obtain copyright permissions where required. Any omissions
and errors of attribution are unintentional and will, if notified in writing to the publisher, be corrected in
future printings.

ISBN 978-0-9954683-7-5

Printed by Swale Borough Council
Swale House, East Street, Sittingbourne, ME10 3HT

A Soldier's Prayer

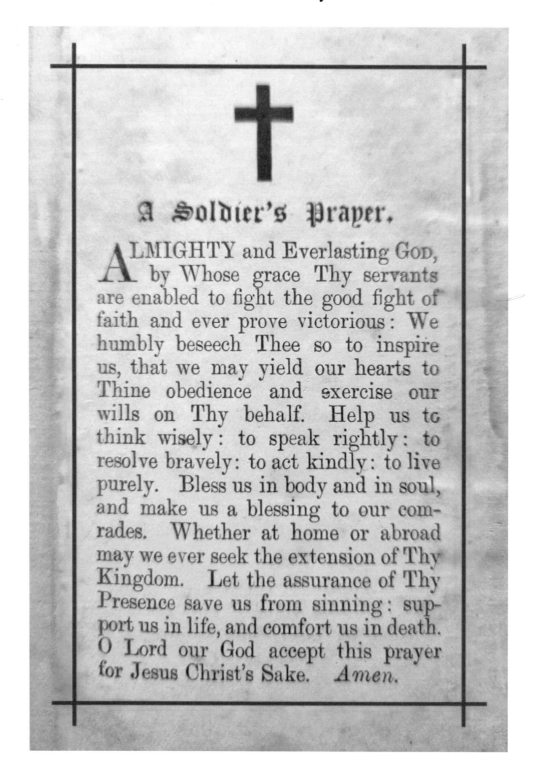

A Soldier's Prayer.

ALMIGHTY and Everlasting God, by Whose grace Thy servants are enabled to fight the good fight of faith and ever prove victorious: We humbly beseech Thee so to inspire us, that we may yield our hearts to Thine obedience and exercise our wills on Thy behalf. Help us to think wisely: to speak rightly: to resolve bravely: to act kindly: to live purely. Bless us in body and in soul, and make us a blessing to our comrades. Whether at home or abroad may we ever seek the extension of Thy Kingdom. Let the assurance of Thy Presence save us from sinning: support us in life, and comfort us in death. O Lord our God accept this prayer for Jesus Christ's Sake. *Amen.*

The Bible Society during the First World War distributed more than nine million Bibles, to the British Armed Forces, and Prisoners of War on all sides.

Printed on the inside front cover was A Soldier's Prayer, which has been replicated above. The Bible was issued to service personnel with their uniform, boots, and helmet. The Bible measured 14cm x 9cm (5.5 inches x 3.5 inches) and so fitted the pocket of the individual.

There are several accounts of the Bible saving a soldier's life, by stopping a bullet. It also appeared to provide solace in the last moments of a soldier's life, as some were found with the Bible alongside them.

Acknowledgments

Edited and proof read by Richard Emmett VR, Theresa Emmett, Janet Halligan, Enya Williams, Patricia Robinson PhD, Don Harris, Jacky Harris, Myles Brown, John Weeks OBE, Lynda Briggs, Sue Burford, Vanessa Kelsey-Jansen, Carole Chapman and Alarni Cherrison.

With input from the many volunteers from the Historical Research Group of Sittingbourne who completed the initial research as part of The War Memorials Project which commenced in 2012.

My thanks also go to the forums and projects whose volunteers and members share their knowledge and information, of which there are too many to mention. The primary ones used in the compilation of this book are:

Remembering the Fallen - ww1cemeteries.com

Great War Forum - www.greatwarforum.org

Sussex History Forum - sussexhistoryforum.co.uk

The War Graves Photographic Project - twgpp.org

Sittingbourne Remembers - pigstrough.co.uk/ww1

New Zealand War Graves Project - www.nzwargraves.org.nz

The Long, Long Trail - www.longlongtrail.co.uk

Some photographs have been included through a Creative Commons Licence and include a CC reference of the appropriate licence. Information on the licences is available at creativecommons.org.

100 Years of Sittingbourne's Living Memorial

The History of the Avenue of Remembrance and Stories of the First World War Men which it Commemorates

by Stephen Palmer

The Soldier

If I should die, think only this of me:
That there's some corner of a foreign field
That is forever England. There shall be
In that rich earth a richer dust concealed;
A dust whom England bore, shaped, made aware,
Gave, once, her flowers to love, her ways to roam,
A body of England's, breathing English air,
Washed by the rivers, blest by the suns of home.

And think, this heart, all evil shed away,
A pulse in the eternal mind, no less
Gives somewhere back the thoughts by England given;
Her sights and sounds; dreams happy as her day;
And laughter, learnt of friends; and gentleness,
In hearts at peace, under an English heaven.

Published in January 1915, The Soldier was written by Rupert Brooke (1887-1915), who was a published poet before the war. He joined the navy at its outbreak. On his way to Gallipoli he died of blood poisoning, probably from a mosquito bite, on a French hospital ship in Skyros, Greece.

Contents

Foreword

by

Deputy Lieutenant of Kent Paul Auston DL

Honorary President – Historical Research Group of Sittingbourne

As President of the Historical Research Group of Sittingbourne, I am particularly delighted to have been asked to write a few words to introduce this book.

The launch of this book coincides with the centenary of the inauguration of the Avenue of Remembrance in Sittingbourne. The Avenue's 'Living Memorial' is now unique across the United Kingdom and the Commonwealth, as it is the only one which remains alongside a main thoroughfare.

The book represents the culmination of the many hours of extraordinary effort and research which has been carried out over eleven years, by members and volunteers of the Historical Research Group of Sittingbourne; as well as other local groups and individuals who provided their research. It is though, testament to the dedication of the author, Stephen Palmer, who saw it as a labour of love to bring together all that research, with that of his own, to compile this book. It tells the unique story of how and when the Avenue came about; and the life stories of all those men who are commemorated along its kerb line. Those individual stories inform the reader about the social history at the time, along with information about their experiences during World War One.

This book is a tribute to those whose names can be seen along the length of Sittingbourne's 'Living Memorial' who perished during World War One. More information on their stories and others from across the borough, may be found in the Heritage Hub and on the website of the Historical Research Group of Sittingbourne – www.hrgs.co.uk.

November 2023

The Avenue's History

Introduction

For 100 years the Avenue of Remembrance in the Kentish town of Sittingbourne, with its lines of trees and memorial tablets, has stood in silent tribute to commemorate 182 local men who gave their lives in the First World War. This book explains how this 'living memorial' was created and the stories behind each of the men that it commemorates.

The Avenue is actually two roads, laid out in a 'T' format. They run east-west from Bell Road to Albany Road (formerly Albany Street) and north-south from Borden Grammar School to Albany Park (formerly Sittingbourne Recreation Ground) and the Cemetery.

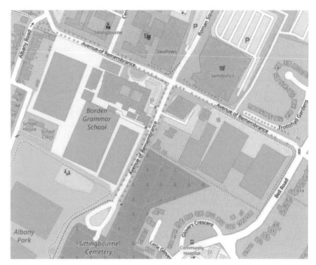

The north-south section is primarily planted with copper beech trees, which were originally planted in 1923, although some have been replaced due to disease. The memorial tablets there are mounted on concrete plinths set into the kerbing.

The east-west section is primarily planted with hornbeams, with the memorial tablets mounted on a metal grid set around the base of each tree. Replacement trees are either beeches or field maples, Acer campestre 'Elsrijk'.

A supermarket development in the 1990s removed 13 trees, which were replaced by a single tree on the corner of the Avenue of Remembrance and Central Avenue. To commemorate the 13 men whose trees were removed a memorial tablet was installed at the base of the tree.

At the time of print a number of trees and tablets are missing, awaiting replacement. This situation is covered later in the book (see page 22).

Development

Initially, the Avenue was intended as a section of a bypass to the town's High Street. It was in fact the bringing together of two separate projects undertaken in the early 1920s by Sittingbourne Urban District Council, which resulted in the road being named the Avenue of Remembrance.

These two projects were the extension to the town's cemetery (shown in blue on the map) and a by-pass to the busy High Street (shown in green on the map).

Discussions on both were made during council meetings, regularly reported in the East Kent Gazette. The council met in the boardroom of Sittingbourne Town Hall, which was located in the High Street.

The council at this time was run by Councillors J R Millen (Chairman), L J Goodhew (Vice-Chairman), H Payne, R A Hadaway, E F Handcock, F Filmer, W E Jarrett, M de L Easton, H E Berry, Mrs French, and Mrs T W Jarrett, together with Mr G H Potter (Clerk), Mr W L Grant (Surveyor), Dr H C Mends Gibson (Medical Officer), and Mr J Varley (Inspector of Nuisances).

The first mention of the two projects, which eventually led to the Avenue of Remembrance, came in a report in March 1921.

At the time of the First World War, Sittingbourne and Milton were two separate towns, with their own council and Town Hall. The boundary between them crossed many of the streets running to the south of West Street and London Road. At number 75 William Street, the boundary ran through the house, with the front bedroom being in Milton and the back bedroom in Sittingbourne. Both Ufton Lane School and St Mary's Church, Park Road, were in Milton.

The two councils amalgamated in April 1930 to become Sittingbourne and Milton Council.

Cemetery Extension

For a number of years, it had been clear that there was not enough space left in Sittingbourne Cemetery. By 1921 the situation had become acute, with only 110 spaces remaining. It was suggested that the cemetery be enlarged by acquiring three acres of orchard to the south of the cemetery. This land belonged to George Hambrook Dean JP, who was a prominent fruit and livestock farmer and had a jam factory in Bell Road. He was also a partner in the brickmaking company of Smeed, Dean and Co Ltd.

At the council meeting a fortnight later it was reported that the orchard was not available as Messrs G H Dean and Co Ltd required it for the extension of the Whitehall Preserve Works.

The council meeting held on 7th June 1921 received a report from the Burial Grounds Committee, which stated that a meeting had been held with agents of Mr Charles Twopeny (pictured right) to buy Little Glovers, which was to the north of the cemetery. Mr Twopeny (1868-1923) was from a prominent family who owned Woodstock Manor. He was a Justice of the Peace and Mayor of Hythe (1919 to 1922) and the son of Tunstall's Vicar, the Reverend Edward Twopeny. He had also served as a Lieutenant in the 3rd and 4th Battalions of The Buffs in the late 1800s.

The land was seven acres and included a cottage and some buildings. The offer for the land was £3,250 (equal to £131,000 today[1]) Although there were concerns about burials being within 100 yards of dwelling houses, the recommendation to buy the land was approved.

At the meeting held on 6th December, the council received an update on the purchase of the Little Glovers land. The landowner Mr Charles Dynley Twopeny was offered £300 (£12,000 today) per acre for seven acres, but he refused since Kent Education Council had paid £400 (£16,000 today) per acre for land proposed for a new school. Councillor Jarrett said it was a vicious circle since Mr Twopeny knew the price of the adjoining land. Therefore, they did not expect the owner to accept a lower price, even though they knew it was an exorbitant price.

The councillors discussed increasing internment rates to cover the land costs and it was suggested they could sell the frontage for building purposes. Afterwards, the council agreed to arrange an interview with the owner's agents.

---

[1] Bank of England. *Inflation Calculator.* bankofengland.co.uk.

At the meeting held on 14th February 1922, the council was informed that agents for Mr Twopeny, Messrs Brown and Son, had offered 3¼ acres for £1,300 (£60,700 today) and the whole site for £3,000 (£140,146 today) instead of £3,250. The 14th March meeting had agreed to pay a tenant compensation, who had wanted the council to buy his property, subject to a valuer's assessment. At the April meeting the council were told that the tenant's compensation was set at £28 3s 0d (£1,308 today). They agreed that once the cost of the extension was known then the burial charges would be reviewed. Councillor Handcock said that £400 had been paid from the poor rate to keep the cemetery.

On 18th May 1922, the St Michael's Parish Church Vestry Meeting discussed the cemetery extension and the need to complete formalities. They were informed the costs were £1,300 for the land, £700 to layout the cemetery, £28 tenant compensation, £10 for the valuer and £60 for legal fees, resulting in a total of £2,098 (£98,009 today). The meeting approved the extension.

An inquiry was held by the Ministry of Health on 20th September 1922, at which the council sought permission to borrow money and purchase the ground for the burial extension. The inquiry was informed the burial ground had 9,550 burials and was becoming overcrowded. The cemetery had opened in 1860, with St Michael's Churchyard closing in 1861, then the cemetery was increased from five acres to seven acres in 1875. The land for the extension was chalk and not subject to flooding.

Sittingbourne Cemetery and Chapel

The inquiry queried the land's high price and the clerk explained that this was driven by the price Kent Education Council paid for adjoining land. The inquiry asked whether alternatives had been looked for elsewhere and the clerk said they had exhausted other options. They also discussed the 1921 census population figure for Sittingbourne, which was recorded at 9,339. At the meeting on 26th September the council was told that the Ministry of Health had completed a site visit and was in favour of the scheme.

Work on the cemetery extension was carried out during 1923, which included a new entrance, with a road to it from the new bypass. At the council meeting held on 23rd October 1923, tenders were reviewed for the cemetery entrance pillars and gates. The contract for the pillars was awarded to F & W Millen, Monumental and General Masons at the cost of £49 10s (£2,289 today), which was £25 less than two other submitted tenders. The contract for the gates was awarded to East Kent Ironworks Company (Mr Green) for £23 10s, £16 cheaper than the next cheapest tender.

At the meeting the following week the council discussed the placement of new trees and shrubs for the cemetery. The contract had been awarded to Clark and Sons of Dover, and it was agreed that Mr Clark should meet with Mr Kemsley, the groundsman at the cemetery, to decide where the new trees and shrubs should be planted. Councillor Thorne then suggested that a tree should be planted to remember each man named on the war memorial. This meant that more trees would be needed than the 150 originally planned. Another suggestion, made by Councillor Millen, was that some of the trees planned for the cemetery should be planted along the new road leading to it to form an avenue. It was decided to have a special meeting on Friday 26th October, at which Mr Clark and Mr Kemsley would be present.

The 6th November 1924 meeting received a report on the site visit by Mr Clark and Mr Kemsley and their recommendations were: (1) copper beech trees on the new road leading to the cemetery; (2) lime trees on the new bypass road from Bell Road to Albany Road; (3) assorted trees on the north and east sides of cemetery; and (4) the layout of the trees to be presented by Mr Clark.

The detailed specifications were reviewed, and Councillor Thorn said there were enough for each of the 182 names on the Cenotaph with some left over. The total cost would be £116 (£5,418 today). The meeting approved and accepted the costs and recommendations.

The Cenotaph was originally inscribed with 181 names, which were published in the East Kent Gazette on 28th May 1921 at the reporting of the unveiling. No records were identified which record how the names to be inscribed were collated or identified.

At the meeting of 18th November 1924, they were advised that the Home Secretary had approved the plans to consecrate the cemetery extension and the next step was to make arrangements with the Dean and Chapter at Canterbury Cathedral.

On 13th July 1926 the burial extension was consecrated by Edward Parry, Bishop Suffragan of Dover, in the presence of a large congregation. The consecration was preceded by a procession from St Michael's Church, which included local parish vicars.

The Southern Bypass

The council meeting held on 1st October 1921 saw the first mention of the new road to bypass the High Street, which was to become the main part of the Avenue of Remembrance. Previous meetings had discussed a new road on the north side of the High Street, running from Shortlands Road to Crescent Street. This proposal was greatly criticised and an alternative scheme on the south side of the High Street from Albany Road (which joined Park Road) to Snips Hill was suggested. The Chairman said that he was inclined to think that the south side was preferable to that to the north.

It was felt that this was a good time for a new road, as it would provide work for the unemployed, which was a serious problem especially at that time of the year. Councillor Handcock thought they should make inquiries as to what grant might be obtained for the work, and the Chairman suggested that this matter be deferred until further information was obtained about the Government's proposal for grants and this was agreed to.

The Unemployment Grants Committee was set up in 1920 to assist local authorities in carrying out approved public works schemes.[2] There was also an Unemployment Relief Works Act aimed to provide

2 Public Records: Records of the Unemployment Grants Committee. The National Archives (UK), Kew, England.

employment by facilitating the acquisition of land for works of public utility.[3] At that time, unemployment in Sittingbourne was 334 men, 69 women, 28 boys and 22 girls.

At the 7th November 1921 council meeting, the Chairman, Clerk and Surveyor reported that on the 3rd they had met with Colonel C H Breasey, of the Roads Department of the Ministry of Transport. They had discussed the suitability of constructing a bypass to provide employment, the dealing with the various interests in land and property on the proposed route and funding. They were informed the Unemployment (Relief Works) Act 1920 did not cover the affected buildings and gardens along the route and that the Council would need to negotiate their purchase. The Council were advised to consider larger schemes with arterial roads under Housing and Town Planning. The Council though could apply for funds from the Unemployment (Relief Works) Act 1920 if they could be recognised as a distressed area, or if unemployment was to significantly increase.

The proposed new south side road was discussed, and the clerk agreed to ask Kent Education Council if they would gift the meadow land by Albany Road from the Masonic Hall to the market meadows. The additional land was owned by Mr Francis Austen Bensted (pictured right), who had already agreed to gift his land to the council. Councillor Handcock suggested the owners of the land from Chilton Avenue to Snips Hill be approached, and they agreed to take this approach.

Mr Bensted, a former trooper in the Royal East Kent Mounted Rifles, was a respected and prominent figure in Kent's agricultural circles. He was a farmer and acknowledged leader in stock breeding and management, judging at several shows. He later became a governor of the new Borden Grammar School and was a Vicar's Warden at Sittingbourne's Holy Trinity Church.

The new year started with a site meeting at Albany Road on 6th January 1922 which was reported on in the newspaper on 21st January. The site meeting discussed the route from the south-west corner of the meadow in Albany Road, to the north-west corner of the meadow in Bell Road, then down Bell Road and up Chilton Avenue terminating in a straight line to the south-west corner of the site of the Council School at Snips Hill. The route passed over land owned by Kent Education Council, Mr Bensted, Mr Twopeny, and trustees of the late Mr R Chapman.

The surveyor said the road was 1,000 yards in length and the chairman said this was a very useful road and a plan should be sent to the landowners. Councillor Goodhew noted that the route would open up a large area of building land. The clerk said that sending the plans to the owners may give them the desire to give up the land. The proposal of sending out a plan to landowners was agreed by the council.

The April 1922 local elections saw the introduction of Councillor T G Thorne to the council.

The first council meeting held in July 1922 reviewed the costs of the new road, which was planned in three sections. The total cost was £5,952 (£278,049 today), with the section that would become the Avenue costed at £706 (£32,980 today) and it was agreed this would be the first section to be built. The council agreed to adopt the scheme and seek a grant from the Unemployment Grants Committee.

The 26th September 1922 meeting was told that the Minister of Labour had responded to the application of a grant for the new road. The Minister stated that the volume of unemployment was not such to justify him issuing a certificate of grant, however if the council considered the volume would increase, they could resubmit their application.

At the 13th February 1923 meeting the then Surveyor, Mr Grant, announced he was retiring. The council thanked him for his services and offered him a position of Consulting Engineer, which Mr Grant

[3] Unemployment (Relief Works) Act 1920. Your World of Legal Intelligence. vlex.co.uk.

accepted. The council had approached Milton Regis Council to have a joint surveyor, but they did not see any advantage in doing so. A new Surveyor, Mr Lashmar, was introduced at the council meeting of 6th March.

Later in the month, the Highways Committee was approached by the building company of Messrs E Bishop and Sons to exchange a strip of land that abutted their premises in the south-west corner of Albany Road, opening up the junction. After a site visit the council agreed.

At the meeting held on 24th April 1923, the council were told that the Unemployment Grant Committee had now approved a grant towards the new road. The meeting gave credit to the clerk and Major Charles Wheler MP for their efforts in obtaining the grant. Councillor Handcock also acknowledged that without the help of Mr Bensted and the Kent Education Committee they would not have had the land.

The surveyor stated that 75% of the men who would work on the new road should be ex-servicemen and from Sittingbourne. A discussion started on the definition of an ex-serviceman and if this included the South African War (1899-1902), Chitral War (1895), and even the Soudan War (1885), as some of the men who had fought in those wars were unemployed. Councillor Spice said that he had been conscripted in the Great War to serve at home in the railway service, and could not leave to join the army and if he had been discharged after the Great War and unemployed then he should be as much entitled as those who were called ex-service. After further talk it was agreed that the surveyor knew the feelings of the council and that there was no hard and fast rule, but consideration should be given to unemployed Great War service men.

At the first meeting in May, it was reported that on 30th April 1923 work was started on the new road between Albany Road and Bell Road and the extension road to the cemetery. There were 41 men employed and Councillor Cowper asked if over 75% of the workforce were ex-servicemen, to which the Surveyor replied that they were. A month later the workforce has increased to 60 men.

Avenue Completion

> **"AVENUE OF REMEMBRANCE."**
>
> With regard to the planting of trees in the Burial Ground extension and the new roads on the south side of High-Street, Councillors Cowper and Thorne reported that, with the Surveyor, they visited the nurseries of Messrs. G. and A. Clarke, Limited, Dover, on the 14th instant, and they recommended : (1) That an amended scheme for lay-out of the Burial Ground Extension, as now submitted, be adopted : (2) That an "Avenue of Remembrance" be made in the new roads bearing that or a similar suitable name, and consisting of 183 trees ; and (3) That laburnum trees be planted between the copper beech trees, along the part provided for a path to the road leading to the Burial Ground.
>
> Messrs. G. and A. Clarke, Ltd., submitted details of the cost, and were prepared to supply and deliver the whole of the trees and shrubs for the sum of £118.
>
> Councillor Thorne explained the scheme, and under motion of Councillor Filmer, seconded by Councillor Handcock, the recommendations were approved, the name of the new roads being agreed to as "Avenue of Remembrance."

History was made at the council meeting of 20th November 1923, which was reported in the East Kent Gazette (reproduced on the left) with the sub-heading "Avenue of Remembrance."

The council had been updated about a meeting held between the Surveyor, Councillor Cowper, and Councillor Thorne, at which they (1) agreed the cemetery extension layout; (2) recommended that an "Avenue of Remembrance" be made or a similar name and consisting of 183 trees.

After Councillor Thorne had explained the schemes, Councillor Filmer proposed the motion, which Councillor Handcock seconded, that the recommendations be accepted and approved. This motion was passed by the council with the name of the new roads agreed as the "Avenue of Remembrance".

The Surveyor reported at the next meeting, on 4th December 1923, that the planting of the trees had commenced, and a fortnight later stated that good progress was made on the planting on both roads.

There was no report in the paper about any grand opening of the new road, and in February 1924 there were still requests for the service rank of some of the men to be sent to the council so that they could be inscribed on their plaques. However, it is clear that the Avenue was being put to good use by the summer of 1924, when it was used for the start of Sittingbourne's Carnival.

The East Kent Gazette edition of 27th December 1924 reported that 162 name tablets had been fixed to the trees, with each tablet bearing the man's rank and name. There were 19 left to fix and information on the ranks was being requested.

Over a year later at the 23rd February 1926 meeting, the council discussed the fact that the tablets were not uniform, with some only inscribed with the soldier's name whilst others included "In Memory of". The suggestion of new tablets with identical wording was put forward and the outcome was to wait until the trees had grown some more. It was also suggested that a nameplate be erected with a statement explaining why the trees were planted.

The 27th July 1926 meeting discussed the provision of a nameplate for the Avenue itself and it was agreed to obtain quotes. The Highways Committee had suggested a second sign to read "The Trees in this Avenue were planted and named in remembrance of fallen residents."

The 24th August 1926 meeting approved a £25 (£1,256 today) quote from Messrs Nicholls and Clarke to supply a bronze plate with raised lettering reading "Avenue of Remembrance. The trees in this avenue were planted and named in remembrance of Sittingbourne men who fell in the Great War."

The nameplate was in place by December 1926 as it is installed in the wall of Lloyd's Club House (see page 16) on the corner of the Avenue junction to the cemetery.

At the first council meeting in 1930 on 7th January, the surveyor reported that the memorial stones and tablets had been fixed to 181 trees. Councillor Jarrett said, "the council should congratulate the surveyor, Mr M W Lashmar, for the excellent way he had carried out the wishes of the council and that the tablets now form a most complete and unique war memorial which would always keep in the minds of all those who used the roads, the sacrifice those men made for their country."

The start of 1930 also saw the completion of footways, and kerbing was installed.

The late 1920s and early 1930 saw the first developments on the Avenue with the construction of two iconic buildings and residential houses. In the mid-1960s, a new civic centre was constructed which was the first impact on the Avenue, then thirty years later the construction of a new supermarket had a profound impact. These developmental changes are covered over the following pages.

Trotts Hall Gardens

The first development on the Avenue was the construction of 32 houses on the corner with Bell Road. The council meeting on 31st May 1927 approved the houses at a cost of £13,022, and it was to be constructed by Blackwell and Meyer, based in Erith, Kent. It was noted that local companies supplied higher quotes of at least £1,900.

The name of the development stemmed from the houses being adjacent to the 18th century *Trotts Hall*, the council approved the name *Trotts Hall Gardens*.

The building of all the houses was completed by the Christmas of 1928 and sold at the price of £515 per house.

In 1974 the hall was dismantled, brick by brick, and rebuilt in the nearby village of Milstead, and still stands today.

Lloyd's Club House

The East Kent Gazette edition of 11th December 1926 announced the opening of the NEW CLUB HOUSE FOR PAPER MILL EMPLOYEES. The building was paid for by Messrs Frank and Harry Lloyd, built for the social recreation of the employees of Sittingbourne and Kemsley Paper Mills.

The building was designed by the same architects as Kemsley Mill, Messrs W L and T F W Grant, MC, FRIBA of Sittingbourne, and London. The club house stands on the junction of the Avenue, which leads to the cemetery. The construction of the building started in August 1925 and took 15 months to complete. The club house was renamed as The Appleyard in 2018, to appeal to all the local residents.

On 4th April 1927, the Club House was visited by Her Royal Highness Princess Helena Victoria of Schleswig-Holstein, the granddaughter of Queen Victoria. The Princess had earlier in the day visited the newly established Kemsley Village and Kemsley Mill.

Borden Grammar School

On 11th October 1929, the new Borden Grammar School opened, on the opposite corner to Lloyd's Club House. This superseded the school in College Road, Sittingbourne. The new school was opened by Lord Harris and the headmaster Mr William Murdock MA, BSc (1870-1951). The headmaster was appointed in 1906 at the old school, and remained until he retired in 1936.

The Avenue shortly after completion.

Remembrance Avenue, Sittingbourne

Postcards of the Avenue of Remembrance from the 1920s and 1930s.

At the opening the chairman of the Governors, Rev R E Harding, in his speech included the following:

"The site of the school had been well chosen in that Avenue of Remembrance. They could never forget the happenings of the War, and so there had been dedicated for all time that Avenue of Remembrance and in that Avenue of Remembrance that day they were opening the door of hope."

The building was designed by Major W H Robinson FRIBA Architect of the Kent Education Committee. The 12th October 1929 edition of the East Kent Gazette reported "the finished building is one of the finest Secondary Schools in England." It noted the bricks, manufactured in Newington, were moulded to a special pattern. It was built by Mr. George Browning of Canterbury at a cost of £30,025 (approximately £1.32m today).

Lord Harris, Colonel George Robert Canning Harris, 4th Baron Harris, GCSI, GCIE, CB, TD, ADC (1851-1932) (pictured right) was a prominent member of the Kent community, who lived at Belmont, Throwley.

He was a former politician and former Governor of Bombay. He was active on the cricket scene having played for Kent and England International and was an administrator for the Marylebone Cricket Club.

Residential Houses

Three residential houses were built near the club house. The first, adjoining the east boundary, was built in the late 1920s and named Berwyn. The second on the section leading to the cemetery, was completed by 1932 and is named Sunnested, with its next-door neighbour, Tynan, built in the 1960s.

The Civic Centre

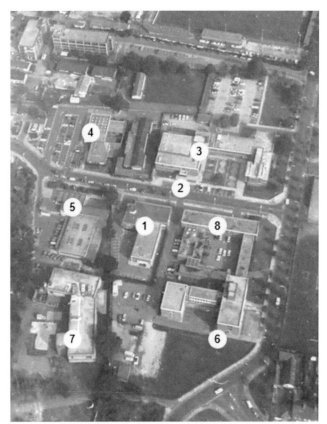

The council had discussed building a new assembly hall, council chamber, and council offices in 1938, but this was put to a stop by the outbreak of the Second World War. The East Kent Gazette edition of 9th July 1948 published the plans for a new Civic Centre, to replace the Town Hall in the High Street, which was not large enough, as the council offices were scattered throughout the town, in Bell Road, King George's Park and atop the Burtons building in the High Street. The centre was to be constructed between the Avenue and the High Street, behind the then Town Hall.

The first building was the Revenue Office (1), now part of the town's Police Station, which opened on 30th June 1954 and included a new road from its car park to the High Street, named Central Avenue (2).

To accommodate access to the Civic Centre (3), Central Avenue was extended in 1962 up to the Avenue of Remembrance. As a result, four trees which stood where the new entrance was built had to be removed. The East Kent Gazette reported on 23rd February 1962 concerns about the trees and the council reported they would replace the trees or provide suitable memorials when the development was completed. However, these trees have never been replaced, nor has a memorial bearing the four names been erected. The trees were in the memory of G W Hadler, K Hadlow, W T Hadlow, and P O Hancock.

Through the 1960s and early 1970s the civic centre saw the construction of a library (4), new council offices (5), a post office (6), automated telephone exchange (7), and police station (8).

The mid-1960s also saw the junction of the Avenue with Albany Road move. This move required the reshaping of the Avenue and removal of a number of the trees. A number of the trees were replaced in the 1980s and late 1990s, so the names of those not replaced were added to a memorial created in the 1990s when a new supermarket was constructed (see page 22). In 1987, the council moved to Swale House in East Street and the council offices were converted into function rooms and a theatre.

Swallows Leisure Centre

The construction of the Swallows Leisure Centre started on 11th January 1988 and was the council's biggest and most expensive project, reported to cost £5.5m.

During the refurbishment and conversion, two more memorial trees were removed bearing the names of G W Hutchens (see page 173) and T Huxted (see page 175). Their trees, to date, have not been replaced.

The leisure centre opened in August 1989 and was visited on 23rd November 1989, by Her Royal Highness Princess Anne.

Sainsbury's Supermarket

The Gazette and Times edition of 7th January 1988 published a notice of the planning application for a supermarket on the site of Sittingbourne Football Club's Bull Ground (pictured right), opposite the Lloyd's Club House. The Co-operative Society was the initial applicant, though at some point during the process this changed to Sainsbury's.

The application would prove to be the most controversial stage in the Avenue's history. The council disclosed that 14 trees would be removed to enable the widening of the Avenue, due to the expected increase in traffic and the implementation of traffic lights at the junction with Bell Road. The East Kent Gazette dated 12th September 1990 reported that the council had "secretly provided niches around the newly moved war memorial for the Avenue tablets that will be removed."

The news of the proposed works resulted in a petition, started by Mrs. June Hammond, and resulted in over 1,700 signatures being handed to Swale Borough Council. This was the start of the Save Our Living Memorial (SOLM) campaign, founded by Mrs. Hammond and Mrs. Ellen Matson.

The campaign received backing from the public, a number of veterans' organisations, conservationists, and Sittingbourne's twin town of Ypres. There was a silent march led by a piper and 1,000 poppies were placed at the base of the trees in November 1990.

The planning documents include a letter dated 29th March 1996, from the Tree Preservation Officer noting that the memorial lime trees were pollarded each year and cost the council 8½ percent of the highway maintenance budget. The Officer added that many trees were decayed, dead, windblown, and leaning over. The Tree Preservation Officer also stated that a more suitable species should be planted.

An agreement was eventually reached between Swale Borough Council, Sainsbury's, and the Royal British Legion to replace all the trees from Bell Road to Albany Road, together with the memorial plaques, which would be mounted on grills set around the base of the trees. The grills and plaques bear the name of Littlewoods who had a foundry in Milton, however, they contracted out the manufacture of the plaques to MJ Allen Fabricators in Ashford. This work was completed in late 1996 and early 1997.

JOIN OUR SILENT PROTEST

We will never forgive if you choose to forget dead

Memorial trees win a reprieve

Lone piper to lead poignant street march

Don't forget war dead

Lost respect for memorial

Poppy protest in fight to save the avenue

Living tribute to war heroes

Victory in sight for avenue protest

Save Our Living Memorial headlines from the East Kent Gazette.

The road widening and development resulted in 13 trees not reinstated. In their place a single tree was planted on the corner of the Avenue of Remembrance and Central Avenue to commemorate the 13 names associated with these lost trees. A commemorative plaque with their names was installed at the base of the tree.

A second plaque was installed on the corner of the entrance to the supermarket car park, reading:

"Avenue of Remembrance, The Great War 1914-1918. Trees planted in 1921 on this site in memory of those from Sittingbourne killed in the Great War have been replaced by Swale Borough Council, J Sainsbury PLC and save our living memorial with the co-operation of the Royal British Legion and local ex-service associations. New trees bear the names on individual tablets. Their names live forever 1996."

The plaque was unveiled on Sunday 9th November 1996 as part of that day's Remembrance Day service.

Present Day

At the time of writing the Avenue has a number of the commemorative plaques either obscured by the growth of the original beech trees or missing. A few of the original beech trees have been replaced or scheduled for replacement, due to disease. These trees are inspected annually by the county council.

In February 2020 Swale Borough Council set up a working party with HRGS, Kent County Council (KCC), Sittingbourne Society, and previous campaigner Ellen Matson, to review the condition of the Avenue, with the aim to make recommendations to the local and county councils. From this the local council held a public consultation in May 2021 that received the highest number of responses for any consultation and showed that the vast majority of the community who responded supported the plan to improve and increase maintenance.

As a result, it was agreed by the working party that the Avenue of Remembrance will be enhanced to mark its centenary. Whilst KCC are responsible for continuing to maintain and care for the trees. A plan was devised and agreed to be delivered in phases; HRGS to supply research details and develop a website to support information on those commemorated along the Avenue; then to produce and erect two information boards on the history of the Avenue; and to erect a plinth to accommodate the two existing plaques plus a plaque listing the names associated with the missing trees.

The above photos, taken in the Avenue leading up to the cemetery, show an original plaque obscured by the growth of one of the original beech trees planted in 1923 and a memorial plaque with a replacement tree, where the original was removed due to disease.

The photos above show one of the replacement hornbeams planted in 1996 as part of the construction of Sainsbury's and the widening of the Avenue, together with the grid with the replacement memorial plaque mounted upon it.

View towards the cemetery from the junction of the two Avenues

View from Central Avenue towards Albany Road

View from junction of two Avenues towards Bell Road

View towards the cemetery from the junction of the two Avenues

24

Avenues of Remembrance Around the World

There are numerous thoroughfares which commemorate those that have fallen or served in conflicts across the ages, though only four others actually named *Avenue of Remembrance*, have been identified around the world according to Google Earth and Google Maps. Only the one in Sittingbourne remains a public thoroughfare.

These avenues are at the following locations:

<u>Charleston, South Carolina, USA</u> – The avenue is located within the grounds of the Citadel, a military college. Their avenue originally consisted of 183 palms dedicated to the men and women that served in World War One. The Avenue is also home to the Citadel War Memorial commemorating 759 alumni killed in all conflicts from 1848 and the *HMS Seraph* memorial, which honours the collaboration between the US and Britain during World War Two through the missions of the *Seraph*, a World War Two British submarine.

<u>Narooma, New South Wales, Australia</u> – Their avenue is a section of the Princes Highway and is dedicated to the men and women who served in World War Two.

<u>Memorial Park, Herne Bay, Kent</u> – An avenue, (pictured below left), created in 1945, leads from a park entrance to the War Memorial, which commemorates World War One, World War Two, Falklands, and Iraqi Wars. The avenue was of Horse Chestnut trees which were felled in 2016 and replaced by hornbeams in 2018-2019 with guards.

<u>Colchester, Essex</u> – This avenue, (pictured below right), was built in 1933 and originally had individual tablets for Boer War and World War One. In 1958 a central memorial was built with the names on larger tablets, due to a large number of the individual tablets being lost. The list of names was expanded to include World War Two and notable citizens.

There are other avenues of trees existing around the world commemorating the First and Second World Wars bearing various names including Memorial Drive, Avenue of Honour, and Remembrance Avenue. The locations of these range from the roadside to cemeteries and parks. The number of trees at these commemorative roads range from a few trees up to several thousand, like on Memorial Drive, Calgary, Canada where over 3,000 trees were planted.

Sittingbourne's dedication to the First World War with a dedicated tree and commemorative plaque to each individual soldier appears to make its Avenue of Remembrance unique in this manner of commemoration.

Credit: Google Street View

Credit: Liz White, Lexden History Group

Research Methods

The research methodology applied for each name on the Avenue of Remembrance utilised some or all of the following datasets and official documents, including both civil and military records, plus on occasions input from families and relations.

The Civil records included censuses, registrations of birth, marriage and death, parish records, and newspapers. These were examined to identify birth, marriage, and death dates and the places of these events, as well as where people lived and newspapers to extract more personal information that was reported.

The Military records included service (both army and navy), medal index cards, registers of soldiers' effects, pension index cards, and war diaries, which provided information about the service of men. This included where they enlisted, the units they served with, as well as where, when and how they died, plus where they served.

Where actual service records exist, they provide information on age, height, as well as, in the naval documents, their eye and hair colour and occupation when joining the navy. Though some of the documents have been lost or subject to destruction since 1918, many still exist.

Where available, Battalion War Diaries provide context to the events at the time of their deaths.

Commonwealth War Graves Commission Database

The Commonwealth War Graves Commission's (CWGC) objective is to commemorate all those that had died while serving with Commonwealth forces during the First and Second World Wars. To achieve this, they had to record the details of all those that fell, including where they were buried or where they had died.

Retired Major-General Sir Fabian Ware was too old to join up for military service during World War One and became commander of a Red Cross mobile unit, arriving in France in September 1914. He became aware that there was no official process to document or mark the location of graves of the fallen, and so created what was to become the Graves Registration Commission. By 1916 this had been changed to the Army Department of Graves Registration and Enquiries.

Fabian, noting that municipal cemeteries were filling up, negotiated with the French and later Belgian governments to purchase land for war cemeteries, which would be granted in perpetuity to Britain for them to maintain. By 1917 various committees believed a formal organisation was needed so with the help of Edward, Prince of Wales, Fabian submitted a memorandum to the Imperial War Conference in 1917. Then on 21st May 1917, through a Royal Charter, the Imperial War Grave Commission (IWGC) was created. In 1960 the commission was renamed to the Commonwealth War Graves Commission (CWGC).

Grave Registration Units were created, and with the Labour Corps, they were to identify and, where required, exhume, and rebury the fallen in the newly created cemeteries. A significant number of casualties were left where they fell and could not be retrieved due to enemy action or were buried close to where they fell in both single graves and clusters. On occasions small cemeteries were created and they were also buried in local churchyards and cemeteries.

The CWGC thus created a database of individuals, which includes some or all the following: service number, initials, forename, surname, service and unit served in, date of death, where buried or commemorated, additional information (normally next of kin) and headstone inscription.

The CWGC database is available online at cwgc.org. At the time of publication, the CWGC are in the process of adding headstone photographs to each individual. All images in this section are produced with the kind permission of the Commonwealth War Graves Commission.

The following research areas include copies of documents, as an example, which relate to a specific Avenue man, Private Charles John Armond (see page 39).

Grave Registration Report Form

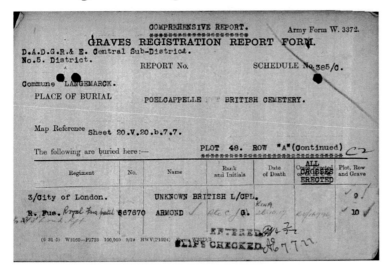

This form records for each cemetery, the cemetery name and location, with a list of those that are buried in that cemetery.

The details include Name, Regiment, Rank, Date of Death, Cross Erected, Plot Number, and some forms include a How Identified column.

The Map Reference on this form 'Sheet 20.V.20.b.7.7.' is a grid reference on typically a Trench Map. These maps can be viewed online at the National Library of Scotland maps.nls.uk.

Headstone Inscription Form

This form records the required inscription for each headstone in the order of Badge Design, Number and Rank, Initials, Name, Honours, Regiment, Date of Death, Age, Religious Emblem, and the family's personal inscription.

Badge Design No. and Layout No.	1st Line.	2nd Line.	3rd Line.	4th Line.		Centre of Stone.	To be stencilled on foot of Headstones below ground level.	
	Number and Rank.	Initials. NAME and Honours.	Regiment.	Date of Death.	Age.	Relig. Emb.	Plot P. Row R. Grave G.	No. of Stone.
(1)	(2)	(3)	(4)	(5)	(6)	(7)	(8)	(9)
1048/1C	67670 PRIVATE	C.J. ARMOND	ROYAL FUSILIERS	26TH OCTOBER 1917	AGE 27	CROSS	48 B 10 48 B 11 TO 48 B 18	954

A second page details what Personal Inscription is to be included on the headstone and includes the name and address of those who provided the inscription, usually a parent or spouse.

Badge Design No. and Layout.	Headstone No.	Line 1.	TEXT. Line 2.	Line 3.	Line 4	No. of Letters in Text.
(1)	(2)	(3)	(4)	(5)	(6)	(7)
1048/1C	954	LOVED AND MISSED	BY ALL AT SITTINGBOURNE (Mr. A. E. Armond, 10, Park Rd., Sittingbourne, Kent.)		9-11	34

Concentration of Graves (Exhumation and Reburials)

These documents record details of individuals who were originally buried in isolated graves or smaller cemeteries, often close to or near the battlefield. After the war, these individuals were moved into designed and purpose-built war cemeteries. This document records: the location of their original burial, normally a Trench Map reference; if there was a cross on the grave; regimental particulars; means of identification; and if any effects were forwarded to base.

11.					LANGEMARCK 337-567.		B/564.	

CONCENTRATION OF GRAVES (Exhumation and Re-burials).

BURIAL RETURN.

Name of Cemetery of Re-burial __POELCAPELLE BRITISH CEMETERY.__ 9.9.20.
Commune:- LANGEMARCK - BELGIUM - Sh.S.E.20. 1/20,000.
V.20.b.7.7.

Plot	Row	Grave	Map Reference where body found	Was Cross on grave?	Regimental particulars	Means of Identification.	Were any effects forwarded to Base?
			Sh.S.E.20. 1/20,000.				
48	B	10	V.15.c.2.2.	No.	667670, ARMOND G. R.Fus.	Disc.	No.
		11	V.15.c.2.2.	"	U.B.S.		"
		12	V.20.b.4.5.	"	U.B.S. Post Officer.	Cap Badge.	"

Civil Records

The use of civil records in the research of the men, provided information about their families and where they lived, when and where they were born, marriages, and occupations. Together with newspaper articles their family story could be told.

Census

The UK Census is held every ten years and records who was living in each household on a specific date. The census records names, relationships, marital status, age, occupations and where individuals were born. The censuses utilised in the research were from 1841 through to 1921, which was the last public census available, as the records are closed for 100 years. The census also captured some military institutions overseas and marine vessels that were in port on the specific date.

Civil Registration

The civil registration records covering birth, marriages and deaths are not open to the public and indexes to the entries are available. The indexes record the names of individuals and the district where the event was registered, which in some cases is different to where the event occurred. To see specific dates of birth, marriage, or death a copy of the certificate of entry is required. For marriages in a church, then a certificate is available in parish records and that is a duplicate of the civil entry. After September 1911, birth indexes provide the maiden name of the child's mother.

East Kent Gazette Newspaper

The East Kent Gazette was the local newspaper for Sittingbourne and Milton Regis and the neighbouring
villages, during the First World War. The newspaper carried reports of those that were wounded or killed, as well as stories from the front. On occasion the reports included a photograph of the individual and additional information on their family and life.

The newspaper published an "In Memoriam" column from families and friends, which often contained additional information about the individual. Many families posted "In Memoriam" for many years after their loved one's death. A few have been included in most of the men's stories to give an insight into how families coped.

Parish Records

The parish records are produced by the church and record baptisms, which on occasion include date of births, marriages, and burials, in that churchyard.

Parish records are in the process of being digitalised for online publishing, though coverage is not complete. More recent records are still held and maintained by the parish church.

Baptism record of Charles Armond's sister Edith

The marriage records include the occupations of those who are being married as well as the name and occupation of their fathers. A copy of the marriage certificate is sent to the General Register Office, for inclusion in the civil registration records.

1939 Register

The 1939 Register was used for the men's family member details and where they were living at the time.

The 1939 Register was taken on 29th September 1939 to produce identity cards and in January 1940, to issue ration books. This is an important resource as the 1931 census for England and Wales was destroyed by fire during the Second World War. Also, due to the war, no census was taken in 1941.

Military Service Records

The Military Service Records include those who served in the Army during the First World War. In the Second World War about 60% of the service records were destroyed when an enemy bomb hit the War Office in 1940. All surviving records and 'burnt records' were digitalised by The National Archives and are also available on subscription genealogy web sites. There is an exception in that service records of the Guards regiments (Coldstream Guards, Grenadier Guards, Irish Guards and Welsh Guards) are only available from the Ministry of Defence.

The service record may contain all or some of the following information: date of attestation, age, birthplace, residence, occupation, physical description and service postings. They occasionally include medical history, misconduct history, correspondence, the names and addresses of relatives, as well as the dates of a marriage and those of the birth of any children.

A number of men commemorated by the Avenue of Remembrance served in the Australian and Canadian military forces. Their records contain similar information to the UK records, and the records for both these countries are available online via:

Canada – Government of Canada > Library and Archives Canada > Personnel Records of the First World War on their website bac-lac.gc.ca.

Australia – National Archives of Australia > First Australian Imperial Force Personnel Dossiers, 1914-1920 on their website naa.gov.au.

Army Battalion War Diaries

During the war, units of the British and Canadian Armies produced daily reports. These recorded the operations they were involved with, together with troop movements; some are more descriptive than others. The content varies by unit and by the officer who wrote the entries. The diaries often include daily losses, with officers named, and occasionally plans and trench maps.

The diaries occasionally mention individuals who were nominated or awarded the Military Medal and other Meritorious Service Medal awards. Sensitive material was redacted before the diaries were handed to The National Archives or the Government of Canada Library and Archives.

The men's stories in this book use extracts from the War Diaries, which are held by The National Archives and are available online nationalarchives.gov.uk, under record set WO-95. Some are held by the regiment or regimental museums.

10 Battalion South Wales Borderers - War Diary WO-95-2562-1.

Army Registers of Soldiers' Effects, 1901-1929

These documents, which are held by The National Army Museum, Chelsea, London, are the War Office Registers that detail the money owed to those that died in service from 1901 to 1929, whilst serving in the British Army. The documents record the soldier's service details including, name, service number, regiment, date of death, and often, the place of death. As the soldier's payments were made to next of kin, their names are included in the order of widow, parent (often the mother), and then siblings. The money was normally made up of two payments; wages and war gratuity, which were calculated based on rank and length of service.

Medal Index Cards

The Award Rolls, and UK, WWI Service Medal, and Award Rolls, 1914-1920 were created by the Army Medal Office. These were created to document a soldier's entitlement, to medals, to be held in a single location.

The award of each medal was based upon fulfilling certain criteria based upon the theatre of war and dates served. The cards typically record the soldier's name, rank, service number, regiment, medals received, theatre of war service, and often include the date posted.

Name.	Corps.	Rank.	Regtl. No.
ARMOND	E. Surr R.	Pte	33996
	3 Lond R.		GS/6464C
	R Fus.		"
Charles J.			

Medal.	Roll.	Page.	Remarks.
VICTORY	TP/104 B21	3040	
BRITISH	----- " ---	------	
STAR			

E 1283

Occasionally additional information can be found. They are held in The National Archives under class WO-372 and on subscription genealogy web sites.

Pension Index Cards

These record where a claim was made for a pension by the soldier or the soldier's next of kin. The card records the rank, name, regiment and date of death of the soldier, and may include cause of death. The name and address of the next of kin is recorded and may include their date of birth. Where a soldier had children, these are named with their date of births.

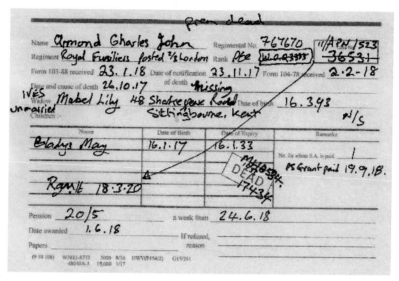

Naval Operations

Information for Naval operations was obtained from the reference sites - wrecksite.eu and uboat.net. Both of these sites include information on the majority of Royal Navy, Royal Naval Air Service, Royal Marines and Merchant Navy vessels, with descriptions of the vessels, crew lists and operations. If the vessel was lost, then they also include geographic location of the site of the wreck.

Royal Navy Registers of Seamen's Services

These records are not as comprehensive as the Army service records and normally consist of a single page. They record the individual's date and place of birth, and occupation. The detail it provides is a listing of the vessels that an individual served on, with dates and their rank whilst serving on that vessel.

In Flanders Fields

In Flanders fields the poppies blow
Between the crosses, row on row,
That mark our place; and in the sky
The larks, still bravely singing, fly
Scarce heard amid the guns below.

We are the Dead. Short days ago
We lived, felt dawn, saw sunset glow,
Loved and were loved, and now we lie
In Flanders fields.

Take up our quarrel with the foe:
To you from failing hands we throw
The torch; be yours to hold it high.
If ye break faith with us who die
We shall not sleep, though poppies grow
In Flanders fields.

Lieutenant-Colonel John McRae (1872 – 1918) was a Canadian surgeon, poet, author, and artist. It is understood he wrote the poem the day after his friend was killed in 1915 and buried on the battlefield with a cross and with wild poppies beginning to bloom around. The poem was published in 1918 after his death from pneumonia.

THEIR STORIES

The names commemorated on the Avenue of Remembrance were taken from the town's War Memorial, formerly in Sittingbourne Recreation Ground, which now stands in Central Avenue. The memorial was moved to the more prominent position and re-dedicated on 2nd September 1990.

Churches, schools, clubs, and employers created their own memorials to their congregation, pupils, members, and employees. As a result, some individuals appear on multiple memorials especially when they moved residences, and attended a different church. In some cases, various family members, grandparents, parents, wives and sweethearts put their names forward, so they appear on various memorials.

This book provides more information on local memorials which commemorate significant numbers of men named on the Avenue of Remembrance (see page 334).

AKHURST, Harry Thomas

G/5015, Private, 2nd Battalion, The Buffs (East Kent Regiment).

Harry was born on 6th June 1875 in Milton, the son of Thomas, a mariner, and Harriet (née Baker). He was the second of five children, named Alfred Bridge (1872-1893), Harriet Fanny, William Baker (1879-1880) and Mabel Phoebe. He also had four older half-siblings, Sarah Ann, Elizabeth, Job Edward, and John, from his father's first marriage to Sarah Ann Bingham, who died in 1870.

Harry was working as a labourer in 1901, living with his parents at 23 Church Street, Milton. He married Emily Isabel Mortlock in Milton in early 1904, and by the 1911 census Emily was boarding at 34 Eastbourne Street, Sittingbourne and working as a laundry maid. They had four children: Donald Harry (born 1905), Harriet Phoebe (born 1908), Charles John Abram (born 1912) and Doris May (born 25th October 1915) after her father had died. According to the East Kent Gazette dated 24th April 1915, the family, at that time, were living at 43 New Road, Milton Regis.

Before he enlisted, Harry had worked as a general labourer in the paper mill.

Harry was involved with The Second Battle of Ypres, which commenced on 22nd April 1915 and ended on 15th May 1915. It was also the scene of the first mass use of poison gas by the Germans.

An extract from the battalion's War Diary[4] for the month before Harry was killed is transcribed here:

WAR DIARY or INTELLIGENCE SUMMARY.		Army Form C. 2118.

<small>Instructions regarding War Diaries and Intelligence Summaries are contained in F.S. Regs., Part II, and the Staff Manual respectively. Title pages will be prepared in manuscript.</small>

<small>(Erase heading not required.)</small>

Date	Summary of Events and Information	Remarks and References to Appendices
14-4-15	*In trenches at ZONNEBEKE. Early morning relieved by 3 ROYAL FUSILIERS and marched to billets at ST JEAN (SINT-JAN).*	
16-4-15	*Took over new line of trenches from ZONNEBEKE RAILWAY to extend. Trenches in very poor state of repair.*	
21-4-15	*Moved to YPRES, as under heavy shelling, moved to open fields dug outs in ST JEAN.*	
22-4-15	*5pm - Sudden sharp outburst of artillery fire...followed by a powerful reek of escaped gas.* *Scattered French troops appeared from nearby fields and apparent something was wrong.* *7pm - Sound of village being hit with machine gun and rifle fire. CANADIANS calmly marched to N&NE passing retreating French.* *Battalion covering N&NE of ST JEAN.*	

[4] War Diary. 2 Battalion Buffs (East Kent Regiment). WO-95-2279-2. December 1914-October 1915. The National Archives (UK), Kew, England.

23-4-15	4am - The battalion marched in early morning broad daylight to WIELTJE, reaching dug-outs and trenches occupied by the CANADIANS. Deployed into open countryside, only to be met by 'furious' machine gun fire and managed to reach a line of trenches a few hundred yards forward.
25-4-15 to 26-4-15	Counter attacking the enemy in ST JULIEN. Trenches shelled all day. Few casualties. Men suffered considerably from the poisonous gas fumes.
27-4-15	Relieved by 4TH BATTALION, RIFLE BRIGADE and moved to VERLOREN -HOEK and made new dug-outs. That evening moved to GRAVENSTAFEL area.
29-4-15	A quiet day much to everyone's surprise.
30-4-15	Draft of 115 men received.
1-5-15 west of Passchendaele	Moved into support trenches near sectors D4 and D5.
2-5-15	Baptism of fire from heavy shelling. Evening - further draft of 34 men joined them.
3-5-15	Early dawn - Germans commenced mortaring and shelling, - relentless and determined manner. By 7.30am many casualties had been reported. Enemy continued fierce shelling with crumps, high explosive shrapnel and whizbangs. Our artillery made little or no reply. State of affairs almost intolerable. 3.30pm - Enemy bombardment of whiz bangs sounded like machine gun fire and their field guns were rapid and incessant. A little later the enemy walked into D5, there being few if any left to resist them... 80 men of "C" Company had occupied the trench and the whole party is now missing and it is believed most of them were killed or wounded." Germans now occupying the woods behind D5, despite a small party of BUFFS and ROYAL FUSILIERS, who were compelled to retire. Germans still pressing forward and taken a portion of the new support trench where it joined D4. Our men and enemy now only a few yards apart, unfortunately enemy are in greater numbers and a far stronger situation. The two last men in D4 are Company Sergeant Major Post and No.7852 Pte Frederick Campbell both of "C" Company. These two bravely kept the enemy off while the others got away, they were able eventually to follow under very heavy fire. Dusk - The battle has quietened down and allowed us to retire further to the woods at POPERINGHE.

Harry lost his life during the events of 3rd May 1915, alongside a further 141 men. Of these 142 losses, all but six are commemorated on the Menin Gate to the missing. Harry was one of the six whose bodies were found. Initially buried in Poelcapelle Cemetery of Honour No 3, also known as the German Cemetery No 3, in Belgium, he was reinterred in Perth Cemetery (China Wall), where his headstone is inscribed "AT REST".

Harry is also remembered on a number of local memorials including Holy Trinity Church, Sittingbourne and Lloyd's Paper Mill Memorials. Harry was remembered by Milton Regis where his name appears on Milton Regis War Memorial, spelt as Ackhurst, St Paul's Church Memorial, spelt as Akehurst and the Old Boys Milton Regis Council Schools Memorial.

His wife, Emily, received his gratuity and pay, and his Victory, British War Medals, and 1915 Star. Emily never remarried, and in 1939 she was living at 22 Eastbourne Street, Sittingbourne. She was listed as the head of the household with her two daughters Harriett and Doris, plus Doris' husband William Marsh, their daughter Maureen and Emily's brother John Mortlock. Emily died, aged 94, in 1975 in Sittingbourne.

ALLEN, Ernest Alfred

166452, Private, 2nd Battalion, Canadian Pioneers.

Ernest was born on 27th May 1896 in Sittingbourne, the third of eight children. His parents were Jesse, a gardener and later a landlord of the Foresters' Arms, in Sittingbourne, and Ann Elizabeth (née Mungham). His siblings were Sidney George Edward, Beatrice Clara, Gladys Gertrude, Dorothy Lilian, Cornelia Blanche (1902-1914), Mabel Constance (1905-1906) and Horace Mawson.

Ernest attended St Michael's School and later was employed by G H Dean at Hempstead Farm. He also played football for Bapchild Football Club. The 1911 census records him, aged 14, as living at 33 Burley Road, Sittingbourne and working as a farm labourer.

In 1913 he emigrated to Toronto, Canada, to join other members of his family. His attestation papers show he was living with his sister Beatrice at 222 Campbell Avenue, Toronto. She had emigrated in 1912, just a year after her marriage to Connor Foley. Another sister, Gladys, emigrated to Toronto in 1914. Ernest recorded his trade as a teamster, which is a horse driver.

Ernest enlisted on 18th October 1915 in Toronto and his Attestation Paper records he stood 5ft 9¼in tall, with brown eyes and dark brown hair. He named his sister Beatrice as his next of kin. He was posted to the 2nd Battalion Canadian Pioneers and on 6th March 1915 the battalion left Halifax, Canada on the Pacific Mail steam ship *Orduna* arriving in Devonport on 14th March 1915. The battalion moved to Hazeley Down Camp, Hampshire, (pictured right) where they trained for almost a year, leaving on 7th March 1916, then on 9th March 1916 he landed at Le Havre, France.

For the next nine months they were involved in working parties, front line duties, and resting. The working parties primarily were involved in reclaiming and repairing trenches and this work was not without incident with several casualties incurred over this period.

Credit: Hampshire and Solent Museums (CCBY-SA 2.0)

The War Diary[5] for December 1917 and January 1918 is transcribed here describing the period leading to Ernest's death:

	WAR DIARY or INTELLIGENCE SUMMARY. (Erase heading not required.)	Army Form C. 2118.
Instructions regarding War Diaries and Intelligence Summaries are contained in F.S. Regs., Part II, and the Staff Manual respectively. Title pages will be prepared in manuscript.		
Date	Summary of Events and Information	Remarks and References to Appendices
1-12-1917	*Battalion stationed at PETIT SERVINS. Polling Booths set up to vote on the Military Service Act.* *Note: The vote was actually a federal election to determine the government, but in effect also determined the outcome of the Military Service Act, which was passed in August 1917, making all male citizens aged between 20 and 45 subject to conscription for the First World War. A change in Prime Minister would veto the Act. The outcome was that Prime Minister Robert Borden retained his position. It was found that eighty percent of front-line soldiers voted in favour of Borden.[6]*	
3-12-17 to 19-12-17	*Moved to the trenches, in the region of LA COULOTTE on the southern edge of LENS. Remained in the trenches and support trenches.*	
19-12-17	*Returned to PETIT SERVINS.*	
20-12-17	*Moved to CAMBLAIN-CHÂTELAIN.*	
25-12-17 to 20-1-1918	*Christmas Day - Battalion was given a holiday. Christmas dinners were served. Time spent on parades, inspections and drills.*	

Ernest first became ill in December 1917, feeling weak and suffering from dizziness, but did not report sick. At the end of January 1918, whilst he was on leave in Sittingbourne, he collapsed and was attended by a doctor from the 3rd Queen's Regiment who were based in the town at the time.

On 7th February 1918 Ernest was admitted to Fort Pitt Garrison Hospital, Chatham and on 10th February 1918, recorded as dangerously ill. A laboratory report dated 21st February records a diagnosis of Lymphatic Leukaemia. Ernest succumbed to his illness at the age of 21 in the hospital on 10th March 1918. His mother had stayed with him for five days before his death.

Ernest's death was announced in the East Kent Gazettes dated 23rd and 30th March 1918, where it reported he had had several narrow escapes, including one where the officer stood beside him was killed. The report also stated Ernest had received flesh wounds during his time in France.

He was buried with full military honours in Sittingbourne Cemetery. with the words "DEATH DIVIDES BUT MEMORY CLINGS" inscribed on his headstone. Ernest is commemorated on Sittingbourne War Memorial and St Michael's Church WW1 Memorial Window.

Ernest's military papers record he was not eligible for the British War or Victory medals, nor the 1914-15 Star.

The East Kent Gazette

SATURDAY, OCTOBER 25, 1919

IN MEMORIAM

ALLEN – In loving memory of my dear son, Ernest Alfred Allen who died at Fort Pitt Hospital, March 10th, 1918.

We oftentimes sit and speak of him,
And old times we recall;
But there is nothing left to answer us,
But his letters and his photo on the wall.

From Mum, Dad, Brothers and Sisters

---

[5] War Diary: 2 Pioneer Battalion. RG9-III-D-3, Volume number: 5010, Microfilm reel number: T-10858, File number: 722. 28 October 1915-31 December 1916. Government of Canada, Library and Archives.

[6] Election of 1917: Military Service Act. Valour Canada. https://valourcanada.ca/military-history-library/election-of-1917-military-service-act/

ANDERSON, Leslie

G/266, Private, 3rd Battalion, The Buffs (East Kent Regiment).

Leslie, and his twin Sydney, were born on 18th August 1895 at 2 Connaught Road, Milton Regis. He also had a younger sister Gladys May and an older brother William Henry who sadly died in infancy. Leslie's parents were William Henry, a brickfield labourer, and Mary Ann (née Martin).

The 1911 census records the family living at 30 Home View, Murston, together with Leslie's grandfather Henry John Anderson. Both Leslie and Sydney recorded their occupations as brickfield labourers.

Leslie joined The Buffs on 22nd August 1914 at Sittingbourne, four days after his 19th birthday, standing 5ft 4in tall.

On the 5th July 1915 he appeared before a medical board, where they found he was *"Unfit for further service."* He was officially discharged on 27th July 1917 as no longer physically fit for war service, as a result of 'Tubercle of the Lung'.

> Military *N'Oxre* | Appeared before a Medical Board. 5·7·15 & was found "Unfit for further service"

Leslie died on 23rd October 1918 at his home, 197 Shortlands Road, of Pulmonary Tuberculosis. He was 23 years old, and his death certificate shows he was a brickfield labourer. Leslie was buried in Sittingbourne Cemetery, together with his parents and brother William Henry, as recorded in the Cemetery Register[7]. William died in 1891, his father died in 1916 and his mother in 1938. No headstone was placed on their grave.

Leslie is also commemorated on St Michael's Church WW1 Memorial Window.

Leslie at the time was not recognised as an official war casualty and therefore his burial place was not marked with a CWGC headstone. This could have been due to either the family not knowing they could apply, or they applied, and their request was denied. As a result, Leslie laid in an unmarked grave.

An appeal was submitted by the author to CWGC in 2021 for Leslie to be considered as a war casualty. The basis was that Leslie's service records stated that his disability started at Christmas 1914 and that Leslie had reported to the army that 'he had always been delicate' and had an attack of pleurisy just before Christmas 1914. A civilian doctor also supported Leslie's case.

On the 5th November 2021 the CWGC accepted the appeal to have Leslie recognised as a WW1 war casualty and added him to the CWGC database. A CWGC headstone was installed on his grave on 20th April 2023 to mark his final resting place. As no family was identified, his headstone does not carry a personal inscription.

7 Sittingbourne Cemetery Register. Burials Office, Swale Borough Council, Sittingbourne.

Leslie's death was announced under the Roll of Honour in the 26th October 1918 edition of the East Kent Gazette, noting he was a twin.

His family posted this touching and emotive "In Memoriam" a year after his death. The family continued to post these for several years on the anniversary of his death.

Leslie's twin brother, Sydney, continued to live in Murston until his death in 1954.

The East Kent Gazette

SATURDAY, OCTOBER 25, 1919

IN MEMORIAM

ANDERSON – In ever loving memory of Leslie Anderson, the beloved twin son of Mrs. Anderson and the late W. H. Anderson, who died October 23rd, 1918, aged 23 years.

Sleep on dear son, your toil is o'er,
We hope to meet on that beautiful shore.
Loved ones were waiting to grasp your hand
As you entered into that heavenly land.

From his sorrowing Mother, Brother and Sister

ARMOND, Charles John

67670, Private, Royal Fusiliers, posted to 2nd/3rd Battalion, London Regiment (Royal Fusiliers).

Charles was born in Sittingbourne in early 1890, the eldest son and second child of Charles John, a labourer, and Eliza Rebecca (née Franklin). His sisters and brothers were Annie Ellen, Albert, Mabel Cooper, Kathleen Esther, and Edith Emma. In 1891 the family was living at 19 New Road, Sittingbourne and by 1901 they had moved to 11 Lloyd Street, Sittingbourne, and his father was working at the local paper mill as a machine minder.

In 1911 Charles, aged 21, and his brother Albert, aged 19, were both dryermen working in Lloyds Paper Mill and lived with their mother and two younger sisters still at 11 Lloyd Street, whilst their father, a gas and steam engine driver, was working away at a paper mill in Eynsford.

In the summer of 1916, Charles married Mabel Lily Wildash, they lived at 48 Shakespeare Road, Sittingbourne and had a daughter, Gladys May, who was born on 16th January 1917.

The East Kent Gazette dated 21st September 1918, reported with the headline ANOTHER PAPER MILL EMPLOYEE KILLED, and that Charles had joined The Buffs on 23rd May 1917, then the East

Surreys before transferring to the Royal Fusiliers. He was posted to France just two months later and reported missing on 26th October 1917. The War Office, on 31st August 1918, officially recorded his death as the day he went missing. Charles was 27 years old.

Charles was originally buried on the battlefield, just 233 metres from his final resting place at Poelcapelle British Cemetery, Belgium. He was identified from his identity disc and his headstone carries the words "LOVED AND MISSED BY ALL AT SITTINGBOURNE." Lying beside Charles is an unknown soldier who had died with him.

Poelcapelle British Cemetery is the final resting place for 7,479 casualties. Sadly 6,230 are 'Known unto God' and the majority of graves date from late 1917, in particular October 1917. The cemetery was created after the Armistice when graves from the battlefield and smaller cemeteries were moved. The cemetery was designed by Charles Holden.

Charles is also remembered on the Sittingbourne War Memorial, Sittingbourne Holy Trinity Church WW1 Memorial and Lloyd's Paper Mill Memorial. He was awarded the British War and Victory Medals. His widow Mabel received his pay and gratuity and remarried in 1920 to Bert Ives, when they moved to Bapchild. Their 19-year-old son, Corporal Walter Eric Ives died in the Second World War on 31st March 1944, in Italy.

In 1939, Charles and Mabel's daughter Gladys, aged 22, was living at home, and working at the Paper Mill as a paper sorter. She married Edward Goodwin, in 1941, and they emigrated to Edmonton, Alberta, Canada in August 1952, where they spent the rest of their lives.

This replica of the East Kent Gazette from October 1919 recalls how his widow mourned his loss.

> ## The East Kent Gazette
> ### SATURDAY, OCTOBER 25, 1919
> ### 'IN MEMORIAM'
> **ARMOND** – In Loving memory of my dear husband, Charles John Armond, who was killed in action in France, October 26th, 1917, aged 27 years.
> God forbade his longer stay,
> God recalled the precious loan;
> God hath taken him away,
> From my bosom to his own.
> Surely what God wills is best,
> Happy in His will I rest.
> From his Wife and little Daughter

ASHBY, David

442, Private, 16th Battalion, Australian Infantry.

David was born on 28th August 1892 at 21 Murston Road, Sittingbourne and was baptised in St Michael's Church on 9th October the same year. He was the son of Alfred, a brick labourer, and Jane (née Kemp) and was one of thirteen children. His siblings were Alice, Eliza Ann, William John, Alfred William, Albert Edward, Henry George, John Raynor, Frederick Isaac, George, Emily Jane, Charles Edward, and Georgina.

In his youth David sang in the St Michael's Mission Room Choir. By 1911 his family had moved to 57 Albion Terrace, Sittingbourne, and David in about 1908 had emigrated to Australia. His parents, together with his brother Henry and five youngest siblings, emigrated to Freemantle, Australia, on the steamship *Demosthenes* on 8th August 1913. By 1926 the remainder of David's siblings had joined them.

David enlisted at Helena Vale, Western Australia on 13th September 1914, giving his father's address as Moora, Western Australia. David's Attestation Paper records that he was 5ft 7in tall and had served in the 4th Battalion, The Buffs (East Kent Regiment), for 13 months, prior to leaving the country.

David sailed from Melbourne on 22nd December 1914 on *HMAT Ceramic* and took part in the Gallipoli landings at the Dardanelles. On 2nd May 1915, he received a gunshot wound to his right side, and then on 4th May, it was discovered he had also been shot in the back and spine, which caused paralysis. He was transferred by hospital train, to No. 2 Australian General Hospital in Ghezireh, Cairo, a main hospital centre for the Gallipoli campaign.

David's parents were informed on 14th May 1915 that he was dangerously ill. A Medical Board, held on 12th June, recommended his discharge as permanently unfit, which was approved five days later.

However, David died at the hospital on 30th June 1915, aged 23. He was buried in Cairo War Memorial Cemetery and his service record shows that a photograph of his grave had been taken. Amongst David's personal effects were his handkerchief, three photos, purse, badges, wallet, testament, prayer book and fountain pen, which were delivered by Messrs Thomas Cook & Son, to his parents. He was awarded the 1914-15 Star, British War Medal, and Victory Medal.

The Midlands Advertiser, Moora, Western Australia, dated 9th July 1915 reported under the headline Roll of Honour – TWO OF THE BEST, the deaths of David and 25-year-old Private Richard Sidney Roberts, who died on 21st June 1915, also at the Dardanelles. They were the first two causalities of WW1 from the district. The article recalled that David was a prominent member of the local British Association and the Moora Football Club.

On 11th July 1915 a memorial service was held at St James Church (pictured left) in Moora. Such was the attendance that the East Kent Gazette of 18th September 1915 mentioned it in their report on the death of David.

The Midlands Advertiser of 16th July 1915 carried a lengthy report of the memorial for David and Richard, opening with the comment:

"Such a gathering of people has rarely, if ever, been equalled at a Church Service in Moora. Before the service began the seating accommodation of the spacious Church was taxed to its utmost, and the aisles of the Church had to be utilised."

On the same day, the Midlands Advertiser also published the Bereavement Notice (reproduced right), from his eldest sister Alice and her husband Frederick Baseden. The Midlands Advertiser included several reports up to 1931, the latest issue available online, of David and Sydney Roberts being remembered on Anzac Day at Remembrance Services, especially as they were the first two killed from Moora.

David is remembered on Sittingbourne War Memorial and Moora War Memorial (below).

© Mike Harris, ww2cemeteries.com

The Midlands Advertiser
PRINTED AT **MOORA**, AND CIRCULATING
July 16, 1915
BEREAVEMENT NOTICE
ASHBY. - In loving memory of David Ashby, who died at Egypt on June 30, 1915, from wounds received at the Dardanelles.

Years may pass away, dear brother,
But your face will never fade,
For we love you just as dearly,
Though you are silent in your grave.
Our life and home are sad and lonely,
While tears they often flow,
Thinking of our dear brother in the cold grave, where he lies.
Loving sister and brother-in-law,
Mrs. and Mr. F. Baseden.

David's younger brother John also enlisted on 7th October 1914 and sailed to Egypt on 27th February 1915. John also took part at Gallipoli, until he was sent to England on 16th September 1915 due to sickness.

After his sickness John spent two months in Egypt and then moved to France, where he served from June 1916 to 21st November 1916. He was wounded in the hip and thigh at Flers, France, and once again he was sent back to England.

John spent five months in hospital and returned home in August 1917.

ASHLEE, Thomas William

9314, Serjeant, 2nd Battalion, South Staffordshire Regiment.

Thomas William was born at Maidstone, in 1893, the son of Thomas Wiles, a farrier and blacksmith, and Mercy Emma (née Wood). Thomas senior also served during the First World War from February 1915 to February 1918, in the Royal Field Artillery, as a shoeing smith in the army.

The family moved around, as censuses showed; Margate in 1891, Maidstone in 1901 and Bromley in 1911. Thomas was the oldest of seven children, and his siblings were Mercy Ellen, Henry Wiles (1896-1901), Edward George (1900-1900), Henry George, Frederick Percy, and Arthur Charles.

Thomas' sister Mercy, enlisted in the Queen Mary's Army Auxiliary Corps on 22nd May 1918. On 11th June 1918 she was posted to Étaples, France. Mercy was discharged on 9th July 1919. At the time of her enlistment Mercy was married to Ernest Cousins, who himself was serving with the Army Service Corps in Egypt, and they had two young children Ernest and Ivy. Ernest served the full duration of the war and survived.

Thomas enlisted in 1914 at Stratford, whilst living in Bromley, and served in France. Whilst on a second period of leave, in February 1916, he married Jean Elizabeth Anderson in Sittingbourne, her hometown. At the time of Thomas' death, Jean was living in Bromley and his parents at 35 Gibson Street, Sittingbourne.

Instructions regarding War Diaries and Intelligence Summaries are contained in F.S. Regs., Part II, and the Staff Manual respectively. Title pages will be prepared in manuscript.	**WAR DIARY** [8] *or* **INTELLIGENCE SUMMARY.** *(Erase heading not required.)*	Army Form C. 2118.
Date	Summary of Events and Information	Remarks and References to Appendices
1-5-1916	*In support at CITÉ CALONNE.*	
4-5-16	*Relieved 1ST KING'S REGIMENT in CALONNE SOUTH.*	
5-5-16	*British fired mortars in preparation for an attack by the KING'S REGIMENT. Two Germans surrendered.*	
6-5-16	*German prisoners wrote letters, which we fired, by bow and arrow, into the German trenches, (though their contents are not recorded.)*	

[8] War Diary: 2 Battalion South Staffordshire. WO-95-1362-2. January 1916-December 1916. The National Archives (UK).

9-5-16	Relieved by 1ST KING'S REGIMENT. Moved to BULLY-GRENAY and tasked with digging facsimile trenches in readiness for practice of proposed raid.
11-5-16	Practised the raid in the morning, afternoon and again at night.
12-5-16	Relieved 1ST KING'S at CALONNE SOUTH.
13-5-16	Heavy German barrage, heavy rain and the lack of trench boards and sump pits, causing the trenches to become very wet and muddy.
14-5-16	Received draft of 77 other ranks, of which about half had seen active service in France or GALLIPOLI. 11pm - ready in the front line, at a point about halfway between GRENAY and LIÉVIN. Telephone lines laid to the 50th and 56TH HOWITZER BATTERIES, Z2 TRENCH MORTAR BATTERY, 6/1 and 6/2 LIGHT MORTAR BATTERIES, HEADQUARTERS. 11.50pm - left the front line, by previously constructed exit points, crawling to the enemy parapets. Machine gun fire laid down and Very Lights (flares) fired to distract the enemy on the flanks of RAILWAY SAP to the left and ROAD SAP to the right. 12.30 orders received to return to the front line, as the element of surprise seemed to have disappeared. Road Sap Party returned, as they had encountered thick wire. RAILWAY SAP Party had not heard the order and managed to enter the enemy trench, to find it unoccupied. After several minutes though they retired, after sending a few bombs further into the trenches.
15-5-1916	There was considerable shelling of our lines probably in retaliation for the Raid and we had several casualties from rifle grenades.

Thomas volunteered for a bombing raid on the German trenches, which was initially refused as his officer deemed him too valuable, but Thomas prevailed and was allowed to go. It was during this action that Thomas lost his life on 15th May 1916, aged 23.

His officer wrote to his family saying:

> "He was a splendid young soldier, always trustworthy and reliable, and had been of the utmost value in the trenches. He added that Thomas himself had killed six or seven Huns before he was shot and killed."

Thomas was originally buried in Cite Calonne Military Cemetery, Liévin, but after the Armistice he was moved to Loos British Cemetery, which consolidated a number of smaller cemeteries and battlefield graves.

He is remembered on the Sittingbourne War Memorial and Sittingbourne Holy Trinity Church WW1 Memorial (see image below).

Credit: ww1cemeteries.com

ASHWOOD, Frank

124218, Air Mechanic 2nd Class, Royal Air Force, School of Technical Training (Halton Camp).

Edward Frank (known as Frank) was born on 13th May 1890 in Tamworth, Staffordshire. Frank was baptised at St Editha Church, Tamworth, on 4th June 1890. He was the son of Alfred Godderidge Ashwood and Sarah Elizabeth (née Waldron). He was the middle child of nine children, Emma Agnes, Ethel Mary, Alfred George, William Henry, Emmie Elizabeth, Alice Maude, Linda Rose, and Doris.

Frank's father had various occupations with the 1891 census recording him as a licensed victualler, at the Horse and Jockey in Tamworth, and in 1901 a mineral water manufacturer, then in 1911 as a carpenter.

By 1911 Frank had left home and was living in South Norwood, Surrey, where he was working as a laundry hand. By 1914 he had moved to Sittingbourne, where he married Edith Dorothy Sage in August 1914. Frank moved to Sittingbourne in connection with a laundry in the High Street, where he later secured a controlling interest. He disposed of his share and opened a laundry in Chalkwell Road, to carry out Government contracts.

Frank joined the Royal Flying Corps (RFC) late in the war, and was in training at RFC Halton (pictured left), Wendover, Buckinghamshire when, on 31st March 1918, his wife Edith was notified that her husband was dangerously ill in Aylesbury Military Hospital. She travelled with her father to the hospital, and 27-year-old Frank died of double pneumonia the following Wednesday, 3rd April 1918, with Edith and Frank's parents present.

The East Kent Gazette of 6th April 1918, on reporting his death, commented that Frank had been in the Royal Flying Corps for just a few weeks. The article noted he was rejected for service several times, and eventually joined in about January 1918, where he was posted to the Royal Flying Corps School of Technical Training at Halton., The report also recorded that Frank's parents were living at Oakdale Terrace, London Road, Sittingbourne.

He was buried in Sittingbourne Cemetery, where his headstone is inscribed with the words "AT REST". He is also remembered on Sittingbourne War Memorial and St Michael's Church Memorial Window.

Frank's brother Henry served in the Royal Fusiliers from May 1915, until he was discharged in June 1916 as he was no longer fit for active service. Henry's 25-year-old son, RAF Sergeant Albert Henry died at RAF Litchfield on 27th September 1941 when the undercarriage on his Wellington bomber broke on landing and the plane caught fire.

RAF Halton continues to be used as a training centre and is home to the Central Training School, though it is scheduled to close by 2027. The base sits on the former Halton estate, once owned by the Rothschild family. The first military aviation manoeuvres in 1913 at Halton occurred when the owner, Alfred de Rothschild, invited No. 3 Squadron of the Royal Flying Corps to practice. The site was purchased to provide a permanent base in 1918 following the death of Alfred de Rothschild.

The ATTWATER Brothers

Brothers Bertie and Ernest were both born in Murston, Bertie in the summer of 1888 and Ernest in late 1896. They were part of a family of ten children, their siblings being Emma Anna Elizabeth, Marshall Ernest Robert (1873-1874), Rosina Jane, Ethel Eliza, Henry Athelstan, Ellen Lavinia, Nora (1891-1891), and Edith (1892-1893).

Their parents were Ernest Mark, a brickfield labourer for Smeed, Dean and Co, and Eliza Ann (née Tyler), who was born in Bobbing.

Ernest and Eliza's golden wedding anniversary was announced in the East Kent Gazette of 4th December 1920. The article reported they wed in Sittingbourne Wesleyan Church on 26th November 1870, that Ernest senior had worked for Smeed Dean since he was a boy, and that Eliza was born in a hop picker's hut near Maidstone, whilst her mother was hop picking.

The brothers had both attended Murston Church (pictured right) Day School and the Wesleyan Sunday School.

ATTWATER, Bertie

10426, Serjeant, 10th Battalion, South Wales Borderers.

Bertie was working for Smeed, Dean and Co. before joining the Royal Army Medical Corps in Chatham in 1909, transferring to the South Wales Borderers after six months and then serving two years in South Africa. He was then posted to China where he was stationed when the war broke out. Whilst there he was involved in the capture of Kiouchau from the Germans, with the Japanese supporting the British Army.

Afterwards he spent time in hospital, then he was sent out to the Dardanelles, as part of the Gallipoli campaign. Whilst there he was wounded and returned home to hospital, where it was reported he had shaken hands with King George V and chatted to Queen Mary during a visit to the hospital.

Bertie spent several months in hospital recovering, and on his release, he was posted to France, only to return shortly after with malarial fever.

In the spring of 1917, in the district of West Derby, Lancashire, Bertie married 20-year-old Harriet Titherington from Liverpool. That October he was once again posted to France.

From the middle of June 1917 through to 19th July 1917 the battalion were alternating between the front line at Mesnil-Martinsart and in reserve at Forceville or Englebelmer. They would spend between two and six days on the front line and the majority of reports in the battalion War Diary record quiet and uninteresting days. From the 20th July 1917 they moved to the reserves in Hérissart, until the 30th when they moved to Acheux-en- Amiénois.

Reproduced below from the South Wales Borderers War Diary are the events after this latest move:

	WAR DIARY[9] or INTELLIGENCE SUMMARY. (Erase heading not required.)	Army Form C. 2118.
Instructions regarding War Diaries and Intelligence Summaries are contained in F.S. Regs., Part II, and the Staff Manual respectively. Title pages will be prepared in manuscript.		
Date	Summary of Events and Information	Remarks and References to Appendices
30-7-1918	Battalion in reserve in ACHEUX-EN-AMIÉNOIS.	
30-7-1918 to 3-8-1918	Time spent cleaning kit and equipment, bathing in the village and battle practise.	
4-8-1918	Formed working parties at nearby BEAUSSART, finished about 12.30pm. Marched back to billets. In the afternoon, the Divisional Horse Show and Steeplechase took place at TOUTENCOURT, where a very fine show was witnessed.	
5-8-1918	The morning was spent in company training until 12.30pm. At 9.30pm marched to SENLIS-LE-SEC where we relieved 10TH BATTALION, WEST YORKS REGT.	
6-8-1918	The men are billeted in the trenches and day passed very quietly and the men were tasked with draining the trenches and making them comfortable.	
7-8-1918 to 17-8-1918	Enemy activity generally quiet, with occasional bursts of enemy fire and shelling. Battalion spent time improving trenches and on working parties.	
18-8-1918 to 19-8-1918	Battalion moved into the front line at Aveluy to relieve 2ND BATTALION. 318 AMERICAN INFANTRY REGIMENT. Days passed quietly, with some enemy shelling at intervals with gas shells. No casualties incurred.	
20-8-1918 to 22-8-1918	Relieved by 14TH WELSH and moved to BOUZINCOURT. Spent time cleaning up and making up deficiencies.	
23-8-1918	9.30pm - Moved to ANCRE to assemble for attack. No time for rest.	
24-8-1918	1.00am - Advanced to the village of LA BOISSELLE, enemy machine gun fire made this impossible. Moved on the flanks, confronted by heavy machine gun fire and successfully took nearby MAMETZ, the enemy quickly withdrew.	
25-8-1918	Holding front line at BAZENTIN-LE-PETIT. Water brought up and was welcomed by the men.	
26-8-1918	Moved to front line from HIGH WOOD to LONGUEVAL. Casualties estimated at 50 ORs.	
27-6-1918	Enemy counter attacked on the flanks with machine gun fire, but quickly held back. An American forced to serve in the German army gave himself up and volunteered valuable information as to enemy disposition.	
28-8-1918	Attacking DELVILLE WOOD, with limited success due to the enemy guns and forced to withdraw to HIGH WOOD.	
29-8-1918	Day spent resting in the trenches.	

[9] War Diary: 10 Battalion South Wales Borderers. WO-95-2562-1. December 1915-May 1919. The National Archives (UK), Kew, England.

Bertie is recorded as being killed in action on 26th August 1918, aged 30. His parents learnt of his death from his wife and, coincidentally, on the same day they received official confirmation that Ernest was buried in Nine Elms British Cemetery.

With crosses marking their graves, Bertie was originally buried on the battlefield with four other South Wales Borderers, about 600m north of his final resting place at Caterpillar Valley Cemetery, Longueville.

Bertie's pay and gratuity were paid to his widow, Harriet. This document records his rank as Corporal, though the Medal Index Card for his award of the 1914-15 Star records him as a Private. The Medal Index Card for his Victory and British War Medals show him as Sergeant, which is how he is officially recognised on the CWGC database.

The East Kent Gazette announced Bertie's death in their 14th September 1918 issue,

Credit: New Zealand War Graves Project

and commented that his sister Rosina Jane was serving in Yorkshire with the Women's Army Auxiliary Corps. Also, their brother Henry served in the Merchant Navy during the war.

Bertie is remembered on Sittingbourne War Memorial and St Michael's Church WW1 Memorial Window.

ATTWATER, Ernest

201075, Serjeant, 7th Battalion, The Buffs (East Kent Regiment).

Ernest was the youngest of the family, with his oldest sibling Emma being 25 years older and his brother Bertie eight years older. Ernest attended Murston National School and was employed at Sittingbourne Paper Mill, where he was an active member of their cricket and football teams.

Ernest was the only child still living at home in 1911.

He joined the Buffs on 5th July 1915 and quickly attained his sergeant stripes. He gained his instructor's certification in musketry, and a certificate in bombing and gas at Hythe, before serving in France.

The War Diary for Ernest's regiment in August and September 1917 has been reproduced here:

Instructions regarding War Diaries and Intelligence Summaries are contained in F.S. Regs., Part II, and the Staff Manual respectively. Title pages will be prepared in manuscript.	WAR DIARY [10] or INTELLIGENCE SUMMARY. *(Erase heading not required.)*	Army Form C. 2118.
Date	Summary of Events and Information	Remarks and References to Appendices
16-8-17	Marched to ERINGHEM area, France, at 5.45pm. Stopped for one hour for dinner.	

---

[10] War Diary: 7 Battalion Buffs (East Kent Regiment). WO-95-2049-1. July 1915-April 1919. The National Archives (UK), Kew, England.

17-8-17 to 28-9-17	Time spent training and practising battle attacks. Also participated in football matches and open-air concerts
23-9-1917	The Battalion arrived at SCHOOL CAMP by 4.40pm (at SINT-JAN-TER-BIEZEN, Belgium)
29-9-1917	Training as previous day. Air Raid on Camp by 1 Aeroplane 4 bombs dropped in the Camp causing the following casualties. Time 7.20pm. Officers _Killed_ — 2/Lt R.E.C. MEAD _Wounded_ — Lt QM T.L. RYE, 2/Lt J.C. TYLER, 2/Lt M.J. MALTON ORs _Killed_ 26 — _Wounded_ 63

Amongst those killed in the air raid was Ernest, aged 20, which was mentioned in the 20th October 1917 edition of the East Kent Gazette under the headline *ROLL OF HONOUR – BUFFS' CASUALTIES FROM AERIAL BOMBARDMENT*. Those killed included, fellow Sittingbourne man, Cecil Aubrey Heuner, who succumbed to his injuries, and he is also commemorated on the Avenue (see page 156). The newspaper also noted that he was engaged to be married to local girl Miss Dora Higgins.

A letter from Reverend Harold Glen to Ernest's parents expressed sympathy and said that he had conducted Ernest's burial which concluded with the 'Last Post'. Another letter from Ernest's platoon commander, Sergeant Hopwood DCM, wrote:

"As his Platoon Sergt. I had every opportunity of knowing him for his value. Indeed, he was a brave boy, knowing no fear of anything, and even in the most trying positions, always kept his men up with his cheery remarks and jokes. I and the men have suffered a great loss by his death."

Sergeant Hopwood explained how he had known Ernest, as he himself was from Sittingbourne and was his sergeant at the Canterbury and Cambridge camps.

In the same edition of the newspaper Ernest's family posted an emotive Roll of Honour reproduced here.

Ernest was buried in Nine Elms British Cemetery, West-Vlannderen, Belgium, which was the main cemetery for the 3rd Australian and 44th Casualty Clearing Station in September 1917, during the Third Battle of Ypres.

Ernest's headstone carries the words "UNTIL THE DAY BREAK AND THE SHADOWS FLEE AWAY", taken from the Bible's Song of Solomon 2:17.

He is remembered on Sittingbourne War Memorial, St Michael's Church WW1 Memorial Window and Lloyd's Paper Mill Memorial.

Just eleven months later the death of Ernest's brother, Bertie, was reported in the 14th September 1918 issue of the East Kent Gazette.

The East Kent Gazette

SATURDAY, OCTOBER 20, 1917

ROLL OF HONOUR

ATTWATER – September 29th 1917 killed in France, by bombs, Sergt. Ernest Attwater, of The Buffs, the dearly beloved son of Mr. and Mrs. E. M. Attwater, of 52, Murston Road, Sittingbourne. aged 20 years and 10 months.

"In the midst of life we are in death.
We did not want to lose him,
But this we surely know,
His King and Country called him,
And his answer was, "I'll go."
He little thought on leaving home,
That he would not return;
But now he lies in a soldier's grave,
And we are left to mourn.
His cheery ways, his smiling face,
Are pleasant to recall.
He had a kindly word for everyone,
And died beloved by all.
From his ever sorrowing Father and Mother,
Brothers and Sisters.

┌───┐
│   │
│   **BAKER, Alfred John**   │
│   │
│   G/48416, Private, 1st Battalion, Royal Fusiliers.   │
│   │
└───┘

Courtesy of Derek Pinckard (great grandnephew) who 'believes' this to be Alfred, from his family album.

Alfred was born in Strood in 1883 the fifth child of Alfred George, a general labourer, and Rosalind (née Stroud). his siblings were Edith, Lilian, Ada Flora, Rosaline, Margaret Emmeline Beatrice, Bertie Reginald (1888-1889), Herbert, Sarah, Annie, Herbert Reginald (1896-1896), and Ernest Edward.

On 2nd April 1904, at Milton Register Office, Alfred married Amelia Steers and they had three children, Ada Florence (born 1905), Alfred George (born 1906) and Amelia Ann (born 1909).

In 1911 the family were living at 20 Flushing Street, Milton and Alfred was employed as a brickfield labourer. By the time of his death the family had moved to 29 The Wall, Sittingbourne.

Alfred joined the 1st Battalion of the Royal Fusiliers and took part with them in the Third Battle of Ypres (31st July 1917 to 10th November 1917).

The Royal Fusiliers' War Diary during their participation in this battle is reproduced here:

Instructions regarding War Diaries and Intelligence Summaries are contained in F.S. Regs., Part II, and the Staff Manual respectively. Title pages will be prepared in manuscript.	**WAR DIARY**[11] or **INTELLIGENCE SUMMARY.** (Erase heading not required.)	Army Form C. 2118.
Date	Summary of Events and Information	Remarks and References to Appendices
28-7-1917	*Relieved 8th Battalion. In the trenches at HEDGE STREET (ZILLEBEKE, BELGIUM) and occupied the tunnels.*	
29-7-1917	*Dull day with thunderstorms and rain.*	
30-7-1917	*Troops served with hot meal and issued with rations including biscuits and chocolate. Preparing for attack on the 31st.*	
31-7-1917	*3.50am - Battalion advanced under cover of artillery barrage, attacking the enemy in the east. Advanced a short distance across SUNKEN ROAD reaching the trenches at BODMIN COPSE. Casualties incurred from machine gun fire and snipers. Reconsolidated at the copse. Casualties 50 killed, 155 wounded, 78 missing.*	
1-8-1917	*SHREWSBURY FOREST - There are a lot of wounded still lying in the shell holes. Owing to the heavy casualties amongst Stretcher Bearers it was difficult to clear the ground of wounded.*	
2-8-1917	*69 Other Ranks arrived to reinforce the battalion*	
3-8-1917	*Relieved by 8TH BATTALION, THE BUFFS. Retired to MICMAC CAMP (near OUDERDOM).*	
4 to 6-8-1917	*Influx of 160 Other Ranks. Re-organising.*	
7-8-1917	*Battalion returned to BODMIN COPSE, relieving the 7TH WEST KENTS and 9TH ROYAL SUSSEX.*	
8 to 9-8-1917	*Incoming artillery fire. No casualties.*	

[11] War Diary: 1 Battalion Royal Fusiliers. WO-95-2207-2. November 1915-May 1919. The National Archives (UK), Kew, England.

Map showing where Alfred fought.

10-8-1917	*4.30am - Line received heavy shelling, owing to operations being conducted on both of the battalions' flanks.* *Casualties - 12 killed and 12 wounded.*
11-8-1917	*Battalion returned to MICMAC CAMP. Replaced by the 9TH ROYAL SUSSEX.*

Alfred was one of those killed on 10th August 1917, just a few months after his mother died. He was 34 years old and buried on the battlefield, north of Bodmin Copse. After the Armistice he was reinterred in Hooge Crater Cemetery, Ypres. He was identified by his identity disc, alongside three other Royal Fusiliers, a Buff and three unknown British soldiers. Hooge Crater Cemetery was designed by Sir Edwin Lutyens, the designer of Whitehall Cenotaph and Thiepval Memorial to the Missing of the Somme.

Alfred is remembered on Sittingbourne's War Memorial and Holy Trinity Church WW1 Memorial.

The East Kent Gazette

SATURDAY, SEPTEMBER 29, 1917
ROLL OF HONOUR

BAKER – August 10, killed in action somewhere in France, Pte. Alfred John Baker Royal Fusiliers, husband of Mrs. Baker, 29, The Wall, aged 36 years.

One of the bravest, one of the best,
Doing his duty was called to rest,
Thy will be done, 'tis hard to say,
When one we loved is called away.
The shock was great, the blow severe;
We never thought the end was near,
Those only who have lost can tell,
How hard it was not saying "Farewell."
We will miss him most that loved him best.
From his sorrowing Wife and Children.

The East Kent Gazette

SATURDAY, AUGUST 16, 1919
IN MEMORIAM

BAKER – In affectionate remembrance of our dear brother, Alfred John Baker, who was killed in action, August 10th, 1917.

Two years have passed
Our hearts still sore,
As time rolls on, we miss him more;
Days of sadness Still come o'er us.
Tears of silence often flow;
But memory keeps the dear one near us,
Although it is two years ago.
From his loving Father, Sisters, and Brother.

BAKER, Ernest
Royal Navy

The plaque on the Avenue of Remembrance does not include the rank of E. Baker, though the East Kent Gazette, dated 7th January 1922, reporting on the dedication of St Michael's Church WW1 Memorial Window notes an Ernest Baker, Royal Navy (died from disease at home).

> Ernest Baker, R.N. (died at home of disease through the war).

The East Kent Gazette in December 1924 and January 1925 published a list of names requesting more information with their ranks and service, and E. Baker was one of those names listed.

Research into Ernest at the time of printing research continues to enable his story to be told.

We remember Ernest, as did those who knew him.

BAKER, Harry John

308151, Petty Officer Stoker, Royal Navy, HMS Pembroke.

Petty Officer Stoker Dress Insignia

The second of eleven children, Harry was born in Rodmersham on 9th June 1885. His parents were Edward, who worked with cattle on a farm, and Elizabeth (née Lurcock). His eight brothers and two sisters were Thomas William, Arthur Edward, Frederick George, Albert James, Ellen Mary, Wilfrid Burgess (1894-1895), Edward Butler (1895-1895), George Butler, Elizabeth May (1899-1900), and Stanley Frank.

Harry joined the Royal Navy on 26th June 1905 as a Stoker 2nd Class. His first ship was *HMS Archeon*, which was in fact a hulk for stoker's training. *Archeon* was a former Monitor-class armoured frigate called *HMS Northumberland*. In the spring of 1914 Harry married Harriett Gandon and they had three children, sadly two died in infancy, Hilda May (born 1915), Harry George (1916-1916), and Violet (1917-1918).

At the outbreak of war, Harry had risen to Stoker Petty Officer and was serving on the destroyer *HMS Lance*, which entered service in August 1914. On 5th July 1915 he was sent to the shore establishment *HMS Pembroke II*, the Royal Naval Air Station at Eastchurch, as it was discovered he had tuberculosis of the lung. Two weeks later, on 14th July 1915 he was discharged from the Navy.

Harry died on 8th November 1918 at home at 29 Shortlands Road, Sittingbourne, of Pulmonary Tuberculosis and Influenza Syncope, aged 33. His pension card records his influenza commenced whilst on active service.

For some unexplained reason Harry is commemorated on the Chatham Naval Memorial to the Missing. In January 2021 the author identified that Harry was actually buried in Sittingbourne Cemetery. Following submission by the author of evidence to the CWGC, they accepted his burial place as an official war grave. On 20th April 2023 a CWGC Gallipoli Marker was installed on his grave.

He is also commemorated on St Michael's Church WW1 Memorial Window and Sittingbourne War Memorial.

Four of Harry's brothers served in the First World War. Thomas served with 437 Agricultural Company, Labour Corps from June 1917 until his discharge in January 1919. Arthur served from July 1909 to February 1919 as a Stoker Petty Officer in the Royal Navy. From October 1917 he served on *HMS Prince Rupert* which was tasked with bombarding German coastal artillery positions in Belgium as part of the Dover Monitor Squadron.

The East Kent Gazette

SATURDAY, NOVEMBER 8, 1918

IN MEMORIAM

BAKER – In loving memory of Stoker Petty Officer Harry John Baker, who passed away, November 8th, 1918.

One year has passed,
My heart still sore,
As time rolls on I miss him more;
Days of sadness still come o'er us,
Tears in silence often flow;
But memory brings the dear one near me,
Although he died a year ago.
What happy hours we spent together,
How sweet their memory still;
But death has left a vacant place,
This world can never fill.
From his sorrowing Wife and Child.

Harry's brother George served in The Buffs and the Queen's (Royal West Surrey) Regiment from December 1914 to February 1919. George served in France, and in August 1916 he was treated for shell shock after a near miss in the trenches. In November 1917 he was posted to Italy and then returned to France, where in March 1918 George was concussed from a gunshot wound, following which he spent 78 days in Sandgate and a Devon hospital. Albert emigrated to Canada in June 1914 and in December 1915 enlisted, serving with the 9th Battalion, Canadian Expeditionary Force in France. He was discharged in March 1919.

BAKER, Percy John

T/2435, Private, 1st/5th Battalion, The Buffs (East Kent Regiment).

Percy was born in 1897 in Bapchild, the first child of Harry, a brickfield labourer, and Alice (née Lombardy). He had two brothers, Harry John, and William Frank, and two sisters, Edith Alice, and Hilda May. His mother died in 1905, when Percy was eight years old. In 1911 Percy was living with his grandmother, Ellen Baker, at 36 Cowper Road, Sittingbourne, with the rest of the family and his uncle Arthur Baker. He was aged 13 and was working as a brickfield labourer at Smeed Dean's brickfields, where his father was also working as a brick sorter. Percy's father remarried in late 1911 to Adelaide Margaret Chapman, who was also widowed. She lived just around the corner from Harry at 56 Shakespeare Road and the family moved in with Adelaide.

According to a report in the East Kent Gazette of 1st April 1916 Percy had attended Murston School and was a member of the Bible Class conducted by Rev. J. G. Easton, Rector of Murston. The report said that Percy was a fine specimen of manhood and had enlisted, just before the war broke out, with E Company (Sittingbourne), 4th Battalion, The Buffs.

Percy was 18 years old when he was killed by a shell on 7th January 1916, alongside fellow Murston lad, 19-year-old Private William Chesson, who lived at the Brickmakers Arms. They were serving with the Mesopotamian Expeditionary Force in Iraq. The 1st/5th Battalion of The Buffs were sent to India in October 1914, where they joined up with the Indian Army. On 31st December 1915, they landed at Basra, Iraq, to relieve the besieged forces at Kut el Amara.

Percy and William were killed on the first day of action at Sheikh Saad on the banks of the Tigris river, together with a reported 249 officers and men. His battalion had been attempting to attack through floodwater but were forced to retreat. By April 1916 the Turkish forces had taken Kut. Both Percy and William were buried in Amara War Cemetery, Iraq. As the salty soil conditions caused the headstones to deteriorate, they were all removed. Instead, the CWGC installed a screen wall inscribed with the names of those who had been buried there.

Percy's pay and gratuity were shared between his father and stepmother. He is also commemorated on the Sittingbourne War Memorial and St Michael's Church WW1 Memorial Window. William Chesson is commemorated on Murston's WW1 Memorial and on a personal memorial in All Saints Church, Murston (pictured right).

THEORE OF THE OPERATIONS BETWEEN BASRA AND CTESIPHON, UP TO THE SURRENDER OF KUT-EL-AMARA.

BAKER, William Thomas

11327, Private, 2nd Battalion, Worcestershire Regiment.

William was born in Strood in 1887, and in 1901, aged 14, was living there with his parents, Alfred, and Emma (née Cheesman). He was the eighth child of ten children with his siblings being Alice, Emma, Edith, Louisa, Ada, Alfred (1882-1900), Percy James, Maud Ellen (1890-1893) and Sarah Jane. William's father was a former labourer on the railways and by 1911 had become a greengrocer.

William joined the 2nd Battalion, Worcestershire Regiment, which left Aldershot in August 1914 and landed at Boulogne, France on 14th August 1914, where they were enthusiastically welcomed by the town's population. The Battalion became involved in what is known as the first great battle, the Battle of Mons, on the Belgium-French border. The British were outnumbered by three to one against the German 1st Army, and both sides claimed victory. The British prevented the Germans from outflanking the French Army, slowing their progress, whilst the Germans had gained a strategic advantage and ground.

Following this battle, William's battalion was involved in further offensives against the Germans. First, at the beginning of September 1914, the First Battle of the Marne, a Franco-British counter offensive which halted the German advance and forced them to retreat. The Worcestershire Regiment then moved into the Battle of the Aisne, in mid-September, which ended in a stalemate with both sides entrenched and refusing to retreat. This was where the first trenches were to appear in France.

The next major offensive was the Race to the Sea, with both sides trying to outflank each other and block off any outflanking opportunities along the coast.

It was during this offensive, on 20th September 1914, that 27-year-old William was killed, when the 2nd Battalion attacked the German lines. The Worcestershire Regiment reported 37 were killed, with all their officers having been either killed or wounded.

William is remembered on the La Ferte-Sous-Jouarre Memorial in France (pictured on the right), which is also known as the Memorial to the 'Missing of the Marne', it commemorates over 3,700 British and Irish soldiers with no known grave, who fell in battle.

He is also commemorated on the Sittingbourne War Memorial and Sittingbourne Holy Trinity Church Memorial. He was awarded the 1914 Star, also known as the Mons Star, as well as the Victory and British War Medals.

BALDOCK, Charles Frederick

9904, Private, 2nd Battalion, East Lancashire Regiment.

Charles, born in 1890 in Milton Regis, was the son of Walter George and Alice (née Freeman) who lived at 12 Rock Road, Sittingbourne. He was the fourth of their nine sons, William Henry, Walter, Harry, Ernest George, Albert Ambrose, Frederick, Leonard, and Harold. His only sister, Queenie Alice was born in 1906, but sadly died in 1907.

In 1911, his father was employed as a Pearl Life Assurance Collector but had previously worked in the brickfields and paper mill. Before the war his brothers William, Walter and Harry worked in the paper mill, and still worked there in 1939, when Leonard was an ARP Warden.

Charles' father, Walter, enlisted with the Royal Army Medical Corps on 6th November 1914 at Sheerness and served at home until 31st March 1920. Their role was to serve and support hospitals. Charles himself had enlisted in 1908 and in 1911 he was with the East Lancashire Regiment in Wellesley Barracks, Mhow, India. Later that year his battalion moved to South Africa, then, when war broke out, they returned to England. According to his battalion's War Diary[12] they arrived at Southampton at 11am on 30th October 1914, then went to Hursley Camp, near Winchester, Hampshire.

On 5th November 1914, the battalion embarked on *SS Lake Michigan* at Southampton and arrived at Le Havre at 7.50pm the following day. They remained overnight on the ship, before transferring to a nearby camp, staying for five days before travelling 266km north-east by train to Neuf-Berquin, France, just 12 km from the Belgium border and 25km south-west of Ypres. On 14th November, they moved into the trenches at Pont-du-Hem. The diary reported sporadic enemy attacks, which were repulsed, and on the 18th the Devonshire and West Yorkshire Regiments arrived to relieve them.

During the following month, there was a cycle of rest and time in the trenches. The 22nd December 1914 found the battalion relieving the Sherwood Foresters in the line, at Neuve-Chapelle. The diary entry for that day recorded heavy and continuous enemy shelling and noted three wounded. The 23rd and 24th were spent exchanging rifle fire.

Christmas Day's diary entry reads:

"The Germans began shouting Christmas Greetings in the early morning and there was no firing throughout the whole day. During the afternoon some of our men and the Germans went into the open outside No 1 Section to bury some German dead which had been lying there for some time."

Events of this nature (depicted above) became known as the Christmas Truce, whereby hostilities ceased on Christmas Day and the British and Germans met in No Man's Land, exchanging gifts, and sang carols[13].

---

[12] War Diary: 2 Battalion East Lancashire Regiment - War Diary WO-95-1719-2. November 1916-June 1916. The National Archives (UK), Kew, England.

[13] *"The Real Story of the Christmas Truce."* Imperial War Museum. www.iwm.org.uk/history/the-real-story-of-the-christmas-truce

At 5pm the battalion were relieved by the Sherwood Foresters and went to billets on La Bassée road, where they rested until the 28th December 1914, when they returned to the line. On arrival they spent their time working to stop 'the influx of water.' The entry in the diary for 29th December 1914, recorded that the water influx had increased despite the use of pumps. It noted that the enemy were 'inactive,' however, it also recorded that there were casualties, including eight killed and four wounded. Charles, aged 24, was one of those killed.

Originally Charles was buried in Edward Road No. 2 Cemetery, Richebourg-l'Avoué, then ten years after his death, in late 1924, he was moved to Cabaret-Rouge British Cemetery. The cemetery was named after

a small red-bricked, red-roofed café, called "Cabaret Rouge" (pictured left), that stood close to the site. His headstone is inscribed "TILL THE DAY DAWN."

He is remembered on the Sittingbourne War Memorial, the Baptist Church WW1 Memorial

(pictured right) and Sittingbourne Holy Trinity Church Memorial.

Charles' pay and gratuity were sent to his mother, as were his 1914 Star with clasp, Victory, and British War Medals.

BALDOCK, Charles William

15067, Private, 2nd Battalion, Royal Munster Fusiliers.

Charles was born in Otterden near Faversham in 1878, the second of the nine children of William and Mary Ann (née Day). His father was an agricultural labourer, and his siblings were Rose (1877-1886), Ellen Maud, Flora May (1884-1909), an unnamed infant (1885-1885), William George, Rosa, and Ethel Gertrude (1895-1916).

Charles was baptised on 29th June 1879 in St Lawrence Church, Otterden, which sits in the grounds of Otterden Place. The family had moved to Lenham by 1891. The 1901 census records the family still living in Lenham and Charles was employed as a carter on a farm.

In 1911 Charles was employed as a gardener and was living at Lime Cottage, Green Street, Lynsted, with his wife Annie (née Gambrill), whom he had married in 1904. They had six children, Norman Charles (born 1905), Percival William (born 1907), Sidney Edward (born 1908), Flora May (born 1910), Alice Mary (born 1911), and Ronald Joseph (born 1912). The family later moved to live at 18 Chilton Avenue, Sittingbourne.

The War Office's Soldiers Died in the Great War, 1914-1919 records that Charles was formerly service number 4740 in the East Kent Regiment.

The War Diary for his battalion for the 1st to 20th March 1918 is recorded as a missing file, though the entry for the period 21st to 24th March is reproduced below.

Instructions regarding War Diaries and Intelligence Summaries are contained in F.S. Regs., Part II, and the Staff Manual respectively. Title pages will be prepared in manuscript.	WAR DIARY[14] or INTELLIGENCE SUMMARY. (Erase heading not required.)	Army Form C. 2118.
Date	**Summary of Events and Information**	**Remarks and References to Appendices**
21-3-1918	4.30am - Battalion positioned between ÉPEHY and MALASSISE FARM. At last the long expected enemy offensive commenced, with gas and heavy shells. The enemy attacked along the LEMPIRE- ÉPEHY road, forcing the battalion to withdraw to ÉPEHY.	
22-3-1918	2am - The Irish troops ordered to withdraw to TINCOURT, where they arrived in isolated parties. Battalion reduced from a strength of 629 Other Ranks to 290.	
23-3-1918 to 24-3-1918	Battalion withdrew further to PÉRONNE and then on to CAPPY.	

Charles was killed during the withdrawal on 22nd March 1918, aged 38. He is remembered, along with over 14,000 other casualties who have no known grave, on the Pozières Memorial in France. They all died when the Allied Fifth Army was driven back across the former Somme battlefields, during March and April 1918. On the same day as Charles, 1,758 other casualties lost their lives, including 24-year-old Private Herbert George Columbine, of the Machine Gun Corps (Cavalry), who was awarded the Victoria Cross for his actions that day.

Charles is also remembered locally on Sittingbourne War Memorial. His widow, Annie, received his pay and gratuity.

BARHAM, Charles William

9047, Private, 1st Battalion, Gloucestershire Regiment.

The WW1 Memorial in Sittingbourne's Holy Trinity Church has a G Barham labelled as having served in the 'Glosters' (Gloucestershire Regiment) and a Charles Barham in the 'Buffs'. Research did not find a record of C Barham in The Buffs, nor a G Barham in the Gloucester's, but did identify a reversal of the regiments, so it is possible that this was an error on the memorial.

Charles was born in Maidstone on 23rd September 1893 and was baptised on 3rd June 1894 at Holy Trinity Church, Maidstone. He was the son of Charles William, a boiler breakers labourer, and

---

[14] War Diary: 2 Battalion Royal Munster Fusiliers. WO-95-1975-4. February-May 1918. The National Archives (UK), Kew, England.

Elizabeth Sarah (née Boswell); he was their fifth child, and his siblings were Elizabeth Sarah, Charles William (1885-1887), George William, Thomas Richard, Edith Emily, and Walter John. In 1911, he was living with them in Church Street, Chatham, and working as a general labourer.

Charles joined the Gloucestershire Regiment and landed in France on 19th December 1914. His battalion fought at the First Battle of Ypres, as part of the Race to the Sea. Both sides were trying to outflank each other to secure the area by the Belgium coast. The battles were fierce and, although his battalion had defended their area, by the end it had been reduced by about two thirds, losing 23 of their 25 officers.

The Battle of Aubers Ridge started on 9th May 1915, at 5.30am the British bombarded the German front line at Richebourg-l'Avoué with high explosive shells. The battalion then went over the top, just 80 yards from the Germans, and were met by heavy machine gun fire, though as ordered they pressed on. Further up the line the Indian Corps had failed to leave the trenches as the German fire was so intense.

The British bombardment advanced on the German line and the British attempted to cross No Man's Land, suffering heavy losses. A hundred men of the Northants and Munsters managed to reach the German trenches but were either killed or captured. Three hours had elapsed. General Haig ordered a new attack for 4pm, which was as ineffective as the morning's attack, with the Germans reported as not even taking shelter. Charles' Battalion sustained 264 casualties including 11 officers. With 12,000 casualties overall the day was described as an unmitigated disaster.

Charles was one of those who had been killed, aged 21 years and he is remembered on the Le Touret Memorial to the Missing in France, together with 13,478 others who have no known grave and were killed on the Western Front. He is also commemorated on Sittingbourne War Memorial and Sittingbourne Holy Trinity Church WW1 Memorial.

Charles was awarded the 1915 Star, Victory, and British War Medals. After the war his pay and gratuity were paid to his mother, since his father had died in 1918.

BARHAM, G

The WW1 Memorial in Sittingbourne's Holy Trinity Church has a G Barham labelled as having served in the 'Glosters' (Gloucestershire Regiment) and a C Barham in the 'Buffs'. Research did not find a record of C Barham in The Buffs, nor a G Barham in the Glosters, but did identify a reversal of their regiments, so it is possible there is an error on the memorial. He is also recorded on the Sittingbourne War Memorial.

Charles Barham's story can be read on page 58, although he had a brother named George, research identified he did not die in the war.

Research into G Barham, has not provided an identity, and will continue to enable his story to be told.

We remember him, as did those who knew him.

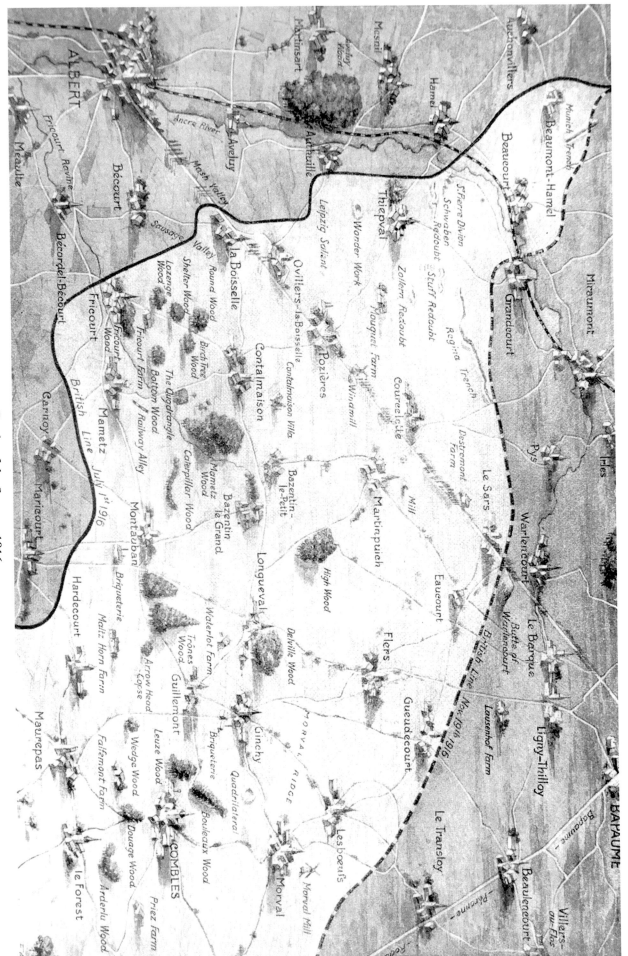

Battle of the Somme 1916

BARNARD, George

960, Corporal, South African Medical Corps.

George was born in Sittingbourne in 1879 and was baptised on 30th March 1879 at Holy Trinity Church, Sittingbourne. He was the second child to William, a printer's compositor, and Rosetta (née Baker). His siblings were William John (1877-1878), and sisters, Gertrude, Elsie, and Nora.

In 1901 the family were living at Apsley House, London Road and George was working as a bricklayer's apprentice, and he was known at Sittingbourne concerts to be a very capable entertainer. By 1911, his parents had moved to 149 Park Road, but George was no longer living there. He may have already emigrated to South Africa, where he continued his entertainment, and became engaged in gold mining work until he had a severe accident, which made his left arm practically useless.

The East Kent Gazette of 27th April 1918 reported that George's family had received some cuttings from the Durban Natal newspaper, from his entertainer partner Tommy Holder. Their act included George's speciality of ventriloquism. Tommy wrote that George was a fine young fellow and gave up his life helping others. The newspaper cuttings included a letter from a friend, Peggy the Showman, who stated that despite George's mining injury, technically making him medically unfit for service, he volunteered for active service with the Expeditionary Force and took part in the invasion of German East Africa. George had said "I can't shoot, but I can help the sick and wounded, as long as they want me". George and Tommy's last public appearance was in June 1917. George entertained the patients in East Africa and was the first to do charitable turns.

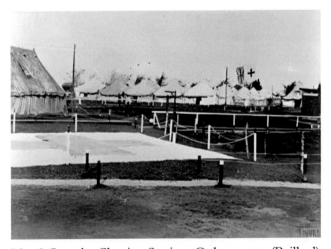

No. 2 Casualty Clearing Station. Oultersteene (Bailleul)

George became ill with enteric fever on 17th January 1918 and was admitted to the 52nd (Lowland) Casualty Clearing Station. Although he appeared to recover, George suffered a very serious complication on 9th February 1918, which required an operation. Sadly, he died the same evening, aged 39. He was originally buried in Mingoyo Cemetery with military honours. After 1968 a number of cemeteries were consolidated due to difficulties in maintaining them, and George was moved to the Dar-es-Salaam Cemetery in Tanzania (formerly German East Africa). He is remembered on the Sittingbourne War Memorial and Holy Trinity Church Memorial.

The East Kent Gazette of 11th May 1918, under the headline "REMARKABLE LETTER FROM A C.O." started the article with "We make no apology for once again referring to the death of George Barnard." They reproduced a letter George's parents had received a few days earlier from Major F. S. Jones, George's commanding officer. The letter explained that he was a cook and looked after the sick and wounded and as soon as he heard a convoy was on its way, proceeded to get scoff ready. He added that George was always cheerful and hardworking and would be missed." Another letter received from a Lieutenant-Commander R.S. Girdwood echoed the character of George and one from Major Geoffrey B. Fleming, Clearing Station Commanding Officer, explaining the facts around George's death.

BARNES, William Alfred

104325, Lance Corporal, 218th Coy, Machine Gun Corps (Infantry).

William was born on 23rd January 1895 in Jubilee Street, Sittingbourne. The son of Herbert George and Harriett (née Hadlow). His father was a former brickfield labourer and fishmonger, and he died when William was just four years old. His mother then married Charles Frederick Batchelor, a cement works labourer, who served in the Royal Garrison Artillery during the war. In 1911 the family were living at 11 Arthur Street, Milton Regis. William was the second youngest of nine children, with his siblings being Herbert George, James Ernest, Harriett Jane, Amelia Emma, John Thomas, Ethel Rose, Henrietta Grace, and Victoria Elizabeth. He also had a stepsister, Mabel, after his mother remarried.

He worked as an errand boy for a Dr. Noble and afterwards a Mr A L Goble. His employers spoke highly of him and said he was well-liked. Just before joining up, he was a waiter in a London hotel.

At St Mary the Virgin Church, Tottenham, he married 20-year-old Dorothy Grace Towner, on 1st August 1915 and they lived at 8 Elizabeth Road, Seven Sisters, Tottenham, North London. He recorded on his marriage certificate that he was employed as a stoker. They had a daughter, Dorothy Florence, who was born on 4th August 1916.

William enlisted on 10th March 1917 and was posted to France on 2nd August 1917. He served with the British Expeditionary Force in France and Flanders. Early in 1918 the 218th Coy, Machine Gun Corps became a part of the 8th Division, 8th Battalion Machine Gun Corps.

The War Diary for his Battalion in March of 1918 is reproduced here:

Instructions regarding War Diaries and Intelligence Summaries are contained in F.S. Regs., Part II, and the Staff Manual respectively. Title pages will be prepared in manuscript.	WAR DIARY[15] or INTELLIGENCE SUMMARY. (Erase heading not required.)	Army Form C. 2118.
Date	Summary of Events and Information	Remarks and References to Appendices
1-3-1918	In the line at PASSCHENDAELE.	
7-3-1918	Relieved by 23RD BATTALION and moved to STEENVOORDE.	
12-3-1918 to 21-3-1918	Moved to LONGUENESSE. Battalion training.	
22-3-1918	Entrained to ROSIÈRES-EN-SANTERRE. Contingent of 37 Officers, 777 Other Ranks, 258 Horses and Mules, 130 Axles and 15 Bicycles.	
23-3-1918	Moved to the line running from BRIE in the north to VOYENNES in the south, following the river SOMME.	
24-3-1918	Enemy attacked.	
25-3-1918 to 27-3-1918	Enemy attack continued forcing battalion withdrawal to ROSIÈRES.	

[15] War Diary: 8 Battalion Machine Gun Corps. WO-95-1702-4. March 1918-March 1919. The National Archives (UK), Kew, England.

28-3-1918	*Withdrawal continued to MOREUIL.*
29-3-1918	*Battalion holding enemy to the east of town.*
30-3-1918	*4am - Battalion moved to LE PARACLET, arriving at 5pm.*
31-3-1918	*Occupying high ground in CASTEL, in action towards the valley on to MOREUIL.* *During these actions, our estimated casualties amounted to* *16 Officers and 300 Other Ranks.* *A large number of the casualties are missing.*

William died on 31st March 1918, aged 23 years, on the 24th Field Ambulance, the day after being wounded in action. The 24th Field Ambulance's War Diary[16] records it had spent the first three weeks of March in the area of Ypres before moving south to Pertain, then west to Sains-en-Amiénois, which is 8km south of Amiens, arriving on 29th March 1918.

The Ambulance set up a Dressing Station near the railway station at Boves and the next few days motor ambulances patrolled and cleared the area, returning the casualties to Boves, where the 10th

Motor Ambulance convoy moved them west to Casualty Clearing Stations at Namps-au-Val. The diary recorded 600 casualties had passed through Boves. The Field Ambulance was relieved on the 2nd April by the French.

William was buried just outside the village of Boves with at least four other British soldiers, with their grave marked with a cross. They were moved in 1920 to Moreuil Communal Cemetery Allied Extension, Somme in France. His headstone is inscribed with the words "FOR EVER IN THE LORD". He is also remembered on the headstone of his mother in Sittingbourne Cemetery, with the inscription "DUTY DONE, LABOURS ENDED, NOW TO WAIT THE TRUMPETS SOUNDING." His mother had received the news of her son's death from a young girl who was a bridesmaid at her son's wedding.

William is remembered on the Sittingbourne War Memorial and by Milton Regis on the Milton Regis War Memorial, Milton Council Boys School Memorial (now located in Milton Court Primary Academy) and St Paul's Church Memorial (now located in Milton's Holy Trinity Church).

William was awarded the Victory and British War Medals and his pay and gratuity were awarded to his wife. A letter to William's wife from his Commanding Officer[17], said: "He was such a fine soldier, and a great favourite with all who knew him. I can speak of your husband personally, as I had been with him ever since he joined the company. He was one of the most reliable and efficient of Non-Commissioned Officers, and it is a tremendous loss to the company."

The family of William remembered him with emotive and poignant words as the "In Memoriams," on the next page, published in the East Kent Gazette, show.

[16] War Diary: 24 Field Ambulance. WO-95-1703-1. November 1914-June 1919. The National Archives (UK), Kew, England.

[17] De Ruvigny's Roll of Honour, 1914-1924. United Kingdom: Navy & Military Press Ltd. 2004. Ancestry.co.uk.

The East Kent Gazette

SATURDAY, APRIL 27, 1918

IN MEMORIAM

BARNES - In loving memory of my dear son, William Alfred Barnes, who died of wounds, in action, on March 31st, 1918. His age was 23 the 28th of last January. Married, leaves a wife and one child. Gone but not forgotten.

We have lost him we loved,
We like others must be brave,
For we know that he is lying
In a British Soldier's grave:
What pains he bore we cannot tell,
We did not see him die,
We only know he passed away
And never said good-bye.

From his loving Mother, Step-Father, Sisters, and Brothers

The East Kent Gazette

SATURDAY, MARCH 29, 1919

IN MEMORIAM

BARNES - In loving memory of our dear son, William Alfred Barnes, who died of wounds received in action, in France, March 31st, 1918. Loved by all.

A call came to him clearly,
That call was not in vain;
On Britain's roll of honour,
You'll find this hero's name.
By shot and shell surrounded,
He bravely did his best;
Died the death of a soldier,
And was taken home to rest.

From Mother, Stepfather, Sisters and Brothers

BARRETT, Frederick Henry Sidney

10082, Private, 144th Coy, Machine Gun Corps.

Frederick was born on 5th July 1893 in Wormshill, the son of Thomas William, a farm labourer, and Florence (née Baker). He was the seventh of twelve children. His brothers and sisters were Elizabeth Florence, William John, Annie Mercy, Emma Eliza, Edith Ethel, Ellen Maria, Louisa Bertha, Thomas William, and Ivy May. Sadly, two of the children died soon after birth and were unnamed. In 1901 the family lived in Shortlands Road, Sittingbourne, but by 1911 his parents had moved to Eastchurch, and Frederick was living with his sister Annie and her husband Arthur John Luckhurst, in 28 George Street, Sittingbourne. Both Frederick and Arthur were employed as brickfield labourers.

When he enlisted at Blandford, Frederick was living at 1 Amelia Cottage, Crayford Road, Erith. Frederick first enlisted with 13th Battalion, The Worcestershire Regiment on 16th November 1915, but was then denied permission by his employer as he was engaged in the making of munitions. So, just two weeks later, he was discharged on 1st December 1915.

Eventually Frederick enlisted as a Private in the Machine Gun Company. Frederick's company War Diary[18] recounts that they arrived in camp north-east of Poperinge on 22nd July 1917 where they rested, cleaned up, overhauled the guns and belts, and dug trenches, due to nearby enemy shelling. A week later, on the 29th, an advance party attempted to move ammunition to the nearby Canal Bank but found it

---

[18] War Diary: Brigade Machine Gun Company. WO-95-2759-3. January 1916-October 1917. The National Archives (UK), Kew, England.

impossible to reach due to enemy high explosive and gas shelling. The following day a barrage was laid, and the company successfully reached the canal bank to achieve their objective. They remained at the bank on the 30th and at 3.30am the following morning they subjected the enemy to over three hours of fire. Later in the day they retired back to camp.

The first five days of August were spent training, until the 6th August when they moved to Dambre Camp, north-west of Ypres. For the remainder of the month, they supported the front line at the Steenbeek river, 10km to the east, with each Section taking turns. On 19th August 1917, Frederick was killed in action, aged 24. He was buried in Vlamertinghe New Military Cemetery in Belgium, alongside four comrades from 144th Company, who were killed the same day.

During this time, it is recorded that the 144th Coy were involved with the Third Battle of Ypres, also known as the Battle of Passchendaele, which occurred from 31st July 1917 to 6th November 1917. The battle inflicted massive losses, estimated at 500,000 killed and wounded, on both sides, with the British

firing about 4.5 million shells. The rainfall for August was twice the normal at six inches of rain, turning Passchendaele into a quagmire. The objective of the battle was to take control of the south and east of Ypres, which was achieved, though a year later the British vacated the ground.

Frederick is remembered on Sittingbourne War Memorial, as several of his siblings lived in the area and on Erith's Christ Church WW1 Memorial Cross (pictured left), as his parents lived nearby. His pay and gratuity were awarded to his mother Florence, and she also received his Victory and British War Medals.

BARTLETT, Albert John

8181, Private, 1st Battalion, Oxford and Bucks Light Infantry.

Albert was born in Sittingbourne in 1888 and baptised in St Michael's Church on 22nd that year. He was the son of Albert John, a brickfield labourer, and Olive Thomasine (née Bartlett) and he had an older brother, William Edwin. His parents had been married in Faversham on 23rd October 1884, but his father died in 1889 when the family were living in Murston Road. Albert's mother remarried in 1892 to James Startup, a general labourer, and they had three children Alice, James Harold, and George Richard, before she died in August 1906 in Sittingbourne.

By 1911 Albert was serving as a Private, in the Oxford and Buckinghamshire Regiment, at Wellington Barracks, Nilgris in India. He served in the Asian theatre and was posted there on 5th December 1914, where the battalion took part in the campaign against the ruling Ottoman forces.

On 26th September 1915 the battle for Kut el Amara, on the bank of River Tigris, Iraq, began and it was captured three days later. Then, in the November, together with the Indian 6th Poona Division, the British attempted to capture Baghdad, but were forced to retreat back to Kut el Amara. This was the beginning of the defence of the town, with both sides suffering heavy losses, until on the 29th April 1916, the British-Indian forces negotiated a cease-fire due to the lack of supplies and sickness.

It is estimated that the force was 8,000 men, including 400 of the 1st Oxford and Buckinghamshire Regiment. Albert was one of the 400 men taken prisoner, only 71 of whom returned to England, bringing with them reports of mistreatment by the Ottomans. Estimates record that about 5,000 British and Indian soldiers, including Albert, died whilst in captivity.

The entry in the Registers of Soldiers' Effects record Albert as being presumed to have died between 29th April and 31st December 1916, with his death being officially recorded as 31st December 1916. He was 28 years old and is remembered on the CWGC Basra Memorial in Iraq and Sittingbourne War Memorial.

Photo by Major P. C. Saunders

KUT, DURING THE SIEGE

The 1915 Star, Victory and British War Medals were awarded to Albert. The Register of Soldier's Effects record that his pay and gratuity were paid to an Edith Phillips. No record of a pension index card or will for Albert were located to identify his relationship with Edith.

Albert's brother Lance Sergeant William enlisted in The Buffs on 12th December 1915, going to France a year later on 16th December 1916. His records show he received a gunshot wound to his left arm on 23rd July 1917 and just over a year later on 27th August 1918 a shrapnel wound to the neck. William was awarded the Military Medal on 24th January 1919 and discharged a month later. He opted to receive his Military Medal by post.

Albert's stepbrother George enlisted in the Royal Army Medical Corps, shortly after his 17th birthday in November 1914. He was posted to France from January 1917 to October 1917 and returned home after being wounded in action. George returned to France from July 1918 to March 1919, being discharged a year later.

BATCHELOR, Thomas Edward

L/8156, Lance Corporal, 2nd Battalion, Queen's Own (Royal West Kent Regiment).

Thomas was born in 1888 in Sittingbourne and was baptised on 9th June 1889 in the parish church of St Michael's. His parents were Robert, a general labourer, and Sarah (née Hopper). He was the fifth of six children, and his siblings were Mary Ann, Robert William, Sarah Elizabeth, Ada Louisa, and George Alfred (1897-1899).

Thomas enlisted in Maidstone and in 1911 was serving in the Queen's Own Regiment, as a drummer, at Roberts Barracks, Peshawar, India. He went with his battalion when it joined the Mesopotamian Expeditionary Force in Iraq in February 1915.

Thomas was in a similar position as the previous story of Albert John Bartlett (see page 65), with his battalion also involved in the defence of Kut el Amara before he was captured.

He died on 9th October 1916 from enteritis, when he was 29, and is buried in the Baghdad (North Gate) War Cemetery. Thomas would have been moved to this cemetery as it was started in April 1917 to consolidate smaller cemeteries and battlefield burials.

At the time of his death, Thomas' home was 15 Shortlands Road and he is commemorated locally on Sittingbourne War Memorial and St Michael's Church WW1 Memorial Window. After his death his pay and war gratuity were divided between his mother, three sisters and brother Robert.

He was awarded the 1915 Star, Victory, and British War Medals.

BEECHAM, George

41230, Private, 2nd Squadron, Machine Gun Corps (Cavalry).

George's father, Charles, had been born in Essex but by 1881 had moved to Milton Regis, where in 1884 at the age of 24, he married 23-year-old local girl Hannah Saddleton. Together they had ten children, of whom George was the second.

George was baptised on 12th September 1886, the year he was born, in Holy Trinity Church, Milton Regis. His siblings were William, Charles, Ellen, Susie, James, Clara Edith, Annie, Florence May, and Henry John. Charles worked in the brickfields as a labourer.

George was 5ft 6½in tall with brown hair and grey eyes when, on 23rd September 1906, he enlisted with the 4th Dragoon Guards at Canterbury. He listed his employment as a brickfield labourer. A year later, on 18th September 1907, he went to South Africa before returning to England on 17th November 1908. On 26th February 1913 he extended his service to complete twelve years.

He married Gertrude Honey on 27th September 1909 in Milton Regis. They had three girls, Dorothy Gertrude (born 1910), Nellie Esmeralda (born 1911) and Georgina Florence (born 1913).

In 1911 he was stationed with the 4th Dragoon Guards at Preston Military Barracks, Lewes Road, Brighton. He was one of the first troops to go to France, joining the Expeditionary Force on 16th August 1914, and served at Mons and in the First and Second Battles of Ypres. On 24th February 1916, still serving as a Private, he transferred to the Machine Gun Corps.

On the night of 25th March 1918 George was hit from shellfire, and died the next day, aged 31. At the time of his death the Machine Gun Corps were involved in countering Operation Michael, a major German offensive which started from the Hindenburg Line (pictured left) on 21st March 1918, with the objective to break through allied lines to the channel ports.

The Battles of Bapaume and Rosières resulted in the German Army gaining these towns by 27th March, and they then commenced to the town of Albert, followed by Arras and Amiens, where their advance was halted.

The 6th April 1918 issue of the East Kent Gazette reported that George's wife, Gertrude, learnt of his death in a letter from a Chaplain of a Casualty Clearing Station, who said he was badly wounded by shell fire on the night of the 25th March, living only a few hours. The Chaplain added that he was given a Christian burial behind the dressing station and his grave marked by a wooden cross. That was next to the Ancre river in the village of Treux, Somme.

George was later reinterred in Ribemont Communal Cemetery Extension, near Amiens, France. A letter in his service record, from the War Office to the Commander in Chief of the Machine Gun Corps, records this re-internment, which occurred in December 1919 and that it was carried out carefully and reverently. The letter concluded with a request to inform the next of kin. On George's headstone the words of a traditional hymn are inscribed "FOR EVER WITH THE LORD."

George is commemorated locally on Sittingbourne War Memorial, Milton Regis War Memorial, St Paul's Church Memorial and Old Boys Milton Regis Council Schools Memorial.

Gertrude received his pay and gratuity, together with his 1914 Star with clasp, British War Medal, and Victory Medal. On 27th April 1918, the East Kent Gazette published a thank you in the personal column, reading "Mrs. George Beecham and Family, of 55 William Street, Milton Regis, wish to thank her many friends, especially her employer and fellow workers, for their kindness and sympathy shown to her on her bereavement."

George's brothers Charles and James both served. Charles, age 26, joined the Royal Naval Air Services from 25th September 1916, transferring to 233 Squadron, Royal Air Force on 1st April 1918, when the Royal Air Force was formed.

The squadron, based at Dover, were responsible for anti-submarine patrols. Charles was discharged on 20th April 1920.

His brother James, aged 18, enlisted on 9th November 1914 joining the Royal Fusiliers and was posted to France in February 1916. In August 1916 he was gassed and in May 1918 he was wounded in the hand from a gunshot, resulting in the amputation of his ring finger. He was discharged in May 1921.

The East Kent Gazette

SATURDAY, MARCH 29, 1919

IN MEMORIAM

BEECHAM - In ever loving memory of my dear husband, Trooper George Beecham Machine Gun Corps, late 4th Dragoon Guards, who died at the 9th Cavalry Field Ambulance Dressing Station, from shock of wounds received in action on the night of March 25th, 1918, aged 32 years. Buried in Amiens.

We know not how he suffered.
One year has passed, our hearts still sore
As times goes on we miss him more:
His loving smile, his welcome face.
For none can fill that vacant place.
Sorrowfully missed by his Wife and Children.

BELSOM, George Henry

6420, Private, 13th Battalion, Duke of Cambridge's Own (Middlesex) Regiment.

George was born in Teynham in 1878 and was baptised there on 2nd June that year in the parish church of St Mary's. He was the son of George, a brickmaker's labourer, and Jane (née Roalf). George was the third of their five children, Robert William, Louisa Jane (1875-1910), William James (1882-1911), and Walter Andrew.

In the summer of 1902, George married 22-year-old Edith Ellen Hickmott in Milton, and they had eight children, Annie, Florence Edith, Gladys Lilian, George Henry Aaron, Mabel Louisa, Walter Henry, Caroline Elizabeth, and Walter George. In 1911 the family were living at 53 New Road and George worked as a brickmaker's labourer. George enlisted in Canterbury in the Middlesex Regiment (Duke of Cambridge's Own) and was in Lapugnoy in March of 1917.

	WAR DIARY[19] or INTELLIGENCE SUMMARY. (Erase heading not required.)	Army Form C. 2118.
Instructions regarding War Diaries and Intelligence Summaries are contained in F.S. Regs., Part II, and the Staff Manual respectively. Title pages will be prepared in manuscript.		
Date	Summary of Events and Information	Remarks and References to Appendices
1-3-1917 to 4-3-1917	At rest in LAPUGNOY.	
5-3-1917	Battalion relieved 2ND BATTALION, 1ST CANADIAN INFANTRY near AIX-NOULETTE.	

[19] War Diary: 13 Battalion Middlesex Regiment. WO-95-2219-1. August 1915-November 1919. The National Archives (UK), Kew, England.

6-3-1917 to 9-3-1917	Remained in the line.
10-3-1917 to 16-3-1917	Battalion tasked with improving Lorette Defences in LENS.
16-3-1917	Returned to the line, relieving 9TH ROYAL SUSSEX REGIMENT, in SOUCHY SECTOR near VIMY RIDGE.
22-3-1917	Relieved by returning ROYAL SUSSEX and moved to billets at SAINS-EN-GOHELLE. Battalion designated Divisional Reserve.
23-3-1917 to 31-3-1917	Time spent in billets. Draft of 43 Other Ranks arrived.
	March casualties – 1 killed and 12 wounded.
1-4-1917	Battalion relieved 46TH and 47TH CANADIAN BATTALIONS in the line in CARENCY SECTOR.
2-4-1917	Preliminary bombardment started at 8am and brought heavy retaliation in return. Trenches in a bad condition.
	No diary entries for the 3rd to 7th April 1917.
8-4-1917	Battalion replaced by the CANADIANS. Moved to CHÂTEAU DE LA HAIE.

George was wounded on 4th April 1917 and died a few days later on 7th April 1917, aged 39. He was originally buried on the battlefield with at least five comrades, near the town of Souchez, with their graves marked with a battalion cross, before they were re-interred in the Canadian Cemetery No. 2 in Neuville-St Vaast. This cemetery was created on 9th April 1917 to cater for the scattered burials from the battle.

Locally, George is remembered on Sittingbourne War Memorial and St Michael's Church WW1 Memorial Window. George's wife received his pay and gratuity, and his Victory and British War Medals.

BLACK, Ralph Edgar

495226, Private, 2nd/2nd Field Ambulance, Royal Army Medical Corps.

Ralph was born in Rainham, Kent in 1897, the fifth of eight children of Alfred, a cement worker, and Emily Maria (née Copping). His brothers and sisters were named Albert Victor, Lilian Clark, Ada Ethel, Harold William, Mabel Ellen, Eva May, and Wilfrid James (1905-1910). In 1911, Ralph was a paper boy with Smith & Son, and was living at 26 Orchard Street, Rainham, with his parents, older brother Harold, who was a grocery assistant at the Co-op Society, and his three sisters, Ada, Mabel, and Eva.

Ralph's father had an accident in the crushing sheds at Smeed Dean cement works, Murston, on 28th May 1915, which was reported in the East Kent Gazette dated 12th June 1915. He was brought home bruised and hurt all over and said he had an accident pulling a rope of an elevator to start it, the rope broke and threw him on his back, and somehow twisted around his legs pulling him eight to ten feet from the ground before he fell. He was attended to by a doctor, but his condition worsened, and he died on 10th June from acute septicaemia due to thrombosis. An inquest determined the cause of death was accidental, with no blame.

Ralph enlisted in Sittingbourne, which is where he was living at the time, and served as a Private (although the plaque in the Avenue of Remembrance has him as Lance Corporal) with the 2nd/2nd Home Counties Field Ambulance, Royal Army Medical Corps.

On 12th May 1917, the Ambulance's War Diary[20] records they moved from Achiet-le-Grand to the eastern edge of Mory and set up a Main Dressing Station. They then set up a number of Advanced Dressing Stations, Registration Aid Posts and Relay Posts to the east of Mory, up to Bullecourt.

The diary recorded that two routes were set up and manned by a total of 24 four bearer squads, with the squads relieved on alternative days. The Field Ambulance on 5th June 1917 moved to Ervillers. Mory is situated between Arras

Regimental Aid Post

and Bapaume and in May 1917 the area was involved in the Battle of Arras, a defence against the Germans. The battle resulted in heavy losses and though seen as a British Victory there was no strategic or tactical gain. It was during this battle that Ralph was killed in action on 17th May 1917.

Under the headline KILLED ON THE BATTLEFIELD, the East Kent Gazette dated 26th May 1917, reported the death of 'another young patriot belonging to Sittingbourne'. The article said that Ralph's mother had been written to by a chaplain informing her that Ralph was performing a gallant deed at the time he met his death. He was carrying a wounded German officer towards the British lines when he was struck in the chest by a bullet and died the next day. The Chaplain, who buried the poor lad, conveyed deep sympathy in his letter. The report also recorded that Ralph's brother Harold was serving with the West Yorkshire Regiment and the family were living at 171 Shortlands Road.

Ralph was laid to rest in Mory Abbey Military Cemetery, Mory, France, at the age of 20. A poignant inscription is engraved on his headstone, reading "ONE OF THE BEST WHOM GOD COULD LEND A LOVING SON A FAITHFUL FRIEND."

Ralph attended Bible classes at Sittingbourne's Congregational Church (pictured right), where he was also a much-liked member of their choir.

He is remembered on both the Sittingbourne and the Rainham Congregational Churches Roll of Honours, sadly the latter has since been lost.

Ralph is also on his father's headstone in the Cemetery at Sittingbourne, and remembered on Sittingbourne War Memorial, Rainham War Memorial (pictured left), and St Michael's Church WW1 Memorial Window.

[20] War Diary: 2/2 Home Counties Field Ambulance. WO-95-2997-4. January 1917-April 1919. The National Archives (UK), Kew, England.

BLACKMAN, Bertie Percy

G/8902, Private, 8th Battalion, The Buffs (East Kent Regiment).

Bertie, known as Bert, was born in Rainham on 26th December 1889, the son of James, a boot and shoemaker, and Amy (née Alexander). By 1901 the family had moved to 9 Short Street, Sittingbourne, where they were still living in 1920. James and Amy had 15 children, but sadly seven did not survive infancy, the children were named Janette Matilda (1871-1871), William James, Annie Maud, George Henry, Stanley Thomas (1880-1880), Arthur (1882-1884), Elias Albert (1883-1884), Kate, Branchet Clara Augustus, Gertrude Louisa (1888-1889), Bert Percy, an unnamed boy (1890-1890), Louisa (1891-1894), Victoria May, and Lily.

Bert was a 5ft 3in tall brick labourer when he joined the army on 11th December 1915 at Canterbury. Bert served in France with the British Expeditionary Force from 10th February 1916. On 15th September 1916 he received a gunshot wound to the scalp and was admitted to No. 6 General Hospital in Rouen, from where he was transported back to England on 18th September 1916. A few months later on 9th December 1916 he was posted to the 3rd Battalion, The Buffs and sent to Étaples, France a month later, then on 21st January 1917 he re-joined the 8th Battalion. On 20th January 1917 he was appointed Lance Corporal, but the stripe was taken away from him in March 1917, after he loaded a live round instead of a dummy during training and injured Private Paterson in the calf of his right leg.

The below extract from his battalion's War Diary covers the period after losing his stripe:

Instructions regarding War Diaries and Intelligence Summaries are contained in F.S. Regs., Part II, and the Staff Manual respectively. Title pages will be prepared in manuscript.	WAR DIARY[21] or INTELLIGENCE SUMMARY. (Erase heading not required.)	Army Form C. 2118.
Date	Summary of Events and Information	Remarks and References to Appendices
27-3-1917	Battalion positioned at CORONS D'AIX (now known as AIX-NOULETTE). Weather dull, wet and cold.	
28-3-1917 to 1-4-1917	Weather dull, wet and cold. Occasional snow. Bosche flew over the trenches and seen off by rifle and machine-gun fire.	
2-4-1917	Relieved by 3RD BATTALION RIFLE BRIGADE and moved to BULLY-GRENAY.	
3-4-1917	Enemy shelled the village.	
4-4-1917	Enemy shelled the village. Enemy aeroplanes flying over the village. The Regimental Concert Party – The Buffellows, gave a concert, in spite of the fact that shells fell very near the Hall all the time.	
5-4-1917	Enemy heavily shelled the village to the extent that the battalion were forced to disperse into cellars and the nearby trenches MECHANICS TRENCH, LES BREBIS and PETIT-SANS. Enemy also fired a number of gas shells, affecting a number of the men for several days.	

[21] War Diary: 8 Battalion Buffs (East Kent Regiment). WO-95-2207-1. August 1915-January 1918. The National Archives (UK), Kew, England.

6-4-1917	*Shelling continued and despite this, the 6th Division 'Fancies' gave a concert.*
7-4-1917	*More shelling and Divisional Band gave a good performance.*
8-4-1917	*Battalion moved to ANGRES relieving 3RD BATTALION RIFLE BRIGADE.* *A number of gas shell craters, and the air very pungent.*
9-4-1917	*British artillery opened up on VIMY RIDGE and continued all day.* *Canadians attacked VIMY RIDGE. We watched the barrage creep forward and knew the Canadians must be gaining their objectives.* *Several Bosche in the trenches opposite us, obviously taken by surprise at the suddenness of the blow at VIMY, stood up – to better see the show – and three of them were promptly knocked out by our sniping officer.*
10-4-1917 to 13-4-1917	*Enemy intermittent shelling and aerial activity.*
14-4-1917	*There is not a sound to be heard, no shelling, no sniping.* *Battalion observers reported enemy trenches looked empty and by 10pm battalion had advanced unopposed to ROLLENCOURT.*
15-4-1917	*Battalion moved to billets in LIÉVIN.*

During the enemy action on 6th April 1917 at Bully-Grenay 28-year-old Bert was killed in action.

He is remembered on the Arras Memorial to the Missing, and locally on Sittingbourne War Memorial and Sittingbourne Holy Trinity Church Memorial.

Bert's mother, Amy, was the sole recipient of his pay and gratuity. She also received his Victory and British War Medals.

His death was announced under the ROLL OF HONOUR, in the Births, deaths and marriages column in the East Kent Gazette of 12th May 1917.

The East Kent Gazette

SATURDAY, APRIL 19, 1919

IN MEMORIAM

BLACKMAN – In loving memory of my dear son, Pte. Bert Blackman, of the 8th Buffs, who was killed in action in France, on April 16th, 1916, in his 26th year.
"Gone, but not forgotten."
> We have lost him we love,
> We like others must be brave;
> For we know that he is lying
> In a British soldier's grave.
> What pains he bore we cannot tell,
> We did not see him die;
> We only know he passed away,
> And never said good-bye.
> From his sorrowing Mother, Sisters and Brother.

The East Kent Gazette

SATURDAY, APRIL 17, 1920

IN MEMORIAM

BLACKMAN - In loving memory of my dear son, Private Bert Blackman, who was killed in action in France, on April 16th, 1916,
> 'Tis just three years ago to-day
> Our own dear boy did fall;
> We did not hear his last farewell.
> Nor hear him faintly call
> His country called him and he went,
> No nobler deed was done.
> And on the battlefield so far way
> There lies my own dear son.

From his ever-loving Mum, Sisters and Brother.

BODIAM, Ernest Percy

G/8594, Private, 6th Battalion, Queen's Own (Royal West Kent Regiment).

Ernest was born on 4th January 1898 in Luton, Chatham and baptised in Christ Church, Luton on 12th August 1898. He was the son of Amos, a farm labourer, and Clara Louisa (née Barrett). His father died in 1900, leaving five children Florence Edith, Alfred Albert, Mabel Louisa, Ernest, and Ethel Olive. In 1903 Ernest's mother married John Richard Wood and they had three children Nelly Elizabeth, Sidney, and Emma. In 1901 and 1911 Ernest was living with his maternal aunt Florence and uncle Ernest at 8 Nelson Terrace, Luton, Kent.

When he enlisted, he was living in Queenborough and had attended Holy Trinity Church, Sittingbourne, where he is remembered. Ernest is also commemorated on Queenborough's war memorial.

The East Kent Gazette of 29th July 1916 under the headline BUFFS & KENT LOSSES – WEST KENT CASUALTIES – WOUNDED lists Ernest, amongst a long list of names.

Prisoner of War documents from the International Red Cross record that Ernest was captured on 19th July 1917 at Monchy, after being wounded in the thigh and transferred to a field hospital. The CWGC records Ernest died on the same day, aged 19.

Ernest was buried in Cabaret-Rouge British Cemetery, Souchez, (below) after he was moved from his original burial place at Dechy Communal Cemetery, as part of a programme to consolidate the fallen from over 100 cemeteries and also battlefield burials. The cemetery holds hundreds of Canadian Infantry killed in the battles at Vimy Ridge and in 2000 an unknown Canadian soldier was taken and re-buried in the Tomb of the Unknown Soldier, at the foot of Canada's National War Memorial in Ottawa.

Ernest is remembered locally on Sittingbourne War Memorial and Sittingbourne Holy Trinity Church Memorial. Both the Victory and British War Medals were awarded to Ernest.

BOLTON, Albert John

T/270198, Private, The Buffs (East Kent Regiment).
"B" Coy. 10th (Royal East Kent and West Kent Yeomanry) Battalion.

Albert, born in 1894, was the youngest child of William Riley, a railway carriage coach painter, and Ellen (née Davis). William and Ellen were a mobile family as they had married in Bristol, and their first child William Harry was born in Northamptonshire. Their next child, Clara Gertrude, was born in Norfolk and then they settled in Ashford, Kent, where George Frederick, Edward Riley, and Albert were all born. The 1911 census showed they were living at 10 Lower Denmark Road, South Ashford, with Albert living at home and working as a grocer's shop assistant.

When Albert enlisted at Canterbury in May 1915, he was 5ft 9in tall and living at 6 Terrace Road, Sittingbourne. He embarked from Gallipoli to Mudros, Greece on the 3rd February 1916. On 21st December 1917 he attended an Aid Post in the field with pleurisy and was admitted to 36th Stationary Hospital in Mohammediya, Egypt, rejoining his battalion in the field on 5th February 1918.

On 1st May 1918 the battalion boarded *HT Malwa* and arrived in Marseilles on 7th May. The battalion War Diary records they spent the next three months in reserve and training, and periods on the front line in August.

This War Diary extract records the events of September.

Instructions regarding War Diaries and Intelligence Summaries are contained in F.S. Regs., Part II, and the Staff Manual respectively. Title pages will be prepared in manuscript.	WAR DIARY[22] or INTELLIGENCE SUMMARY. (Erase heading not required.)	Army Form C. 2118.
Date	Summary of Events and Information	Remarks and References to Appendices
2-9-1918	8.45am - Assembled north of the RIVER SOMME. Area shelled all day with high explosive and gas.	
3-9-1918	Company moved into the line from MOISLAINS to ALLAINES.	
4-9-1918	Moved to the Front Line, at CANAL DU NORD, to the east, relieving 224TH BRIGADE.	
5-9-1918	Battalion advanced east and captured MIDINETTE TRENCH at 1.15pm. Continued 2km from the canal and halted by enemy machine gun fire.	
6-9-1918	8am - Battalion advanced (with Albert's company in reserve). 3/45pm - Reached final objective at LONGAVESNES.	
7-9-1918 to 9-9-1918	Battalion consolidated position in the line and salvaging the trenches.	
10-9-1918	Battalion returned to the Front Line at ÉPEHY	
11-9-1918	Front Line very wet. Considerable Machine Gun and Artillery fire during the day.	
12-9-1918 to 13-9-1918	Battalion remained in the line under enemy artillery fire.	

22 War Diary: 10 Battalion East Kent Regiment (Buffs). WO-95-3153-2. May 1918-May 1919. The National Archives (UK), Kew, England.

14-9-1918	*Battalion relieved and moved near to LONGAVASNES.*
17-9-1918	*Returned to Front Line at TEMPLEUX-LE-GUÉRARD relieving the 15TH SUFFOLKS. 59 Other Ranks from draft were taken on strength.*
18-9-1918	*Albert's company moved under barrage at 8.30am advancing on CONNOR POST and SUNKEN ROAD, and 'C' COMPANY on CARBINE ZOGDA TRENCH.*

During the action on 18th September 1918, 24-year-old Albert was killed.

Albert's service record was damaged as a result of a fire in the Second World War, but it includes correspondence between Albert's father, his regiment, and the Imperial War Graves Commission. Some areas of the documents are missing and therefore the information is incomplete. Albert's father wrote to his regiment asking where he was buried, and his letter was passed to the Imperial War Graves. Their response was that Albert was buried on the battlefield, in the vicinity of Hargicourt, East-North-East of Peronne. They added that they were carefully and systematically searching the battlefields for any graves.

Further correspondence noted that his burial location could not be found and stated that the 10th Battalion had been in position at Connor Post, which is located just north of Hargicourt, Aisne, France.

Sadly, as Albert's grave was not located, he is listed on CWGC's Vis-en-Artois Memorial to the Missing. He is also commemorated on St Michael's Church WW1 Memorial Window and Sittingbourne War Memorial.

Albert's father, William, received his pay and gratuity, together with his 1915 Star, Victory, and British War Medals.

BONNETT, Frank John

36040, Private, East Surrey Regiment, posted to London Regiment (First Surrey Rifles).

Frank was born in 1895 in Sittingbourne, and was the son of Edward, a bricklayer, and Minnie (née Russell), and he had two older sisters, Florence Electra, and Minnie Lily, both of whom had been born in the United States of America. Florence in 1887 in Whitewater, Wisconsin, and Minnie in 1890 in Beloit, Wisconsin. Frank unusually was baptised twice at St Michael's Church, firstly on 30th May 1895 and again on 16th July 1899, with his sisters.

In the 1901, census, Frank is noted as living with his parents and sisters at 109 East Street. Ten years, later one sister has left the household, and they have a boarder at 13 Connaught Road, Milton.

The 14th September 1918 edition of the East Kent Gazette reported on Frank's death with the headline AN ONLY SON KILLED. Frank was expected home on leave when his parents received the sad news. The night before receiving it, his mother had a premonition and dreamt that she was attending Frank's funeral.

The news was conveyed in a letter from medical orderly Sergeant A. Boughton, which said: "I regret to inform you of the death of your son Frank, who died on August 23rd whilst collecting wounded. The Section join me in offering you our heartfelt sympathy in your bereavement. I assure you he was one of our best stretcher bearers, and it is a great loss to us. He is buried by his comrades."

The report noted that Frank was well known and had attended the Wesleyan Day School before working in the paper mill and rising to the position of dyer-man.

The article explained that Frank had joined the army in January 1917 and entered the Royal Flying Corps as a mechanic, passing out as a 2nd Class Air Mechanic at RFC Halton, Wendover. Six months later he was transferred to the Rifle Brigade, London Regiment, and posted to France on 23rd August 1917. The following March 1918, after a long spell as a stretcher bearer, he was on his way home and actually on-board ship at Boulogne, when the German offensive started. All the men were then recalled back to their units.

On 6th April, Frank was slightly wounded and severely gassed, initially being treated at No. 3 Casualty Clearing Station, which was based at Gézaincourt, France, before a four-month hospital stay. Following his hospital discharge he re-joined his regiment and six weeks later was killed aged 23, on 24th August 1918, a year and one day after being posted to France.

Frank was buried in Bray Hill British Cemetery, in Bray-Sur-Somme, France and he is also remembered on the Sittingbourne War Memorial, St Michael's Church WW1 Memorial Window and Lloyd's Paper Mill Memorial.

Bray Hill British Cemetery is a small cemetery with 105 casualties, of which 33 are unknown. With the exception of four casualties who died in March 1918, all the known casualties died within an eight-day period from 22nd to 28th August 1918. Sixty-five of the casualties were associated with the London Regiment. Frank's plot number denotes that he was re-interred in this cemetery after originally being buried in the battlefield.

His family chose the inscription "GONE FROM SIGHT BUT NOT FROM MEMORY" for his headstone.

The Victory and British War Medals were awarded to Frank.

Mrs Bonnett's brother, Private Alfred Warren Russell of the Royal Fusiliers, was reported missing for several months, and then declared officially as Missing, Killed in Action on 15th June 1917, in France. Her daughter, Minnie, was married to Corporal Charles Gordon Hancock, in the Royal Engineers, who was a despatch rider and served in France for the last two years of the war and survived.

BOWER, Herbert

5446, Private, 2nd Battalion, Honourable Artillery Company.

Sittingbourne War Memorial is inscribed with the name 'H Bowes' and St Michael's Church WW1 Memorial Window commemorates a 'H Bowers.' The East Kent Gazette dated 7th January 1922 reporting the window's dedication records an H Bowers serving with the H.A.C. The only recorded casualty in the CWGC database that is a close match to these names and regiment is Herbert. Though at the time of printing no connection to Sittingbourne could be found for Herbert, Research is ongoing to identify his connection to the town and here we tell Herbert's story.

Herbert was born in 1892, in Poplar, Middlesex, and was the middle child of nine children of Henry Herman Stillgebauer and Catherine Jane (née Whitehorn). The family name was Stillgebauer, and all the children's births were registered with this surname, though in all later records they use Bower. His siblings were named Adelaide Catherine (1885-1887), Ada Annie, Henry Ernest, Edith, William Edward, Alice May, Arthur Alfred, and May Bessie.

Herbert's father, Henry, was born in Sheffield, Yorkshire, the son of Heinrich Herman Franz Stillgebauer and Mary Ann Cooling from Limehouse, Middlesex. In the 1881 census Henry recorded the family's surname as Bower, which was a common adaptation of the German surname Bauer. Herbert's grandfather Heinrich Herman Franz Stillgebauer was born in 1836 in Switzerland.

`The 1911 Census records the family living at 18 Ettrick Street, Poplar, East London. Herbert, aged 19 years, was listed as a library assistant and his father as an engine fitter.

Herbert was 5ft 7in tall when he enlisted on 22nd November 1915. He arrived in Le Havre, France on 3rd October 1916, then proceeded to the Front the next day. He served as a 'Bomber' and was home on leave from 17th to 27th August 1917. His battalion's War Diary once he returned to the field is transcribed here:

Instructions regarding War Diaries and Intelligence Summaries are contained in F.S. Regs., Part II, and the Staff Manual respectively. Title pages will be prepared in manuscript.	WAR DIARY[23] or INTELLIGENCE SUMMARY. (Erase heading not required.)	Army Form C. 2118.
Date	Summary of Events and Information	Remarks and References to Appendices
30-8-1917	Battalion travelled from HENDECOURT-LÈS-RANSART to EECKE.	
31-8-1917 to 2-9-1917	Training on Lewis Guns, Gas Drills and practising attacks.	
3-9-1917	Battalion moved to HONDEGHEM. Fine and sunny. Company Training.	
8-9-1917 to 27-9-1917	Moved to STAPLE. Rested and took part in inter-company competitions for Best Turnout and Route Marching. Training and lectures. Battalion spent time in BANDRINGHEM and QUELMES.	
28-9-1917	Battalion entrained to CAËSTRE.	

---

[23] War Diary: 2nd Battalion Honourable Artillery Company. WO-95-1662-1. 1 September 1916 – 30 November 1917. The National Archives (UK), Kew, England.

29-9-1917	Marched over Belgium border to DICKEBUSCH.
30-9-1917	Fine and warm.
	Battalion moved into support at the railway dugouts at ZILLEBEKE by 6.30pm. Seven casualties caused by enemy aeroplanes en route.
1-10-1917	Relieved 2ND ROYAL WARWICKSHIRES in nearby Ritz Trench.
2-10-1917	Returned to DICKEBUSCH.
3-10-1917	Weather cooler and showery.
	Carried duckboards to RITZ TRENCH at HOOGE.
4-10-1917	5am Battalion moved to ZILLEBEKE LAKE. Served breakfast on arrival.
	Awaiting orders to move later in the day. Orders did not appear.
5-10-1917	Very cold and wet.
	Battalion moved back to DICKEBUSCH to the SCOTTISH CAMP and ordered to stand by to move. Orders did not appear.
7-10-1917	Stormy and very wet day.
	Battalion moved into shelters at ZILLEBEKE and were served a hot dinner and tea. At 4.30pm the same day the battalion moved into the front line at HOOGE CRATER, completing the move at 2.45am.
8-10-1917	Tape laid out for attack towards REUTEL, south of POLYGON WOOD.
9-10-1917	5.20am Attack started. 5.25am Enemy counter barrage started.
	5.55am First objective of JUDGE COTTAGE and CEMETERY and JUNIPER COTTAGE reached. Remainder of the day patrols sent out.
10-10-1917	Battalion relieved and moved to ZILLEBEKE LAKE.

It was during the attack on the 9th October 1917 that Herbert died, aged 25 years, together with 84 men from his battalion and they are amongst the 34,991 names commemorated on the Tyne Cot Memorial to the Missing.

He is remembered on Sittingbourne War Memorial, spelt as Bowes, and St Michael's Church WW1 Memorial Window spelt as Bowers.

Herbert's personal effects were sent to his father, and they included his identity disc, letters, photos, cards, and wallet. Herbert was awarded the Victory and British War Medals, and they were also sent to his father.

Herbert's brother Henry served with the Princess Charlotte of Wales's (Royal Berkshire) Regiment and his brother William served as a Gunner, with the 330th Brigade, Royal Field Artillery.

Tape path laid to the front

BRAY, Gordon Victor

G/614, Corporal, 6th Battalion, The Buffs (East Kent Regiment).

Gordon was born in Sheerness on 29th April 1897 and was baptised in the dockyard church of St Paul's on the same day, which also happened to be the fourth wedding anniversary of his parents. At the time of Gordon's birth his father, James, was a Church of England Temperance Society Police Court Missionary and a short time later was licenced as a Lay Preacher, prior to that he was a coal miner in Cumberland. James was to become Kent's first probation officer, he opened Britain's first remand home, was a Justice of the Peace and a town councillor from 1922 to 1942. Gordon's mother, Alice, was recorded to be a Preventive and Rescue Worker in the 1911 census.

Gordon was the second son of James and his second wife Alice Louisa May (née Peake) whose other children were Charles (1895-1898), Arthur, Albert Edward, and William James. He also had a stepbrother and sister, from his father's first marriage to Margaret Ann Banks (who died in 1891, aged 24) John (1889-1905), and Polly Margaret (born 1891).

Gordon went to Milton Regis Council School and in 1911 the family were living at 152 Park Road and Gordon was an errand boy.

Before he enlisted, Gordon, who was 5ft 4½in tall with blue eyes, had worked for Smeed Dean and Co as an apprentice fitter. He had worked for them for 207 days and they had given him permission to enlist. When he enlisted in Canterbury, on 31st August 1914, he gave his age as 19 years and 154 days, although his true age was two years younger. Gordon embarked for France on the 1st June 1915 and ten weeks later on the 15th August 1915 he was appointed Lance Corporal.

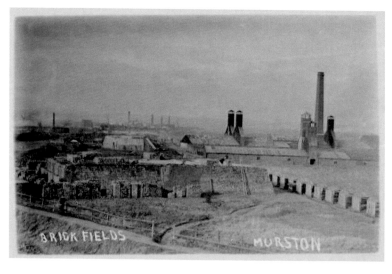

On 1st January 1916 Gordon was mentioned in the Commander in Chief Field Marshall Sir John French's despatch for gallantry and distinguished conduct in the field, which was reported in the East Kent Gazette of 8th January 1916. On 16th September 1916 he was appointed Corporal, but just three weeks later, Gordon was posted as wounded and missing.

His battalion's War Diary[24] records that on 6th October 1916 the battalion had relieved the 6th Queens in the front-line trenches at Gueudecourt, 15km north-east of the town of Albert. The next day orders were received to attack the line to the east of the village, with the 6th Royal West Kent Regiment on their left. At 1.30pm the enemy opened with heavy machine gun fire and fifteen minutes later the attack

---

[24] War Diary: 6 Battalion Buffs (East Kent Regiment). WO-95-1860-3. September 1916-December 1917. The National Archives (UK), Kew, England.

commenced. By midnight the first objective was taken, though with heavy casualties. The battalion were then relieved and moved into bivouacs at Longueval Valley. The diary recorded 347 Other Ranks killed, wounded, or missing. Gordon was officially recorded as being 'Missing presumed Killed in Action' that day, 7th October 1916, aged 19.

The 5th May 1917 issue of the East Kent Gazette published a report entitled BELIEVED TO BE DEAD.

> BELIEVED TO BE DEAD.—We regret to learn that Corpl. Gordon Bray, son of Mr. J. Bray, of Chatham (formerly of Sittingbourne), is now regarded as having died from his injuries on the battlefield. He was reported wounded and missing in October last, and it is feared that a shell blew him to pieces. Mr. Bray has also learnt that his son-in-law, Corpl. H. Uings, of the Royal West Kents, was wounded on Easter Monday, and is now in hospital at Richmond, Surrey. Gordon Bray was well known at Sittingbourne, and his many friends will regret to learn of his sad end.

Gordon was 19 years old and was awarded the 1914-15 Star, Victory, and British War Medals. His pay and gratuity were paid to his father. Gordon was also awarded a Meritorious Service Medal, for gallantry.

He is one of the 72,333 casualties commemorated on the Thiepval Memorial to the Missing in France.

Locally he is remembered on Sittingbourne War Memorial, Milton Regis War Memorial, St Paul's Church Memorial and Old Boys Milton Regis Council School Memorial.

In June 1920 his father was sent his medal, and he wrote to ask if there had been a mistake;

> 'Should it not read Corporal or Lance Corporal and not Private? I don't know that it matters much, we mourn him just the same. It was my other boys that cause me to write.'

BRENCHLEY, William Edward Charles

A/200337, Corporal, 11th Battalion, King's Royal Rifle Corps.

William was born in Sittingbourne in 1895, the son of Emily Brenchley. In 1901 he was living with Emily's parents, Edward Brenchley, a brick sorter, and Sarah, with his name recorded as William Miller.

In 1911 he was living with his father and mother William and Emily Miller as their son, but with the surname Brenchley, at 14 Lloyds Square, Sittingbourne. They had five other children alive at the time, George, Clara, Edith, Nelly, and Hilda. The census records that three other children had died, though research has not identified their names.

William attended Milton Council School and Holy Trinity Church, Sittingbourne, then worked at Lloyd's Paper Mill as an assistant reelerman. In Spring 1915, William married Rhoda Smith, in Milton Regis, and they lived with Rhoda's parents at 14 Goodnestone Road, Sittingbourne.

William enlisted at Sittingbourne in December 1914 and joined The Buffs. He then served in the King's Royal Rifle Corps as a Corporal. His battalion's War Diary[25] placed them at the end of August 1917 in Prattle Camp in Proven, north-west of Poperinge, Belgium, where they received a draft of 79 other ranks. On 3rd September 1917 a further 23 other ranks arrived and the following day the battalion moved just over the French-Belgium border to Herzeele. Here the battalion started training for platoon attacks, until 8th September when they returned to Proven, following a further reinforcement of 40 other ranks.

---

[25] War Diary: 11 Battalion King's Royal Rifle Corps. WO-95-2115-2. July 1915-March 1919. The National Archive (UK), Kew, England.

On 11th September 1917 the battalion moved to Divisional Reserve at Roussol Farm, north-west of Ypres. The next week was spent training for attacks. At 3am on 20th September they moved to the tape line on the eastern side of Langemark-Poelkapelle, relieving the Kings Own Yorkshire Light Infantry. The diary for the day records they lined up in three waves without a hitch and prepared to attack. At 5.40am the barrage started, and the front line moved to within 50 yards of their objective, Eagle Trench (pictured below). The right of the trench was found to be strongly held by at least six machine guns and a large number of Germans and the line was held up by severe bombing and suffering heavy losses.

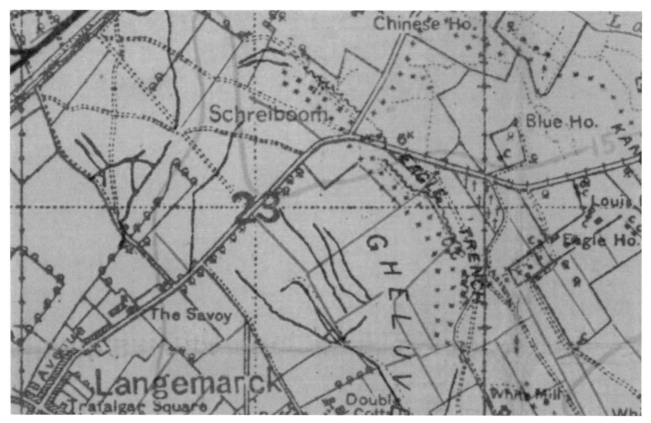

The left side of the trench was reached without opposition and occupied. The platoon continued and took up positions, in shell holes, 80 yards short of Chinese House, where they were stopped by machine gun fire. They remained here until dusk and were then withdrawn, back to Eagle Trench.

At 11pm an order was received from Brigade to withdraw the battalion to the west of the Steenbeek, where they remained the following day and the next day, they returned to Roussol Farm. The diary recorded the losses as 42 killed, 43 missing and 139 wounded. The CWGC database shows of the 85 killed only 8 were recovered for burial.

It was during this action on 20th September 1917 that 22-year-old William was killed and listed as missing.

His death was reported in the East Kent Gazette edition of 27th October 1917. He is remembered on the Tyne Cot Memorial in Belgium and locally on a number of memorials including Sittingbourne War Memorial, Lloyd's Paper Mill Memorial, Sittingbourne Holy Trinity Church, St Michael's Memorial Window, and in Milton Regis on the Milton Regis War Memorial, St Paul's Church, and Old Boys Milton Regis Council Schools Memorials.

His wife Rhoda received a letter after his death from Lieutenant C G Webb of his regiment who wrote: "The deceased was waiting in a trench ready to move forward, when a shell burst close by and killed him and another man instantaneously. He was a very good soldier, well-liked by his men, and the loss you have sustained is also a great loss to us, as he was a very good NCO (Non-Commissioned Officer)." The officer concluded by asking Mrs Brenchley to accept his sincere sympathy in her bereavement. Rhoda received William's pay and gratuity.

BREWER, George William

9791, Private, 7th Battalion, East Surrey Regiment.

George was born in Melton, Hampshire, in August 1887, the second child of George William and Sarah Alice (née Williams), who had five children, Alice Audrey, Elsie Lilian, Arthur John aka Jack, and Emily Esther Maud.

George also had three stepsiblings named Benjamin Francis, Samuel Frederick Charles, and Florence Mary (aka Florrie) whose father was Frank Douch. The 1901 census records all the children had the surname Douch, and in the 1911 census they went by the name of Brewer. George, like his father and stepfather was an engine driver.

His family had moved around the country, Great Missenden, Buckinghamshire in 1891, Hanwell, Middlesex in 1901 and Coedffranc, Glamorgan, South Wales in 1911. At the time George enlisted on 14th July 1915 he was living at 13 Station Street, Sittingbourne, with his sister Alice. His mother was in Higher Irlam, Lancashire, though his service record shows she had moved to live with Alice.

George was 5ft 9¼in tall and a month short of his 28th birthday when he enlisted on 14th July 1915 at Hounslow, Middlesex stating he was a steam locomotive driver. He arrived in Étaples, France on 1st December 1915.

Oxford & Bucks Camp at Martinsart Wood

The CWGC and service record for George record he was killed in action on 29th July 1916. The War Diary[26] for the 7th Battalion, East Surrey Regiment records that they were being held in reserve at Martinsart Wood near Thiepval. As George was posted missing and the date was unknown, the army officially recorded his death as 29th July, but it is therefore probable that George was killed at the beginning of July, when the battalion, with The Buffs, The Queens and West Kents, were involved in an attack on the towns of La Boisselle and Ovillers. The attack started on the 1st and lasted for six days with over a thousand casualties, of which 50 plus were East Surrey Regiment.[27]

---

[26] War Diary: 7 Battalion East Surrey Regiment. WO-95-1862-2. 1916. The National Archives (UK), Kew, England.

[27] The Queen's Royal Surrey Regiment. *War Diary, 7th Battalion, East Surrey Regiment-July 1916.*
www.queensroyalsurreys.org.uk/war_diaries/local/7Bn_East_Surrey/7Bn_East_Surrey_1916/7Bn_East_Surrey_1916_07.shtml

George was killed just before his 29th birthday and is remembered on the Thiepval Memorial to the Missing in France and locally on Sittingbourne War Memorial.

George's mother received his wallet and photos after his death, and he was awarded the 1914-15 Star, Victory, and British War Medals.

On 1st July 1916, just four weeks before George's death, La Boisselle (pictured below) was the worst battlefield in British military history, with 6,380 casualties, and of the 2,267 who died only 340 are named. This was the start of the Battle of the Somme, and is recognised as the bloodiest day, which resulted in over 57,000 casualties, including 19,240 fatalities.

Also, on this first day the largest man-made explosion occurred just 1.7km from La Boiselle when a mine was exploded at 07.28am, two minutes before Zero Hour. The mine was laid by the British Army's 179th Tunnelling Company Royal Engineers, with 60,000lbs (27 tons) of explosive. This resulted in the creation of Lochnagar Crater, measuring 100m wide by 21m deep.

The period from the 1st to 13th July 1916 were entitled the Battle of Albert.

Credit: National Army Museum NAM. 2001-01-277-4

In 1915, having lied about his age, George's 15-year-old stepbrother Samuel Brewer (aka Douch), (pictured left), was serving with A Coy, 4th Platoon, 53rd Bedfordshire on the Rhine. Samuel reached his 16th birthday whilst serving on the Somme. In 1942 he is recorded as serving in the Home Guard with 42nd County of Lancaster (Irlam) Battalion.

Samuel's own 20-year son, Reginald Brewer, served as a Private with 2nd Battalion, North Staffordshire Regiment, and was killed on 8th February 1944 in Italy. He is buried in Anzio War Cemetery.

BROWN, Edward Thomas

G/5604, Private, 6th Battalion, The Buffs (East Kent Regiment).

Edward was born in Sittingbourne in 1879 and was baptised at the parish church of St Michael on 6th April that year. He was the eldest of the eight children of Richard Milliner Brown, a brickfield labourer, and Clara (née Spice). His siblings were Richard Milliner, Amos William (1882-1883), Stephen Amos, Catherine (1889-1911), Mary Ann (1891-1893), Edgar Belsom, and Dorothy May.

Edward married Emily Frances Reuben in January 1909, and they had three daughters, May Winifred (born 1909) and Lilian Clara (born 1910) and Florence Katherine (born 1913). By then he was working as a fitter's labourer at the paper mill.

When Edward enlisted in Sittingbourne on 22nd January 1915, he recorded the family as living at 3 Lorne Place, Sittingbourne. He joined The Buffs and landed in France on 12th May 1915.

His battalion's War Diary[28] records that they were at Ivergny and Arras, training, from mid-June 1917 to 9th July before moving into the trenches to the south-east of Arras relieving the East Surrey Regiment. The diary entry for the 11th records an enemy attack at their position in Long Trench, after "a heavy bombardment of all calibres. Smoke and Liquid fire was used." It was also recorded that enemy aeroplanes flew low over the trenches with little opposition. By noon, 63 casualties were noted.

On the 13th the battalion was relieved by the Royal West Kent Regiment and moved to nearby Wancourt Line, spending the next five days on working parties and a day in the baths. The rest of the month was occupied on working parties.

The 1st August saw the battalion move to the Brown Line, being relieved by the 6th Battalion, The Queens. The following day "The whole battalion had baths at Tillroy." On the evening of the 3rd the battalion sent 100 Other Ranks to the line at Hooks Trench to the north-east, to support the Queens and Royal West Kents due to an enemy attack. The next day further reinforcements of 130 men from the Transport Details, consisting of "Drums, Storemen, Grooms etc" and the Divisional Depot Battalion arrived. Edward was one of those sent to Hooks Trench, where he was killed in action on 3rd August 1917, aged 38.

The East Kent Gazette carried both a notice, under the ROLL OF HONOUR and report of Edward's death. The report was headlined:

DIED OF GUNSHOT WOUNDS – A SITTINGBOURNE HERO'S DEATH.

[28] War Diary: 37 Infantry Brigade: 6 Battalion Buffs (East Kent Regiment). WO-95-1860-3. September 1916-December 1917. The National Archives (UK), Kew, England.

The report reproduced several letters that Emily had received, with the first dated 29th July 1917, from Base Hospital No.4, Camiers, Matron Grace E Allison, notifying her that he had been wounded.

Dear Mrs. Brown – I am sorry to write that your husband Pte. Brown, 5604, has arrived at hospital suffering from a gunshot wound of the back. He is very sick, although not considered in immediate danger, but we hope for the best. I wanted you to know that we are doing all we can for him in every way, and that he is having good care. Please accept my deepest sympathy. – Very sincerely.

Matron Allison sent a second letter dated 31st July 1917, which read:

I am sorry to tell you that Pte. Brown has been placed on the danger list and is considered to be a very sick man; in fact, I doubt very much if he will survive the next twenty-four hours. He came to us a few days ago suffering from a gunshot wound of the back and has had a change for the worse in the last twelve hours, since I wrote to you. I am, indeed, very sorry to write you this sad news. With deepest sympathy, I am, sincerely yours.

The last letter from Matron Allison was on 3rd August 1917 and arrived with an additional letter, from the hospital Chaplain. The matron wrote:

My Dear Mrs Brown, - I am very sad to write you that Pte. Brown passed away this morning at nine o'clock. He had been unconscious for the past twenty-four hours and did not realise his condition. My heart aches to send you this sad message, and I hope you feel our sympathy. He will be buried to-morrow, having a military funeral. I am enclosing a lock of his hair, and his personal effects will be sent to you by registered mail of the Government Department. I assure you we did all we could to save him. In deepest sympathy.

The second letter from the Church of England Chaplain to the Forces, C H P Hodges, read:

Dear Mrs Brown, - Please accept my deep sympathy in your loss. I had the privilege of ministering your husband. It was a great shock when he took a turn for the worse. I had just begun to prepare him for Confirmation, but when he became seriously ill, I gave him the sacrament of the Church. He lingered for several days and knew me each time I went to him. He was not, I feel sure, in pain, although at times his mind went back a bit to the trenches. I am sure he was really peaceful. Every care and ease possible was given him. I shall take funeral to-morrow. You would like the cemetery where our dead lie, and the work of planting flowers and making the graves beautiful goes ahead day by day. May God grant you His own comfort, and give light and rest to your husband. – P.S. – Will be buried August 4th, at Saint Severs Cemetery, Rouen.

Edward was 38 years old when he was buried in St Sever Cemetery Extension in Rouen. Rouen during the First World War was a primary location for hospitals, which included eight general, five stationary, one British Red Cross and one labour hospital, and No. 2 Convalescent Depot. The great majority of those that died there are buried in St Sever Cemetery and the extension which was added in September 1916.

Credit: New Zealand War Graves Project

Emily, Edward's wife, was sent his personal effects of photos, letters, cards, cuttings, testament, 'The Soldier's Friend', metal mirror, tobacco pouch, ring, pipe disc, 2 cap badges, 2 silver stripes and a purse. She also received his pay and gratuity and his 1914-15 Star, British War Medal, and Victory Medal. Edward is commemorated on Sittingbourne's War Memorial and Holy Trinity Church WW1 Memorial.

The lady who wrote the letters, Matron Grace Evelyn Allison, was a 27-year-old American nurse from Lakeside Hospital, Cleveland, Ohio, who had arrived in France on 8th May 1917. She served until 23rd November 1918. Grace died in 1966 aged 85 and is buried in the military Arlington National Cemetery in Washington DC, USA. In March 1919, she wrote articles which told of her experiences during the war published in the American Journal of Nursing: 'Some Experiences in Active Service – France' then in August 1919 one entitled 'What the war has taught us about nursing education'.

BROWN, Percival

290583, Private, 1st/1st Battalion, Cambridgeshire Regiment.

Percival was born in Teynham, in 1884, and was baptised on 21st May that year in the parish church of St Mary's. He was the son of Henry John, an agricultural labourer, and Sophia (née Percival) who died in 1890 when Percival was just six years old. One of nine, Percival was the seventh child, his siblings were Alice Kate, Ernest, Henry (1875-1876), William Charles, Alfred, Edith Sarah (1881-1882), Martha Eleanor, and Harry George (1888-1911). In 1901 Percival was working as a carter in the brickfields.

On 25th January 1908 he married 23-year-old Emily Alice Maybourne in Lynsted. They moved to 35 Cowper Road, Sittingbourne, where the family were still living when Percival died. Emily had their only child on 15th January 1911, Percival William. Percival enlisted with the Suffolk Regiment in Sittingbourne and served with them as a Private.

An extract from the battalion's War Diary[29] leading up to the death of Percival is transcribed here:

	WAR DIARY or INTELLIGENCE SUMMARY. (Erase heading not required.)	Army Form C. 2118.
Instructions regarding War Diaries and Intelligence Summaries are contained in F.S. Regs., Part II, and the Staff Manual respectively. Title pages will be prepared in manuscript.		
Date	Summary of Events and Information	Remarks and References to Appendices
1-8-1918	Reconnaissance carried out of support lines at BUIRE-SUR-ANCRE and RIBEMONT.	
2-8-1918	Embussed at 12.30pm – debussed on CONTAY-FRANKVILLERS ROAD and marched via ROUND WOOD and FRANKVILLERS to support lines at RIBEMONT	
3 to 6-8-1918	Usual trench work – improving trenches at RIBEMONT	
7-8-1918	6pm – Battalion moved to BALLARAT and BENDIGO lines south of RIVER ANCRE	
8-8-1918	4.20am – Battalion attacked and captured enemy position W of MORLANCOURT	
9-8-1918	5.30pm - Battalion attacked and captured MORLANCOURT	
10 to 15-8-1918	In reserve in trenches. Reorganised and reequipped	
16 to 18-8-1918	10pm – Relieved 5TH R BERKS in right of subsection K4b and K5 of MORLANCOURT	

---

[29] War Diary: 1 Battalion Cambridgeshire Regiment. WO-95-1850-2. May 1918-March 1919. The National Archives (UK), Kew, England.

19-8-1918	Relieved by 9TH ESSEX REGIMENT and moved into Div. reserves in VILLES-SUR-ANCRE
20-8-1918	In reserve in K1C. Reconnaissance carried out
21-8-1918	9pm – Moved into position in front line in E4b – E5a & c preparing for attack
22-8-1918	4.30am – Assembly completed on tapes laid out. Made difficult owing to counter preparation from the enemy and several casualties.

4.45am – barrage started and advance commenced with objective of BRAY-MEAULTE road. Thick mist and smoke from barrage made it most difficult to maintain direction. Considerable opposition from four machine guns in shell holes. The objective was reached at 6.20am and consolidated.

About 15.20 – M-Gs were captured with two 77mm guns. There was considerable hostile shelling throughout the day and at about 7pm became intense on the right flank. The situation was obscene and eventually cleared up by the reserve brigade, supported by tanks.
There were 12 officer casualties and a great strain devolved on the remaining officers. |
| 23-8-1918 | Consolidating positions |
| 24-8-1918 | 2am - Relieved by 6th R W KENT REGIMENT and moved to sunken road MORLANCOURT- MEAULTE road |

Percival died, aged 34, on 22nd August 1918. He was buried in Meaulte Military Cemetery in France, which was designed by Sir Edwin Lutyens.

Percival's headstone carries the wording "PEACE PERFECT PEACE". His pay and gratuity were paid to Emily, and she also received his Victory and British War Medals.

Locally, Percival is remembered on Sittingbourne War Memorial and St Michael's Church WW1 Memorial Window.

In 1919 his widow, Emily, married Douglas Bertie Jarrett in Milton, and they moved to Hampshire.

The East Kent Gazette on 23rd August 1919 carried "In Memoriams" from Emily and Percival's parents, reading:

German shelling Meaulte on 23rd August 1918

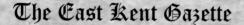

The East Kent Gazette

SATURDAY, AUGUST 23, 1919

IN MEMORIAM

BROWN – In ever loving memory of Percival Brown who was killed, August 22nd, 1918.

They miss him most
Who loved him best.
From Mother, Father, and Sisters-in-law.

The East Kent Gazette

SATURDAY, AUGUST 23, 1919

IN MEMORIAM

BROWN – In ever loving memory of a devoted husband and father, Percival Brown, 1/1st Cambridgeshire Regt., killed in action in France, August 22nd, 1918.

Oh, why was he taken so young and so fair?
Taken from home and those who loved him dear;
Only those who have lost can ever tell the pain
at our hearts at not saying farewell.
From his sorrowing Wife and Child, Dad, Sisters, and Brothers.

BROWN, Sydney John

TR10/38181, Private, 98th Battalion, Training Reserve.

Sydney was born in 1898 in Sittingbourne, the son of Sydney, a journeyman sail maker, and Susan Jane (née Harris). He was their fourth child, and his siblings were Ellen Jane, Edith Emily, Amelia, George Harry, Edward Redvers, Harold William (1904-1917), and Norman (1905-1909).

Tragedy beset the family with the death of Sydney's youngest brother, Norman, who at the age of four years old died in 1909. Then in the space of three years Sydney lost both his parents, his father in 1914, his mother in 1915 and then his second youngest brother, 13-year-old Harold in July 1917 who died at Keycol Sanatorium, Sittingbourne (pictured below) from consumption.

According to the report of his death, in the East Kent Gazette of 26th January 1918, Sydney and the family lived at 60 East Street, Sittingbourne. Sydney, before enlisting in October 1915, had been employed by Smeed Dean and Co He was a member of the Sittingbourne Congregational Church and their Young Men's Bible Class.

The newspaper reported he was 'rather delicate of health,' though he completed his military training and in June 1917 was sent to the front, but just a month later he was returned home, as the conditions were too much for him. On 16th January 1918 in Brompton Hospital (below), after being transferred from a military hospital in Norfolk, Sydney died, aged 20 years, from consumption, as did his brother Harold.

Brompton Hospital

Sydney's body was returned to his family for burial, and his coffin was transported on a gun carriage along East Street, which was lined with people. Following the carriage, the band and drums of the 3rd Battalion, Wiltshire Regiment played Handel's Dead March. At Sittingbourne Cemetery, Sydney was buried with full military honours, during a ceremony conducted by Baptist Minister Reverend John Doubleday, at the Congregational Church, who was standing in for Reverend T Peroy Phillips.

His family added the words "PEACE PERFECT PEACE" to his CWGC headstone.

Sydney is also remembered on the Sittingbourne War Memorial and Congregational Church Memorial.

Sydney's brother, George, served as a private in the 4th Queen's Regiment. and survived the war. As did his eldest sister Ellen's husband, Sapper Albert John Kenwood of the Royal Engineers, who at the time of the funeral, was in hospital after being shot in the right arm, paralysing it below the elbow.

BROWN, William Robert

G/20038, Private, 7th Battalion, The Buffs (East Kent Regiment.

William, also known as Robert, was the eleventh of the thirteen children of Robert and Ann Chapell (née Rossiter), was born in Sittingbourne on 24th February 1887. His brothers and sisters were Flora Ann, Alfred Robert, Robert (1873-1874), Belinda Mary, Ellen Rose, Annie Amelia, Lily, Violet (1881-1881), Ethel Daisy (1884-1884), Adelaide Kate, Frank Walter, and Walter Richard.

In 1901 the family were living in Gibson Street, and 14-year-old William was working as a brickfield labourer, the same as his father. Three of his sisters, Annie, Lily, and Adelaide were all working in the collar factory, in nearby Ufton Lane. William's father died in 1908 and the 1911 census shows his mother still living in Gibson Street. Just Adelaide and Walter were living with her, and Adelaide was still working at the collar factory.

At the age of 20, William was 5ft 4¼in tall when, on 2nd May 1907, he joined the Royal Navy as a Stoker 2nd Class, rising to Stoker 1st Class by the time he left on 11th February 1911. He then enlisted in Sittingbourne, joining the Royal West Kent Regiment and he served with them in India. Later he transferred to The Buffs and was serving with them as a Private in France when he died.

On 17th January 1917 his battalion's War Diary[30] recorded they had arrived in Hédauville, France and the entries for the following month read "Parades under company arrangements". There was the occasional entry for cable laying working parties.

Road Building Working Party

The East Kent Gazette

SATURDAY, FEBRUARY 23, 1917

IN MEMORIAM

BROWN - In ever loving memory of a dear Son and Brother, William Robert Brown, "The Buffs," second son of Mrs Anne Brown, of 19, Gibson Street, Sittingbourne, who died in France, on February 23rd, 1917.

He gave his life, What grander sacrifice?
From his Mother, Sisters, and Brothers.

On 11th February, his battalion moved to Warwick Huts, 11km east to Ovillers-la-Boisselle. Eleven days later, on the 22nd, they relieved the 7th Queens in the trenches to the south of the nearby village of Grandcourt. The next day they took over the front line from the 7th Royal West Regiment in Boom Ravine, a long Y-shaped ravine, named by the British, that snaked its way from near the village of Grandcourt towards the high ground close to Courcelette. During the relief, his battalion was heavily shelled and incurred about 20 casualties. It was that day, 23rd February that William was killed, the day before his 30th birthday.

[30] War Diary: 7th Battalion Buffs (East Kent Regiment). WO-95-2049-1. July 1915-April 1919. The National Archives (UK), Kew, England.

William's body was originally buried on the battlefield with at least eight fellow soldiers, both British and Canadian. It was moved 800m south to Regina Trench Cemetery, Grandcourt, France, on 28th March 1919 by a Canadian Burial Party. Locally, William is remembered on Sittingbourne War Memorial and Sittingbourne Holy Trinity Church WW1 Memorial.

William is listed on the CWGC database as R. Brown.

BURDEN, George

K/27957, Stoker 1st Class, Royal Navy.

Stoker Dress Insignia

George was born in Sittingbourne on 19th January 1894, the son of Henry George, a general labourer and former carter at the paper mill, and Bertha (née Boakes). George was their eighth child, and his siblings were William Henry, Thomas Alfred (1880-1907), Annie Eliza (1882-1907), Edwin (1884-1906), James Frederick (1886-1889), Sidney Stephen (1889-1890), Eliza Bertha, Frederick, Albert Victor, and Alfred Walter.

George's family were hit with the tragic deaths of his mother, a brother and sister in 1907 and a year later another brother. This was on top of the loss of two brothers, in infancy, a few years earlier. Sadly, his father and two youngest brothers were in Milton Union Workhouse in 1911. George was living at 25 Eastbourne Street, with his brother William and his family. William served in the Merchant Navy for the duration of the war.

In the autumn of 1914, George married Esther Mary Ann Spice and they had two sons, Edward George Alfred (born 7th July 1915) and Harold Reuben (born 18th June 1917).

George was 5ft 8in tall and had been working as a labourer at Smeed Dean's brickfields when he joined the Navy on 6th August 1915. On 27th October 1915 he joined the monitor ship *HMS General Wolfe* (pictured above), which was attached to the Dover Patrol, whose primary role was to stop enemy shipping, especially submarines, from entering the English Channel, and involved in fighting at Ostend and Zeebrugge.

George served on the *General Wolfe* until his death on 21st July 1918, when he died at the Haslar Royal Naval Hospital, in Gosport (pictured right), from pneumonia, aged 24.

The East Kent Gazette of 3rd August 1918 reported that: 'The young sailor had been on leave and was quite well in health. However, on the Saturday following his return from leave, he was taken ill with pneumonia and died the following day."

George's body was returned to his family and his cortege left his maternal grandparent's home at 30 Shakespeare Road, where he had lived. The cortege included the band and drums of the Queen's Regiment playing Chopin's "Funeral March." The pallbearers were his messmates, brought up from Portsmouth. As the cortege reached Sittingbourne Cemetery the drums played "Farewell my Comrade". His burial, with full military honours and firing party, was conducted by Wesleyan minister Reverend W. Gregory.

George is remembered on St Michael's Church WW1 Memorial Window, Sittingbourne War Memorial and Old Boys Milton Council Schools Memorial. His headstone is inscribed "GOD IS LOVE."

After the war, in 1919, Esther married George Butler Baker, whose brother, Stoker Petty Officer Harry John Baker (see page 52), is also commemorated in the Avenue, after his death from influenza on 8th November 1918. George himself served with the Queen's (Royal West Surrey) Regiment from December 1914 to March 1919, and in April 1918 had suffered from concussion after he was shot.

BURLEY, Edward

210809, Lance Corporal, 15th Division Signal Coy, Royal Engineers.

Edward was born in Sittingbourne in the autumn of 1887, and he was baptised at St Michael's Church on 16th October that year. He was the eldest child of Edward Felton Burley and Elizabeth (née Wood), and his siblings were Gordon, Elizabeth Hilda, Alfred Thomas, Wilfred, and Mary Christine.

In 1911 the family were living at 7 East Street, where they had lived for at least 40 years. Edward was working as a Post Office Clerk, after joining as a learner in 1903. His father was a master tailor, a profession his own father had whilst living at the same address. Edward's brothers Alfred and Wilfred were assistant tailors.

On Wednesday 27th August 1913 Edward married Florence Nellie Millen at St Michael's Church, Sittingbourne, which was reported on in the East Kent Gazette dated 30th August 1913. Together they had two daughters, Joyce Millen Burley (born 30th August 1914) and Stella Millen Burley (born 1915).

Edward died of wounds as the result of being gassed, aged 30, on 30th July 1918 at the 63rd Casualty Clearing Station, Senlis, France. He was buried in Senlis French National Cemetery, which contains 135 CWGC burials from 24 different regiments, of which 133 were killed in a three-week period from the 23rd July to 11th August. The remaining two burials were from April 1918 and November 1918.

Locally, he is remembered on Sittingbourne War Memorial, St Michael's Church WW1 Memorial Window, and the Post Office Memorial. His probate was granted to his widow, Florence Nellie, who was living at 24 Albany Road.

The East Kent Gazette headline "POSTMEN AND THE WAR – RETURNED SITTINGBOURNE MEN ENTERTAINED" in the 27th March 1920 issue, reported on a welcome meeting at the Masonic Hall for demobilised members who had served in the war. The Postmaster Mr. F. Shackleton thanked them all and the temporary staff brought in whilst the men were away serving. He went on to mention the loss of three established members, Edward Burley (Overseer), Barnard Gray and Frederick Charles Mead (see page 209) saying that they were good and faithful servants, and it was a matter of deep regret that their lives had been cut short. Mr. Shackleton said that when he arrived at the Post Office, as a stranger, it was Edward who was of inestimable value to him and became a good friend, adding "he was one for whom I would forever entertain a personal regard and affection."

The three men are remembered on a brass plaque memorial in Sittingbourne Post Office with the inscription "FAITHFUL UNTO DEATH."

Private Barnard Gray, The Buffs (East Kent Regiment), was 33 years old when he died on 27th March 1918. He is commemorated on the Pozieres Memorial to the Missing and Bobbing Church WW1 Memorial, though not on the Avenue of Remembrance.

Private Frederick Charles Mead, who is commemorated on the Avenue, served in The Buffs (East Kent Regiment). He was 26 years old when he died on 20th December 1915 and he was buried at Duhallow A.D.S. Cemetery, Belgium. (A.D.S. = Advanced Dressing Station).

Sittingbourne Post Office Memorial

BUTCHER, George Leslie

45290, Rifleman, King's Royal Rifle Corps,
attached to 12th Battalion, London Regiment (The Rangers).

George was born in Sittingbourne in 1899, the son of George Richard Ralph and Edith Emma (née Pettitt). He was the second of six children, his siblings were Sybil Lillie, Bessie Gladys, Reginald John, Hedley Owlett, and Sydney George, who sadly died in infancy age 2 years old, in 1908. George's mother died in the spring of 1906, around the time Sydney was born.

In 1908, George's father married Edith Oram, who had been widowed in 1904 when her husband Alfred Bedelle, a tobacconist and newsagent of 5 Milton Road, had died. Edith and Alfred had three children Edith Harriett, Alfred James, and Robert Baden Powell (aka Baden). George senior, a baker and confectioner, and his children moved in with Edith and took over the shop, with Edith and her daughter Edith assisting.

George enlisted in Maidstone and served as a Rifleman in the King's Royal Rifle Corps. His military records show that at the time of his death he was attached to the London Regiment. The London Regiment's War Diary[31] recorded that on 31st August 1918 they had moved from the trenches to Méricourt-sur-Somme, south of the town of Albert. The 1st September entry read "bathed in the river Somme."

The next four days were occupied with range practice before they moved 34km east to Liéramont Trench at Aizecourt L'Abbe. On the 7th the diary noted that the Brigade had advanced 7000 yards, before withdrawing to Liéramont during the darkness the following day

Battle of Épehy September 1918. IWME(AUS) 3252

and spending the 9th at rest. The 10th September 1918 saw them back in the line at nearby Épehy and for the next two days they came under enemy barrage, before being relieved by the Suffolks on the 13th.

George's death is recorded as occurring on 12th September 1918.

The East Kent Gazette

SATURDAY, OCTOBER 12, 1918

ROLL OF HONOUR

BUTCHER. – Killed in action somewhere in France, Sept. 12th 1918, George Leslie Butcher, eldest son of G. R. Butcher, aged 18 years.
"Thy Will be done."

A week later the East Kent Gazette published a report of George's death, which mentioned he was an old Trinity School boy, and was employed by the Strood Co-operative Society and had been living with a sister.

George had enlisted in December 1917 and trained in Northampton, before proceeding to France in May 1918. The report concluded that George's stepbrother, Baden, had died earlier that year, details of his death were not yet known and "Much sympathy is felt for the bereaved family."

---

[31] War Diary: 1/12 Battalion London Regiment (Rangers). WO-95-3009-8. February 1918-May 1919. The National Archives (UK), Kew, England.

George is remembered on the Vis-en-Artois Memorial to the Missing in France and on Sittingbourne War Memorial, as well as those in Sittingbourne Holy Trinity Church and the Baptist Church. George is also commemorated on a family headstone for his mother and father, brother Sydney, and grandparents George and Francis Butcher, in Sittingbourne Cemetery.

George's pay and gratuity were paid to his father, who also received his British War Medal and Victory Medal.

Alfred James Bedelle, George's 22-year-old stepbrother served as a Lieutenant in the Queen's (Royal West Surrey) Regiment, from March 1918 to March 1919. His other stepbrother, Baden, died at the age of 17 on 28th February 1918 and his death and well attended funeral were reported in the East Kent Gazette on 2nd March 1918.

A further report dated 22nd June 1918 entitled "DEDICATION OF A HOSPITAL COT" in memory of Baden at the Whitehall Red Cross Hospital (pictured right), Bell Road, Sittingbourne. The report mentioned that the cot was "a pretty wooden bed with a special hair mattress" in Rose Ward which was covered in flowers and roses. The dedication, conducted by Reverend John Doubleday, was attended by Baden's family, and consisted of prayers and Bible readings.

The first occupant of the cot was 26-year-old local Milton boy Private Stanley Marsh, who had had his foot amputated. The East Kent Gazette of 8th July 1916 reported that Stanley had been hit in the legs by a shell splinter during an advance.

BUTLER, Stanley Mack

G/68510, Private, 23rd Battalion, Royal Fusiliers.

Stanley was born in Milton Regis in 1897, the youngest of the eight children of George, a brickfield labourer, and Lucy Ann (née Sands). He was baptised on 11th October 1897 in St Mary's church, Milton Regis. His siblings were William Durrant (1883-1916), George Sands, Sarah Stirling (1887-1891), James Leonard, Richard Edmund, Sidney (1893-1913) and Alice Rosetta.

In 1911 Stanley was working as a guard on a paper mill engine and the family were living at 5 Laburnum Place, Sittingbourne.

Stanley's brother Sidney was also a guard on the paper mill railway and on 25th November 1913 he jammed his right leg between the buffers of two trucks, fracturing his fibula and bursting a vein. He was taken home first and later taken to Rochester Hospital. Following an amputation of his leg, Sidney died from shock on 27th

November 1913, aged 21. Another brother, William, had emigrated in 1909 to Toronto, Canada and died on 30th January 1916 at Western Hospital of heart failure.

Four of Stanley's siblings emigrated to Ontario, Canada, George in 1904 aged 19, James in 1910 aged 20, Richard in 1911 aged 20, and Alice in 1913, aged 18.

George enlisted with the 220th Battalion, 12th York Rangers on 6th May 1916 and a month later, on 5th June 1916, his brother James joined the same Battalion. Both had served in France before their discharges in early 1919. During James' service he received a chest flesh wound, on 14th October 1918, from a gunshot and spent a month in hospital.

Stanley enlisted on 2nd October 1917 in Herne Bay, joining the Queen's Royal West Surrey Regiment. Two days later on the 4th he transferred to the Royal Fusiliers. October 1917 saw his battalion fighting at Cambrin, before they moved to billets at Raimbert, where they spent the remainder of the month and the first few days of November in training. The battalion War Diary[32] recorded that; 234 reinforcements had arrived to add to the 613 Other Ranks. From the 5th October the battalion marched 60km north via Busnes, Merville, Eecke to Herzeele, arriving on the 8th. Their time there was spent continuing training.

On 26th November, after a 125km train journey south, they arrived at the front line at Bourlon Wood (pictured left), just to the west of Cambrai, relieving the King's Own Yorkshire Light Infantry. Two days later they themselves were relieved by the 1st Royal and moved in support. The last day of November saw a heavy enemy attack, and the battalion moved to the line to assist the Royal Berkshire Regiment. Later the same day they counter attacked the enemy who had gained a footing to the right of the line. With valuable assistance from the 17th Royal Fusiliers, carrying bombs and ammunition, the battalion re-established the line.

His battalion's diary entry on 1st December 1917 noted that the 'Line re-adjusted,' with the 1st Royal Berks to the left and the Fusiliers to the right. The following day saw a push forward at 8.30pm, gaining all objectives, and it was in this action that Stanley lost his life on 2nd December 1917, when he was 20 years old.

Stanley is remembered on the Cambrai Memorial, Louverval, France, which commemorates those that died in the Battle of Cambrai in November and December 1917, whose graves are unknown. The battle started on 20th November 1917 and lasted for 18 days. It is renowned for the first major use of tanks in battle, and it is recorded that about 180 tanks were lost. The Memorial is inscribed with 7,122 names from the Commonwealth and South Africa.

Locally, Stanley is remembered on Sittingbourne War Memorial and Sittingbourne Holy Trinity Church Memorial. His father received his Victory and British War Medals, together with his pay and gratuity.

---

[32] War Diary: 23 Battalion Royal Fusiliers. WO-95-1372-3. November 1915-July 1919. The National Archives (UK), Kew, England.

Clifton was born in Sittingbourne in 1898, the son of John William, a brickfield labourer, and Eliza Ann (née Slarks). In 1901 the family were living at 3 Thomas Street and by 1911 they had moved to 9 George Street, Sittingbourne. Clifton had an older sister, Hilda Annie Mary, and a sister Elsie May, who was seven years his junior.

He attended St Michael's Church and worked at Lloyds paper mill. He enlisted at Herne Bay and at one point served with the Norfolk Regiment, before transferring to The King's (Liverpool) Regiment.

Clifton's enlistment date is not known. The War Diary for his battalion for the month before he was killed is transcribed below.

Instructions regarding War Diaries and Intelligence Summaries are contained in F.S. Regs., Part II, and the Staff Manual respectively. Title pages will be prepared in manuscript.	WAR DIARY [33] or INTELLIGENCE SUMMARY. (Erase heading not required.)	Army Form C. 2118.
Date	Summary of Events and Information	Remarks and References to Appendices
1-10-1918	TRENCHES NEAR VILLERS GUISLAIN. Fine weather. Reconnoitring parties sent forward to Canal De L'ESCAULT.	
2 to 4-10-1918	Fine weather. Battalion in Brigade reserve and re-organising.	
5-10-1918	Fine weather. Battalion moved to PIGEON QUARRY.	
7-10-1918	Wet weather. Reinforcements joined 76 Other Ranks.	
8-10-1918	Showery weather. Battalion moved to line east of HONNECOURT in evening.	
9-10-1918	Fine weather. Moved into line at CLARY.	
10-10-1918	Fine weather. Moved to River SELLE. Enemy put up strong opposition.	
11-10-1918	Showery weather. In the line on banks of river.	
12-10-1918	Showery weather. Battalion relieved and moved back to CLARY arriving at 15.00 hrs.	
13-10-1918	Showery weather. Church parades. Battalion at baths.	
14-10-1918	Fine weather. Battalion at baths. Armourer inspected arms of battalion.	
15 to 17-10-1918	Wet weather. General Officer Commanding-in-Chief inspected Battalion.	
18 to 19-10-1918	Showery weather. Lewis gun training.	
20-10-1918	Wet weather. Church parades. Message rocket training to ALL officers and N.C.Os.	
21-10-1918	Wet weather. Battalion moved to TROISVILLES.	
22-10-1918	Wet weather. Battalion moved to assembly place prior to attack on FOREST.	
23-10-1918	Fine weather. Battalion attacked and moved through FOREST to CROIX.	

[33] War Diary: 4 Battalion King's Liverpool Regiment. WO-95-2427-1. November 1915-November 1919. The National Archives (UK), Kew, England.

24-10-1918	Fine weather. Battalion continued in attack towards ENGLEFONTAIN.
25-10-1918	Fine weather. Battalion continued in operations.
26-10-1918	Fine weather. Battalion attacked ENGLEFONTAIN – capture completed. Battalion relieved and returned to billets at MONTAY arriving 18.00 hrs.
27-10-1918	Fine weather. Battalion at baths and cleaning up generally.

Clifton was killed in action, aged 20, on 23rd October 1918, and he was originally buried in Montay-Amerval Road Cemetery, created by the 38th (Welsh) Division for 31 men who fell in the week of 23rd October 1918. Clifton was reinterred in Montay-Neuvilly Road Cemetery, Montay in France, where his headstone is inscribed with these words chosen by his family "HIS WORK WELL DONE."

Locally he is remembered on Sittingbourne War Memorial, St Michael's Church WW1 Memorial Window and Lloyd's Paper Mill Memorial.

Clifton's pay and gratuity were paid to his father, who also received his Victory and British War Medals.

On the first and third anniversaries of Clifton's death the East Kent Gazette published the following "In Memoriams."

The East Kent Gazette

SATURDAY, OCTOBER 25, 1919

IN MEMORIAM

CARRIER – In ever loving memory of our only dear son and brother, Pte. Clifton Carrier, killed in action in France, October 23rd, 1918.

One year has gone
Since Heaven gained.
He bravely answered his country's call,
He gave his life for one and all;
But the far away grave is the bitter blow,
None but the aching hearts can know.
One of the bravest, one of the best,
Doing his duty was called to rest.
Sadly missed by Mum, Dad, and Sisters.

The East Kent Gazette

SATURDAY, OCTOBER 22, 1921

IN MEMORIAM

CARRIER - In ever loving memory of a dear son and brother, Pte. Clifton Carrier, who was killed October 23rd, 1918.

Three years have passed,
Our hearts still sore,
As time rolls on, we miss him more;
His loving smile, his cheerful face;
There are none can fill his vacant place.
From Mum, Dad, and Sisters.

CASTLE, Frederick Frank

2355, Private, Royal East Kent Yeomanry.

The plaque in the Avenue reads D. F. Castle, though the Sittingbourne War Memorial has F. F. Castle inscribed and this is the name reported in the East Kent Gazette of the memorial names. The inscription on the Avenue is considered to be an error.

Frederick, with his twin brother Albert, were the youngest of a very large family of 17 children. Born in Sittingbourne in 1896, the records do not indicate which twin was the first born. Their parents were James Edward Ambrose and Ellen Frances (née Chapman). James was an engine driver in the brickfields and the family lived at 23 Station Street, Sittingbourne in 1911.

Their children were Thomas William, Ellen Celia (1873-1874), Edward Ambrose, Elizabeth, John, Ellen Florence, Catherine Chapman, Clara Edith (1883-1885), Arthur, Rose, Alfred Victor (1887-1887), Lilian, Daisy, George, and Edith May.

Before the war Frederick had belonged to the Sittingbourne Swimming Club and was in the employ of Mr. Henry Filmer, corn and seed merchant, being recorded in the 1911 census as a corn-factor's assistant.

Albert, his twin brother, had previously joined the same regiment and survived the war.

Frederick's death was reported in the East Kent Gazette on 4th March 1916 under the headline "SAD DEATH OF A YOUNG SOLDIER".

The report explained that several months previously he had fallen from his horse and fractured his spine, causing paralysis, whilst training at Maresfield, Sussex. He had been taken to the VAD Hospital in Brighton before transferring to King George's Hospital, Waterloo, London. Despite receiving the best advice and care, Frederick died on 28th February 1916, aged just 19.

Frederick was buried in Sittingbourne Cemetery and is remembered on Sittingbourne War Memorial. Frederick, or members of his family are likely to have attended Holy Trinity, Sittingbourne, as well as the Baptist church in Sittingbourne, as he is remembered on these memorials. His pay and gratuity were paid to his father.

CHAPMAN, Frederick

K/25557, Stoker 1st Class, Royal Navy, HMS Vanguard.

Stoker Dress Insignia

Frederick, the eighth of thirteen children, was born on 2nd June 1878 in Eastling. He was the son of William, the landlord of the White Hart Inn in Crown Quay Lane, Sittingbourne in 1911, and Frances (née Trigg). His siblings were Emily, John, Jane Elizabeth, Henry, Ann (1874-1874), Mary Ann, William Thomas, Alfred (1880-1881), Albert, Thomas, and Amy.

In 1911, Frederick was a temperer for Wills and Packham brickmakers and barge owners, but by 1915 he was working as a gas stoker for the Metropolitan Gas Works in East Greenwich.

When he first tried to enlist in Greenwich, he was rejected due to a 'slight defect', so he went with some workmates to Whitehall where he was successful. He was 5ft 10in tall, with blue eyes and brown hair, when he joined the Royal Navy on 22nd April 1915 as a Stoker 2nd Class. On completing his training at *HMS Pembroke II* on 8th July 1915 he joined the crew of *HMS Vanguard*. On 17th February 1916 Frederick was promoted to Stoker 1st Class.

Frederick was a Stoker 1st Class, aged 39, when he died on his ship *Vanguard*, which sank on 9th July 1917, at Scapa Flow, Scotland.

The East Kent Gazette of 21st July 1917 reported his death in both the "ROLL OF HONOUR" and in an article, with the headline "SITTINGBOURNE'S DEATH TOLL – TWO BROTHERS IN ONE FAMILY". The headline reflected the fact that two brothers, also commemorated in the Avenue, were also killed on *HMS Vanguard*, and they were Clarence Victor (see page 205) and William Luckhurst (see page 205). They were also stokers. The article started "Bereavement has fallen heavily on many families in this part of Kent by the sinking of *HMS Vanguard*."

The East Kent Gazette

SATURDAY, JULY 21, 1917
ROLL OF *HONOUR*

CHAPMAN. – In loving remembrance of our dear son and brother, Frederick Chapman, who lost his life on H.M.S. Vanguard, July 9th, 1917, aged 39 years.

From his sorrowing Brothers, Sisters, Mother, and Father, White Hart, Sittingbourne.

The Admiralty wrote to Mrs. Chapman on 12th July 1917 informing her of the sinking and telling her that Frederick must be regarded as lost. The article recorded how Frederick was unable to get home for his parent's golden wedding in August 1915 but had home leave in December 1916. His last letter home dated 8th July 1917 said he was hopeful of receiving home leave for August.

HMS Vanguard (see page 206) was a dreadnought class battleship launched in 1909. Her role during the First World War was primarily to patrol the North Sea, although she was involved in the Battle of Jutland in May 1916. On the night of 9th July 1917, the Vanguard was anchored in Scapa Flow, Scotland, when shortly before midnight one of her magazines blew, caused by a detonation of cordite charges. The reason for the explosion is though unclear. The ship sank instantaneously with the loss of 843 men, three of those on board survived, though one died shortly afterwards. Only 22 of the bodies were recovered, with 17 being buried in Lyness on the Isle of Hoy, Orkney, Scotland.

All three local men are remembered on the Chatham Naval Memorial, Sittingbourne War Memorial and St Michael's Church WW1 Memorial Window.

HMS Vanguard

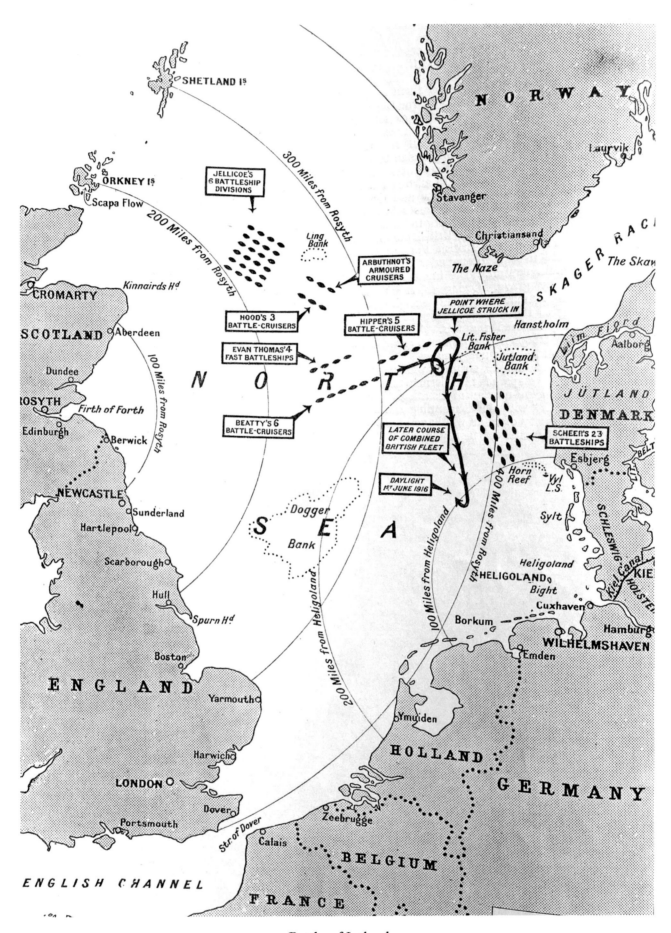

Battle of Jutland

CLACKETT, Frederick Sherlock

Shipwright, H.M. Dockyard (Sheerness), HMS Princess Irene.

Credit: David Hughes

Frederick was the second child of Edward and Emma Jane (née Sherlock), whose other children were Bertram Frank, Grace Emma, and Charles Edward. Frederick was born on 2nd August 1885 in Sittingbourne and was registered at birth as Frederick Sherlock Brunger, which was his father's registered name. The family adopted the use of Clackett, which was Frederick's paternal grandfather's name, from about 1891; though on some official records Edward and some of the children used Brunger.

In 1911 Frederick's father was a brickfield labourer, although by the 1901 census he was the landlord of the Cumberland Arms Inn in Mill Street, Sittingbourne. Frederick was a gas fitter's apprentice in 1901, then in 1911 he was employed as a shipwright at the dockyard. He was boarding at 11 Ranelagh Road, Sheerness with fellow shipwright Benjamin Harris, age 29, and his wife Florence. Benjamin sadly was killed alongside Frederick, leaving his widow and son Arthur (born 1910).

Frederick married Kate Balch (née Ford) and they lived at 3 Ranelagh Road, Sheerness. He had been working in Sheerness Dockyard for seven years when he was killed, age 29, when *HMS* Princess Irene exploded on 27th May 1915.

He is remembered on Sittingbourne's Holy Trinity Church Memorial, the Sheerness War Memorial, the memorial in Holy Trinity Church, Sheerness, and on the Chatham Naval Memorials.

HMS Princess Irene (pictured right) was an ocean liner, built in 1914, which was requisitioned by the Royal Navy and converted into a minelayer. On 27th May 1915 she was moored at Saltpan Reach in the Medway Estuary, 3km west of Sheerness Docks. Whilst the ship was being loaded with mines an explosion occurred at 11:14 GMT, causing her to

disintegrate and wreckage was found 20 miles away. Three hundred and fifty-two of those on board, including 76 civilian dockyard workers were killed. A Court of Inquiry found that mines were primed on board and a faulty primer was blamed for the explosion.

Frederick's family posted "In Memoriam" in the East Kent Gazette for at least three years on the anniversary of his death. The first was published on exactly the first anniversary, with poignant words (shown on the next page).

The East Kent Gazette

SATURDAY, MAY 27, 1916
IN MEMORIAM

CLACKETT – In ever loving memory of our dear son, Frederick Sherlock Clackett, who was killed in the explosion on H.M.S. Princess Irene at Sheerness, on the 27th of May, 1915, aged 29 years.

Thy voice is now silent. Thy heart is now cold,
Where thy smile and
Thy welcome oft met us of old;
We miss thee and mourn thee in silence
unseen,
And dwell on the memory of joys that have
been.
Had He asked us well we know,
We should cry, "O spare the blow";
Yes, with streaming tears, should pray,
"Lord, we love him, let him stay."

The East Kent Gazette

SATURDAY, MAY 25, 1918
IN MEMORIAM

CLACKETT - In ever loving memory of our dear son, Frederick Sherlock Clackett, who lost his life on the ill-fated H.M.S. Princess Irene at Sheerness, on the 27th of May, 1915, aged 29 years.

Oh, how our hearts do ache.,
When we think of how you died;
To think we could not say "Goodbye,"
Before you closed your eyes.
We think of you in silence,
No eyes may see us weep;
But treasured in our inmost hearts,
Your memory still we keep.
From his ever-loving Mother, Father,
Brothers, and Sister, Frank, Charlie and Grace.

COOMBES, Samuel Henry

G/51518, Private, 2nd/10th Battalion, Middlesex Regiment.

Samuel was born in Milton under Wychwood, Oxfordshire in 1882 and was baptised at St Mary's Church, Shipton under Wychwood on 21st February that year. He was the third child and oldest son of Samuel Bolt Coombes, a carpenter, and Martha (née Playne), whose other children were Edith (1878-1878), Martha Louise, Frank Risby, William Edwin, Charles Edward (1888-1917), Harold John (1889-1890), Alexander, Rebecca Margery, and Herbert Cyril.

In 1907 he married Edith Emma Greensted, who had been born in Borden. By 1911 they were living in Oxfordshire with their children, twins Hilda Edith and Leonard Henry (born 20th May 1907), Gerald (born 6th February 1910) and Dennis (born 22nd December 1911).

Samuel enlisted in Sittingbourne, joining the Middlesex Regiment. His battalion fought in Gallipoli from 1st August 1915 and moved to Egypt on 19th December 1915. However, it is unclear whether Samuel fought in these events, as his enlistment date is unknown.

In early December 1917 his battalion, as part of 53rd (W) Division were involved in the Battle of Jerusalem advancing towards Bethlehem[34].

---

[34] Captain Cyril Falls, *History of the Great War: Military Operations, Egypt and Palestine*, Vol II, *From June 1917 to the End of the War*, London: HM Stationery Office, 1930/Imperial War Museum and Naval & Military Press, 2013.

4th Battalion, Royal Sussex Regiment march through Bethlehem.

On the 8th the battalion together with the 2/4th Queen's advanced under shellfire to the hills at Belt Hill, arriving to discover them unoccupied. Two weeks later, on 21st December, his battalion were involved in fierce fighting, with bombs, bayonets, and clubbed rifles, near Jericho and a Turkish post named White Hill.[35].

Samuel died of wounds on 22nd December 1917, when he was 35 years old, and was buried in the Jerusalem War Cemetery, Israel (pictured below).

Just a month before Samuel's death, his younger brother 28-year-old Charles was accidentally shot and killed whilst serving with 6th/7th

Royal Scots Fusiliers. He is buried in Level Crossing Cemetery, Fampoux, France.

Locally, Samuel is remembered on Sittingbourne War Memorial, Sittingbourne Holy Trinity Memorial and St Michael's Church Window Memorial.

After Samuel's death, his pay and war gratuity went to his widow who was living at 15 Bassett Road, Sittingbourne. She also received his Victory and British War Medals.

COUCHMAN, Robert

40, Private, 28th Battalion, Australian Infantry, Australian Imperial Force.

Robert was baptised on 27th May 1877 at St John the Evangelist Church, Ickham, after having been born in Hucking the same year. He was the son of Robert, a market gardener, and Rose (née Tyler). They had seven children of which Robert was the third child and eldest son, their names were Rosabella, Edith Emily, Nellie, George, Reginald Charles, and Bertie. In 1911 Robert's parents were living at 20 Harold Road, Sittingbourne.

Robert's brother George, with his wife Mary, emigrated to Toronto, Ontario, Canada in 1903, followed by his youngest brother Bertie, with his wife Jane and their three children in 1911.

---

[35] Everard Wyrall, *The Die-Hards in the Great War*. A History of the Duke of Cambridge's Own (Middlesex Regiment), 2 Vols, London: Harrison, 1926 and 1929.

Robert himself, age 33, emigrated to Australia, travelling on the *SS Armadale* (pictured right), and arriving in Freemantle, Western Australia on 27th December 1910.

Robert enlisted at Blackboys Hill in Western Australia on 24th February 1915. He was 5ft 8in tall and had been working as a farmer, in Donnybrook, Western Australia. He sailed initially for Gallipoli on 4th September 1915, arriving in Alexandria, Egypt, on 10th January 1916. Then he sailed to Marseilles to join the British Expeditionary Force, arriving on 21st March 1916.

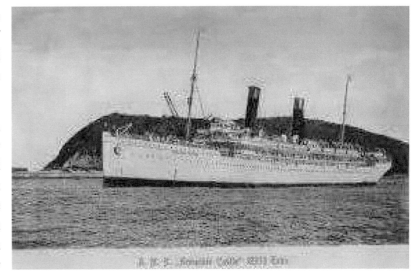

The battalion War Diary reproduced below records the month before Robert's death.

Instructions regarding War Diaries and Intelligence Summaries are contained in F.S. Regs., Part II, and the Staff Manual respectively. Title pages will be prepared in manuscript.	**WAR DIARY**[36] or **INTELLIGENCE SUMMARY.** (Erase heading not required.)	Army Form C. 2118.
Date	Summary of Events and Information	Remarks and References to Appendices
1-7-1916	*12.30am - Battalion in the locality of MESSINES TRENCHES and STINKING FARM. Our trench shelled by enemy artillery.*	
3-7-1916	*5pm - Enemy shelled STINKING FARM with 5.9" High Explosive shells.*	
5-7-1916	*11.30pm - Our artillery shelled MESSINES trenches heavily for 45 minutes. Enemy's retaliation very weak.*	
6-7-1916	*10pm - Battalion marched to SAUSAGE VALLEY, arriving on 27th (distance of 110km, staying overnight in billets and bivouacs).*	
28-7-1916	*6pm - Marched to POZIÈRES, ready for advancement planned to start at 11pm.*	
29-7-1916	*12.10am - Enemy opened up with high explosives, shrapnel, and machine guns, inflicting heavy casualties.* *Our artillery laid down a barrage. As soon as this was lifted the men rushed forward in perfect order and were met by heavy fire from an enemy which was 'intact and very strong'.* *2.45am Battalion was withdrawn back to SAUSAGE VALLEY.* *CAUSALTIES for July 1916*	

CAUSALTIES for July 1916

	KILLED	*WOUNDED*	*Sick to Hospital*	*MISSING*
Officers	*5*	*6*		*1*
Other Ranks	*58*	*145*	*52*	*256*
	63	*151*	*52*	*257*
			Total Casualties	*523*

[36] Australian Imperial Force unit war diaries, 1914-18 War: 28th Infantry Battalion. AWM4 23/45/16. July 1916, Australian War Memorial awm.gov.au

It was on 29th July 1916, that Robert was reported as missing in action. A Court of Inquiry[37], held on 4th January 1917, decided that he had been killed in action on that day, aged 39.

Robert is remembered on the Memorial at Villers-Bretonneux, which commemorates all Australian soldiers who fought and died in France and Belgium, especially those that have no known grave, and is classed as an Australian National Memorial.

The memorial was designed by Sir Edwin Lutyens and unveiled by King George VI on 22nd July 1938. The memorial records 10,982, and at the time of print, the burial place of 253 have been found.

At the time of Robert's death, the 28th Battalion had just become involved in the Somme's Battle of Pozières, the objective of which was to retake the town and subsequentially defend it. Their first operation was to assault German lines, in a night-time attack, but they became entangled in heavy wire which should have been destroyed in aerial bombardments and suffered heavy losses. It is probable that Robert was lost during these attacks.

The Australian Red Cross Society Wounded and Missing Enquiry Bureau Files 1DRL/0428 records a statement made by Corporal Robert Etty (Service Number 619) which read:

"I was lying wounded with him in a shell hole and in trying to get back he was killed by a shell – badly mutilated – no grave. He was in my Company (A), and I knew him intimately."

Australian War Memorial, Canberra

Honorary Captain Charles Bean, who was Australia's official correspondent and historian witnessed the events at Pozières and his diary entry reads " Pozières is one vast Australian cemetery." Charles conceived a museum memorial dedicated to remembrance, but the outbreak of World War Two caused a rethink, due to the expectation of additional losses. As a result, the Australian War Memorial was built and opened on Remembrance Day 1941, which commemorates conflicts from 1885 to the present day.

Robert is remembered on the Sittingbourne War Memorial, St Michael's Church WW1 Memorial Window, the Australian War Memorial in Canberra and the Western Australian War Memorial in Perth.

Robert was awarded the 1914-15 Star, Victory, and British War Medals, which were sent to his father, together with a leaflet entitled "Where the Australians Rest".

---

[37] First Australian Imperial Force Personnel Dossiers, 1914-1920. B2455. COUCHMAN, Robert. National Archives of Australia, Canberra, Australia.

William was born in the spring of 1896 in Upchurch and was baptised in the parish church of St Mary the Virgin (pictured below) on 19th July the same year. He was the son of Henry John and Florence (née Saunders), and his parents had married in Upchurch on 6th November 1892, and all his siblings were born there.

William was the third of eight boys, George, Henry John (1894-1895), Edward (1898-1898), Henry Thomas, Albert Edward, John, and Thomas (1910-1910). Though the 1911 census indicates there were 10 children, no record could be located for two of the children, and it may be that they did not live long enough to be registered.

In 1901 the family were living at Station Road, Rainham and by 1911 they were living at Brices Cottages, Upchurch. William, his father, and brother George were all working as labourers in brick manufacturing.

William initially enlisted in Sittingbourne on 27th November 1915, standing 5ft 7in tall. As his occupation was a waterman, he was posted to the Inland Waterways and Docks, Royal Engineers. However, the next day he was assigned to the Army Reserves, most probably under the Derby

deferment of Service Scheme. William was then called for service on the 22nd of April 1918 at Canterbury, but only served 118 days on home service, he was discharged on 17th August 1918 as he was considered to be unfit for service.

A medical report dated 10th July 1918 recorded that William was suffering from TB Lungs (Tuberculosis), which had started in the January. The report adds that he had been suffering from a cough, and he was losing weight and strength. He was admitted to Sandwich Military Hospital on the 20th June 1918 before being discharged. At the time he was living at 23 Eastbourne Street, Sittingbourne.

William died on 26th February 1919, aged 23 years, and is buried at Sittingbourne Cemetery, together with his parents. His mother, Florence, died in 1926 and father, Henry, died in 1934. The inscription on their headstone reads;

THOU ART NOT FORGOTTEN, DEAREST ONES

NOR WILT THOU EVER BE,

AS LONG AS LIFE AND MEMORY LAST;

WE WILL REMEMBER THEE

CRAYDEN, Henry

G/9489, Private, 3rd Battalion, The Buffs (East Kent Regiment).

Henry, known as Harry, was born in Sittingbourne in 1884, the son of Henry Alfred, a brickfield labourer, and Sarah Ann (née Waters). He was the eighth of nine children, his siblings were Samuel, James, William, George, Joseph, Harriet, Esther, and Mary. Though the 1911 census indicates there were 10 children, no record could be located for a tenth child, and it may be that they did not live long enough to be registered.

On 2nd September 1906 Harry married Maud Mary Wyman at the Canterbury Registry Office and they had four children, Georgina May in 1907, John Henry in 1909, Evelyn Maud in 1911, and George Alfred in 1914.

When Harry enlisted in Sittingbourne on 7th March 1916, he was 6 foot tall and living at 46 High Street, Milton Regis. He was working as a general labourer, but he had previously served for three months in the 3rd Battalion, The Buffs, before purchasing his discharge. Sadly, before the end of the month, he died, aged 32, on 30th March 1916.

Harry was buried in St James' Cemetery, Dover.

The doctor's report into his death said:

> "He died from adhesions of the bowels of long standing, following an old attack of peritonitis. This man's disease was not caused by military service but would certainly be aggravated by the same."

Harry's widow and family were living in Canterbury when she received a pension of 22s 6d a week and his personal effects. He is remembered on Sittingbourne War Memorial and Sittingbourne Holy Trinity Church Memorial.

The East Kent Gazette

SATURDAY, APRIL 8, 1916

DEATHS

CRAYDEN - On March 30th, 1916, at Dover formerly of 24 Frederick Street, Sittingbourne, Private Harry Crayden, of the 3rd Battalion Buffs, aged 32 years.
Gone but never forgotten.

The East Kent Gazette

SATURDAY, APRIL 6, 1918

IN MEMORIAM

CRAYDEN – In loving memory of Harry, the beloved son of Henry and Sarah Crayden, who died suddenly, at Dover, March 30th, 1916.
"God's will be done."

His family continued to be beset with tragedy, with the deaths of both Harry's parents and his wife in a three-year period. First his mother Sarah died in the summer of 1918 aged 73, then in May 1919 his 33-year-old wife Maud, and lastly in spring 1920 at the age of 78, his father Henry. In addition, Harry's sister Esther had married William Jury, who died on *HMS Hawke* on 15th October 1914, and he is remembered on the Chatham Naval Memorial.

CROUCHER, Robert

410719, Private, 38th Battalion, Canadian Infantry.

Robert was the fourth son and seventh child of the eleven children of Elisha and Mary Ann (née Goodhew) of 21 New Road, Sittingbourne. Robert's brothers and sisters were George William, Caroline Matilda, Mary Ann Harriett (1882-1904), William Edwin, Elisha, Frances Jane, Harty, Edwin Thomas, Flossy, and Thomas John (1901-1906). Robert was born in Sittingbourne on 7th January 1891 and was baptised in St Michael's Church on 1st February that year. His father worked in the paper mill, and Robert worked in the brickfields of Smeed Dean and Co Ltd and was well known and much liked.

When he was 20, Robert emigrated to Canada, arriving at Montreal on 30th April 1911, settling in Toronto and working for a gas company until war broke out.

When he enlisted at Lindsay, Ontario on 7th May 1915, Robert was 5ft 10in tall. He joined the 38th Battalion, Canadian Infantry, and after a few months he was posted to Bermuda. He arrived from Bermuda to Plymouth, England on 9th June 1916 and embarked for France on 13th August 1916.

Robert's battalion had moved to the front line at Souchez on Vimy Ridge on Christmas night 1916, where they remained until April 1917. During that time, they also sent patrols into No Man's Land.

Robert, just four days before his 26th birthday, with fellow soldier, 25-year-old Private William Henry Wilson from Toronto, Canada, were killed in action on 3rd January 1917. They were buried together on the battlefield between Souchez and Petit Vimy, west of Vimy.

After the war the two young men were re-interred, side by side, at the Canadian Cemetery No. 2, Neuville-Saint Vaast, France.

The Taking of Vimy Ridge, Easter Monday 1917 by Richard Jack

Robert's headstone is inscribed with the words "BE THOU FAITHFUL UNTO DEATH AND I WILL GIVE THEE A CROWN OF LIFE," which is from the Bible, Revelations 2:10.

The WW1 Memorial tablet in Sittingbourne's Holy Trinity Church includes Robert's name.

Credit: ww1cemeteries.com

CROW, Hubert Stanley

19272, Lance Corporal, 11th Battalion, Queen's Own (Royal West Kent Regiment).

Hubert was born on Christmas Day 1877 in Canterbury, the oldest of the four children of John, a cutler, and Sarah Denne (née Bingham). He had two sisters named Alice and Hilda Maud, and a brother Arthur Leslie. Hubert's mother died in December 1914, by which time Hubert was 36 years old.

On 30th August 1905, at St George's Church, Canterbury, Hubert, married Florence Lily Gaywood, daughter of Edward Gaywood, who was a confectioner and restauranteur in Canterbury. Hubert and Florence had moved to Sittingbourne by the time the first of their three daughters were born in 1907. Their names were Margaret, Norah (born 1908), and Phyllis (born 1910).

In 1911 the family were living at 59 Park Road, Sittingbourne, and his brother Arthur was a cashier at Canterbury's Union of London and Smith Bank (taken over by National Westminster bank).

Hubert was a bank cashier at Martin's Bank, Sittingbourne (taken over by Barclays) (pictured right). Hubert's occupation allowed him to employ a domestic servant, 19-year-old Elsa Maylam from Sittingbourne. The Scouts Roll of Honour shows Hubert was a Scoutmaster before the war.

When Hubert enlisted on 28th November 1915, he was 5ft 10in tall and had been a volunteer in The Buffs for 4½ years. He joined the Kent Cyclist Battalion, attached to 11th Battalion, Royal West Kent Regiment.

The events in the month leading to Hubert's death were recorded in his battalion's War Diary, reproduced here:

Instructions regarding War Diaries and Intelligence Summaries are contained in F.S. Regs., Part II, and the Staff Manual respectively. Title pages will be prepared in manuscript.	**WAR DIARY**[38] or **INTELLIGENCE SUMMARY.** (Erase heading not required.)	Army Form C. 2118.
Date	Summary of Events and Information	Remarks and References to Appendices
6-6-1917	Battalion stationed at SAINT-ÉLOI.	
7-6-1917	Battalion successfully attacked WYTSCHAETE-MESSINES RIDGE.	
8-6-1917	5am - Battalion relieved by 73rd Infantry Brigade and proceeded to OLD FRENCH TRENCH.	
12-6-1917	Battalion took up position in the trenches south of YPRES-COMINES CANAL, relieving the 8th and 17TH BATTALIONS LONDON REGIMENT.	
13-6-1917	In the trenches.	

[38] War Diary: 11 Battalion Queen's Own (Royal West Kent Regiment). WO-95-2634-4. May 1916-October 1917. The National Archives (UK), Kew, England.

14-6-1917	Battalion successfully attacked OBLIQUE ROW and OPTIC TRENCH, in HOLLEBEKE, with 18TH KING'S ROYAL RIFLE CORPS to the right and 24TH DIVISION to the left.
15-6-1917	4.45pm - Enemy counter-attacked but were repulsed.
17-6-1917	battalion relieved and moved for rest and bathing. Week's casualties - 3 officers and 37 other ranks, with 7 officers and 200 other ranks wounded.

It was on 13th June 1917 that Hubert was wounded by machine gun fire, which caused a compound fracture of his left elbow and right knee and wounds to his right elbow, left foot and left first finger. He was taken to No. 2 Canadian Casualty Clearing Station (pictured right), at Remy Sidings, Lijssenthoek, but sadly died two days later on 15th June 1917.

At the time of Hubert's death, he was 39 years old, and his family were by then living at 42 Albany Road, Sittingbourne. He was buried in the Lijssenthoek Military Cemetery, Belgium, and a memorial service was held for him at St Michael's Church, where his name appears on their Memorial Window.

Credit: © King's Printer for Ontario, 2022

Lijssenthoek was on the main communication line between the battlefields of Ypres and the rear military bases and became a natural place to create casualty clearing stations. It is the second largest cemetery in Belgium, containing 9,901 Commonwealth WW1 burials, of which 24 remain unidentified.

The death of Hubert was reported on 30th June 1917 in the East Kent Gazette, the article mentioned that he was held in high esteem and respect. It went on to say he was a keen cricketer and was an honorary secretary of Gore Court Cricket Club. Hubert was one of the first to join the Volunteer Training Corps, rising to Platoon Commander and becoming an efficient officer.

Hubert is remembered on Sittingbourne War Memorial. He was awarded the Victory and British War Medals. Among his personal effects, returned to wife Florence, was clothing, scissors, a thimble, a Devotional Book and poignantly, a lock of hair, perhaps his wife's.

The East Kent Gazette on 5th October 1918 reported:

"Boy Scouts Rally.

This was followed by the presentation of the challenge trophy of the old Sittingbourne Cycling Club, which had been given to the Sittingbourne Troop in memory of Hubert Stanley Crow, the former scoutmaster, who had given his life for his country, while fighting in France."

George James was born in Canterbury in 1879 and was baptised in St Mary Northgate Church on 28th March 1880. He was the son of George and Elizabeth Frances Bailey, who at that time were living with Elizabeth's parents, James, and Sarah Taylor, at 10 Artillery Gardens, Canterbury.

On 15th April 1882 Elizabeth married James Thomas Davis in Hougham, Kent. George adopted the use of his surname Davis after his mother's second marriage. James and Elizabeth, moved around before settling in 1891 in Milton Regis at 27 Crown Road. Their first two children James Edward and John Thomas were born in Portland, Dorset, then Marion Eliza, born in 1887 in County Cork, Ireland. Their last two children were born in Sittingbourne, Albert William, and Sydney Harold. Sadly in 1904, George's mother, Elizabeth died, aged 44, in Milton Regis.

When George married Margaret Marjorie White, on 1st July 1905 at St Mary the Boltons Church, West Brompton, London (pictured right), he was a Sergeant in the army, based in Aldershot. Their first son George Taylor was born 28th September 1906 in Andover, Hampshire.

In 1911 George, Margaret, and George junior, aged 4, were living in married quarters at Ebrington Military Barracks, Londonderry, Ireland. The 29th July 1911 saw the birth of their second son John Arthur in Londonderry and their third child, Thomas Hector, was born on 3rd December 1917 in Wayland Norfolk.

cc-by-sa/2.0 - St Mary, The Boltons... by John Salmon - geograph.org.uk/p/2715208

At the start of April 1918 George's battalion's War Diary[39] records they had moved to Auchel, after providing Brigade support. For the next three days they spent their time re-organising, before moving on to Houchin and spending the next five days training reinforcements.

On 11th April 1918, his battalion had moved, by bus and by marching, from Houchin to Avelette bridge crossing the La Bassée Canal. In the early afternoon of 12th April German troops were spotted in nearby Locon moving heavy machine guns on carts. The officer in charge called up artillery support, which continued for an hour or so. The Germans could be seen trying to outflank the battalion but with the use of four Vickers guns the German fire was suppressed; though the Vickers teams ran out of ammunition and sustained heavy casualties. In the evening the order was given to retire back to Avelette bridge.

George's battalion continued to be under fire for the whole day, and at 11pm, they retired to a point south of the bridge and canal, to the Sevelingue line. The following day, 13th April, the battalion suffered

---

[39] War Diary: 1 Battalion Royal Scots Fusiliers. WO-95-1422-3. April 1916-May 1919. The National Archives (UK), Kew, England.

some heavy shelling, though no casualties were reported. Sunday 14th April was reported as a quiet day and that night they were relieved by the King's Own and moved to Annezin. In the period from 11th to 14th April, 10 men were killed, 169 wounded and 151 reported as missing.

George was killed in action, aged 40, on 12th April 1918 and buried in Pont-Du-Hem Military Cemetery, La Gorgue, France. He is designated as one of nine Special Memorials, denoting his actual burial location is unknown, though records indicate he is buried in the cemetery amongst the 1,500 plus casualties.

Adorning his headstone is the inscription "THEIR GLORY SHALL NOT BE BLOTTED OUT" from the Bible Sirach (Ecclesiasticus) 44:13. It is the second half of the phrase "Their seed shall remain for ever, and their glory shall not be blotted out." Ecclesiasticus is also known as the Wisdom of Jesus the Son of Sirach, and contains practical and moral rules, and exhortations. At the time of his death his family were living in 36 Epps Road, Milton Regis. His pay and gratuity were paid to his wife and three children.

George was awarded the Distinguished Conduct Medal, which was announced in The London Gazette dated 3rd September 1918, suggesting he may not have known about the award before he died. The announcement read:

5301 R.S.M. G. J. Davis, R. Scots Fus. (Dersingham, Norfolk)

For conspicuous gallantry and devotion to duty. During an attack he organised battalion headquarter details and a machine-gun, taking up a position which checked the enemy, who were threatening the flank of the retiring companies. After covering the withdrawal, he brought his party back to the reserve line.

George was also awarded the Croix de Guerre for gallantry, which was announced in The London Gazette dated 12th July 1918 under the headline "Decorations conferred by HIS MAJESTY THE KING OF THE BELGIANS. Croix de Guerre."

George's widow, Margaret, died in 1923, aged 41, at 36 Epps Road, Milton Regis. Their eldest son, George Taylor, died at 65 Bell Road, Sittingbourne in 1972, aged 65. Their middle son John Arthur emigrated to Australia sometime before 1933, as he married in Australia and served in the Second World War from 3rd July 1941 to 22nd February 1943. Their youngest son Thomas Hector was a waiter at the Royal Oak Private Hotel Rosthwaite, Keswick in 1939 and died in Carlisle in 1988, aged 70.

DEVERSON, Harry

T/240659, Private, 5th Battalion, The Buffs (East Kent Regiment).

Harry was the second child of William Henry and Rosina Elizabeth (née Hull), and was born in 1896 in Sittingbourne. He had nine siblings, of which sadly three did not survive infancy, and their names were William Henry, Gladys May, Ernest Edward, John Thomas, unnamed twins (1906-1906), Julia Ann (1908-1912), Ida Mary, and Rosina Elizabeth.

Harry's father was a canal boat captain in 1901 in Brentford, Middlesex, and his children's birth places show the family moved around a lot. Harry's first three children were born in Sittingbourne, as that was Rosina's hometown, followed by Hertfordshire, Staffordshire, Warwickshire, and then the family moved back to Milton Regis in 1913.

In 1911 the family were in Nuneaton, Warwickshire and Harry's father was employed as a miner and Harry himself as a brickmaker. By the time of his death Harry was living at 4 Eastbourne Street, Sittingbourne.

He served as a Private in The Buffs and joined the Mesopotamia Expeditionary Force. His brother William was also in The Buffs, as part of 8th Battalion.

Harry was reported missing on 16th February 1916 and was confirmed as having been killed in action on 21st January 1916 at the age of 19.

It is understood that Harry was in the same action as another man remembered in the Avenue, Percy John Baker (see page 53). Both were serving with the Mesopotamia Expeditionary Force in Iraq in the 5th Battalion, The Buffs. They were sent to India in October 1914 joining up with the Indian Army. Then on 31st December 1915 they landed at Basra, Iraq, to relieve the besieged forces at Kut el Amara.

One of the events to break the siege which started on 21st January 1916, the day that Harry was declared as 'missing presumed killed in action', was the Battle of Hanna. This was situated 30 miles downriver of Kut el Amara and involved a 600-yard advance across no-man's land, which was flooded. The Ottoman army was well prepared with well sited machine gun posts, this forced the British to abandon the assault after suffering heavy losses.

Harry is remembered on the Basra Memorial to the Missing and locally on Sittingbourne War Memorial, Milton Regis Memorial Cross, and St Paul's Church Memorial.

DORRELL, Frederick Thomas

14060, Private, 7th Battalion, Bedfordshire Regiment.

Frederick was born in Sittingbourne in 1895, the son of Frederick William and Alice Ann (née Saxby). He had two younger sisters, Alice Caroline, also known as Cissie and Dorothy Emily, who were both born whilst the family lived at 66 Ospringe Road, Faversham. Frederick attended Holy Trinity School in Sittingbourne.

In 1911 Frederick's parents and sisters were living at 22 Laburnum Place, Sittingbourne and his father was employed in the paper mill. Frederick himself, was employed as one of the two live-in servants of Dr John Francis Grayling and his wife May Maria, of 119 High Street, Sittingbourne. The other servant was 27-year-old Ethel Frances Eastman from Rodmersham.

Frederick then moved to work in Derbyshire, before he gained employment as a footman for Baron Dimsdale of Essendon Place, Buntingford, Hertfordshire. He enlisted at the outbreak of war, with the 7th Battalion Bedfordshire Regiment, also known as 'The Shiny Seventh'.

His employer, Baron Charles Robert Southwell Dimsdale, tragically lost two sons in the war. They were 31-year-old Captain Edward Charles, Rifle Brigade, who died on 8th May 1915 and is commemorated on Ypres (Menin Gate) Memorial; and 30-year-old Lieutenant Reginald Thomas, Royal Navy HM Submarine *E22*, who died on 25th April 1916 and is commemorated on the Portsmouth Naval Memorial.

Frederick was serving with his battalion in France on 27th September 1916, when they were in trenches south of Thiepval and received the order to attack the last untaken part of the village in the north-west. At 5.45am, on an extremely dark morning, the British swept across the untaken ground, and despite being under heavy machine gun and rifle fire, advanced on the German trenches. The attack was successful and the village of Thiepval taken, with 36 German men taken prisoner. It was an important victory as the village was a strategic location in the lines and one of the German's strongest positions. Frederick's regiment suffered the loss of two officers and about 110 other ranks.[40]

Frederick was one of those who lost his life on 27th September 1916, from machine gun fire and unusually named in the casualty list in the battalion War Diary[41], which normally only listed the names of commissioned officers. Frederick was 21 years old when he was buried at the Connaught Cemetery, Thiepval. He is remembered on Sittingbourne War Memorial, Sittingbourne Holy Trinity Church WW1 Memorial and Milton Regis War Memorial.

The East Kent Gazette of 14th October 1916 reported that Frederick had become an officer's servant and was highly spoken of by everyone who knew him. The article refers to letters of condolence, including one from his commanding officer, Second Lieutenant Cartwright, sent to his parents which said that although Frederick was small of stature, he had the heart of a lion.

Frederick's father received his pay and gratuity, together with his 1915 Star, Victory, and British War Medals.

The 24th November 1993 edition of the East Kent Gazette in a supplement to commemorate the 75th anniversary of the end of the war reported on a visit to Frederick's grave by his niece, Phyllis Bridges, and her husband. Mrs Bridges is quoted as saying Frederick's parents were heart broken and unable to afford to visit his grave and so this visit was a very emotional moment.

---

[40] The Bedfordshire Regiment in the Great War. 1916 *War Diary*. www.bedfordregiment.org.uk/7thbn/7thbtn1916diary.html

[41] The Bedfordshire Regiment in the Great War. *War Diary, 1916 War Diary Appendices, September onwards*. www.bedfordregiment.org.uk/7thbn/7thbtn1916appendices2.html

DOUBLEDAY DSC, George Hambrook Dean

Lieutenant, Royal Naval Reserve, HMS Cullist.

George was the son of the Reverend John Doubleday and Jessie Vincent (née Dean), and he was named after his maternal grandfather George Hambrook Dean, with whom he lived for most of his life, before joining the Royal Navy as a Cadet.

George's father was born in Lincolnshire and became the minister for Sittingbourne's Baptist Church in 1881, where he officiated for the next 40 years. His father married his mother, Jessie, in 1884. Jessie's father was one of Sittingbourne's industrialists, owning a brick and cement works, and a jam factory in Bell Road.

The seventh of nine children, born on 17th November 1895 in Tunstall, Kent, his siblings were Hilda Jane, Leslie, Lilian Vincent, John Eric, Georgina Smeed, Jessie Margaret, Stuart Mead, and Marion Bessie.

George, as a cadet pupil in Nautical School, trained on the schooner *Harriet Thompson* and cadet ship *HMS Worcester*, where he was one of five cadets to be nominated for the King's gold medal. On 10th August 1912 he gained the rank of Midshipman. He then joined the P&O line, sailing to and from Australia.

During the war he served in the Royal Naval Reserve. The UK Navy List for October 1916 listed George as an Acting Sub-Lieutenant, which was made permanent on 28th January 1917. The Navy List 1918 records George as an acting Lieutenant, in the section entitled Officers and men killed in action.

George was awarded the Distinguished Service Cross, on 29th August 1917[42], for "The good shooting, during the action with an enemy submarine on 13th July 1917 was largely due to him, and he afforded valuable assistance on the bridge during the action."

The East Kent Gazette reported his award in its 1st September 1917 edition, with the headline "A SITTINGBOURNE NAVAL OFFICER DECORATED BY THE KING". The article mentioned that he was the first Sittingbourne officer to gain this particular honour. It would appear they attempted to obtain details behind the action as they reported "Wild horses will not drag from the young officer more

than the barest details of what was a thrilling piece of work." They added that the King shook hands, congratulated George, pinned on his medal and wished him success.

Sadly, just five months after winning his DSC, 22-year-old George was killed in action on 11th February 1918 when his ship *HMS Cullist* (pictured left) was torpedoed in the Irish Sea. *HMS Cullist* was previously known as the *Westphalia*, when on 7th March 1917 she entered service as a "Q" ship. A "Q" ship was

---

[42] Admiralty, and Ministry of Defence, Navy Department: Medal Rolls. Class: ADM 171 ; Piece: 83 ; Page 149. National Archives (Great Britain), Kew, England.

essentially a disguised merchant ship, with concealed weapons, used to hunt and attack submarines by luring them to the surface. The ship was sunk by the German submarine U-97, 11.3km north of Anglesey, Wales. The ship lost 43 of the 70 crew, with the survivors being picked up by the trawler *James Green*.

The 16th February 1918 edition of the East Kent Gazette reported his death, saying that George's "career was more or less veiled in secret." They added that it was no secret that George sunk the first of five U-boats, that the ship had sunk in a single day, as it had been mentioned by Prime Minister Lloyd George in the House of Commons. On another occasion he had been responsible for saving a convoy, when he changed its route and called up destroyers which sank four German submarines.

A week later on 22nd February 1918, George was posthumously Mentioned in Despatches[43], with the citation "The high gunnery and running of this ship is due entirely to his zeal and energy."

Like many young men who served in the war he would not speak of his experience, but it was known that 'the brass case of a shell fired in a fight' had been kept as a souvenir of the 'something' that had happened.

George is commemorated on the CWGC Portsmouth Naval Memorial to the Missing, Tunstall's Roll of Honour (pictured right), and Sittingbourne's Baptist Church Memorial. The latter was unveiled on 3rd December 1919, by Mr. George Kemsley, who lost three sons, all commemorated on the Avenue (see page 192). George's own father, as the Pastor of the church, read an invocation prayer and read out the 34 names on the tablet.

DOWNING, Percy Albert William

915746, Gunner, "D" Battery, 223rd Brigade, Royal Field Artillery.

Percy, known as Paw (because of his initials), was born in New Brompton, Gillingham, in 1895, the son of Walter, a general labourer, and Catherine, known as Kate (née Hill). He was the middle of their five children and his siblings were Walter Edward, Maud Beatrice, Catherine (Kate) Caroline Ethel, and Daisy Elizabeth.

By 1901 the family had moved to Milton Regis, where, in 1909, his father died. By 1911 the family were living at 13 Milton Road, Sittingbourne, and the following year Percy's mother married George Cockell. Percy had attended St Michael's School before working for the Co-operative Bakery at Murston.

Percy's sisters Kate and Maud (pictured right) worked at Ridham Dock Salvage Depot during the war.

43 Admiralty, and Ministry of Defence, Navy Department: Medal Rolls. Class: ADM 171 ; Piece: 83 ; Page 223. National Archives (Great Britain), Kew, England.

Percy was killed by an explosion of a defective shell on the howitzer gun that he was manning on 20th April 1917, aged 22. His death was reported by the East Kent Gazette of 5th May 1917. It said that Percy had joined the Howitzer Brigade in Sittingbourne in August 1915, whilst they were in training at Otford, Sevenoaks, and arrived in France in early 1916. The brigade had fought in all the Somme battles. On the day of his death, the brigade was in Gavrelle, near Arras.

The CWGC database and the Kent & Sussex Courier, dated 15th June 1917, record that Percy was killed alongside his fellow soldier, Ashley Cyril Tully. They were buried side by side (pictured below) in Bailleul Road East Cemetery, Saint-Laurent-Blangy, France. Ashley, aged 20, was from Capel, Kent, and sadly left his young widow Florence May and nine-month-old son, Cyril Frederick. Three other soldiers were injured when the gun exploded.

Percy's family chose the phrase "UNTIL WE MEET AGAIN" to be inscribed on his headstone.

The battery commander, Lieutenant G. S. Dixon, wrote to both families, saying they did not suffer "thank God" and that they would be greatly missed. He added that they were buried with full military honours.

Percy's schoolteacher, Sergeant Frank Morris, served in the same battery as Percy, and he was killed on 30th March 1918, near Amiens.

Percy's brother Corporal Walter Downing was in The Buffs and lost his right leg after being wounded. At the time of Percy's death Walter was waiting to attend Roehampton Hospital, for the fitting of an artificial leg.

Percy's mother received his Victory and British War Medals, together with his pay and gratuity.

Two emotional "In Memoriams" were published in 20th April 1918 edition of the East Kent Gazette.

The East Kent Gazette

SATURDAY, APRIL 20, 1918

IN MEMORIAM

DOWNING – In ever loving memory of our dear brother, Gunner Percy Downing R.F.A., attached to R.N.D., who was killed in action in France, 20th April 1917.

Oh, why was he taken so young and so fair,
Taken from home
and those that loved him so dear;
For one so loving and dear to our hearts.
When others return, we will miss you more;
Only those who have lost can ever tell
The pain at our hearts at not saying farewell.
From loving Sister and Brother, Maud and Arthur.

The East Kent Gazette

SATURDAY, APRIL 20, 1918

IN MEMORIAM

DOWNING – In ever loving memory of our dear son and brother, Gunner Percy Downing R.F.A., attached to R.N.D., who was killed in action in France, 20th April 1917.

If I had but seen him at the last and watched his dying bed.
Or heard the last sigh of his heart or held his drooping head.
My heart I think would not have felt such bitterness of grief.
But God has ordered otherwise and now he rests in peace.
From loving Mum, Dad, Sisters and Brother.

Percy is remembered on Sittingbourne War Memorial, Sittingbourne Holy Trinity Church WW1 Memorial and Milton Regis War Memorial.

Two months later the family again placed an "In Memoriam" in the East Kent Gazette, signed off with "Deeply mourned by his Mum, Dad, Sisters and Brother".

These touching and poignant words surely expressed the emotions and feelings of every mother, and father, who lost a son in the First World War and all other conflicts.

The East Kent Gazette

SATURDAY, APRIL 19, 1919

IN MEMORIAM

DOWNING – In ever loving memory of our dear boy, Gunner Percy Downing R.F.A., attached to R.N.D., who was killed in action, April 20th, 1917.

It's only a mother who knows the sorrow,
It's only a mother who knows the pain,
Of losing her son, she loves so dearly,
And to know she will never see him again.
He sleeps beside his comrades,
in a hallowed grave unknown;
But his name is in letters of love,
in the hearts he has left at home.
Deeply mourned by his Mum, Dad, Sisters, and Brother.

DRAKE, William Edward Roger

298941, Stoker 1st Class, Hood Battalion, Royal Navy Division.

Stoker Dress Insignia

William was from a large family of thirteen children, and he was the fifth in line, sadly some of his siblings died in infancy. His parents were James, an iron moulder, and Sarah Jane (née Pankhurst).

William's siblings were James William David (1875-1903), Annie Maria, George Henry, Louisa Alice (1880-1882), Albert (1885-1885), Frederick Charles, Albert Thomas, Ernest Edgar, Florence May, twins Alice Phoebe and Arthur David (both 1894-1895), and Bertha Agnes.

William was born in Sittingbourne on 3rd November 1882 and his father died in 1912. In 1911 the family were living in Frederick Street, where they had lived for at least 20 years.

When William signed up for 12 years in the Royal Navy at Chatham, on 11th November 1901, he was 5ft 7in tall with brown hair and grey eyes. He served on more than a dozen different ships, being promoted to Stoker 2nd Class in 1904 and to Stoker 1st Class a year later.

On 15th November 1913 he was transferred to the Royal Fleet Reserve and re-joined on 2nd August 1914. The following month, on 17th September, he was posted to Royal Naval Division Hood and was sent to Gallipoli.

Royal Naval Division Charge

The campaign at Gallipoli was to last for eight months with Commonwealth and French forces landing there on 25th-26th April 1915. In the south the 29th Division landed at Cape Helles and the Australian and New Zealand Corps (Anzacs) landed on the west coast. The objective was to try to force Turkey out of the war in order to open a supply route to Russia. The forces moved inland to take a ridge at Achi Baba, some 9km north-west of their landing point, but fatigue forced them to stop short. In early May the Turkish forces counter attacked but were repulsed. Small gains were made, though heavy losses were taken. During May, the 29th Indian Infantry Brigade and 42nd (East Lancashire) Division landed at Helles, to reinforce the existing divisions.

On 4th June 1915 the reinforced forces attacked to try and push forward but were stopped. This was the day that William lost his life, aged 32. Further attacks were made for the remainder of 1915, but the positions remain unchanged, and in January 1916 the peninsula was evacuated.

William is buried in Redoubt Cemetery, Helles, Turkey. The Royal Navy and Royal Marine War Roll records William's cause of death as 'killed or died as a direct result of enemy action'. Although his grave was never identified, a special memorial headstone for him was installed with the words "BELIEVED TO BE BURIED IN THIS CEMETERY" across the top, and his father chose the words "THEIR GLORY SHALL NOT BE BLOTTED OUT" to be inscribed on his headstone. The words were taken from the Bible's Ecclesiasticus 44:13.

An article headed "PATRIOTIC SITTINGBOURNE FAMILY – SIX SONS AND EIGHT NEPHEWS SERVING THE KING" in the East Kent Gazette dated 20th February 1915, details the service of William and his brothers. They are listed as: George in the 9th Battalion, The Buffs and served eight years in the 16th (Queen's Own) Lancers and three years in Africa; Frederick also in the 9th Battalion, The Buffs; Albert, at that time, had just joined the 4th Home Counties Howitzer Brigade, Royal Field Artillery, who were headquartered in Sittingbourne; Ernest had served six years, and was in the 2nd South Lancashire Regiment and in France since the previous August; James, who died in 1903, had served five years in the Navy Chatham Division and finally, adopted son Roland Brown had been a Petty Officer in the Navy for 12 years. All the brothers had worked for Smeed Dean and Co. Limited before volunteering and all, bar William, survived the war.

The article adds that of the eight nephews, one was in the Royal Engineers, three in the Royal Marines and four in the Navy.

A few months later "A LETTER FROM THE KING" was the sub-heading in the East Kent Gazette, published on 17th July 1915, under the main heading "PATRIOTIC SITTINGBOURNE FAMILY." The article reminded readers that William's mother lived at 86a Murston Road, Sittingbourne and that she had six sons serving their King and country.

The article added that she had recently lost William, one of the six. The letter read:

BUCKINGHAM PALACE

Privy Purse Office,
Buckingham Palace, S.W.,
14th July, 1915.

Madam, - I am commanded by the King to convey to you an expression of His Majesty's appreciation of the patriotic spirit which has prompted your five sons to give their services to the Army and Navy. The King was much gratified to hear of the manner in which they have so readily responded to the call of their Sovereign and their country, and I am to express to you and to them His Majesty's congratulations on having contributed in so full a measure to the great cause for which all the people of the British Empire are so bravely fighting.

I have the honour to be,
Madam,
Your obedient servant,
F. M. PONSONBY,
Keeper of the Privy Purse.

A "DEATH" announcement in the 26th June 1915 edition of the East Kent Gazette, shows William's death as 18th June 1915. William's Service Record implies this date was when his death was reported and also records his death as 4th June 1915, as does the Admiralty Casualties Book[44] and the CWGC database.

On the anniversary of William's death, in 1916 and 1917, the East Kent Gazette printed an "In Memoriam" from his family to him.

EDWARDS, John

42892, Private, 1st/5th Battalion, Northumberland Fusiliers.

The WW1 Memorial in Sittingbourne's Holy Trinity Church records a J. Edwards, North. Fus. Research identified one name that matched this inscription, John Edwards who was born in Wexford, Ireland. John's pension card records that he was in the 1st Battalion, Royal Dublin Fusiliers, Service Number 17936, before transferring to the Northumberland Fusiliers.

The East Kent Gazette has several articles concerning the Royal Dublin Fusiliers being billeted in Gore Court, Sittingbourne, including their fielding a football team against local opponents. The edition of 6th November 1915 records that the 5th Battalion departed from Sittingbourne, after an eleven month stay, and that the 4th Battalion had seen them off.

[44] The National Archives of the UK ; Kew, Surrey, England ; Admiralty: Naval Casualties, Indexes, War Grave Rolls and Statistics Book, First World War. ; Class: ADM 242 ; Piece: Piece 008 ; Piece Description: Piece 008 (1914-1919)

It was probably during the period of their stay in Sittingbourne that John made an impression that he was remembered by someone from the town and church after his death. This War Diary of the Royal Dublin Fusiliers provides some background information:

Instructions regarding War Diaries and Intelligence Summaries are contained in F.S. Regs., Part II, and the Staff Manual respectively. Title pages will be prepared in manuscript.	WAR DIARY[45] or INTELLIGENCE SUMMARY. (Erase heading not required.)	Army Form C. 2118.
Date	Summary of Events and Information	Remarks and References to Appendices
1-4-1918	Battalion dug-in on a crest near DOMART-SUR-LA-LUCE with enemy holding the line over LA LUCE. 8am - cavalry charge took the whole line. Despite heavy shelling the battalion suffered one loss.	
1-4-1918 to 4-4-1918	Battalion moved to GONNEHEM, near BÉTHUNE. (Using a combination of marching, buses, and trains to travel the 150km distance.)	
5-4-1918 to 7-4-1918	Battalion bathed, cleaned and re-organised.	
8-4-1918	Marched to LE SART. heavy bombardment on the way.	
9-4-1918	Early morning – Battalion ordered to stand to at ESTAIRES. On arrival Battalion moved to TROU BAYARD and along the line of RIVER LYS to PONT SAILLY. More bombardment on the marches.	
10-4-1918	German forces attacked both right and left flanks using trench mortars and machine gun fire. Enemy crossed the LYS at PONT SAILLY. Battalion held them at TROU BAYARD.	
11-4-1918	Battalion lost ground. Entrenched in NEUF-BERQUIN.	
12-4-1918 to 17-4-1918	Withdrew to LA MOTTE. Battalion working parties on the trenches in the locality.	
18-4-1918 to 24-4-1918	Battalion marched to REBECQ. Bathing, cleaning, and training.	

John lost his life during the German attack on 10th April 1918 and is remembered on the Ploegsteert Memorial, near Ypres in Belgium. The memorial commemorates more than 11,000 United Kingdom and South African men who died in the region and have no known grave. The majority of the names were not involved in major offences, but were killed in smaller engagements and trench warfare, usually supporting the major offences. On the same date as John, there are 90 additional names from his regiment.

He is also remembered on Sittingbourne War Memorial as well as Sittingbourne Holy Trinity Church WW1 Memorial, and he was awarded the Victory and British War Medals.

---

[45] War Diary: 5 Battalion Northumberland Fusiliers. WO-95-2828-2. April 1915-July 1918. The National Archives (UK), Kew, England.

EDWARDS, John Arthur

1017, Private, 1st Battalion, Northumberland Fusiliers.

John was born in 1884 in Sittingbourne to Hampshire born German Edwards (1846-1891), a tobacconist and carriage painter, and Alice Catherine (née Trimmer). John was the middle of their five children, and his siblings were Henry German, who carried on the family name of German, William John, Emily Louisa (1886-1904) and George Samuel (1888-1901). In 1881 and 1891 the family were living at 27 Station Street, Sittingbourne. John's father died when he was just six years old, in 1891.

In 1897 John's mother married Frederic Beresford Simpkin, a farm stockman, in Milton Regis. Sadly, Frederic died in 1909, leaving Alice a widow for a second time, and in 1911 she was living in William Street, Milton Regis, with three daughters, John's half-sisters Mary Victoria, Alice Helena, and Katie Elizabeth.

In 1901 John was working as a news boy and living with his employer, Samuel Snelling, a newsagent, and shop keeper, in Newington. By 1911, the census shows that John was stationed at West Ridge barracks (pictured right) in Rawalpindi, India (now Pakistan) as he had enlisted and was serving with the Northumberland Fusiliers. His regimental number indicates that he had joined the army in 1905.

John's brother William emigrated to New York in 1904, followed by Henry in 1912, who went to Boston and moved back to Sittingbourne before 1939, as he was recorded then as a 58-year-old unmarried butcher and living at 21 Dover Street, Sittingbourne.

The War Diary for John's regiment in August 1914 is reproduced below:

	WAR DIARY[46] or INTELLIGENCE SUMMARY. (Erase heading not required.)	Army Form C. 2118.
Instructions regarding War Diaries and Intelligence Summaries are contained in F.S. Regs., Part II, and the Staff Manual respectively. Title pages will be prepared in manuscript.		
Date	Summary of Events and Information	Remarks and References to Appendices
13-8-1914	Left Cambridge Barracks, PORTSMOUTH.	
14-8-1914	Battalion arrived at LE HAVRE.	
23-8-1914	In the line at MONS, under heavy shell fire.	
24-8-1914	In the line at MONS. Fell back to FRAMERIES, followed by German forces.	
25-8-1918	Long and tiring march in drenching rain arriving at INCHY at 6pm.	

---

[46] War Diary: 1 Battalion Northumberland Fusiliers. WO-95-1430. August 1914-June 1915. The National Archives (UK), Kew, England.

26-8-1914	Proceeded to prepared trenches which were unsuitable and before new trenches dug German opened fire with little harm and digging continued.
27-8-194 to 31-8-1914	Brigade moved from AUDENCOURT through HARGICOURT, VERMAND, CRESOLLES, RESSON LE LONG arriving in billets at VAUCIENNES.
1-9-1914 to 8-9-1914	Marching continued through BOUILLANCY, PENCHARD, VILLEMAREIL, CHATRES, LUMIGNY, LA MARTROY, ORLY arriving in billets at LA FAUCHERE.
9-9-1914	4.30am Crossed the MARNE. Delayed all day fighting in the woods near VENTRELETT.
10-9-1914	5.30am Marched out and met rear guard at VERILLY and ordered to clear the woods. There was a chasm in the middle, waist deep, which had to be forged. 12 snipers killed or captured, with no casualties. Six hundred of the enemy were taken prisoner, and signs of hasty retreat.
	4pm Battalion billeted at DAMMARD.
11-9-1914	7.15am marched to GRAND ROZOY and set up outposts. It was a very wet night.
12-9-1914	Battalion saw no action whilst marching to BRENNEL.
13-9-1914	Left 7.0am and crossed the AISNE in single file as bridge had been broken. Nearly midnight when arrived at billets at VAILLY.
14-9-1914	5am moved to ROUGEMAISON FARM, VAILLY, encountered strong enemy force. Due to our position, unable to call in artillery support. Remainder of the day was spent fighting the enemy. Towards midnight the enemy made a half-hearted attack.
	Our casualties this day were very heavy.
15 to 21-9-1914	Battalion remained in the trenches.
22-9-1914	Moved out to COURCELLES.

The War Diary records that 31-year-old John was wounded on 14th September 1914 at Vailly, and the CWGC records that he died that day. John was one of Sittingbourne's earliest casualties of the war, being killed just 43 days after war was declared and after just six days of fighting.

John is commemorated on the La Ferte-Sous-Jouarre Memorial to the Missing, which is in France, which commemorates 3,740 men who lost their lives at the battles of Mons, Le Cateau, the Marne, and the Aisne. John is also remembered on the Sittingbourne War Memorial and Sittingbourne Holy Trinity Church WW1 Memorial.

John was awarded the 1914 Star with clasp, and the Victory and British War Medals. His pay and gratuity were divided between his mother, his half-sisters, who were all living at 14 Cockleshell Walk in Sittingbourne, and his brothers, though his brother Henry gave his share to his mother.

G/5405, Private, 8th Battalion, The Buffs (East Kent Regiment).

Henry was born in Swanscombe in 1880, the son of William, a cement labourer, and Sarah Ann (née Winch). He was the second of their nine children, his siblings were William Thomas (1877-1907), Elizabeth, Susan Ellen, Charlotte, William Thomas, Alice, Ruth, and James.

Henry's father died in 1902 and his mother remarried in 1902 to George Winch, though sadly he died five years later, and she had moved to Sittingbourne by 1911.

In 1900, Henry married Sarah Jane Ford in Strood, and they had two daughters, Violet Ethel (born 1901) and Ivy Gladys (born 1903). Just five years after they married, tragedy struck, and his wife died in 1905.

Henry remarried, in Milton Regis in 1909, his second wife was Ada Mary Waller. They had three children, Ada Ellen (born 1910), Henry Thomas (born 1914) and Elizabeth Annie (born 1916). In 1911 Henry was a general labourer in the cement works and the family lived at 4 Cross Street, Sittingbourne.

When Henry enlisted in Sittingbourne, he was a cement burner at Smeed Dean, and he arrived in France on 7th October 1915.

The War Diary for Henry's regiment for August 1916 has been reproduced below:

		Army Form C. 2118.
Instructions regarding War Diaries and Intelligence Summaries are contained in F.S. Regs., Part II, and the Staff Manual respectively. Title pages will be prepared in manuscript.	**WAR DIARY**[47] or **INTELLIGENCE SUMMARY.** (Erase heading not required.)	
Date	Summary of Events and Information	Remarks and References to Appendices
1-8-1916	Battalion arrived at the SAND PIT at MÉAULTE.	
2-8-1916 to 3-8-1916	Battalion practised a signalling scheme with a patrol aeroplane from No 9 Squadron of the Royal Flying Corps.	
4-8-1918 to 8-8-1916	Training	
8-8-1916	Moved to the front at BERNAFAY WOOD at CARNOY.	
13-8-1916	Battalion relieved by ROYAL FUSILIERS.	
14-8-1916	Working party created new communication trench at TRONES WOOD.	
15-8-1916	Nothing of importance to report. Fine all day.	
16-8-1916	Nothing of importance to report. Fine all day.	
17-8-1916	Battalion relieved ROYAL FUSILIERS in the line at WATERLOT FARM (located between LONGUEVAL and GUILLEMONT.)	
18-8-1916	2.45pm Battalion joined RIFLE BRIGADE, 6TH BATTALION SOMERSET LIGHT INFANTRY and the 3RD ROYAL BERKSHIRE.	

[47] War Diary: **8 Battalion Buffs (East Kent Regiment).** WO-95-2207-1. August 1915-January 1918. The National Archives (UK), Kew, England.

18-8-1916 continued	Under cover of barrage, left trenches and attacked DELVILLE WOOD. Met strong resistance from machine guns and a sniper, who was disposed of by one of the Bomb Squads. By the end of the attack 60 prisoners had been taken. CASUALTIES - Officers: 1 killed, 6 wounded. Other Ranks: 38 killed, 297 wounded, 16 missing. Communication was kept up with the most remarkable completeness of Runners. No case has yet come to light in which any message failed to reach its objective.

Henry was killed during this action, aged 36, on 18th August 1916, leaving behind a widow and five children, the youngest was five months old, having been born after he had left for France.

CWGC records show he was originally buried in Mametz Wood, with a number of casualties. He was later moved to Delville Wood Cemetery, where many people buried in July, August, and September 1916 were reinterred. The cemetery was designed by Sir Herbert Baker and created after the Armistice, with the casualties being consolidated from smaller cemeteries and isolated graves. It is the final resting place for 5,523 burials of the First World War of which 3,592 (65%) are 'Known unto God'.

Henry is remembered on Sittingbourne War Memorial, and was awarded the 1914-15 Star, Victory, and British War Medals. His widow Ada received his pay and gratuity.

ELLIOTT, Frank

270263, Private, 10th (Royal East Kent and West Kent Yeomanry) Battalion,
The Buffs (East Kent Regiment).

Frank was born in Rye, Sussex in 1895, the youngest child of Henry Simon, a musician, and Sarah Ann (née Heneker). Frank's brothers and sisters were Grace Mary, William George, Alice, Kate, and Annie (1893-1893).

In 1899 his mother died and in 1901 and 1911 he was living at 37 Pembury Street, Sittingbourne, with his maternal aunt and uncle Henry Robert and Sophia Smith. An "In Memoriam" in the 13th September 1919 and 18th September 1920 editions of the East Kent Gazette, say "the beloved nephew and adopted son from infancy."

In 1901, his father was living in Ashford with Frank's brother, and sisters Alice and Kate. In 1911 his father was living in Maidstone. Frank was working in the paper mills when he enlisted in Sittingbourne on 26th October 1914, and he was sent to France on 24th September 1915.

WAR DIAR[48]

or

INTELLIGENCE SUMMARY.

(Erase heading not required.)

Instructions regarding War Diaries and Intelligence Summaries are contained in F.S. Regs., Part II, and the Staff Manual respectively. Title pages will be prepared in manuscript.

Date	Summary of Events and Information	Remarks and References to Appendices
10-9-1918 ÉPEHY	Battalion moved into front-line trenches. Took over from 14th R.H. 23 Other Ranks from Hospital taken in strength.	
11-9-1918	Front trenches very wet. Considerable sniping. Considerable machine gun and artillery fire during the day.	
13-9-1918	Usual enemy artillery fire. One Other Rank killed.	
14-9-1918	Relieved by 24th W.R.	

Credit: RutlandRemembers.org

The death recorded for 13th September 1918 was Frank, who died of wounds aged 23 years. He was buried in Bronfay Farm Military Cemetery, Bray-sur-Somme, France. Frank's headstone carries the family's chosen words "IN GOD'S KEEPING". The cemetery was designed by Sir Edwin Lutyens.

Frank's service record is one of those burnt during the Second World War, but does show that some of his personal effects including letters, photos, wallet, and cap badge, were sent to his father. His father also received his 1914-15 Star, Victory, and British War Medals, together with his pay and gratuity. He is remembered on Sittingbourne War Memorial and Sittingbourne Holy Trinity Church WW1 Memorial.

FAGG, William John

13028, Private, 7th Battalion, The Buffs (East Kent Regiment).

William was born in Faversham on 5th February 1899 and was baptised there on 1st March 1899, at the parish church of St Mary of Charity. He was the youngest of the two children of John Robert, a wine merchant, and his second wife Caroline Day (née Cornford), and his sister was named Marie Helen. William had five half-siblings from his father's first marriage to Barbara Ann (née Kirkhouse), who died in 1885; their names were John Kirkhouse (1878-1878), Bessie Maud, Nellie Mildred, Annie Kirkhouse, and Thomas Walter.

When William enlisted, on 17th December 1914, he was 5ft 10in tall and was living at Collingdale, London Road, Sittingbourne. He joined the 2/1 Battalion of The Buffs, and was posted to Étaples, France on 21st September 1916. Then on 11th October he was transferred to the 4th Battalion before being posted to the 7th Battalion.

[48] War Diary: 10 Battalion The Buffs. WO-95-3153-2. May 1918-May 1919. The National Archives (UK), Kew, England.

Documents from the Red Cross show that William was captured on 15th December 1917 at Poelcapelle, Belgium and that on 28th January 1918 he was being held at Dülmen in Germany.

The East Kent Gazette edition of 19th January 1918 reported that his parents received the glad news that he was alive, although a prisoner in Germany. He had been listed as missing in action for a while and his parents had been afraid that he had been killed. When he was captured, he was the battalion runner carrying messages from HQ to the line. It was assumed he lost his way, which is how he fell into the hands of the Germans.

The 7th December 1918 edition of the East Kent Gazette reported the sad news of William's death on 24th October 1918, aged 19. The report stated that a Private Keall of Dover Street, Sittingbourne, was the first to inform William's parents that he had died from pneumonia, whilst in a German Prisoner of War Camp. Private Keall himself had just been released from the same camp. The article also provides additional information that, when William was captured, he was taken to Lemburg and then to Münster, Westphalia, where he had died, from pneumonia following influenza.

A Prisoner of War Camp at Friedrichsfeld near Cologne, Germany

William was buried in Cologne Southern Cemetery, Germany, which is the burial place for over 1,000 servicemen who died while prisoners of war. During the First World War almost 300,000 servicemen were taken prisoner on the Western Front. Although the Geneva Agreement afforded POWs certain rights, Germany was not equipped to house, feed, and clothe these large numbers.

The Red Cross monitored camps and treatment of prisoners and ensured food, clothing, and personal letters, sent from Britain, reached the men. It is estimated that 12,000 servicemen died in the camps, with the common cause being disease, especially in 1915 with typhus and the 1918 influenza epidemic.

William is remembered on Sittingbourne War Memorial and Sittingbourne Holy Trinity Church WW1 Memorial. His father received his pay and gratuity, and his Victory and British War Medals.

FISHER, Sidney

L/9444, Private, 2nd Battalion, The Buffs (East Kent Regiment).

Sidney was born in Milton Regis in the summer of 1892. The youngest of the four sons of Thomas Henry Fisher and Sarah Jane (née Morgan). His brothers were James, George Edward, and Walter John, and he also had four half-siblings from his mother's first marriage to Frederick Blaxland in 1875: Rhoda Jane, Thomas Henry, Alfred, and Richard. In 1881 his mother was living in Gas Road, Milton, with Rhoda, Thomas, Alfred and Thomas Fisher. By 1891 they were living in the same house and her children by Frederick Blaxland had the surname, Fisher.

Sidney was 18 when he enlisted at Canterbury on 6th January 1911 and joined The Buffs. He had been working as a carman, and he was 5ft 5in tall with blue eyes, brown hair, and a tattoo on his right forearm.

He served with the regiment in Dublin until January 1913 when he joined the 2nd Battalion and sailed for India, where he served until November 1914, at which time he returned to England.

His battalion landed in Le Havre on 18th January 1915 and moved to Hazebrouck, by the French-Belgium border, travelling by train in cattle trucks. On the 1st February they marched to Rouge-Croix, arriving at 8am. They remained there until the 2nd February when they travelled, via army omnibuses, to Ouderdom, 6km south-west of Ypres. Two days later the 34th Brigade were attacked west of Ypres and the battalion were ordered to move to Ypres,

where they arrived at midnight with the 3rd Middlesex and ammunition limbers. They returned to Ouderdom the next day at 6.45am. The following day, the 6th, they marched with the East Surrey Regiment to Ypres and had moved into position by 8pm.

On 7th February the battalion moved to Ferme Chapelle. The battalions War Diary[49] records that the trenches were in a bad condition, with water knee deep and the parapets were not bulletproof. One 'Other Rank' was killed, which was probably Sidney, as his death is recorded as 9th February 1915.

Sidney's body was never found, and he is one of the 54,595 recorded in Belgium on the Ypres (Menin Gate) Memorial to the Missing. After his death his effects were returned to his father who was also given Sidney's war medals.

[49] War Diary: 2 Battalion, The Buffs. WO-95-2279-2. December 1914-October 1915. The National Archives (UK), Kew, England.

Locally, Sidney is remembered on Sittingbourne War Memorial, St Michael's Church Memorial Window and Sittingbourne Holy Trinity Church WW1 Memorial. Sidney is also commemorated by Milton Regis on their War Memorial, and St Paul's Church and Old Boys Milton Council Schools Memorials.

FOSTER, Alfred

T/200835, Private, 1st/4th Battalion, The Buffs (East Kent Regiment).

The fourth of six children, Alfred was born in 1893 in Sittingbourne, and was baptised in the parish church of St Michael's on 12th March 1893. His parents were Henry, a brickfield labourer, and Harriet Sarah (née Green). Alfred had five brothers Henry George, Frederick Isaac, Albert Thomas, and Ernest Edward, and one sister who died, Elizabeth Annie (1888-1888).

In 1911 he was working as a cement labourer at Smeed, Dean and Co., whilst his father and older brothers were brickfield labourers, probably also for Smeed Dean.

He joined the Territorials in November 1914 and volunteered for overseas service. The 1st/4th Battalion had embarked from Southampton to India on 30th October 1914 and nine months later on 26th July 1915 they were sent to Aden. In February 1916 they returned to India and spent the remainder of the war in India.

Alfred died, in India, of appendicitis, aged 24, on 6th April 1917, and was buried in Bareilly Cemetery. He is remembered on Sittingbourne War Memorial and St Michael's Church WW1 Memorial Window. His father received his pay and gratuity.

Alfred's brother Frederick was a stoker on a dockyard tug and his death certificate records he died on 31st October 1918, from Influenza, aged 29. The East Kent Gazette edition of 28th April 1917 reported on the Easter vestry at St Michael's Mission Room and said that a letter of sympathy would be sent to Alfred's family as he had been a choir boy and bellringer at the Mission Room. In the same edition and the previous week's, the family and Alfred's sweetheart, Emily Collar, had printed a thank you to "all kind friends for their heart-felt sympathy in their sad bereavement."

Personal.

MR. and Mrs. Foster and Family, and Miss Collar, of 59, Albion Terrace, Canterbury Road, Sittingbourne, wish to thank all kind friends for their heartfelt sympathy in their sad bereavement of their dearly-loved son so far away.

Exactly a year after Alfred's death two poignant and emotional "In Memoriam" (reproduced on the next page) were placed in the East Kent Gazette, one from his family and one from his sweetheart and her family.

His family's words are the first verse of the hymn On the Resurrection Morning, where it is listed in The English Hymnal (1906) as a hymn for Easter, as Alfred died on a Good Friday. Emily was four months older than Alfred and the records show that she did not marry after Alfred's death.

Alfred was obviously well loved and missed, by both his family and sweetheart, as an "In Memoriam" was published every year for him until at least 1929.

The East Kent Gazette

SATURDAY, APRIL 6, 1918

IN MEMORIAM

FOSTER - In loving memory of Pte. Alfred Foster, who died, the 6th April, 1917, in Bareilly, India, the dearly-loved third son of Mr. and Mrs. Foster, 59, Albion Terrace, Canterbury Road, Sittingbourne.

On the Resurrection morning
Soul and body meet again;
No more sorrow, no more weeping,
No more pain!
From his loving Mother, Father, and Family.

The East Kent Gazette

SATURDAY, APRIL 6, 1918

IN MEMORIAM

FOSTER - In ever-loving memory of my dear sweetheart, Pte. Alfred Foster.

His cheerful smile and loving face,
Are pleasant to recall;
He always had a kindly word,
And died beloved by all.
From Emily and Mr. and Mrs. Collar and Family.

FREEBORN, Ernest Archibald

11871, Private, 7th Battalion, Queen's Own (Royal West Kent Regiment).

Ernest was born in Sittingbourne in 1895, the fifth of the ten children of Albert Edgar, a barge captain, and Rosina (née Furminger). His siblings were Rosina Hannah (1889-1889), Joseph (1889-1889), Albert Edgar, William Edward, Olive Gertrude (1898-1901), Baden Powell Mafeking, Henry Thomas, Nellie Mary, and Beatrice.

The family lived at 8 Dover Street, Sittingbourne, from at least 1891 and the will of Ernest's father in 1951 shows they were still living at the same address. In 1911 Ernest worked as a labourer at the paper mill. He was 5ft 9in tall when he enlisted in Maidstone on 10th December 1915, and living in Chatham where he was working as a packer. The next day he was posted to the Army Reserve in the 1st Battalion.

A comment on Ernest's Medical History was made on 24th January 1916, which read "Fit for:- Field Service at Home, Defective Vision." Though this did not stop him being mobilised on 22nd June 1916 and sent to France on 22nd July 1916. Ernest was wounded twice in less than a fortnight after he arrived in France, on the 7th and 16th September 1916. The following month, on 7th October, he was transferred to 7th Battalion.

At the beginning of November 1916, his battalion were billeted in Warloy-Baillon and given orders to march the 10km east to the town of Albert, on 4th November.

Nos 10 and 8 Dover Street

The East Kent Gazette

SATURDAY, DECEMBER 23, 1916

DEATHS

FREEBORN - Nov. 18th, 1916, Ernest Archibald Freeborn, son of Albert and Rosina Freeborn, killed in action somewhere in France.

In a foreign, but friendly land, he lies,
Far away from friends and home;
No kindred round his grave doth weep,
But to the Lord we trust his keep,
And say, Thy will be done.
Billeted there by death,
Quartered to remain,
Until the last trumpet call shall sound;
Then they'll rise and march again.

On the afternoon of 6th November 1916, they received further orders that they would be taking battle positions on the 7th, but at close to midnight these orders were cancelled. However, on the 7th they were ordered to relieve the 7th Queens in Fabick Trench, where they remained for three days before returning to the town of Albert.[50]

On the 13th they then relieved the Berkshire Regiment on the front line, in preparation for an attack on Desire Trench, just south of Grandcourt. Although the attack was postponed twice, his battalion finally attacked the trench on 18th November 1916. Three days later, after occupying Desire Trench, on the 21st they were relieved by the 2/5th Gloucester Regiment and spent the next week moving west to Domvast, a distance of about 70km.

Ernest was killed in action, on the first day of the attack on 18th November 1916, aged 21. He was buried in Stump Road Cemetery, Grandcourt, together with 16 other men from his battalion, and 87 from The Queen's (Royal West Kent Regiment) and The Buffs (East Kent Regiment) who fell on the same day. The East Kent Gazette edition of 23rd December 1916 printed an announcement of his death. The same words were published for the anniversary of his death in the 15th November 1919 edition.

The Personal Effects form in his service record and his Pension Card, indicate Ernest was a Lance Corporal, though his Medal Card and the CWGC database record him as a Private. It is probable that Ernest was an Acting Lance Corporal and when he lost his life his promotion was not confirmed.

Albert, Ernest's brother, served in the Royal Navy as a Probationary Air Mechanic Class 1, from 8th

March 1916 to 31st March 1918, after which he joined the Royal Air Force. His records state he was a police constable, and he remained in the police force until 1939 when he retired with the rank of inspector.

Ernest is remembered on Sittingbourne Holy Trinity Church WW1 Memorial, and both Sittingbourne and Milton Regis War Memorials. He was awarded the Victory and British War Medals, and his mother received his pay and gratuity.

Ernest was also remembered through the East Kent Gazette "In Memoriam" over the years.

---

[50] War Diary: 7 Battalion Queens Own (Royal West Kent Regiment). WO-95-2049-2. July 1915-December 1917. The National Archives (UK), Kew, England.

GAMMON, Alfred Thomas

18439, Private, 11th Battalion, Queen's Own (Royal West Kent Regiment).

Alfred was born in Plumford, near Faversham, on 20th June 1897, and was baptised on 5th August at the parish church of St Peter and St Paul. He was the son of Edward, an agricultural labourer, and Caroline (née Burrows). He had two brothers, Edward, who served in Mesopotamia and survived and Albert. He also had a half-brother, George, and a half-sister, Maud, from his mother's first marriage to William Goodwin, a barge captain, who died between 1886 and 1891. In 1911 the family were living at Fox Hill Cottages, Stones Farm, Bapchild. His mother, Caroline, died in 1916, aged 56.

When Alfred enlisted in Sittingbourne on 28th September 1914, he was 5ft 9in tall and working as a skilled farm labourer for a Mr E B Gascoyne. He gave his age as 18 years and 3 months, a year older than his actual age, and he joined the Royal East Kent Mounted Rifles (Reserves). Just under two years later on 21st September 1916 he embarked for France and was posted to 11th Battalion Royal West Kent's on 14th November 1916.

On 1st February 1917 Alfred's battalion were resting at Reningelst, according to the battalion's War Diary[51]. The next day they relieved 11th Battalion, Royal West Surrey Regiment at Sint-Elooi, where they remained until 9th February when they were relieved by the same battalion they had replaced.

On 8th February, the battalion carried out a raid on the German trenches, taking 16 prisoners. A second raid later in the day failed to get into the trenches. During this action Albert sustained gun-shot wounds to the abdomen and right lower chest, which fractured his ribs.

A statement in the War Diary, by Second Lieutenant R.S. French, states they formed in No Man's Land and crawled out 50 yards, where the shells were falling short, stopping the men moving forward. On the sight of a red light the men rushed forward and the Bosche were disorganised and offered no resistance, though our central group suffered badly, mainly from our own fire. During the action Second-Lieutenant French was wounded and awarded the Military Cross for his actions.

A Casualty Clearing Station

Alfred was taken to No. 3 Canadian Casualty Clearing Station for treatment, but died three days later on 11th February 1917, aged 19 years old. He was buried in Lijssenthoek Military Cemetery in Belgium.

Locally, he is remembered on the memorials in St Laurence Church, Bapchild, and Holy Trinity Church, Sittingbourne, as well as on Sittingbourne War Memorial.

His father received his pay and war gratuity, his personal possessions – letters, photos, wallet, testament, and a broken knife, together with his Victory and British War Medals. According to Alfred's Pension Card he was living at 4 Faith Street, Sittingbourne.

---

[51] War Diary: 11 Battalion Queen's Own (Royal West Kent Regiment). WO-95-2634-4. May 1916-October 1917. The National Archives (UK), Kew, England.

GANT (De GANT), Cecil Edwin

8994, Serjeant, 1st Battalion, Welsh Regiment.

Cecil was born in Barrackton, Cork, Ireland, on 15th July 1890, the son of Corporal David Gant and Elizabeth (née Ryan). Cecil's surname is recorded as De Gant, in his army service records.

His father had married Charlotte Luckhurst in 1884 in Maidstone and they had two children, David (born 22nd October 1884, Leeds, Kent) and Ellen (born 24th December 1887, Maidstone), before he enlisted, joining the Welsh Regiment in Portsmouth on 22nd July 1887.

According to Cecil's father's Attestation Papers he married Cecil's mother Lizzie Ryan on 17th January 1889 at Molash, Kent, whilst appearing to still be married to his first wife Charlotte. The army records show that Lizzie was 'brought on [to the] married establishment on 12th August 1892', showing they recognised their marriage.

Cecil's father was posted to Ireland, where Cecil was born, before being posted to Trichinopoly, Madras, India (pictured right) on 13th September 1892. His wife, Elizabeth, joined him there and Cecil's sister, Theodosia Vida Jane, was born on 22nd May 1893, but tragically died on 12th February 1894. By then his mother, Elizabeth, had died of tuberculosis and dysentery and was buried on 29th July 1893.

On 24th January 1895, Cecil's father, who held the rank of Sergeant, returned to England and he returned to his first wife Charlotte, and they had three more children Maude Jane (born 1896, Sheldwich, Kent), who lived to be 102 years of age, Andrew Edwin (born 1899, Boughton-under-Blean) and Frank (born 1902 - died 1903, Milton Regis).

David was discharged from the army on 21st July 1899 and by 1901 he was working at Sittingbourne Paper Mill and was living in William Street with Charlotte and their four children. Cecil was living in Denton with his paternal grandmother, Jane, who by this time was married to her second husband, John Rogers.

Cecil enlisted in his father's regiment before 1911, where the census records him as a drummer and stationed at the main barracks in Abbassia, Cairo, Egypt. Cecil went to France on 18th January 1915.

Cario Barracks.
Credit: Australian War Memorial, P02321.047

134

The War Diary for his regiment in October of that year is reproduced here:

	WAR DIARY[52] or INTELLIGENCE SUMMARY. (Erase heading not required.)	Army Form C. 2118.
Instructions regarding War Diaries and Intelligence Summaries are contained in F.S. Regs., Part II, and the Staff Manual respectively. Title pages will be prepared in manuscript.		
Date	Summary of Events and Information	Remarks and References to Appendices
1-10-1915 VERMELLES	*8pm - Attacked LITTLE WILLIE TRENCH in AUCHY-LES-MINES. Battalion proceeded to go over the parapet in complete silence. Officers in the centre of the line.* *Reached to within 100 yards of the PRUSSIAN GUARD enemy before being discovered and met with machine gun fire. Within 20 seconds 250 men and officers were on the floor.* *Battalion entered enemy trench and forced Prussians to retreat using bayonet fighting and firing.* *Battalion secured some bombs and during the night proceeded to work on securing the flanks.*	
2-10-1915	*10am - Germans began serious counterattack. No more bombs left, but Germans had their own supply.* *Germans came in on both flanks, Congestion in the trench, with no way out. A bomb landed and six men would disappear. The fighting and bombing continued into the afternoon. Battalion attempted to move into a communication trench with fixed bayonets.* *6TH WELSH managed to stop the machine guns and bombers. With trench taken the 1ST BATTALION moved into the next trench OLD BRITISH LINE.* *Operations carried out with tired troops who had been in the trenches and moving for 8 days and nights, and that all officers behaved magnificently.* *Losses severe with 370 men and 15 officers missing.*	
3-10-1915	*Battalion relieved.*	
4 to 20-10-1915	*Marching and resting to reach BÉTHUNE.*	

Cecil was declared missing, presumed dead, on 2nd October 1915. He was 27 years old and is remembered in France on the Loos Memorial. Locally, he is remembered on Sittingbourne and Milton Regis War Memorials, together with St Mary's Church, Sittingbourne Holy Trinity Church, St Paul's Church Memorials, and in the Welsh National Book of Remembrance.

Ironically a newspaper article in the East Kent Gazette, also dated the 2nd October 1915, records that Cecil was 'mentioned in despatches' and was being put forward for a promotion, for a commission.

He was awarded the 1915 Star, Victory, and British War Medals. His pay and gratuity were awarded to his father.

Credit: New Zealand War Graves Project

[52] War Diary: 1 Battalion Welsh (Welch) Regiment. WO-95-2277-4. January 1915-October 1915. The National Archives (UK), Kew, England.

GEE, Frederick Ernest

CH/17626, Lance Corporal, 1st Royal Marine Battalion Royal Navy Division,
Royal Marine Light Infantry.

Frederick was born in 1898 in Rochester, though the British Army archives[53] record his birthdate as 21st April 1895, showing he lied about his age. He was the son of John Thomas, who was a crane driver at Sittingbourne Paper Mill and Jane Elizabeth (née Weller). In 1911 he was living at 53 Cowper Road, Sittingbourne, with his parents and siblings. He was the second child, and his siblings were John Charles, Margaret Frances (1899-1903), Albert Edward, Violet Aileen, and Doris Jane (1907-1916).

He attended Holy Trinity School, Sittingbourne, then worked at the Paper Mills for 12 months before joining the Royal Marine Light Infantry (Chatham Division) on 14th October 1912, aged just 14.

His battalion went to Gallipoli on 17th August 1915 and were evacuated in January 1916. They arrived in Marseilles on 19th May 1916 and the remainder of the month was spent in Longpré, resupplying and retraining. In June they were stationed at Hersin, providing working parties for the trenches. On 26th June, they arrived in Frévillers where they carried out battle training until 12th July.

On 15th July 1916 the battalion moved to Ancre and provided support and relief to the front line until mid-September. During the remainder of September and October they were based in Diéval and Varennes, where they took part in more battle and company training, The last two weeks of October were spent in Hamel trenches, creating more trenches, and clearing others, and can be read about here:

	WAR DIARY[54] or INTELLIGENCE SUMMARY. (Erase heading not required.)	Army Form C. 2118.
Instructions regarding War Diaries and Intelligence Summaries are contained in F.S. Regs., Part II, and the Staff Manual respectively. Title pages will be prepared in manuscript.		
Date	Summary of Events and Information	Remarks and References to Appendices
13-10-1916	Battalion provided a Funeral Guard, of 200 other ranks, to Major E.P. Sketchley R.M.L.I. at FORCEVILLE MILITARY CEMETERY. (Major Ernest Frederick Powys Sketchley DSO was 35 years old and the son of Reverend E.P. and Mrs. Sketchley of West Kensington, London, and was twice Mentioned in Dispatches.)	
1-11-1916 to 5-11-1916	Battalion stationed in VARENNES, on working parties cleaning the camp and roads.	
6-11-1916	Relieved the ROYAL DUBLIN FUSILIERS at HAMEL sector.	
7-11-1916	Remained in sector.	

53 Admiralty: Naval Casualties, Indexes, War Grave Rolls and Statistics Book, First World War. ADM 242/1-15. www.ancestry.co.uk

54 War Diary: 1 Royal Marines Battalion. WO-95-3110-1. May 1916-April 1919. The National Archives (UK), Kew, England.

10 to 12-11-1916	Moved to the VARENNES TRENCH and preparing for an attack.
13-11-1916	5.45am - 188TH INFANTRY BRIGADE to our left and 1/7 GORDON HIGHLANDERS on our right, advance began. Advance through thick mist in four waves, with one platoon of each company per wave, together with military support. Every company commander killed before reaching the German trenches, which were almost destroyed by the artillery barrage. Advance across No Man's Land difficult due to deep and muddy shell holes and the condition of the ground. British barrage started. Germans replied almost immediately with artillery fire. Battalion suffered very heavy losses due to machine gun fire. Estimated 50% of losses during the advance. During the night the German lines were taken.
14-11-1916	Reinforcements arrived.
15-11-1916	Afternoon - Battalion withdrawn to PUCHUILLERS by lorries.

There were a shocking number of casualties. The advance was 420 strong, but only 138 returned, 47 were killed, 210 wounded and 85 missing. Of the 22 officers, only two returned, six were killed, 11 wounded and three missing.

Frederick was killed, aged 18 years, during the main attack on 13th November and was buried in the Ancre British Cemetery, Beaumont-Hamel; 538 of the casualties buried in the cemetery fell on the same day as Frederick, including 62 more RMLI men. This battle became known as the Battle of Ancre.

His family decided on the words "GONE BUT NOT FORGOTTEN FROM HIS SORROWING MUM, DAD BRO'S, SISTERS" to be inscribed on Frederick's headstone. The abbreviated BRO'S was used as families were limited to the number of characters they were allowed to use for personal inscriptions.

Locally Frederick is remembered on the Sittingbourne War Memorial and St Michael's Church WW1 Memorial Window.

The GOATHAM Brothers

The Goatham brothers, Archibald William (and Charles Henry were the sons of Edward, a carpenter and joiner, and Emma (née Cassam). They were the second and third born of seven children: Maylia Rose (1884-1884), Archibald William (1885-1916), Charles Henry (1888-1915), Beatrice Ruth (1889-1976), Phyllis Rosetta (1891-1958), Edward Arthur (1894-1970), and May Victoria (1897-1981).

The family are recorded in the 1891 and 1911 census as living at 23 The Wall, Sittingbourne and this was still their home in 1939, when May Victoria was living there, after her mother died the same year.

Pictured is a section of the street called The Wall

GOATHAM, Archibald William

Civilian, Faversham Gunpowder Works

Great Explosion Memorial
Faversham Cemetery

The memorial tablet in the Avenue is inscribed with PTE A J GOATHAM, though Sittingbourne's War Memorial is inscribed A W GOATHAM.

Research identified an Archibald William Goatham, who was the older brother of Charles Henry Goatham (see page 139), as the name to be remembered on the memorials.

Archibald died in home service, in an explosion at Faversham Gunpowder Works, labelled The Great Explosion.

Archibald, known as Ben, was born in the autumn of 1885 in Milton Regis. In 1901 he was living with his parents and siblings at 23 The Wall. He was employed as a cutter boy at the paper mill, and he continued to work there until going to work at the Faversham Gunpowder Factory during the war.

In the summer of 1909, he had married local girl Jessie Young, and in 1911 they were living at 33 Milton Road. Archibald and Jessie had two daughters, Evelina Doris, and Adelaide Bertha.

Archibald was killed on 2nd April 1916 in the Great Explosion at Faversham Gunpowder Works in Uplees (pictured right). At the outbreak of the war the gunpowder factory in Faversham was requisitioned and expanded by the Admiralty.

At the time of the explosion a storage building contained about 150 tons of ammonium nitrate and 15 tons of TNT. Empty linen TNT bags were also stacked against the building. The previous night, patrolmen spotted a small fire between the building and the boiler house that stood about 50 feet away, the fire was put out.

Many of the staff had stopped for lunch at 12.00 and the clerk of works noticed some of the empty bags had caught fire. The works fire brigade was called, and the Works Manager decided to remove the boxes of TNT, from what was now blazing sheds. Despite the fire brigade and staff passing buckets of water, an explosion occurred at 1.20pm, quickly followed by two more. The result destroyed, beyond trace, five buildings and left a crater 150 feet in diameter and 15ft deep, plus within a 225-yard radius of the explosion every building of conventional light construction was destroyed.

The official death toll was put at 108, though the final number is uncertain. As the explosion occurred on a Sunday no women were killed, as it was their day off. Sixty-nine of the casualties, including Archibald, were buried in a mass grave in Faversham Cemetery.

A 'message of thanks' printed in The East Kent Gazette on 15th April 1916, recorded that his family were living at 8 St Paul's Street, Milton Regis.

Great Explosion Plot - Faversham Cemetery

GOATHAM, Charles Henry

L/8558, Lance Corporal, 2nd Battalion, The Buffs (East Kent Regiment).

Charles was born in Sittingbourne in February 1888. When he enlisted on 26th June 1907 at Canterbury, he was 5ft 8in tall, with brown hair and eyes, and joined the 2nd Battalion, The Buffs, and on 29th July 1914, he extended his service for an additional two years.

He served in the Far East, including Hong Kong in 1910, Singapore in 1912 and India in 1914. His service record is one of the records burnt during WW2 so the dates of when he served in each country are unreadable.

Charles returned to England with his regiment at the end of 1914 and joined the British Expeditionary Force on 17th January 1915. On 2nd February 1915 he was taken to hospital after he had been shot in the thigh, and he stayed there until 20th March 1915. He wrote a letter home to his mother about his experience, saying:

'It was rather rough out there, we were up to our knees in water in the trenches. I was picked to go out of the trenches to Brigade HQ to bring back a Company of Fusiliers who were to relieve our Company. On the way back from HQ, I was shot by a sniper, and unable to walk. I was carried back to HQ.'

Charles was appointed to the post of Lance-Corporal on 8th May 1915, then, less than three weeks later, he was reported missing in action.

In May 1915 his battalion was stationed in Poperinge, Belgium. On the 20th the Commander in Chief, Field Marshal Sir John French, addressed the troops in eulogistic terms and thanked all the ranks for the

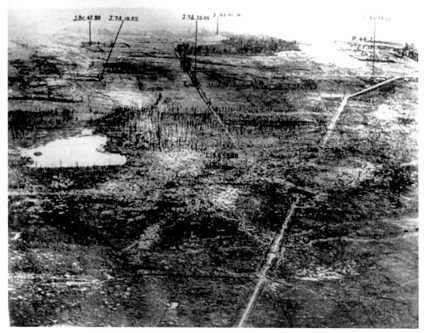

good work done. The next day they returned to the trenches just north of the Menin Road, understood to be east of Ypres. For the next two days they came under intermittent shelling.

In the early morning of 24th May 1915, the enemy opened fire and a gas cloud was seen coming from their trenches. Orders were then received to reinforce the 3rd Royal Fusiliers in the trenches on both sides of the Menin Road. During the move the battalion came under heavy fire from rifles, machine guns and shelling, causing heavy casualties.

Menin Road, Bellewaarde Ridge in the background

The War Diary[55] noted that the "enemy appeared to be in great strength." Further orders were received to reinforce the Fusiliers at a railway and level crossing, and it was recorded that this area was a 'death trap' and the enemy fire was 'terrific'. By nightfall a counterattack was attempted, but this failed due to the terrific fire. The diary entry read "It was a case of digging in all day and night, some trenches knee deep in water".

On the 25th the enemy relaxed its offensive and when night fell, many of the wounded were collected and carried away. The following day The Buffs occupied new trenches, running north from the level crossing towards Verlorenhoek (pictured right). The 27th and 28th were reported to be quiet days, with the occasional sniper. On the 29th May the battalion marched back to billets east of Poperinge.

Charles was posted missing and presumed killed, with his death, aged 27, being officially declared as 28th May 1915. His body was found in Railway Wood about halfway along the main highway between Ypres and Zonnebeke. He was identified by his clothing and Certificate of Education which he had in his possession.

Charles was buried in the area, but was reinterred, on 19th November 1928, in Sanctuary Wood Cemetery, Ypres, Belgium. His headstone carries the inscription "EVER IN OUR THOUGHTS LOVE, MUM."

His mother received his pay and gratuity, as well as his 1914-15 Star, Victory Medal, and British War Medal. Locally he is remembered on the Sittingbourne War Memorial, where he is recorded as G H Goatham, and the Sittingbourne Holy Trinity Church WW1 Memorial.

[55] War Diary: 2 Battalion The Buffs (East Kent Regiment). WO-95-2279-2. December 1914-October 1915. The National Archives (UK), Kew, England.

GOATHAM, James Walter

70123, Private, 16th Battalion, Sherwood Foresters (Notts and Derby Regiment).

James was born in Sittingbourne in 1884 and baptised on 4th October 1885 in the parish church of St Michael's. He was the ninth of the eleven children of Charles, a brickfield labourer, and Jane (née Goodson). James' siblings were Charlotte Ann, Charles, Elizabeth Jane, William, Edwin, Margaret (1876-1894), Annie Rebecca (1878-1880), John Thomas, George Stephen, and Benjamin Richard.

James was living with his parents in 1911 at 80 West Street, Sittingbourne, and was working as a brickfield labourer. However, he enlisted in Newark, Nottinghamshire.

James' battalion's War Diary[56] records that at the start of October 1916 they were billeted at Bertrancourt, halfway between Amiens and Arras. On the 3rd they marched 9km south-east to Martinsart Wood, and two days later relieved 7th Battalion, The Buffs in Schwaben Redoubt, 3km east of the wood. Whilst moving the battalion came under heavy shelling, with 26 men wounded, one missing and one killed.

The 7th and 8th October saw the enemy putting a heavy barrage (pictured right) on Thiepval and attacking Schwaben Redoubt, which was repelled. On the 9th James' battalion attacked the German trenches, although they sustained a large number of casualties, they were successful in meeting some of their objectives in taking ground. Later that day they were relieved by the Kings Royal Rifles. Four officers and 26 other ranks were killed, 141 wounded and 67 missing. James was one of those who died during the fighting and was recorded as losing his life on 8th October 1916, aged 32 years, though some documents show 10th October.

James and at least 14 other soldiers were originally buried in a small cemetery about 700m east of Connaught Cemetery, Thiepval, to which they were moved in the summer of 1919. A simple inscription adorns James' headstone reading "PEACE PERFECT PEACE."

James's pay and gratuity, as did his Victory and British War Medals, went to his sister Elizabeth, as both his parents died in 1915. Locally he is remembered on Sittingbourne War Memorial and Sittingbourne Holy Trinity Church WW1 Memorial.

James' nephew Walter, the son of his sister Elizabeth, was also killed in the war and his story is next.

---

[56] War Diary: 16 Battalion Sherwood Foresters (Nottinghamshire and Derbyshire Regiment). WO-95-2587-1. March 1916-June 1919. The National Archives (UK), Kew, England.

GOATHAM, Walter George Henry

8312, Private, 1st Battalion, Oxford and Bucks Light Infantry.

Walter was born in the autumn of 1889 in Sittingbourne, the son of Elizabeth Jane Goatham, the sister of James Walter, whose story appears above. His mother married Harry Christie in 1890 in Lewisham and in 1891 she was living in Camberwell, Surrey, whilst Walter was living with his maternal grandparents, Charles, a brickfield labourer, and Jane Goatham, at 2 Orchard Lane, Sittingbourne.

Walter was still living with his grandparents in 1901 at 80 West Street, Sittingbourne, although he was recorded as their son.

Walter enlisted in Chatham before 1911, as by then he was stationed at Wellington Barracks, Nilgiris, India. At the outbreak of the war his battalion was stationed at Ahmednagar, India as part of the 17th Brigade of the 6th (Poona) Division.

On 7th November 1914 they deployed to Mesopotamia. The battalion was involved in the battle for Kut el Amara, Iraq, which began on 26th September 1915 and lasted for a few days until the Ottoman forces retreated on 28th September.

The next major offensive was the Battle of Ctesiphon, from 22nd to 24th November 1915. The objective was to capture Baghdad, but they were defeated by the Ottomans. The 6th Division, including Walter's battalion, had moved back to Kut el Amara by 3rd December, where they were besieged by the enemy four days later. This battle lasted until 26th April 1916 when the British-Indian forces surrendered, mainly due to lack of supplies and sickness amongst the troops.

Walter died of beriberi on 11th December 1915, aged 26, whilst onboard the Hospital Ship *HMAT Takada* (His Majesty's Australian Transport - pictured right), on route in the Persian Gulf to Bombay.

The *Takada* was launched in 1913 as a passenger and cargo liner for the British India Steam Navigation Company to serve the Far East. She was converted into a 450 bed Hospital Ship in August 1915 and served until April 1918 primarily for the Mesopotamian Campaign.

Walter is remembered on the CWGC's Basra Memorial to the Missing, Iraq, Sittingbourne War Memorial and Sittingbourne Holy Trinity Church WW1 Memorial. His mother received his pay and gratuity, as well as his 1915 Star, Victory, and British War Medals.

GORELY, Reginald Bertram

12737, Private, 6th Battalion, King's Shropshire Light Infantry.

Reginald was born in Sittingbourne in 1889, the son of Frank, a grocer, and Martha Louisa (née Rich). His siblings were Frank Henry Victor (1887-1908), Dorothy Louise Rich, Spencer George, Marjorie Edith Morton, Leslie Fordwich, and Violet Strutton.

The family in 1911 were living at 42 High Street, Sittingbourne, though Reginald was living as a boarder in Derby, as a commercial traveller for Reckitt's Blue. He had left Queen Elizabeth's Grammar School in Faversham, in 1904. Reckitt's Blue was a laundry product used in a wash as a whitener, to delay yellowing.

He enlisted in Shrewsbury, which is where the 6th Battalion was raised in September 1914. They moved to Aldershot, Hampshire and then in April 1915 to Larkhill, Wiltshire for final training, and then to France on 22nd July 1915.

The War Diary for his battalion in July to September 1916 is reproduced here:

Instructions regarding War Diaries and Intelligence Summaries are contained in F.S. Regs., Part II, and the Staff Manual respectively. Title pages will be prepared in manuscript.	WAR DIARY[57] or INTELLIGENCE SUMMARY. (Erase heading not required.)	Army Form C. 2118.
Date	Summary of Events and Information	Remarks and References to Appendices
28-7-1916	HÉBUTERNE - Relieved 17TH BATTALION ROYAL WELSH FUSILIERS in the trenches.	
29 to 30-7-1916	Hostile artillery activity.	
31-7-1916	Enemy rifle grenade, with the pin still inserted, fired into the trench. Attached was a red label where on one side "Much Pleasure" was written and on the other side "VORSTECKER VOR ABSCHUSS HERAUSRICHEN", (which translates to "Pull out the pin before firing".)	
1 to 5-8-1916	Battalion reinforced and improved front line, support and communication trenches. Enemy quiet.	
6-8-1916	Relieved by 17TH KING'S ROYAL RIFLES. Moved into billets at COURCELLES.	
7-8-1916 to 13-8-1916	Time spent bathing, inspections and forming working parties in the front lines and support trenches.	
14-8-1916 to 26-8-1916	Moved to the Craters at MÉAULTE. Travelling via COIGNEUX, AMPLIER, FIENVILLERS and SAND PIT CAMPS. At each location cleaning kit, assault practice and on working parties.	
27-8-1916	Relieved the 17TH BATTALION KING'S LIVERPOOLS in the trenches north of CARNOY.	
28 to 31-8-1916	Subjected to heavy artillery fire.	
1-9-1916	Relieved by 7TH BATTALION LEINSTER REGIMENT. Moved to bivouacs at CARNOY.	
2-9-1916	52 men on sick parade from the effects of gas and bad feet due to the wet weather.	

[57] War Diary: 6 Battalion King's Shropshire Light Infantry. WO-95-2122-1. July 1915-April 1919. The National Archives (UK), Kew, England

3 to 5-9-1916	Moved into trenches in BERNAFAY WOOD. Battalion attempted to lay wiring and extend the trenches but were hampered by a lack of tools and water.
6-9-1916	Battalion relieved 6th Oxford and Bucks at ARROW HEAD COPSE. During the afternoon an 8-inch shell hit a water party, killing five and injuring three.

Reginald's death is recorded as 6th September 1916. Letters received by Reginald's parents, from his comrades, imply that he was one of the working parties.

One letter read:

> "There was not a better fellow in the company than he – always ready and willing to do his duty. ... He was carrying fresh water for our use in the trenches, when a shell dropped in the middle of the party killing five and wounding others."

A second letter read:

> "I am happy to tell you that his death was in no way marred by pain, as it was instantaneous, the result of a high-explosive shell bursting practically beside him. ... Your son was extremely popular with all ranks. As his Company Commander may I tell you that I had the highest opinion of him, knowing him as I did for the best part of two years. His death has left us the poorer, for men such as he can be ill spared, especially now, when we have need of the best and the bravest. Up to his death he had done some magnificent work; he was fearless in everything. He was amongst those who by their work have made our Regiment, and our Battalion one of the most highly spoken of in the field of battle. Beloved by all of his comrades, thought extremely highly of by all of his officers, his death has been keenly felt, and has cast a gloom over all."

Reginald is commemorated on a number of memorials including Thiepval Memorial, Sittingbourne War Memorial, St Michael's Church WW1 Memorial Window, Faversham War Memorial and Faversham Wreight's School Old Boys Memorial, which is now located in Queen Elizabeth's Grammar School, Faversham.

Pictured left is Wreight's School,

Reginald also has an individual memorial in St Michael's Church (pictured right) as a remembrance to him being in their choir, which has the inscription:

I have fought a good fight

I have finished my course

I have kept the faith.

The memorial plaque was dedicated on 28th May 1917, by the vicar Reverend A B Parry-Evans.

After his death a special service was held for him in St Michael's Church and his father Frank Gorely, a grocer, received his probate.

The original Avenue of Remembrance memorial tablet (pictured below) from the 1920s is now on the wall in Queen Elizabeth's Grammar School in Faversham, which replaced Wreight's School.

Reginald's brother Leslie served in the Royal Fusiliers London Regiment from September 1914 to March 1917 and his other brother, Spencer, served in the Second World War as a Major in the Royal Army Service Corps Canteen Service. He was a Japanese Prisoner of War from at least 1942 to September 1945.

HADLER, George William

G/12385, Private, 1st Battalion, Queen's Own (Royal West Kent Regiment).

Born on 7th January 1886 in East Farleigh, George was the son of George Hadler, a furnace stoker in the paper mill, and Sarah (née Heyburn). His eight siblings were Thomas John, Julia Harriett, Henry Thomas (1880-1880), Edith Annie, Alice Mary Ann, Henry Ernest, Florence Kate, and Mabel Agnes, also known as May.

In 1889 the family were living in Unity Street and by 1911 they had moved to 26 Burley Road, Sittingbourne. George was known as "Nip" and he played full-back for Milton FC and sometimes for Sittingbourne FC.

The report of his death in the East Kent Gazette of 23rd September 1916, noted that he was working in the paper mills before emigrating to Canada for a short time. On his return, he was employed by the Imperial Paper Mills at Gravesend.

George had trained in Shoreham and had only been in France for about ten weeks before his death.

His battalion had spent the last couple of days of August 1916 and the first day of September resting and cleaning, when on the 2nd they moved out to trenches to the west of Angle Wood, near Guillemont, which were not visible by the Germans, but in range and under constant shell fire. The next day his battalion War Diary[58] commented "the whole front was extraordinary quiet, and our men could be seen walking out of the trenches with impunity."

---

[58] War Diary: 2 Battalion The Buffs (East Kent Regiment). WO-95-2279-2. December 1914-October 1915. The National Archives (UK), Kew, England.

George's battalion was on standby to provide support and men to attack the nearby Falfemont Farm (pictured right), which was under German occupation and guarded by machine guns. Their position was given to the Artillery Firing Officer, but no action was taken. The 15th Royal Warwickshire enclosed the farm but were pushed back by the machine guns. The following day, the 4th, the 1st Cheshire's approached the farm through German trenches and were receiving

British advance on Falfemont Farm

artillery support. The Germans could be seen retiring towards Leuze Wood, 3km north, and by mid-afternoon the enemy were surrendering. Falfemont Farm had finally been taken on the night of the 5th/6th.

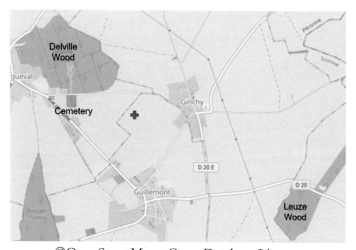
©OpenStreetMap - Open Database Licence

Late on the 4th the men had reached a point 200 yards south of Leuze Wood and dug a new trench, with some ease, in places to a depth of 5ft. During the day the battalion sent parties into the woods, there they encountered the enemy in shell holes and suffered some casualties. The diary notes that the 5th was a fairly quiet day and the troops had acquired souvenirs from the machine gun pits and dug outs. Later that day the battalion retired to a camp about 9km south-west near Fricourt. The diary entry for the day concluded with the casualty number of 21 killed and 174 wounded or missing.

George's death is recorded as 6th September 1916, age 30, though it is more probable that he died during the previous two days, as he is buried in a small cemetery 500m to the east of his final resting place of Delville Wood Cemetery. His original burial was marked with a wooden cross (shown on the map with a cross), with his name slightly mis-spelt as W Hodler. He was buried with at least 12 other fallen.

George is remembered on Sittingbourne War Memorial, and Sittingbourne Holy Trinity Church and St Mary's Church Memorials. He is also remembered by Milton Regis on their War Memorial and St Paul's Church Memorial.

George was commemorated on Gravesend's Imperial Paper Mills Memorial (pictured right), which was mounted on the exterior of their head office, The White House. In 2014 the memorial was stolen and remains unrecovered, and a replacement was erected in 2023, though made of non-ferrous material.

He is also commemorated on his parent's headstone in Sittingbourne Cemetery, with the inscription "PEACE PERFECT PEACE."

A letter from a Lance Corporal G. Tierney, from George's company written to his father said that he was killed instantly without any pain. 'He was a good soldier, and very well-liked by all the men that knew him and bear up in the knowledge that he died a soldier's death and that of a hero.'

George was awarded the Victory and British War Medals. After his death probate was granted to his father.

The "In Memoriam" reproduced below expresses the loss his family still felt two years after his death.

The East Kent Gazette

<u>**SATURDAY, SEPTEMBER 7, 1918**</u>

IN MEMORIAM

HADLER - In ever-loving memory of our dear (Nip) George William Hadler, who was killed in action, in France, Sept. 6th, 1916.

Two years have passed,
but still to memory dear,
We think of him and shed a silent tear,
Friends may think the wound is healed,
But sorrow 'neath a smile lies oft concealed.
From his sorrowing Mother, Father and Family.

The East Kent Gazette

<u>**SATURDAY, SEPTEMBER 7, 1918**</u>

IN MEMORIAM

HADLER - In fond and loving memory of our dear brother, George William (Nip) Hadler, who fell mortally wounded in France, Sept. 6th, 1916, in his 31st year.

Yet again, we hope to meet him,
When the day of life is fled;
Then, in Heaven, we hope to greet him,
Where no farewell tears are shed.
From Tom and Cis.

HADLOW, Karl

TR13/64015, Rifleman, 53rd Battalion, King's Royal Rifle Corps.

Karl was born at 85 William Street, Sittingbourne on 26th August 1900; his registered name was Karol Hadlow. His parents were William George, a postman in the town, and Edith Emma (née Reeve). He was the youngest of three boys, his brothers were George Alfred and Leslie (1899-1904).

Karl's brother, George, emigrated to Oswego, New York, USA in 1910, where there was a large population of British emigrants, many of them from Sittingbourne.

Before joining up in Canterbury, Karl had spent a year working at Ridham Dock. Prior to that he had sung in the choir at St Michael's Church and worked in the outfitting department at the Sittingbourne Co-operative.

An article in 19th October 1918 edition of the East Kent Gazette, entitled, "SUDDEN DEATH OF A YOUNG SOLDIER", reported that Karl had joined the army just a month before his death. He was training in Northampton when he contracted pneumonia and pleurisy, after a bout of influenza. Karl was admitted to Abington Avenue VAD Hospital, and soon took a turn for the worse. His parents were summoned, but sadly on 14th October 1918 he died at the age of 18. At the time his family were living at 21 Thomas Road, Sittingbourne.

The short but poignant words "PEACE PERFECT PEACE" are inscribed on Karl's headstone. The words are the start of the title of the hymn, written by Minister Edward Henry Bickersteth DD. in 1875, and are understood to be derived from the Bible's Isaiah 26:3 "You will keep in perfect peace those whose minds are steadfast, because they trust in you."

Karl was buried in Sittingbourne Cemetery and is remembered on Sittingbourne War Memorial and St Michael's Church WW1 Memorial Window.

HADLOW, William Thomas

260161, Private, 9th Battalion, Royal Sussex Regiment.

William was born in 1893 in Vange, Essex, but by 1901 the family had moved to Sittingbourne High Street. His parents were John and Elizabeth (née Mullinger). His father had worked in the brickfields when they moved to Sittingbourne, but in 1911, when the family were living at 14 Pembury Street, he was a labourer at a Chemical Manufacturers, and William a student teacher.

William had three older sisters, Elizabeth Charlotte, Caroline Martha (1886-1908) and Matilda Harriett. He also had five younger siblings, John Edward (1895-1900), Maude Clara, Laurence Henry, Frederick Charles (1903-1909), and Robert Frank (1905-1909).

Under the headline "SERGT. W. T. HADLOW, THE BUFFS – A SITTINGBOURNE SCHOOLMASTER" in the 4th May 1918 issue of the East Kent Gazette, was the report of the death of William. The article explained that William, affectionally known as "Billy", had attended Milton Council School and at the age of 13, gained a County scholarship to Borden Grammar School.

On 11th February 1911, after passing his exams, he enrolled in Goldsmith's College, New Cross, London (pictured right), and passed with first-class honours two years later. After college William became an assistant master at Bethersden Council School and acted as a Scout Master, before moving to Rainham Council School.

On 7th June 1915 he left the school and enrolled in the Army. The following year, on 7th March 1916, he left Crowborough Camp for France.

Instructions regarding War Diaries and Intelligence Summaries are contained in F.S. Regs., Part II, and the Staff Manual respectively. Title pages will be prepared in manuscript.	WAR DIARY[59] or **INTELLIGENCE SUMMARY.** (Erase heading not required.)	Army Form C. 2118.
Date	Summary of Events and Information	Remarks and References to Appendices
1-3-1918	*Camped in field TEMPLEUX QUARRIES and HARDY BANKS, by the village of TEMPLEUX-LA-FOSSE.*	
2-3-1918	*Battalion marched to HANCOURT through a blizzard.*	
3-3-1918 to 19-3-1918	*Provided working parties to 258 TUNNELLING COY.*	
20-3-1918	*Battalion moved to HESBÉCOURT.*	
21-3-1918	*Morning – Battalion stood to and taken up positions through a rather heavy gas cloud. Afternoon - Subjected to heavy enemy bombardment.*	
22-3-1918	*6am - Enemy attacked through the mist. Noon – Enemy surrounded one trench, troops had withdrawn down a shallow trench.* *Throughout the day enemy attacked on the flanks.* *Midnight - our position was untenable and withdrew. Rear-guard of about 30 men fighting on the high ground south-west of HERVILLY, eventually managing to retreat to BERNES.*	
23-3-1918	*Battalion moved to FALVY on the bank of the RIVER SOMME. Relieved by 72nd Infantry Brigade. Moved across the river to LICOURT.*	
24-3-1918	*Battalion marched west to CHAULNES. Singing along the way.* *Took up positions in the line.*	
25-3-1918	*Marched south to DRESLINCOURT to support the French in counterattack. Attack unsuccessful, battalion forced to withdraw.*	
26-3-1918	*Another attempt made to advance. Forced to withdraw to MÉHARICOURT.*	
27-3-1918	*Enemy attacked and entered trenches. Battalion managed to hold them back.*	

On 27th March 1918, William was reported as having died from wounds, aged 25.

The East Kent Gazette newspaper mentioned that a chum had sent a letter explaining that;

> "Sergeant Hadlow went into the line for the first time at three a.m. on March 22nd, was wounded on the 24th, and died on the 27th."

According to military records William was a Private in the Royal Sussex Regiment, so he may have been recently promoted or a mistake was made. His medal card records he had also served in 2/4th Battalion, The Buffs (East Kent Regiment), as regiment number 201053.2.

Unusually, his battalion's War Diary contained a Casualty List for March 1918, listing all men by number, rank, and name and whether they were killed, wounded, missing or prisoner of war. William's name does not appear in the list, though some names appear to have been handwritten and added at a later date. The war diaries normally only listed commissioned officers by name and rank.

---

[59] War Diary: 9 Battalion Royal Sussex Regiment. WO-95-2219-2. August 1915-May 1919. The National Archives (UK), Kew, England.

William was buried in St Sever Cemetery Extension in Rouen, which was a main hospital centre during the war, with eight general, five stationary, one British Red Cross and one labour hospital, and No. 2 Convalescent Depot, being located there.

He is remembered on a number of memorials locally including Sittingbourne War Memorial, Borden Grammar School, Sittingbourne Holy Trinity Church, Milton Regis War Memorial, St Paul's Church, and Old Boys Milton Regis Council Schools.

William had married Ellen Elizabeth Lanning in the summer of 1915, in Milton Regis, where she worked as a teacher at Sittingbourne Council Schools. Five months after William's death, on 11th August 1918, their daughter Ruby Nita was born. Ellen remarried in Maidstone in 1920 to hairdresser William Henry Snashford, who had served in the Royal West Kent Regiment from 1907 to 1920, being in India for the duration of the war. He was declared 20% disabled when he was discharged as a result of malaria and a gunshot wound to the stomach.

William's wife received his pay and gratuity as well as his Victory and British War Medals.

HANCOCK, Percy Oak

204388, Private, 7th Battalion, Somerset Light Infantry.

Percy's parents, John, a grocer and draper, and Ellen (née Oake) were born and married in Cambridgeshire, though the family were recorded in different counties through the censuses. They lived in Sussex in 1871, Essex in 1881, then they settled in Sittingbourne where John was running a clothing and draper's shop at 24 East Street in 1891. John died in 1900 and his wife continued to run the business as a boot shop, with Percy and his two sisters Mary and Alice assisting in the business in 1901 and 1911.

Percy was born in Newport, Essex on 2nd September 1879, and baptised at the parish church of St Mary the Virgin on 15th March 1880. The tenth of eleven children; his siblings were John Thomas, Edward Ernest, Mary Jane, Eliza Jane (1866-1867), Frederick William, Alice Maud, Louisa Agnes, Ellen Esther (1876-1895), Edith May and Eveline Margaret.

In the autumn of 1915 in London, Percy enlisted in the Bucks Hussars, before being transferred to 6th Battalion, Dorset Regiment. He was then posted to the Somerset Light Infantry when he went to France on 17th December 1917. The East Kent Gazette of 11th May 1918 reported that Percy had been missing since 23rd March and it was hoped that he was a prisoner of war. An update was published in 28th September 1918 edition, stating that as of 8th April, Percy was in hospital at Avesnes, France as a German prisoner of war. Sadly though, the following week the paper reported that his mother had been informed by the Geneva Red Cross, of his death on 8th April 1918 from tetanus, aged 37. The report added that he had been captured 16 days earlier and was wounded and slightly gassed at the time.

Percy's battalion War Diary[60] reported that for the first three weeks of March 1918 they had been billeted first at Fréniches, 56km south-east of Amiens, and then Curchy. On 21st March 1915 the battalion was bussed 25km east to the south of Saint-Simon and took up battle positions to the south of the St Quentin Canal (pictured below).

Credit: National Army Museum (1953-03-31-191)

On the 22nd the enemy were seen entering the town. On the day Percy went missing, 23rd March 1917, the Germans had captured the right flank towns of Jussy and Flavy, forcing the battalion to retire from the line.

Percy was announced as killed in action and was buried in the Avesnes-Sur-Helpe Communal Cemetery, France, and he is remembered on Sittingbourne War Memorial and St Michael's Church WW1 Memorial Window. He is also remembered on the headstone of his parents and sister, Ellen, in Sittingbourne Cemetery, with an inscription "Greater Love Hath No Man."

After his death the probate from his will was divided between his sisters Mary Jane and Alice Maud Goldsmith (widow). He was awarded the Victory and British War Medals.

Percy's nephew, the son of his sister Louisa, was also killed in the war. He was 20-year-old Lieutenant Leslie Reginald Parnell of the 13th Kensington Battalion, London Regiment, who died on 9th October 1917 and is commemorated on the Tyne Cot Memorial to the Missing. Leslie's father (Percy's brother-in-law) was Major Edward Louis Parnell, who served with the same regiment during the war and was also a silver medallist in the 1912 Olympics for the team military rifle competition.

[60] War Diary: 7 Battalion Somerset Light Infantry. WO-95-2127-1. July 1915-May 1919. The National Archives (UK), Kew, England.

HARRIS, Arthur Henry

6352, Rifleman, 18th Battalion, London Regiment (London Irish Rifles).

The middle of nine children, Arthur was born in Tunstall in the autumn of 1881, and was baptised at Tunstall's St John the Baptist church on 27th November 1881. He was the son of Thomas, a coachman and ostler, and Jane Ann (née Gray). He had four older siblings Frederick William, Annie Florence, Edward Thomas, and Montague Charles, and four younger sisters, Marian Irene, Emmeline Jane, Francis Charlotte (1888-1888), and Dicy Gray. The family, in 1911 and 1917, lived at 65 High Street, Sittingbourne.

In 1911 Arthur was living with his brother Frederick and family in Camberwell, Surrey, where he was employed as a draper's clerk. He then worked in London business houses before the war, returning to Sittingbourne to enlist. He joined The Buffs, then later transferred to the London Regiment, serving as a Private with them in France from 31st August 1916.

Arthur's battalion War Diary[61] describes the events following Arthur's arrival in France. From 15th September 1916 the battalion were involved in fighting at High Wood, near Longueval, with relief occurring on the 21st when they moved 20km south-west to Bresle to rest and re-equip. On the 27th they returned to the High Wood area and the next day relieved the Northampton Regiment.

Over the next few days, the London Irish attacked the Flers Line and the village of Eaucourt L'Abbaye, just north of High Wood. Despite heavy enemy fire the London Irish took their objectives on 3rd October 1916. They held the line and were relieved in the early morning of the 5th, moving 10km west to Becourt Wood.

The next day they moved to nearby Mametz Wood (pictured left), which was a jumble of smashed trees, tangled undergrowth, abandoned equipment, and dead horses, with the atmosphere reeking of chloride of lime and putrefaction. Artillery based in open pits were constantly firing.

The diary records the battalion left Mametz Wood on 7th October 1916 and marched to Franvillers, where they entered the Corps reserves and rested. Though on that day 34-year-old Arthur, died during an operation to amputate one of his legs, after he was wounded in both.

---

[61] War Diary: 1/18 Battalion London Regiment. WO-95-2737-2. March 1915 – February 1919. The National Archives (UK), Kew, England.

He was buried in Dernancourt Communal Cemetery Extension, France. The cemetery was adjacent to the XV Corps Main Dressing Station, formed in July 1916, when the extension was opened. From September 1916 to March 1917 the 45th and 56th (1st/1st South Midland) Casualty Clearing Station was based here. The cemetery is home to 1,997 casualties and was designed by Sir Edwin Lutyens.

Locally, Arthur is remembered on Sittingbourne War Memorial and St Michael's Church WW1 Memorial Window. His pay and war gratuity went to his youngest sister, Dicy Grey.

Credit: ww1cemeteries.com

HARRISON, George Alick

WR/504046, Lance Corporal, Inland Water Transport, Royal Engineers.

George was born in Faversham in 1885 and baptised in St Mary of Charity church on 19th June 1885. He was the son of Henry Aird and Isabel (née Marryott). His father had held a variety of occupations from a gas worker, shipyard labourer to the publican of the Golden Lion, at 47 Milton Road, in 1911.

George was from a large family of twelve children, although sadly five of them did not survive infancy, with three dying before they could be named. His siblings were Herbert Aird, William Thomas, Isabel, Harry (1883-1888), Horace, Bertie (1890-1890), Daisy, and Robert.

His brothers served in the war with the exception of William, who was considered to be unfit to serve. Herbert served the duration of the war as an able seaman, having joined the Royal Navy in 1895, aged 18 years, before entering the reserves in 1905 and re-joining in 1910. Horace served from May 1915 to June 1919, as a driver in the Royal Field Artillery. At the time of George's death, Horace was in hospital suffering from a fractured fibula, incurred in January 1917, and he returned to France in September 1918. George's youngest brother, Robert served with the Royal East Kent Mounted Rifles.

The 4th May 1918 edition of the East Kent Gazette reported George's death. The newspaper reported that he had been employed on Lloyds Wharf before joining up in 1916. He was promoted to Lance Corporal in December that year, at the same time as he was sent to France and placed in charge of a barge, working between French ports.

On 17th April 1918 he was seen on the deck of his craft in Calais Harbour, then later his body was found in the water. It was presumed to be an accident. He was buried, aged 33, in the Les Baraques Military Cemetery Sangatte, Calais, France, which was designed by Sir Herbert Baker. George's headstone is inscribed with the opening words from the Bible's Song of Solomon 2:17, "UNTIL THE DAY BREAKS".

Locally George is remembered on Sittingbourne War Memorial and Milton Regis War Memorial, and his pay and gratuity were paid to his father.

On 30th July 1921, the East Kent Gazette printed an "In Memoriam" from George's parents, to two of their sons.

George was well thought of by a friend who signed F.D., as an "In Memoriam" was published in the East Kent Gazette for at least the following three years, to commemorate the anniversary of his death. Each with the short phrase "Not forgotten."

The East Kent Gazette

SATURDAY, JULY 30, 1921

IN MEMORIAM

HARRISON - In loving memory of our dear sons, William (Scamp) Harrison, who died on July 29th, 1920, and George (Uncle) Harrison, drowned in Calais Harbour, France, on April 18th, 1918.

Death divides,
but remembrance lasts for ever.
From loving Mother and Father.

HENDERSON, Harry Josiah

343786, Ship's Steward, Royal Navy.

Harry Josiah Henderson was born in Devonport on 23rd July 1877 and baptised in Devonport's St Paul's Church on the 5th August 1877. His parents were William, a Navy pensioner, and Mary Ann Elizabeth (née Ruddon). Harry was the third of four children, whose names were William Henry, Lily Beatrice, and Kate Sophia (1879-1884). The Navy records[62] Harry's date of birth as 21st July 1878, rather than the date recorded in the baptism register.

The family was hit with tragedy over a short period of three years with the death of Harry's brother in February 1914, then Harry himself in 1917, followed by both his parents in the spring of 1917.

Harry was 5ft 3in tall, when he joined the Navy, as a ship's steward, on 14th September 1900. He served for 12 years, then extended this to the full 22 years. He was 22 years old when he enlisted and had been working as a teacher. After training, and before he married, he served on *HMS Nile*, *HMS Terror* and *HMS Tribune*.

On 2nd August 1905, Harry married Lilian Jane Bowen, in St Barnabas Church, Devonport. They had seven children, who were born where Harry was based, with Henry (Harry) Bowen, born 1906 in St Budeaux, Devonport; Lilian Kate Bowen, born 1907 in Harwich, Essex; Mary Bowen, born 1909 in Gillingham, Kent; both Richard Bowen (born 1910) and Agnes Ethel (born 1912), in Sheerness; and both Dorothy Bowen (born 1913) and Ruth Bowen (born 1915) having births registered in Milton Regis.

After his marriage, Harry served on *HMS Speedwell*, *HMS Leda*, and *HMS Acteon*. The 1911 census shows that Harry was on board *HMS Caesar* at Devonport, whilst Lilian was at 31 Ranelagh Road in Sheerness, with their children, and a 16-year-old nurse girl, Lilian May Slaughter.

---

[62] Naval Casualties, Indexes, War Grave Rolls and Statistics Book. ADM242. Piece 008 (1914-1919)

On 1st April 1911 Harry was drafted to the battleship *HMS Formidable* (pictured left). The ship left Sheerness on 30th December 1914 to take part in a gunnery exercise off Portland, Dorset.

On Friday 1st January 1915 at 02:00 and 03:05 she was struck by two torpedoes from the German U-boat, U-24, the ship sank with the loss of 547 lives from her complement of 780.

She went down in a little over two hours, about 35 miles from Lyme Regis. Some of her crew were rescued by the light cruisers *HMS Diamond*, *HMS Topaze* and by the trawler *Provident* from Brixham. More than 71 men took to the battleship's sailing pinnace, which drifted away in the darkness. It was soon swamped with water, making it difficult to row for those who could, as they had to bail sea water continuously with their boots. It was 11pm on New Year's Day before the boat reached Lyme Regis, in freezing conditions.

During the terrible journey, fourteen men died and were lowered over the side to lighten the boat and increase chances of survival. Forty-eight were brought ashore alive, six were dead, and three men subsequently died. Harry Henderson was one of those buried at sea by his shipmates.

The Western Morning Times reported on the inquest into the sinking on the 4th and 5th January 1915.

The report included:

> "On the Saturday following, an inquest was held on the nine men whose bodies had been brought to Lyme. The body of a 10th man, Ships' Steward Harry Henderson, had been disposed of over the side of the pinnace during the journey.
>
> There were just three witnesses at the inquest – Master-at-Arms Albert Cooper, Petty Officer Bing and Seaman Mickie Carroll. Bing added to his evidence, the information that when they last saw *Formidable*, the men were assembled on the quarter deck smoking and were perfectly calm."

The following information was from Vernon Rattenbury, the great grandson of the family who laid out the bodies in the theatre.

A remarkable thing happened that night to one of Harry's comrades, Able Seaman John Cowan. The Daily Mail dated 30th December 2014, reported that author Eric Knight was inspired to write the 1938 novel Lassie Come Home, which paved the way for the subsequent TV shows and films. This Lassie was owned by the landlord of the Pilot Boat (pictured right), a public house in the port of Lyme Regis, Dorset, that was being used as a temporary mortuary.

When the bodies had been laid out on the stone floor, Lassie, a rough-haired collie dog owned by the pub owner, found her way down amongst the bodies, and she began to lick the face of Able Seaman John Cowan (pictured left with Lassie). She stayed beside him for more than half an hour, nuzzling him and keeping him warm with her fur. To everyone's astonishment, Cowan eventually stirred, and he went on to make a full recovery.

Harry was aged 37, when *HMS Formidable* was torpedoed on 1st January 1915 – the first British battleship to be sunk in the war. He is remembered on CWGC's Chatham Naval Memorial, Sittingbourne War Memorial, and Sittingbourne Holy Trinity Church WW1 Memorial.

Along with Lyme Regis' own fallen there are six sailors from *HMS Formidable* buried in the cemetery and a Service of Remembrance takes place at their graveside every year on Remembrance weekend and has done every year since 1915. A centennial service was held on 6th January 2015, the anniversary of their burial.

Harry's wife Lilian moved to 30 Albany Road in Sittingbourne, and died in the Milton area in 1921, aged just 44. Their eldest son Harry (Henry) Bowen Henderson would have been 15. Harry junior in 1934 married Mabel Freeman, at St Mary Abbot's church, Kensington, London. Harry junior went on to fight in the second World War and became an American citizen in 1951 and died in 1976. He is buried in Colorado America.

HEUNER, Cecil Aubrey

G/13041, Private, 7th Battalion, The Buffs (East Kent Regiment).

Cecil was born in Plumstead, Kent on 11th March 1897, the son of Frederick Augustus Alfred, a bookstall clerk, and Maria Rose (née West). He was the fourth of six children, his siblings were Ernest Frederick Alfred, Alfred William, Marguerite Helena, Gertrude Isabel, and Ronald (1901-1901).

In 1901 Cecil attended Childeric Road School, New Cross, Kent. The family moved to Sittingbourne and by 1911 they were living at 39 Albany Street, Sittingbourne.

Cecil attended Trinity School, then, before enlisting in the East Kent Yeomanry in October 1914 in Sittingbourne, he was employed in the butchery department of the Sittingbourne Co-operative Society. He was transferred to The Buffs when he was posted to France in July 1916. He had been wounded three times and was due home on leave on the day he died of wounds on 29th September 1917.

His battalion had been billeted at Eringhem since 15th August 1917 training. On 24th September 1917 they moved to Sint-Jan-Ter-Biezen for further training. The battalion War Diary[63] records that at 7.20p.m. on 29th September 1917, there was an "Air Raid on the camp. One aeroplane, dropped four bombs

---

[63] War Diary: 7 Battalion The Buffs (East Kent Regiment). WO-95-2049-1. July 1915-April 1919. The National Archives (UK), Kew, England.

causing casualties." Twenty-seven were killed and 66 wounded. One of those who was mortally wounded, was 20-year-old Cecil. He was taken to No. 61 Casualty Clearing Station, where sadly he died the same day. Another local Sittingbourne man Ernest Attwater (see page 47), was also killed in the same raid.

The 20th October 1917 East Kent Gazette reported on Cecil's death and said that Cecil's platoon officer, Second Lieutenant Searles, wrote to his parents conveying his "deepest sympathy for the great loss they have sustained."

Cecil was buried in the Dozinghem Military Cemetery, in Belgium, which was next to a number of Casualty Clearing Stations, including Nos. 4, 47 and 61.

He is locally remembered on the Sittingbourne War Memorial and on the St Michael's Church WW1 Memorial Window.

No. 2 Casualty Clearing Station. Oultersteene (Bailleul).

HIGGINS, Harry

300545, Gunner, 4th Division Ammunition Column, Canadian Field Artillery.

Harry was born in Sittingbourne on 28th February 1891, the son of William George, a waterman, and Sophia Elizabeth (née Eaglestone). He was the ninth of twelve children; his siblings were Eliza Elizabeth Jane, William George, Annie Elizabeth, Selina (1880-1880), Alice Amelia, George (1884-1884), Sidney Thomas, Osborne David, Dorothy May, Percy, and an unnamed infant. In 1911, he was living with his family at 42 Cowper Road, Sittingbourne. He was working as a waterman, as was his brother Osborne.

Harry emigrated to Toronto, Canada in 1912. He was not the only member of his family to emigrate; Sidney went to Niagara Falls, New York, USA in 1908; William (in 1909) and Annie (in 1910) went to Toronto; Alice (in 1911) went to Quebec; and finally, Osborne went to Toronto in 1913.

Two of his brothers also served in the war. Osborne enlisted with the 75th Battalion, Canadian Expeditionary Force, on 29th June 1916. He had been wounded twice before he was discharged in April 1918, following a gunshot wound to his buttocks. Percy, Harry's youngest brother served with the Royal Field Artillery in Mesopotamia and was in France at the time of Harry's death.

When Harry enlisted in Toronto on 17th August 1915, he was 5ft 6in tall with blue eyes and brown hair and had been working as a labourer. He landed in France on 19th January 1916.

Instructions regarding War Diaries and Intelligence
Summaries are contained in F.S. Regs., Part II,
and the Staff Manual respectively. Title pages
will be prepared in manuscript.

WAR DIARY [64]
or
INTELLIGENCE SUMMARY.
(Erase heading not required.)

Army Form C. 2118.

Date	Summary of Events and Information	Remarks and References to Appendices
10-8-1918	*Column moved to CAIX and BEAUFORT WOOD.* *Objective to create forward ammunition supplies.*	
15-8-1918	*Sent out salvaging parties.* (The diary does not provide any further information on what they were salvaging, or where.)	
24-8-1918	*9pm – Unit moved to AUBERCOURT.* *10.30pm – Stopped in the shadow of some trees at a crossroads. There was a delay in moving on whilst an infantry column crossed in front of them. At this point an enemy plane, aiming for the infantry, dropped two bombs, killing three men and seven horses, and wounding ten men and five horses. Three wagons were also put out of action, though they were recovered.*	
25-8-1918	*Column stayed in AUBERCOURT all day. Buried dead.*	

Harry was killed in the plane attack on 24th August 1918 and was buried in Aubercourt Churchyard, together with 26-year-old Corporal Courtney McBride Johnstone, from Victoria, British Columbia, Canada and 33-year-old Bombardier Thomas Fielding, originally from Bolton, England. They all served and died together, and their burial was marked by a single headstone. After the war they were reinterred side by side at Hourges Orchard Cemetery, Domart-sur-la-Luce.

Belgium Ammunition Column

The East Kent Gazette dated 14th September 1918 reported on Harry's death. The report noted he had emigrated and that he was working as a labourer when he enlisted. The report added that he had been on leave to England about a year before he was killed, and he was expected home again soon. It was mentioned that Harry had attended St Michael's School and worked for Messrs Smeed, Dean and Co. before leaving for Canada.

The family had seen another tragedy that year, when his sister Alice lost her husband Frederick Barter in April 1918, following his death from an electric shock at work.

Harry is remembered on Sittingbourne War Memorial and St Michael's Church WW1 Memorial Window. On the anniversary of his death "In Memoriam" in the East Kent Gazette was published in 1919 and 1920.

Harry's personnel file records he had a son, Albert Harry Fuller, who was born on 1st October 1911. His mother, Daisy Fuller, lived in Stockwell, London, and was awarded Harry's pension.

64 Library and Archives Canada. War Diary. RG9-III-D-3, Volume number: 4979, Microfilm reel number: T-10808, T-10808, File number: 587.

HOLDSTOCK, Sidney John

G/1304, Private, 7th Battalion, The Buffs (East Kent Regiment).

Sidney (Sydney) was born in Brixton, Surrey on 16th April 1897, the eldest child of John and Annie Elizabeth (née Clayton). His parents then moved to Sittingbourne, and Sidney was baptised on 3rd July 1897 in St John the Baptist Church, Tunstall (pictured below).

In 1901 the family was living at 155 East Street, Sittingbourne, and in 1911 they had moved to nearby 37 Harold Road. His father was employed as a steam engine fitter at the brick and cement works. His younger siblings were Millie, Dorothy Lydia (1899-1902), John Edward, and Frank Henry, who served in the RAF from 1923 to 1963.

Sidney, before the war was employed as a clerk. He enlisted on 7th December 1914 at Herne, joining the Royal East Kent Mounted Rifles. His Attestation Papers record he was 5ft 8in tall and had 'hammer toes on both feet'.

Sidney was admitted to Herne Bay's Military Hospital for 26 days from 5th February 1915 to 3rd March 1915 with bronchial catarrh.

On 22nd September 1916 he landed in France and was posted to the 7th Battalion, The Buffs.

The battalion's War Diary is reproduced below:

Instructions regarding War Diaries and Intelligence Summaries are contained in F.S. Regs., Part II, and the Staff Manual respectively. Title pages will be prepared in manuscript.	WAR DIARY [65] or INTELLIGENCE SUMMARY. (Erase heading not required.)	Army Form C. 2118.
Date	Summary of Events and Information	Remarks and References to Appendices
26-3-1917	Battalion in billets at BOËSEGHEM.	
27-3-1917 to 19-4-1917	Training.	
20-4-1917	Battalion marched to billets in BERGUETTE.	
24-4-1917	Moved to LA BOURSE.	
27-4-1917	Moved to BÉTHUNE.	
28-4-1917	Entrained to NEUVILLE VITASSE.	
1-5-1917	Battalion relieved the 7TH QUEENS at the front to support trenches north-east of the town.	

[65] War Diary: 7 Battalion, The Buffs (East Kent Regiment). WO-95-2049-1. July 1915-April 1919. The National Archives (UK), Kew, England.

3-5-1917	Midnight - Battalion commenced to take up battle positions, 12TH MIDDLESEX REGIMENT on the right and 8TH EAST SURREY REGIMENT on the left.
	3.15am - All in position. Impossible owing to the darkness, to see the lines of men until within 2 or 3 yards of them.
	The battle was to commence at 3.45am, but artillery barrage started early, causing Germans to return heavy rifle and machine gun fire.
	Because of the darkness, the three regiments became intermingled by the time they reached the German front trench in CHERISY. They encountered a number of Germans in the trench, killing a number and capturing seven prisoners. As they progressed down the deep and narrow trench, the enemy opened up with machine gun fire, taking out two Lewis gun detachments. By then it was about 6.30am.
	For the next three hours the fighting continued in CHERISY and along the RIVER SENSEE, with heavy machine gun fire from the enemy. Some of the ground that had been gained had then been lost due to the heavy firing.

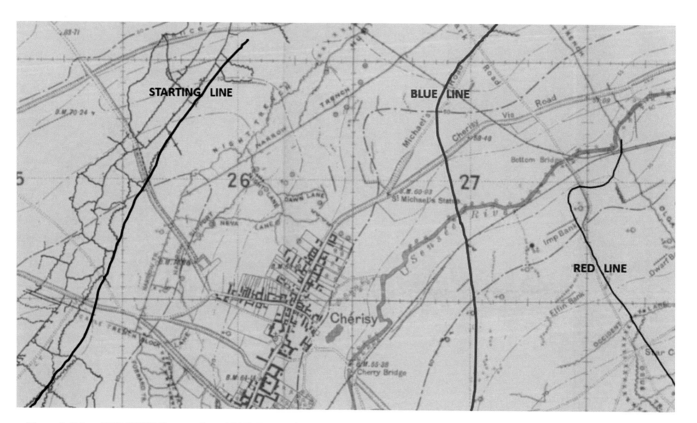

Trench Map 51B.SW.2 September 1917. Reproduced with the permission of the National Library of Scotland

3-5-1917	9am - It was reported that the "BLUE LINE" had been reached and orders were received to consolidate the line and advance on to the "RED LINE". (The diary does not specify the locations of these lines.)
	11am - Reports were received that a general retirement was taking place, and it soon became apparent that the whole line was coming back. The enemy established an intense bombardment on to the front line and the enemy machine gun fire was heavy. By this point the 7TH BUFFS had become intermingled with German troops. A number of officers in the front and support line rallied the troops to move forward to the trenches again, and half an hour later the trenches were strongly held. The enemy shell fire continued to be very heavy until about 3pm.

	5.30pm - Orders received that the 7TH QUEENS would attack the southern portion of the village with a barrage. The 7TH QUEENS formed in the front line with the 7TH BUFFS in a support trench, from which they were to advance into the front-line trench as soon as the QUEENS attacked. However, at the designated time of 6.15pm, the QUEENS remained where they were as the barrage had not opened up.
	7.15pm - The barrage started, and the QUEENS attacked, with the BUFFS moving into the front trench. Because of heavy enemy fire the attack did not succeed, and by dark the 7TH QUEENS were back in the front line.
	The 7TH BUFFS manned the front line during the night, which passed quietly.
4-5-1917	*Relieved by 6th Royal Berkshire Regiment and moved to BEAURAINS.*
	Casualties of 7TH BUFFS for 3rd and 4th May as 380 killed, wounded and missing.

Sidney was reported as one of the missing and almost a year later on 4th April 1918, the War Office declared that Sidney was presumed to have died on or since 3rd May 1917.

Sidney is commemorated on the Arras Memorial to the Missing in France. Locally, he is remembered on the St Michael's Church WW1 Memorial Window and Sittingbourne War Memorial. He was awarded the British War and Victory medals.

HOOK, Ernest William

T/200839, Private, 6th Battalion, The Buffs (East Kent Regiment).

Ernest was born in 1896 in Sittingbourne, the son of George William and Elizabeth (née Harman). His father was a wheelwright for a brick manufacturer and the family lived at 18 West Lane, Sittingbourne. Ernest was their fourth child of eight, although sadly four of them did not survive infancy. His siblings were Herbert (1889-1889), Jesse (1890-1891), Sydney George, Lucy Elizabeth (1898-1904), Amy, Percy (1901-1901), and Harold.

Ernest attended Holy Trinity School, Sittingbourne and was an active member of the choir at the Congregational Church. He worked on the clerical staff at Sittingbourne Co-operative before enlisting in November 1915.

Royal Fusiliers marching to the front.

At the beginning of October 1917 his battalion relieved the 6th Royal West Kent Regiment, in the front line and support trenches near Guémappe, 10km south-east of Arras, on the road to Cambrai.

The battalion War Diary[66] records for October 1917 that they rotated between the front line, support, and reserve lines, with most days reported as quiet, though the weather at times was "frightfully cold and wet".

November began in billets at Vacquerie-le-Boucq. They stayed there cleaning and training, some of which was with tanks, until 17th November. With a combination of marching and train journeys they arrived near to Gonnelieu, at 3.30am on 20th November 1917. Three hours later they attacked Brown and Blue lines, the diary does not record the actual locations of these lines. The last entry for that day reads "All Objectives were taken by about 12 noon with very few casualties. Our casualties were 5 Officers and 105 Other Ranks." Ernest was one of those wounded that day.

"YOUNG SITTINGBOURNE SOLDIER DIES FROM WOUNDS" was the article headline in the East Kent Gazette for 5th January 1918. The report noted it was a sad Christmas for Ernest's parents, as they were aware that he was lying seriously wounded in hospital. On 30th December they were informed he had died. The report said that during a big push, which broke through the Hindenburg Line (pictured left) at Cambrai, he received severe bullet wounds in his thigh from machine gun fire and lay in the open for several hours before being taken to a military hospital at Étaples.

Ernest was 21 when he died on 27th December 1917, at No. 26 General Hospital, Étaples (pictured below) and he was buried in Étaples Military Cemetery.

Ernest's brother, Company Quarter Master Sergeant Sydney Hook, who was serving in the same battalion, managed to arrange leave from the front to see him, and was with him when he died.

66 War Diary: 6 Battalion The Buffs (East Kent Regiment). WO-95-1860-3. September 1916-December 1917. The National Archives (UK), Kew, England.

Letters of sympathy from the Chaplain and the nurse who attended Ernest, were sent to his parents:

"I am grateful that I was able to be with him during his last hours, although he was not conscious of my presence, after Christmas Day. Up till then I was with him almost continually, and he did not want me to leave him; so, I had meals in the ward with him. When I went in about eight o'clock on Christmas morning, he was only partially conscious, and from that time he gradually sank. I stayed until eleven o'clock on Christmas night and was by him the next day until he passed away at 4.30 on the morning of the 27th. He was quite unconscious to the end. I am quite satisfied that he had the best attention he could possibly have had; both nurses and doctor were splendid, and wonderfully sympathetic."

They also received one from Sydney:

"The doctor told me that the real cause of death was poisoning, resulting from wounds, and said it was impossible to amputate his leg to stop the poison from getting into his system, owing to his extreme weakness caused by so much loss of blood, so that he could only try to prevent it by medicine. Ernie was buried at 10.30 on the morning of the 28th, in the cemetery near the hospital, by Captain Carrol, the Canadian Chaplain. I went to the funeral and have taken the number of the grave; it is W345. The graves are well looked after there, and when spring comes and the flowers are in bloom, we shall be able to get a photograph of it taken. The Captain commanding our Company has asked me to send his deepest sympathy to you; also our Company Sergt.-Major, and the other N.C.O.s especially asked me to tell you how sorry they are."

During the war the area around Étaples was full of reinforcement camps and hospitals, including eleven general, one stationary, four Red Cross, and one convalescent depot. These could manage 22,000 wounded and sick service personnel. The area was situated amongst sand dunes and was remote from attack, except for the occasional air attack. Railways from both the north and south served the area.

Ten months after Armistice, the convalescent depot and three hospitals were active. The cemetery is the resting place for 10,771 burials, of which only 35 are unidentified.

Locally he is remembered on Sittingbourne War Memorial, St Michael's Church WW1 Memorial Window and Sittingbourne Congregational Church Memorial. Ernest's father received his pay and gratuity as well as his Victory and British War Medals.

Following the news of his death, the Congregational Church remembered Ernest in their day services on Sunday 30th December 1917, then in the evening they draped the communion table with the Union Jack and placed red and white flowers on it. Ernest is commemorated on the headstone of his parents and sister Lucy, in Sittingbourne Cemetery.

A portrait of Ernest was published in 12th January 1918 edition of the East Kent Gazette, together with the poem, reproduced right. Research has tried to establish who Kath Tatham was and whether she was his sweetheart. There was a Kathleen Tatham born in Faversham in 1898, maybe she wrote this poignant poem about him.

"And praise God still,
Through good and ill,
Whatever He may send."
Can I praise God
For the chastening rod,
The death of my friend?

For this dear boy
Was my heart's joy,
Dear as my own life's breath;
How can I learn
To God to turn,
And praise Him for his death?

But still I know,
The world below
Is ruled by laws Divine;
So when I pray
I'll try to say,
"Thy will, oh Lord, not mine."

You've done your part,
Sleep on, Dear Heart,
Sleep on and take your rest;
And though I grieve,
I will believe,
The Lord above knows best.

God grant to me
To follow thee,
When from the world I go;
I know you wait
Within the Gate
For those you loved below.

KATH TATHAM

On 20th April 1918, the East Kent Gazette reported that Ernest's brother Sydney had been seriously wounded, when a shell burst close to the trench that he was in. It reported that he suffered severe leg injuries, which included a part of his muscle being blown away, and that he was in a hospital in Birmingham. He had been in France since May 1915, and previously worked as a shipwright at Messrs Wills and Packham Ltd. Sydney survived the war and lived in Sittingbourne until his death in 1960.

HOOK, William John

202111, Private, 2nd/4th Battalion, Queen's Own (Royal West Kent Regiment).

William was born in Faversham in 1877 and baptised in the parish church of St Mary of Charity on 5th October 1877. He was the ninth of thirteen children of David John and Mary Ann Eliza (née Payne). His siblings were Rebecca Ann (1862-1863), David John, Alfred William (1866-1910), Thomas Edmund, May Ann, Sarah Ann, Ellen Frances, Charles Bishop, Elizabeth Ann (1879-1884), Alice Fanny (1881-1881), George Henry (1883-1917), and Emma Jane.

The family often moved, probably as his father was a mariner, and the censuses reflect this. In 1871 they were in Whitstable, then Faversham, Northfleet and in 1911 back to Faversham, where his father was recorded as retired.

In 1901 William was a brickfield labourer, but by 1911 he had become a barge master and was, together with his wife, Elizabeth, on the barge the 'Mark Lane' which was moored at Gravesend. He enlisted in Gravesend and by 1917 was serving in Egypt.

On 26th March 1917, the Egyptian Expeditionary Force attacked and surrounded Gaza, in what became known as the First Battle of Gaza. By late afternoon the town was almost captured, but the arrival of Turkish reinforcements and approaching nightfall, caused the attack to be halted.

From the 17th to 19th April, the Second Battle of Gaza occurred. Between the two battles, the Ottoman forces had greatly improved their defences, which spread for almost 20km, and included well concealed and sighted guns. The British had also brought in additional regiments.

British tanks parked at Gaza

The attack which started at 4.30am on 17th April 1917 involved artillery, tanks, cavalry, and aerial bombardments. Initially the right flanks were attacked, and some successes were made, with the capture of some outposts and trenches. The next day the infantry consolidated their positions, whilst an artillery duel was going on, including from the sea., causing heavy casualties.

The 20th April 1917 saw attacks made from the coast, west and east, starting with a two-hour bombardment. The enemy defences proved to be too strong, and by late afternoon it was realised that there was no chance of success on the front lines. Reports said that the troops were fatigued, ammunition was low and there had been heavy casualties. The allied forces then withdrew.

The casualty figures estimated up to 400 Ottoman were killed, 1,347 wounded and 247 missing, whilst the allied casualties were 509 killed, 4,359 wounded and 1,534 missing.

William was killed, on the last day of the battle, aged 39, on 19th April 1917, and was buried in Gaza War Cemetery.

He is remembered on the memorial in Sittingbourne's Holy Trinity Church and on Sittingbourne War Memorial, where his name is inscribed as W S Hook.

William was also listed in the Roll of Honour, The Queen's Own Gazette.[67]

William's pay and gratuity went to Elizabeth Emily Wakyord, who was living at 50 Brunswick Road, Gravesend. Army records show that they were unmarried, although in 1911 they had been living together as husband and wife for seven years.

The status of 'unmarried wife' was acknowledged by the state in 1916, to recognise relationships and provide separation allowance and war widows' pension to the named recipient. She would also have received his Victory and British War Medals.

William's father also died in 1917, with his death being registered in the April to June quarter. Then William's brother, 23-year-old George Henry, who was a Corporal in the 2nd Battalion, Worcestershire Regiment (service number 12299) died on 21st May 1917. George is commemorated on the Arras Memorial to the Missing in France (pictured right).

[67] *The Queen's Own Gazette*, No. 503, June 1917. http://thequeensownbuffs.com/wp-content/uploads/2018/04/2-QO-Gazette-Jan-17-Dec-19.pdf

The HORSFORD Brothers

The Horsford family lived primarily in Sittingbourne, they then moved to Teynham around 1875, before returning to Sittingbourne by 1889, where they lived at 19 Shortlands Road. Two of the children, Guy and Leonard, died in the war.

Their parents were Alpha James Steel Horsford and Emma Lydia (née Tucker). Alpha in 1871 was a mariner and by 1881 was a shipwright. Alpha suffered from chronic rheumatism and was unable to work on a regular basis.

Alpha and Emma's children were Polly Edith, James Steel (1868-1886), Charles Walter, Lily Steel, Florence Steel (1874-1875), Hedley Vicars Steel, Gertrude Steel, Leonard Steel, Laura Steel, Alpha Rowland Steel (1882-1886), Mable Steel (1884-1884), Beatrice Steel (1885-1885), Guy Steel, Ray Steel, and Hilda May Steel (1890-1891). The middle name spelling of the Horsford family is sometimes spelt 'Steel', and more latterly as 'Steele'.

Alpha died on 29th August 1902, aged 57. His widow, Emma, in 1911 was boarding at 26 Darnley Terrace, Milton and in 1921 she was living on her own at 13 Station Street, Sittingbourne. She died in 1925.

HORSFORD, Guy Steele

G/54887, Lance Corporal, 2nd Battalion, Royal Fusiliers.

Guy Steele was born in Teynham in 1886, being baptised at the parish church (below) on 11th August that year. In 1901 he was a machine boy at the Sittingbourne Paper Mill. In 1911, Guy and his brother Leonard, were boarding at 118 Charlotte Street and they were both employed as papermakers.

In the summer of 1911 Guy married Mildred Marcy Bond, they had two children James Steele (born 1914) and Joyce Steele (born 1917).

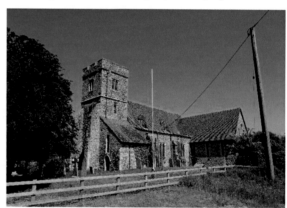

On 3rd July 1917, he enlisted in Faversham, joining the 13th Battalion, Royal Fusiliers, then on the 20th of the same month he was posted to the 2nd Battalion.

Here is the War Diary for Guy's battalion in August 1917:

Instructions regarding War Diaries and Intelligence Summaries are contained in F.S. Regs., Part II, and the Staff Manual respectively. Title pages will be prepared in manuscript.	WAR DIARY 68 or INTELLIGENCE SUMMARY. (Erase heading not required.)	Army Form C. 2118.
Date	Summary of Events and Information	Remarks and References to Appendices
1-8-1917 to 16-8-1917	Battalion billeted in the small hamlet of LA KREULE. Time spent cleaning and training.	

---

[68] War Diary: 2 Battalion Royal Fusiliers. WO-95-95-2301-3. February 1916-March 1919. The National Archives (UK), Kew, England.

17-8-1917	Battalion unsuccessfully attacked LYNDE FARM. Attacked and took control of OUTTERSTEENE RIDGE.
19-8-1917 to 21-8-1917	Took control of LABIS FARM, capturing 111 prisoners. Battalion pushed on with little opposition. No reported casualties. Relieved in the evening, after setting up outposts, and moved to the transport lines.
22-8-1917 to 27-8-1917	Battalion spent time taking baths and performance of a concert party. Battalion Training.
28-8-1917 to 3-9-1917	Returned to the line near GANDER CROSSING and OUTTERSTEENE. Sending out scouts and patrols. Expanded patrols to NOOTE BOOM.
4-9-1917	Relieved by 1ST ROYAL DUBLIN FUSILIERS and 1ST LANCASHIRE FUSILIERS.
5-9-1917	Battalion pushed forward, (though the diary does not record where to). Sent out patrols. Came under very heavy shelling. CASUALTIES – 10 killed, 20 wounded and 9 missing.
9-9-1917	Battalion moved to OUTERSTEENE for rest.

One of those killed on 5th September 1918 was Guy, who was aged 32. He is commemorated on the Ploegsteert Memorial to the Missing in Belgium, which commemorates 11,392 British and South African forces, who died in this sector. The majority of the names are of those who were killed in day-to-day fighting, rather than the major offenses.

Locally, Guy is remembered on Sittingbourne War Memorial and Holy Trinity Church WW1 Memorial, Sittingbourne. His wife received his pay and gratuity, Victory and British War Medals.

HORSFORD, Leonard Steele

L/7587, Private, 1st Battalion, The Buffs (East Kent Regiment).

Leonard Steele was born in Teynham in 1879 and was baptised there on 20th January 1880 in St Mary's church.

Leonard served in the 3rd Battalion, The Buffs from 1st March 1900 to 29th September 1902, but then purchased his discharge. His service record shows his occupation as a blacksmith. He joined again in Canterbury on 27th March 1904, first for three years, then for a further nine.

On 25th November 1904 an Inquiry was held at Dover, where he was stationed, into how a medal awarded to him had been lost. There were in fact two medals, the King's, and Queen's South African Medals. Leonard gave evidence that he had been wearing them, attached by a brooch to his tunic, when he went out on a pass on 15th August 1904. He had gone for a walk with a lady to Kearsney and, when he had returned, they were missing. He said that he had looked for them but had not reported the loss to the police as on 17th August he had been admitted to hospital.

The Inquiry concluded that Leonard had lost them but should pay to have them replaced. In giving evidence his Captain stated that Leonard's character was 'indifferent' and there are reports of his being late, absent, drunk and of improper conduct to an NCO.

Leonard was posted to the 1st Battalion on 24th August 1914 and joined the British Expeditionary Force on 7th September 1914. In 1915, he was in the trenches near La Brique:

Instructions regarding War Diaries and Intelligence Summaries are contained in F.S. Regs., Part II, and the Staff Manual respectively. Title pages will be prepared in manuscript.	**WAR DIARY** [69] or **INTELLIGENCE SUMMARY.** (Erase heading not required.)	Army Form C. 2118.
Date	Summary of Events and Information	Remarks and References to Appendices
11-7-1915 to 26-7-1915	In trenches near LA BRIQUE.	
27-7-1915	Relieved by 3RD BATTALION RIFLE BRIGADE. Battalion moved to some huts in sector A.30. (According to trench maps[70] these were located mid-way between YPRES and POPERINGE, north of the road that connected the towns.)	
31-7-1915	Battalion ordered into reserve on the south side of the YPRES to POPERINGE ROAD. Remained in trenches all day: weather fortunately fine.	
5-8-1915	Major-General Congreve V.C., (Commander of the Battalion's Division) addressed the battalion pointing out the need to retake the trenches at HOOGE. He added that this division had been selected as it was the best one in his command and said, "the Battalion would remember their past record and that the eyes of Kent were upon them." The battalion remained in billets.	
8-8-1915	6.30pm – Battalion marched to HOOGE and in position by 1am.	
9-8-1915	2.45am - Artillery bombardment started. 3.15am - Attack commenced and proved successful. 6.45am – Daylight started, trenches subjected to enemy heavy bombardment and obliterated. Attacks successful along MENIN ROAD, taking over the trenches. Expected night-time German counterattack did not occur.	
10-8-1915 to 11-8-1915	Attacks continued, and counterattacks repulsed.	
12-8-1915	Battalion moved to ramparts at MENIN GATE. _CASUALTIES_ KILLED 25, WOUNDED 162, MISSING 5.	

[69] War Diary: 1 Battalion The Buffs (East Kent Regiment). WO-95-1608-1. August 1914-December 1915. The National Archives (UK), Kew, England.

[70] _British First World War Trench Map._ Sheet 28NW, Scale 1:20000 Edition B Series. 1 April 1917. National Library of Scotland. maps.nls.uk/view/101464906

Leonard, aged 35, was killed on 9th August 1915. He is commemorated on the Menin Gate Memorial to the Missing, Ypres (pictured below), as well as on Sittingbourne War Memorial.

Leonard was awarded the 1914 Star with Clasp, which showed that he had served under fire in November 1914, as well as the Victory and British War Medals. His mother and siblings each received a share of his pay, whilst his mother received his gratuity.

The memorial was designed by Sir Reginald Blomfield with a sculpture by Sir William Reid-Dick. The memorial is inscribed with the names of over 54,000 casualties with no known grave from Australia, Canada, India, South Africa, and United Kingdom. Those from the United Kingdom died before 16th August 1917, after this date they are commemorated on Tyne Cot Memorial. New Zealand casualties are commemorated at memorials in Buttes New British Cemetery and Messines Ridge British Cemetery.

Leonard and Guy's nephew Ray Steele Horsford, the son of their brother Ray and his wife, Lilian Primrose (née Busbridge), was killed in the Second World War. Ray was born on 12th January 1916 in Milton Regis, and married Doris Hunt in 1942. They had two children, George (born 1943) and Doris Ada (born 1944).

Ray became a Flight Sergeant, with 75 Squadron, Royal Air Force Volunteer Reserve, serial number 1387835 during WW2. He was a crew member of Lancaster bomber HK568, which crashed in Robertsau Forest, near Strasbourg, France, on the night of 24th July 1944.

The crew were buried side by side in Cronenbourg French National Cemetery, Strasbourg, and his headstone is inscribed "GOLDEN MEMORIES SILENTLY KEPT OF ONE WE LOVED AND WILL NEVER FORGET."

The HORTON Brothers

Two brothers, 23-year-old George and 24-year-old Sydney, of the Horton family were killed just 48 days apart. They were the sons of James Horton and Emma Monk, who married on 12th July 1868 in Faversham. Before 1869 they had moved to Elmley on the Isle of Sheppey where their first child Alice Mary was born.

By 1881 they had moved to 71 Shortlands Road, Sittingbourne, and James was employed as a labourer at the cement works (below). Living with them were their children, Alice, Arthur James, John William, Ernest Alfred, and Harriett Jane. They sadly lost one infant Horace Benjamin (1877-1878), but later had Emily Eliza, George Frederick, Clara May, Agnes, Lily Grace (1893-1893), and Sydney Aldrick.

In 1911 they were still living in Shortlands Road, at number 92, and James was working as a brickfield labourer. Tragically, Emma died in the summer of 1914, followed by their daughter, Harriett, later that year. Then in 1918 came the deaths of George and Sydney in the war, and then their father James late in the year.

A number of the family emigrated to Ontario, Canada; John, Ernest, and George in 1906, Agnes in April 1911 and Emily in June 1914. John enlisted with the 83rd Battalion in August 1915, sailing to England in April 1916. He was discharged on 31st December 1917, due to illness. His service record shows his service was all in England at various camps. Ernest enlisted on 1st November 1915 with the 84th Battalion and served in France from 27th August 1916. On 16th October 1916 he was shot in the chest and received treatment in England, before returning to the field. Ernest received a shrapnel wound to the jaw on 31st March 1918, before his army discharge on 27th February 1919.

HORTON, George Frederick

725121, Corporal, 38th Battalion, Canadian Infantry.

George was born in Sittingbourne on 15th April 1885. In 1901 he was working as a brickfield labourer, then in May 1906 he emigrated to Canada, together with his older brother Ernest, his wife Ada, and their children.

On 9th September 1911, George married 28-year-old Helen (Ellen) Sarah Milgate, in Toronto. At that time, he recorded his occupation as a brickmaker. Ellen had been born in Bethnal Green, London and emigrated to Canada in 1911. George and Ellen had one daughter who was born in 1913, Mabel Annie Emma.

When George enlisted, in Lindsay, Ontario, on 7th January 1916, he was

5ft 10in tall with blue eyes and light brown hair. He had been working as a brickmaker and living at Lansing, Toronto. George's unit sailed from Halifax on 25th July 1916 for England. On 10th December 1916 he arrived in Le Havre, France. His promotion to Corporal occurred on 11th May 1918. Exactly three months later he was killed, on 11th August 1918, aged 23.

The Canadian War Graves Register (Circumstances of Casualty) for George, records the circumstances as "killed in Action.[71] During the attack through Rosiers towards Hallu, he was struck in the lungs and instantly killed by a bullet from an enemy sniper's rifle."

1. NO.	2. RANK OR RATING	3. SURNAME	4. CHRISTIAN NAMES
725121,	Corporal,	HORTON,	George Frederick,

5. UNIT OR SHIP	6. DATE OF CASUALTY	7. H.Q. FILE NO.	8. RELIGION
38th Battalion.	11-8-18.	649-H-16041.	Church of England.

9. CIRCUMSTANCES OF CASUALTY	10. NAME, RELATIONSHIP AND ADDRESS OF NEXT OF KIN
"Killed in Action." During the attack through Rosieres towards Hallu, he was struck in the lungs and instantly killed by a bullet from an enemy sniper's rifle.	

War graves registers and related documentation - George Frederick Horton, Casualty Record. © Government of Canada. Reproduced with the permission of Library and Archives Canada (2022).

According to his battalion War Diary[72] on 1st August 1918 they had been relieved by English troops at Fampoux, near Vimy Ridge. They then spent four days travelling by light railway and marching to billets at Bougainville, 85km to the south-west and 18km west of Amiens. On arrival they were told that they "were not expected" and no billets were available. Good shelter was obtained, and the diary noted "the climax to this humorous situation, was when the colonel was accused by a French lady of "salvaging" the razor of her beloved spouse." Over the next two days they marched 35km east to Gentelles, reporting ideal conditions, arriving at 9pm on 7th August.

At 4.20 am on 8th August 1918 the battalion joined the attack on the enemy, which lasted for the next four days. They started moving south-east, with cavalry and Whippet tank (pictured left) support, advancing 15km over the first two days, with little opposition, to the village of Caix. On the 10th they entered Rosières, 5km further on, where they came under machine gun and light artillery fire. They managed to proceed to the Lihons-Chilly road, another 2km west, but were met with a trench network and wire, which halted progress. The next day, the 11th, the Germans attacked the flanks and inflicted many casualties, but they were repelled. The battalion remained on this front line until the night of the 13th when they were relieved.

[71] Library and Archives Canada/Ministry of the Overseas Military Forces of Canada fonds/Vol. 31829_B016693, page 167

[72] War Diary: 127 Heavy Battery Royal Garrison Artillery. WO-95-397-4. August-October 1916. The National Archives (UK), Kew, England.

George was killed on 11th August 1918 and is remembered on the Vimy Memorial to the Missing as well as on Sittingbourne War - Memorial and St Michael's Church WW1 Memorial Window. He is also commemorated in the Canadian Books of Remembrance (see page 342).

Standing 110 metres tall Vimy Memorial is situated on Hill 145, the highest point of Vimy Ridge which was captured by Canadian forces on the first day of the Battle of Vimy Ridge on 9th April 1917. The memorial commemorates over 60,000 Canadians who gave their lives in France and its base is inscribed with the names of 11,285 who have no known grave.

HORTON, Sydney Aldrick

317381, Gunner, 1st/1st (Kent) Heavy Battery, Royal Garrison Artillery.

Sydney, the youngest in the family, was born in 1896, and although his middle name was registered as Aldrick, all further documents record his name as Aldrich or Alderich. By 1911 he was working as a reeler boy in the paper mill. In the spring of 1915, he married 21-year-old local girl, Edith May Carpenter, and their only child, Lily May, was born on 27th July 1917.

The report of his death in 19th October 1918 edition of the East Kent Gazette noted that Sydney, before he enlisted in 1915 in Faversham, had worked at the Queenborough Chemical Works. He served in France from 29th December 1915 and was last home on leave in November 1917.

On 14th September 1918 his battalion's War Diary[73] noted that the guns were moved to Neuville-Bourjonval, 19km south-west of Cambrai.

For the following 12 days the battery dug out gun pits and trenches, with recesses for ammunition and accommodation. The record stated that this was excellent work, done at speed and with great lines.

At 9pm on the 27th, after moving a thousand rounds, the battery started firing from the north-west corner of nearby Gouzeaucourt Wood.

RGA moving a 60 pounder Mark I Gun

---

[73] War Diary: 127 Heavy Battery Royal Garrison Artillery. WO-95-397-4. August-October 1916. The National Archives (UK), Kew, England.

It was noted that the enemy returned harassing fire with gas and high explosive shells, all through the night, with 20 men being wounded and one killed.

Sydney was one of those who was wounded and was taken to No. 4 Casualty Clearing Station. He died there, aged 24, the following day, 28th September 1918, and was buried in the Thilloy Road Cemetery, Beaulencourt.

The cemetery was created by the 53rd Field Ambulance in early September 1918, and used by Nos. 3, 4, and 43 Casualty Clearing Stations. There are 239 burials in the cemetery from a six-week period, between 29th August and 9th October 1918, plus two more from men who died in 1916.

Sydney's wife received letters of condolence from the battalion's Chaplain and a Sergeant A. Webb, who was the first to attend to Sydney when he was wounded.

Locally, he is remembered on the Sittingbourne War Memorial and St Michael's Church WW1 Memorial Window (pictured right). Sydney was awarded the 1915 Star, and Victory and British War Medals. His wife, Edith, received his pay and gratuity. She remarried in Milton in 1921 to Arthur Burbidge.

> ## The East Kent Gazette
>
> ### SATURDAY, OCTOBER 19, 1918
> ### ROLL OF HONOUR
>
> HORTON - Sept. 28th, 1918, died of wounds in No. 4 Casualty Clearing Station, France, Gunner Sydney A. Horton, of No. 10, Railway Terrace, Sittingbourne, aged 24 years.
>
> If we could have clasped his dying hand,
> And heard his last farewell;
> It would not have been so hard to part
> With one we loved so well.
> From his sorrowing Wife and Baby.

H. M. ARMY.
K. Hadlow.
P. O. Hancock.
A. H Harris.
C. A. Heuner.
H. Higgins.
S. J. Holdstock.
E. W. Hook.
G. F. Horton.
S. A. Horton.

HUTCHENS, George William

200013, Regimental Quartermaster Serjeant, 1st/4th Battalion, The Buffs (East Kent Regiment).

George was born in 1880 in Milton Regis and baptised in the parish church of Holy Trinity on 29th August 1880. He was the eldest of the five children of George, a paper mill labourer, and Amy (née Wakefield). His siblings were Osborne, William James, Mary, and Nellie. The family lived in Hythe Road, Sittingbourne, from the 1880s.

George's brother Osborne emigrated to Toronto, Canada, arriving on 1st April 1910, followed by William the following year. Finally, his parents and both his sisters emigrated to Canada, leaving Liverpool on 27th June 1912.

George attended Milton Council School and in 1901 was working as a carpenter for Messrs Bowes and Son of Milton and Mr H Tidy of Sittingbourne. On 19th October 1907 he married 21-year-old Lilian

Edith Gorf at All Saints Church, Murston. They had two daughters, May (born 1908) and Eva (born 1910), and they lived at 193 Shortlands Road, Sittingbourne.

In the early 1900s George had joined the Volunteer Force, which became the Territorials in 1908, by which time he had attained the rank of Corporal, then in 1912 was promoted to Colour-Sergeant. At the outbreak of war, he was appointed Regimental Quartermaster Sergeant and went out to India in the autumn of 1914. He held a long service medal for continuous service in the Volunteers and Territorials for 15 years.

On 7th August 1915, the East Kent Gazette published "AN INTERESTING LETTER", from George. In the letter he mentioned that the battalion were in Mhow, Central India, contrary to belief they had been all over India. The battalion had taken the "Kitchener's Test", an annual test in shooting and marching, receiving a high merit in Musketry, which the C.O. hoped would lead to him taking the battalion across a bullet-swept area. George added that they had a furlough period and visited Delhi, Agra, and Cawnpore.

The battalion were involved in training and entrenching and spent their down time playing sports. They had been entered into the Calcutta Cup for football, which drew crowds of 20,000. George went on to mention the death of Sittingbourne man Private B Williams, from appendicitis, and that he had had a military funeral. He concluded that they were being looked after, especially against malaria and that they had left Sittingbourne for training a year previous on 26th July 1914. The letter ends "And what a year!"

By November 1915 the battalion had moved to Aden. The East Kent Gazette dated 13th November 1915 reported that funds to provide comforts and necessities for local units serving around the world had been organised. It also noted that the Sittingbourne and Milton lads serving in Aden had not been provided for, and so the "Lest We Forget" fund was organised by the East Kent Gazette. The following week's edition of the newspaper reported an excellent start, with gifts and monetary donations being received, and were planning to send out the first batch of parcels that week.

How dear to us does our home in Kent become when so full a tide of sympathy, good wishes, and generosity flows out to us across the thousand miles of sea. Words cannot express our gratitude. We can only tell you that we will do our utmost to uphold the honour of Sittingbourne and Milton Regis in the midst of our Regiment.

The newspaper published a thank you letter from George on 22nd January 1916 (reproduced left), following the receipt of gifts and that every Sittingbourne man received something. Letters were often published providing news from the battalion and lists of donations, as George administered the fund, and keeping accounts showing subscribers how the gifts had been allocated.

The 22nd September 1917 edition of the East Kent

Gazette, under the headline "SAD DEATH IN INDIA", reported that his wife, expecting his weekly letter, was shocked to receive one from the War Office notifying her of George's death on the 12th September 1917. The newspaper added that he was a model non-commissioned officer, possessing the entire confidence of both officers and men. He carried out his important duties with tact and discretion, and the younger men would do anything for him.

St Paul's Church Memorial

The newspaper also stated that his death was sudden and further details were awaited regarding the circumstances, which was subject to an inquiry. At the time of print research had not identified any documents relating to the inquiry.

George's pension card records his cause of death as "Com(mitted) suicide while in a state of temporary insanity due to disease while on active service."

George was 37 years old and was buried in the Bareilly Cemetery, Uttar Pradesh, India. Bareilly Cemetery is a civilian cemetery with 37 CWGC burials, from September 1914 to August 1921.

Locally he is remembered on St Michael's Church WW1 Memorial Window, Sittingbourne War Memorial, and on memorials in Milton Regis, including their War Memorial, St Paul's Church (pictured left), and the Old Boys Milton Council Schools Memorials.

George's executor, Ernest Edward Smith, who was his brother-in-law, received his pay and gratuity. George was awarded the Victory and British War Medals.

HUXTED, Thomas

WR/26886, Pioneer, 345th Road Construction Company, Royal Engineers.

Thomas was born in Murston in 1884, the son of Thomas, a brickfield labourer, and Caroline Rhoda (née Bartlett). They had a large family of 12 children, though sadly by 1911 five had died. Thomas' siblings were William Edward Thomas, Celia Lucy (1877-1878), Nellie (1879-1880), Sarah Emma, Solomon James, Ann Caroline (1886-1886), Clara Maud (1887-1888), Caroline Rhoda, Albert John (1891-1918), Eliza May, and an unnamed infant. Thomas was baptised at St Michael's Church, Sittingbourne, on 7th September 1884.

He attended Murston Church of England School and in 1901 was living at 63 Murston Road, Sittingbourne.

On 27th May 1909, at Sittingbourne Register Office, Thomas married Ada Court, and they had two children Hilda May (born 14th July 1909) and Thomas Stephen (born 12th January 1913). In 1911, Thomas and his family were living with his mother-in-law, Eliza Court, at 70 William Street; his military documents record his address as 60 William Street.

175

Thomas had been working as a stoker, at the Sittingbourne Paper Mill, when he enlisted in Sittingbourne on 10th December 1915, the next day he was posted to the reserves, and was mobilised on 2nd May 1917. Just three weeks later he was sent to France.

On 3rd July 1918 Thomas was admitted to the 30th General Hospital in Calais partially unconscious and coughing up huge quantities of frothy mucus. He was very restless and fought for breath, he died, aged 34, at 4.45am on 4th July 1918. The cause of death was given as bronchitis due to gas exposure whilst on active service.

The East Kent Gazette of 13th July 1918 reported Thomas' death under the heading "A MORTAL ILLNESS", it said that his wife had received the news in a letter from Chaplain J. Herbert Diner, at 30th General Hospital, where Thomas died. The Chaplain said they prayed together the night he was admitted.

The article also printed letters from Thomas's commanding officers expressing their regret of his death. The newspaper later published two "In Memoriam" articles about Thomas.

Thomas was buried in Les Baraques Military Cemetery, Sangatte. His headstone is inscribed "AT REST." The cemetery was positioned close to several hospitals, which could accommodate 2,500 beds. It was opened in September 1917 and designed by Sir Herbert Baker, and is the final resting place for 1,546, including 203 Chinese Labour Corps, 237 Germans, and seven World War Two soldiers.

Thomas is remembered on Sittingbourne War Memorial, Lloyd's Paper Mill (below), and Sittingbourne's Holy Trinity Church and Congregational Church Memorials. His wife received his pay and gratuity.

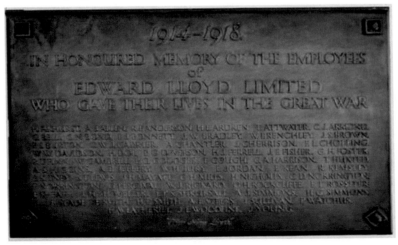

After his death his widow asked a local Justice of the Peace to write asking for his personal belongings, and she was sent his disc, letters, cards, photos, religious books, a metal watch and chain, a bead necklace, a purse, three wallets, a razor strop and two notebooks.

Sadly, just seven months later, Ada was hit with the tragic death of their son, Thomas, on 16th December 1918, a month short of his sixth birthday.

The East Kent Gazette

SATURDAY, JULY 5, 1919
IN MEMORIAM

HUXTED - In ever-loving memory of our dear son and brother, Thomas Huxted, who passed away at the 30th General Hospital, France, July 4th, (sic) 1918.

Duty called and he was there,
To do his bit and take his share;
His heart was good, his spirit brave,
He's sleeping now in a hero's grave.
Mum, Dad, Brothers and Sisters

The East Kent Gazette

SATURDAY, DECEMBER 20, 1919
IN MEMORIAM

HUXTED - In ever-loving memory of our dear little grandson and nephew, Thomas Stephen Huxted, who died, December 16th, 1918.

Oh, why was he taken, so young and so fair,
Taken from those who loved him so dear;
Anchored by love, that death cannot sever,
Dearly we loved him and shall do for ever.
From his loving Grandma and Grandad,
Aunties, and Uncles.

HUXTED, William George

105748, Private, 41st Ambulance Train, Royal Army Medical Corps.

William was born in December 1896 in Sittingbourne, with his surname registered as Huxsted, though all his military documents record his surname as Huxted, which is how the family later spelt their name. He was a cousin of Thomas Huxted (see page 175).

He was the son of Albert, a brick labourer, and Elizabeth (née Furminger) the third of nine children. His siblings were Elizabeth Mabel (1894-1894), Albert Edward, Edward Charles, Thomas James (1901-1908), Frederick (1903-1923), George Henry, and Dorothy Ann. In 1901 the family were living at 40 Shakespeare Road, Sittingbourne and by 1911, still called Huxsted they were living at 11 Murston Road, Sittingbourne.

The Red Cross records[74] show that two of William's brothers volunteered with him. Albert from 14th October 1914 to 18th October 1915, when he enlisted with the Royal Army Medical Corps until his discharge in March 1919. Edward from January to March 1917, before enlisting with the 3rd Bedford Regiment.

William volunteered with the Red Cross from 26th February 1915 until he enlisted with the Royal Army Medical Corps on 21st December 1915 in Sittingbourne. He was 5ft 6in tall and had been working as a cement worker. He went to France in November 1917 then to Italy on 27th December 1917. He returned on 19th February 1918 on a train, with patients, but then went back to Italy. He died in No. 62 General Hospital in Bordighera, Italy, from influenza, aged 21, on 19th November 1918.

---

[74] British Red Cross. *First World War Volunteers.* vad.redcross.org.uk

William was buried in the Bordighera British Cemetery, Italy. The cemetery is located across from the civilian cemetery and close to the 62nd General Hospital, which was in Bordighera from January 1918 to January 1919. The cemetery contains 72 Commonwealth burials and 12 Austrian burials.

The dedication on his headstone reads "WE CANNOT LORD, THY PURPOSE SEE, BUT ALL IS WELL THAT'S DONE BY THEE". These are from the first verse of the hymn O Let My Trembling Soul Be Still by Sir John Bowring, author of 88 hymns, a politician, and former Governor of Hong Kong.

William was awarded the Victory and British War Medals, and locally is remembered on St Michael's Church WW1 Memorial Window and Sittingbourne War Memorial.

The East Kent Gazette

SATURDAY, NOVEMBER 20, 1920

IN MEMORIAM

HUXTED – In loving memory of a dear son and brother, Private William George Huxted, who died in Italy, November 19th, 1918.

Two long years have passed,
And we pictured his face returning;
We longed to clasp his hand,
But God has postponed the meeting.
Till we meet in a better land.
From his ever-loving Mum, Dad, Sisters, and Brothers.

IRVIN, Ernest Sydney

293174, Stoker 1st Class, Royal Navy, HMS Hermes.

Stoker Dress Insignia

Ernest was born on 30th June 1880 in Chislet, near Canterbury; the middle child of the fifteen children of William, a harness maker, and Charlotte (née Goodwin). His siblings were William Alias, Henry Walter, Emma Elizabeth, unnamed boy (1875-1875), Edwin Arthur, Kate, Louis John, Charles Edgar, Minnie, Bertie, Ellen Lilian (1889-1889), Nellie (1891-1891), Lilian Charlotte, and sadly an unnamed child who died in infancy. Some of their birth registrations spelt the surname as Irven, which is how his father spelt their surname, though Ernest and his own family used Irvin. Ernest's surname was spelt incorrectly as Ervin on his plaque on the Avenue of Remembrance.

Ernest was an engine cleaner when he signed on for 12 years with the Royal Navy on 26th September 1899, aged 19. He was 5ft 4¾in tall, with brown hair and blue eyes and served as a stoker. On 3rd October 1903 he married Eliza Russell (1883-1947) in Milton Regis. By 1911 they were living at 27 New Road, Sittingbourne and on 26th September 1911, having served his 12 years, he joined the Royal Fleet Reserve.

Ernest and Eliza had four children, Ernest Sydney (born 1904), William Frederick (born 1906), Henry Arthur (born 1909) and Lilian May (born 1915).

On 2nd August 1914, Ernest was recalled to the navy and three weeks later on the 23rd posted to *HMS Hermes*, a cruiser assigned to the reserve fleet in 1913. During that year she was converted as the first seaplane carrier in the Royal Navy, and successful trials were carried out. In August 1914 she was recommissioned to operate as an aircraft ferry and depot ship to France, for the Royal Naval Air Service.

On 30th October 1914 *Hermes* (pictured below) arrived in Dunkirk with one load of seaplanes. The following day she had started her return to England, when she was notified that a German submarine had been reported in the area. Despite taking avoiding manoeuvres, by zigzagging, she was torpedoed by *U-27*, and she sank in the Straits of Dover at Ruylingen Bank, about half-way between Dover and Dunkirk. Twenty-two of her 123 crew lost their lives. Her wreck lies upside down in approximately 30 metres (98 feet) of water.

Credit: Kurt von Schleinitz (1859-1928) - Frankfurt University Library

One of those who died on 31st October 1914 was 34-year-old Ernest. He is commemorated on Chatham Naval Memorial, Sittingbourne War Memorial and Sittingbourne Holy Trinity Church Memorial.

At the time of his death Ernest and his family were living at 14 The Wall, Sittingbourne, and his widow received his 1914-15 Star, Victory, and British War Medals. His widow and three sons remained in the Sittingbourne area, all working in the local paper mill.

JARMAN MM, William Thomas
2822, Lance Corporal, 6th Battalion, The Buffs (East Kent Regiment).

William was born on 17th May 1893 in Sittingbourne, the son of William Thomas, a gas stoker, and Eliza (née Winn). His name at birth was registered as Winn William Thomas, though his forename Winn was not used in any further documents. The third of six children, William's siblings were Eliza, Winn Lily Rosetta (1891-1891), Rose Hannah (1895-1895), Winn George, and Winn Florence. In 1911, the family were living at 18 Goodnestone Road, Sittingbourne, and William was working as a brickfield labourer. William's mother died in 1911.

He enlisted in Sittingbourne, joining the 8th Battalion, The Buffs, and arrived in France on 31st August 1915. In the autumn of 1916, he married 26-year-old Emma Rose Weeks, in Reigate, Surrey.

The London Gazette dated 14th November 1916 announced the award of the Military Medal (8th Battalion) to William. Research has not identified a citation, or the action William was involved in to gain his nomination.

179

The War Diary for his battalion is reproduced here:

Instructions regarding War Diaries and Intelligence Summaries are contained in F.S. Regs., Part II, and the Staff Manual respectively. Title pages will be prepared in manuscript.

WAR DIARY [75]
or
INTELLIGENCE SUMMARY.
(Erase heading not required.)

Army Form C. 2118.

Date	Summary of Events and Information	Remarks and References to Appendices
7-10-1918	Battalion moved to front line near MERICOURT. QUIET.	
8-10-1918 to 12-10-1918	In the line. QUIET. Patrols sent out.	
15-10-1918	Moved to billets at FOSSE 3, (Trench maps[76] locate it as near the village of CARVIN.)	
16-10-1918 to 20-10-1918	Moved to AUBY and FLINE. Battalion repaired roads and bathed.	
21-10-1918	In the front line. Heavy rain.	
22-10-1918	Moved to support trench by the RIVER SCARPE. All civilians evacuated by the Germans.	
23-10-1918	Battalion advanced to CUBRAY.	
24-10-1918	Battalion attacked strongly held villages of BURIDON and BRUILLE, surprising the enemy. Established the line on the banks of the RIVER ESCAULT. (They were the first battalion to reach the river on the whole front line. For this action the battalion received a Commendation from Lieutenant-General Weston, Commander VIII Corps.	
25-10-1918	Relieved by 6TH QUEENS and moved to support trenches.	

William was killed in action, aged 24, on 24th October 1918. He is buried in Sameon Churchyard, France (pictured below), alongside five other fallen. All died within a few days of each other, with one from the Royal Field Artillery, three from the Cambridgeshire Regiment and a fellow Buff and Milton Regis lad, 20-year-old Harold Stephen Dale, whose family lived at 45 Church Street. William is second from the right and Harold on the far right.

William is remembered on Sittingbourne War Memorial and St Michael's Church WW1 Memorial Window. His pay and war gratuity were paid to his widow Emma, who lived in Newnham. She also received his 1915 Star, Victory, and British War Medals.

---

[75] War Diary: 6 Battalion The Buffs (East Kent Regiment). WO-95-1860-4. January 1918-March 1919. The National Archives (UK), Kew, England.

[76] Trench Map 36c. Grid reference 36c.l.12.c.6.8. Tmapper.com

William's 19-year-old cousin, Private Harry John Simmons (see page 266) was killed just a month earlier on 19th September 1918 in the Battle of Épehy. Harry was the son of William's aunt Elizabeth, his father's sister.

The JARRETT Brothers

Two brothers of the Jarrett family were killed in the war, Herbert, and Rupert. They were the sons of George and Eliza (née Hunt). George was a brickfield labourer and his family had lived at 21 Cheapside, Milton Road, Sittingbourne since his marriage to Eliza in the summer of 1887.

George and Eliza had six children, though tragically three did not survive infancy, Edith May (1893-1894), Percy William (1897-1897) and Alma Elizabeth (1900-1900). A fourth child, William Thomas (1881-1891), died at the age of nine years old.

Herbert Horace was born in 1889 and Rupert George in 1894, both in Milton Regis. They were both living with their parents in 1911, with Herbert employed as a shop assistant at a London gent's outfitters and Rupert an apprentice at the paper mill.

JARRETT, Herbert Horace

Second Lieutenant, 5th Battalion, North Staffordshire Regiment.

Herbert had attended Holy Trinity School, Sittingbourne, and according to 15th December 1917 edition of the East Kent Gazette which reported his death, he had an excellent school record. The newspaper added that when the war broke out, he enlisted with the 5th Lancers, and had served in Gallipoli, where he was wounded. He was then transferred to the 1st Royal Münster Fusiliers, (regimental number 5764) and attained the rank of Sergeant.

Herbert gained a commission and was promoted to Second Lieutenant on 29th August 1917, which was announced in The London Gazette, dated 21st September 1917. He then joined the North Staffordshire Regiment.

On 2nd December 1917, Herbert was supervising the repair of a trench, damaged by shell fire, when he was hit in the back by a sniper, injuring his spine.

Herbert's mother and his fiancée, Miss Minter, of Ash, Canterbury, went to visit him in No. 8 General Hospital, Rouen (pictured on next page), as he was dangerously ill. However, he had died, aged 28, on 6th December 1917, and sadly they arrived three hours after he was buried in the St Sever Cemetery,

Rouen. The words "TO LIVE IN THE HEARTS THEY LEAVE BEHIND IS NOT TO DIE DAD AND MUM" are inscribed upon his headstone.

AUSTRALIAN WAR MEMORIAL   A03235

The East Kent Gazette article reported Herbert's mother Eliza had remarked how she and Miss Minter, and others on the same sad mission were well looked after and cared for by the authorities.

Locally, Herbert is remembered on the Sittingbourne and Milton Regis War Memorials, as well as at Holy Trinity Church at Sittingbourne.

Herbert had left a will, and his probate went to farmer Reginald Henry Minter, who in 1911 was living with his widowed mother and four unmarried sisters at Overland Court, Ash. It is likely that one of them would have been Herbert's fiancé and the money may have been for her benefit. Herbert was awarded the Victory and British War Medals.

JARRETT, Rupert George

G/28589, Lance Corporal, 6th Battalion, Queen's Own (Royal West Kent Regiment).

As a child, Rupert attended Holy Trinity School, Sittingbourne, and sang in the church choir. Before the war, he had captained the Sittingbourne Football Team.

In the summer of 1916, Rupert married 23-year-old Edith May Spencer at Faversham. On 27th September 1917 their only child, Walter George, was born. They were living at 50 High Street, Milton Regis, when Rupert joined up in October 1917 and he had been working for the Cotton Powder Company in Faversham. He arrived in France on 24th February 1918.

His battalion's War Diary[77] records them billeted and training at Prouzel for the second half of July 1918. On 30th July they moved by train to Saint-Léger-lès-Domart, 25km to the north, then on 2nd August they were bussed 30km east to Round Wood, on the Behencourt – Franvillers road, to relieve the 9th Battalion London Regiment. The next few days they experienced some shelling which resulted in a few casualties and the diary reported "much hostile aerial activity."

---

[77] War Diary: 6 Battalion Queen's Own (Royal West Kent Regiment). WO-95-1861-7. July 1918-July 1919. The National Archives (UK), Kew, England.

On 8th August 1918 the battalion moved to billets in nearby Franvillers, having been relieved by American troops from 132nd Regiment. They were held in readiness to move on half-hour's notice, in preparation for a planned attack. Later that evening they were moved to Ballarat Line. The next day they formed up along the Morlancourt-Ville-sur-Ancre road (pictured below), and at 1pm orders were received to attack at 5pm. Some casualties were sustained during assembly. The War Diary does not specify the exact position attacked, though it records it was successful, penetrating 2000 feet into enemy positions. It added that 12 machine guns were captured and 10 more destroyed, with 40 prisoners taken.

AUSTRALIAN WAR MEMORIAL   E04831

Leading his section on an advance to the German lines, Rupert was shot through his hand. He was on his way back to the dressing station when he was hit a second time and fell mortally wounded, aged 24, on 9th August 1918.

Rupert was buried in the Ville-sur-Ancre Communal Cemetery Extension. The cemetery extension is the final resting place of 106 burials, of which 54 remain as "KNOWN UNTO GOD". Alongside Rupert, lie 43 men who were killed in a nine-day period from 7th August 1918. On the day he was killed 13 other men of the Queen's Own gave their lives.

Rupert was awarded the Victory and British War Medals and he is remembered on Sittingbourne War Memorial and Sittingbourne Holy Trinity Church WW1 Memorial. His wife, Edith, was paid his pay and gratuity.

When Rupert died, two of his wife's brothers were serving. Alfred Charles Spencer with the Army Service Corps, though at the time of Rupert's death he was in a Tonbridge hospital after being wounded in France. Walter Frederick Spencer was in the Royal Navy as a Stoker 2nd Class, serving on *HMS Yarmouth*.

JARVIS, Edward John

68773, Gunner, 115th Battery, Royal Field Artillery.

Edward was born in Sittingbourne in 1890 and baptised on 20th July 1890 at Holy Trinity Church, Sittingbourne. He was the middle of the five children of Edward, a bricklayer's labourer, and Harriett (née Baldock). His siblings were Olive Maud, Unnamed brother (1889-1889), Archibald Charles, and Albert James.

In 1907 his father died and in 1911 his mother was employed as a private nurse, and the family were living at 36 New Road, Sittingbourne. Edward was employed as a reeler's assistant in the paper mill. Edward's mother remarried in 1913 to widower and bricklayer Leonard William Hammond.

Edward enlisted in Chatham on 5th February 1912, and his battery arrived in France on 18th August 1914. Their War Diary[78] notes they boarded *SS Victorian* (pictured right) at Southampton and had a calm passage to Le Havre, though the ship was very crowded.

The battery was part of 25 Brigade with 113, 114 and 116 batteries and they initially moved to billets in Boulogne. The battery's first action occurred on 24th August, at Feignes, near Mons. The rest of August was spent moving south 130km to Soissons.

By mid-September the brigade had moved to Moulins, just 45km from the German border. The diary entry for every day to 5th October 1914, reads "Battle continues" with an occasional comment on counter attacks. The brigade remained in Moulins until 16th October when they were given orders to withdraw and be relieved by 32nd Regiment French Artillery. The 18th and 19th October were spent travelling by train to Saint-Omer.

18-pounder gun batteries in action.
Photo by David McLellan

The battery had little rest and within a week had moved to Ypres, arriving on 24th October 1914. They moved to billets at Halte, just outside Hooge, and were being held in reserve. The diary entry for 5th November records heavy bombardment of Ypres and the next day the 115th battery was in action.

---

[78] War Diary: 115 Battery 25 Brigade Royal Field Artillery. WO-95-1248-4. August 1914-April 1919. The National Archives (UK), Kew, England.

At 4pm on 7th November 1914 a heavy German attack was recorded, causing the French to fall back, with covering fire provided by the 113th and 115th batteries. The batteries then counter attacked and "resolved the situation." For the next fortnight the battery remained in action, until relief from the French on 19th November.

Edward was killed on 14th November 1914 and is commemorated on the Menin Gate Memorial to the Missing at Ypres. He is also remembered on Sittingbourne War Memorial and St Michael's Church WW1 Memorial Window.

Edward's mother and sister Olive received pay and gratuity. His mother would also have been sent his 1914 Star, Victory, and British War Medals.

Michael Day (Flickr CC BY-NC 2.0)

JENNER, Samuel

2502, Trooper, Household Battalion.

The middle of five children, Samuel was born on 27th June 1890, in Wouldham and was baptised in the parish church of All Saints, a month later on 27th July. His parents were James and Eliza Jane (née Durrant), and his siblings were Caroline Ellen, Edgar Henry (1888-1888), Eliza Jane, and Violet.

In 1911 the family were living in Aylesford, with Samuel employed as a waggoner on a farm and his father as a cement labourer.

On 1st June 1914, Samuel married Annie Capon at Aylesford. Samuel and Annie's daughter, Annie Violet May, was born on 30th December 1917. Sadly, Samuel did not live to see his daughter as he died two months before her birth.

Samuel's sisters married brothers of Annie, with Eliza marrying Walter Frederick Capon in 1911, and Violet marrying Robert John Capon in 1918. Both Walter and Robert were also cement labourers. It is probable they were employed by Peters Wouldham Hall Cement Works, as they resided in the Wouldham area.

Samuel was 5ft 7in tall when he enlisted at Sittingbourne on 15th November 1915. At that time, he was employed as a kilnsman at Smeed, Dean and Co. Ltd. Cement Works (pictured right). He arrived in France on 5th May 1917.

The War Diary of Samuel's battalion around his death reads:

Date	Summary of Events and Information	Remarks and References to Appendices
	WAR DIARY [79] *or* **INTELLIGENCE SUMMARY.** (Erase heading not required.)	Army Form C. 2118.
1 to 3-10-1917	Battalion at SOULT CAMP, working on the trenches and preparing kit for battle.	
4-10-1917	Moved to IRON CROSS, situated just to the west of LANGEMARK-POELKAPELLE.	
6-10-1917	Battalion returned to SOULT CAMP.	
8-10-1917	Moved to JOLIE FARM in preparation for attack on 9th.	
9-10-1917	5.20am - 12TH BRIGADE attacked area near BIRD HOUSE, south-east of LANGEMARK-POELKAPELLE. 9am - Battalion moved to support them. Under heavy fire. 9pm - Moved back to JOLIE FARM.	
10-10-1917	Battalion relieved 2ND ESSEX REGIMENT to the right of 12TH BRIGADE. 45 Casualties incurred from heavy barrage on POELKAPPELLE-SCHREIBOOM road. Relief proved specifically difficult, due to recent taking of the line and heavy artillery shelling.	
11-10-1917	No movement of troops.	
12-10-1917	50 casualties from heavy shelling.	
13-10-1917	CASUALTIES for 4th to 13th 4 Officers killed, 9 Wounded 65 Other Ranks Killed or Died of Wounds, 278 Wounded, 44 Missing, 7 Missing believed killed.	

Instructions regarding War Diaries and Intelligence Summaries are contained in F.S. Regs., Part II, and the Staff Manual respectively. Title pages will be prepared in manuscript.

An entry dated 28th October 1917 in Samuel's service record records him as "Missing believed Killed" on 12th October 1917.

It was not until 5th January 1918 that he was declared as "Killed in Action" on the 10th/11th October, and his wife Annie was officially notified on 10th January 1918. He is commemorated on the Tyne Cot Memorial to the Missing.

Samuel was awarded the Victory and British War Medals, and his pay and gratuity were paid to his wife Annie.

He is remembered locally on Sittingbourne War Memorial and St Michael's Church WW1 Memorial Window.

Samuel's nephew, Clarence Leslie, the son of his youngest sister Violet, died in the Second World War on 9th March 1943, aged 21. Clarence was serving on *MV Rosewood (London)*, in the Merchant

The East Kent Gazette

SATURDAY, OCTOBER 11, 1919

IN MEMORIAM

JENNER – In ever loving memory of our dearly beloved only son and brother, Tpr. Samuel Jenner, Household Batt., who was killed in action, October 11th, 1917.

To-day recalls sad memories
Of our loved one gone to rest.
We think of him, Talk of him, shed
many a silent tear.
Those who think of him to-day
Are those who loved him best.
From his loving Dad, Sisters, and Brothers-in-law.

[79] War Diary: Household Battalion. WO-95-1481-1. November 1916-February 1918. The National Archives (UK), Kew, England.

Navy. It was part of a convoy south of Iceland when the convoy was attacked by German submarine *U-409*. The *Rosewood* was hit by a torpedo and sunk with the loss of 42 crew. Clarence is commemorated on CWGC's Tower Hill Merchant Navy Memorial.

JULL, Edward George

G/47134, Private, 8th Battalion, Royal Fusiliers.

Edward was the first of eleven children born in Ickham in 1890, to John Edward and Eliza Emily (née Taylor). Sadly, John and Eliza lost seven of their children in infancy, their names were Lilian May (1894-1894), Daisy Emily (1896-1896), Walter Charles (1898-1899), Rose Eveline (1899-1900), Frederick John (1901-1901), William Hubert (1905-1905) and Ernest James (1906-1907). Their surviving children were Winifred Annie (1893-1911), Alfred Thomas (born 1897) and Arthur Henry (born 1903).

Edward was baptised in Ickham on 2nd April 1890 in the parish church of St John the Evangelist. By 1911 the family had moved to 33 Shakespeare Road, Sittingbourne, with both Edward and his father employed as general labourers.

He enlisted in Sittingbourne, joining the 9th Battalion, Royal Fusiliers, and arrived in France on 28th December 1916. Two weeks later, on 15th January 1917, he was posted to the 8th Battalion. The War Diary for the battalion during the period of Edward's death is transcribed here:

	WAR DIARY [80] or INTELLIGENCE SUMMARY. (Erase heading not required.)	Army Form C. 2118.
Instructions regarding War Diaries and Intelligence Summaries are contained in F.S. Regs., Part II, and the Staff Manual respectively. Title pages will be prepared in manuscript.		
Date	Summary of Events and Information	Remarks and References to Appendices
2-4-1917	Battalion at ARRAS providing working parties of 420 to the ROYAL ENGINEERS.	
3 to 8-4-1917	Moved into cellars, due to heavy shelling, in PETIT HALL, (which was the Town Hall.)	
9-4-1917	3am - Moved out of cellars and gathered east of ARRAS CEMETERY. 9TH ROYAL FUSILIERS on the right and 8/10TH GORDONS to the left.	
	Zero hour - Under cover of barrage, attack commenced on the BLUE LINE. Barrage very close and excellent. No casualties.	
	Attack advanced 1km to second objective, BLACK LINE. 10am line taken, 129 German prisoners.	
	11am - Battalion digging in and consolidating trenches.	
10-4-1917	Quiet Day. Consolidation of position.	
11-4-1917	Moved to MONCHY-LE-PREUX, to support 7TH ROYAL SUSSEX.	

---

[80] War Diary: 8 Battalion Royal Fusiliers. WO-95-1857-1. June 1915-February 1918. The National Archives (UK), Kew, England.

12-4-1917	*Battalion relieved and moved to RONVILLE CAVES (now known as the WELLINGTON CAVES).*
	Note – The caves beneath ARRAS were a series of 17th century cellars which were worked on to house 11,500 troops. These were further extended by the NEW ZEALAND TUNNELLING COMPANY and linking them, adding accommodation for 13,000 additional troops.

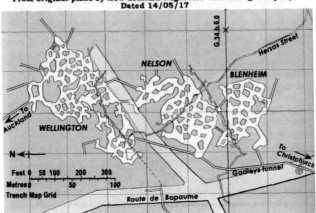

16-4-1917 to 25-4-1917	*Arrived at GRENAS after 30km march.* *Time spent cleaning, training and re-organising.* *Football match between the brigade officers and 11TH MIDDLESEX officers, resulting in a draw.*
26-4-1917 to 29-4-1917	*Battalion at FEUCHY. Working parties with the ROYAL ENGINEERS to consolidate the BROWN LINE.*
30-4-1917	*Relieved ROYAL BERKS on front line at MONCHY-LE-PREUX.* *(MONCHY-LE-PREUX had been held by the Germans since October 1914 before being taken during the battles earlier in the month. At the end of April, the British made an attempt to capture nearby RŒUX, as well as RIFLE and BAYONET TRENCHES, but were pushed back by heavy fire.*

Trench advance - Reproduced with the permission of the National Library of Scotland

1-5-1917	*British and German artillery very active. Germans laying down heavy barrage between 5pm and 8pm.*
	Battalion was now in trenches alongside RIVER SCARPE preparing to attack.
3-5-1917	*3.45am - Battalion moved towards SCABBARD TRENCH, under machine gun fire from RŒUX. Small proportion managed to get into the trench and bombing the enemy. Reinforcements arrived and successfully pushed enemy down the trench line. Battalion successfully attacked and captured BAYONET and RIFLE TRENCHES.*
	CASUALTIES
	42 killed, 147 wounded, 93 missing

This period of action in and around Arras became known as The First Battle of Scarpe.

On 3rd May 1917 one of those killed was Edward, who died of wounds, aged 27. Edward's Medal Index Card records that he was attached to the Royal Engineers, as part of a working party from 12th March 1917 until his death, though the Commonwealth War Graves Commission records that he was with his battalion.

Edward was buried in the Duisans British Cemetery, Etrun, France, which is near Nord-Pas-de-Calais. The site of the cemetery, designed by Sir Reginald Blomfield, was chosen for the 8th Casualty Clearing Station in February 1917.

The cemetery is the final resting place for 3,206 Commonwealth servicemen. The first line of the Bible's Psalm 33-12 is inscribed upon Edward's headstone, "BLESSED IS THE NATION WHOSE GOD IS THE LORD."

Locally, Edward is remembered on Sittingbourne War Memorial and St Michael's Church WW1 Memorial Window. He was awarded the Victory and British War Medals.

KEANE, Roland John

28830, Serjeant, 16th Brigade Ammunition Column, Royal Garrison Artillery.

Roland was born on Spike Island in County Cork, Ireland, in 1894, the son of James and Emily (née Lambert). Roland's father was a career soldier having enlisted in 1887 with the Royal Artillery, aged 22. Where his siblings were born, reflects the fact that the family moved often. Roland was the second of five children, and his siblings were Leonard Lambert Keane (b. 1892 Isle of Wight), Sherelye Moore (b. 1898 Bengal, India), Dudley Wilfred (b. 1901 Pembroke, Wales), and Reginald Thomas (b. 1904 Sheppey).

Roland's father died in 1905 in Hampshire and two years later his mother married George Walter Curtis in Sheppey, where Roland's stepsister, Olive Lambert Keane Curtis was born in 1908. Sadly,

Emily was again widowed in 1910, and by 1911 she was living at 33 Frederick Street, Milton Regis with her two youngest sons and daughter Olive, and employed as a general shop keeper. Roland was living in Blue Town when he enlisted at Sheerness.

Roland's Brigade's War Diary[81] records that they took command of a number of Heavy Battery units on 4th May 1916 at Englebelmer, France, which is halfway between Amiens and Arras. Each day's entry recorded the time each battery engaged and the activity, with occasional details on the actual location targeted and hostile artillery action. Every day was recorded, and the artillery activity looked relentless.

Roland died of wounds, aged 22, on 6th July 1916, though details of which battery he was assigned to are undocumented, nor are the details of when and where he was wounded. The diary for 5th July noted that 25 Heavy Battery (HB) had received hostile artillery.

The diary entry for 6th July 1916 recorded:

13th day of operations

(previous day's entry was : 4th Army + Reserve Army between River Somme and Serre)

12 noon 6/7/16 to 12 noon on 7/7/16

<u>*19 HB*</u> *– Engaged 11 enemy batteries on orders from Group – 176 rounds – support to X Corps operation*

<u>*25 HB*</u> *-   8 enemy batteries   "   "   130 rounds   "   "*

<u>*139 HB*</u> *-   7 enemy batteries   "   "   100 rounds   "   "*

<u>*1/1 Welsh HB*</u> *-   11 enemy batteries   "   "   20 rounds   "   "*

<u>*1/1 Highland*</u> *-   10 enemy batteries   "   "   134 rounds   "   "*

+ shelled 1 enemy Op

<u>*60 S.B*</u> *– Cross roads in L.33C (MIRAUMONT area) – 3 rounds*

<u>*Hostile Artillery*</u> *– Howitzers active on first line in trenches, and on Q3 c+b (AUCHONVILLERS area), and throughout afternoon and evening – much activity at THIEPVAL – with lachrymatory shell (tear gas) Shell trenches between SERRE and BEAUMONT HAMEL.*

Otherwise, a quiet day on the front.

The East Kent Gazette

SATURDAY, JULY 5, 1919

IN MEMORIAM

KEANE – In ever loving memory of Roland John Keane (Rollie), Sgt. R.G.A., who was killed in action, July 6th 1916.

Three years have passed since heaven gained

One of the finest earth contained.

From Mother, Brothers and Sisters

Roland was buried in Étaples Military Cemetery, France. Étaples was the site for 16 hospitals and therefore it is probable that he died in one of these. His headstone is inscribed "IN SACRED MEMORY."

Locally he is remembered on Sittingbourne War Memorial, Sittingbourne WW1 Church Memorial and Milton Regis War Memorial.

His mother received his pay and gratuity and would have been sent his Victory and British War Medals.

This reproduction of the East Kent Gazette shows the family's feelings for Roland.

---

[81] War Diary: Army Troops. 16 Brigade Royal Garrison Artillery. WO-95-216-6. January 1916-August 1916. The National Archives (UK), Kew, England.

Battery of British 6-inch 26 cwt howitzers firing

Roland was part of an Ammunition Column for the Royal Garrison Artillery, which was a key component of a Siege Battery, comprising of four 6-inch Howitzers. The Howitzers were capable of firing a 100 pound (45kg) to a maximum range of 6,000 yards (5,500 metres). The battery was one of four, which together formed a Brigade[82].

The table below shows the structure of a typical Siege Battery.

	Personnel		Horses			Transport		
	Officers	Other Ranks	Riding	Draught	Heavy-Draught	1 Horse Cart	2 Horse Cart	4 Horse Wagon
Battery (x4)	5	177	17	6	80	-	3	10
Ammunition Column	3	104	113	2	72	-	1	16
Brigade HQ	7	137	21	5	72	1	2	16

Note: Ammunition Column - Each non-ridden horse carried eight 18-pounder artillery shells.

82 War Office: *Field Service Book*. 1914. London: printed by Harrison & Sons under His Majesty's Stationery Office authority.

The district of Swale's recorded loss from WW1 was just over 3,000. The Kemsley family suffered the greatest individual loss, with all three sons of the family losing their lives during the war. All three brothers are commemorated on the Avenue.

George, William, and Arthur

The Kemsley family was headed by George, who was born in 1846 in Bredgar and married Agnes Eliza Milgate, from Eastling, in Faversham in 1874. Shortly after marrying they moved to Sittingbourne, and in 1881 they were living at Bassett Road, with their first three girls, Ellen (Nellie) Grace (born 1875), Agnes Eliza (born 1877), and Minnie Gertrude (born 1879).

By 1891 George had become employed by the council as a gardener and caretaker of Sittingbourne Cemetery and living in the lodge (below) at the entrance to the cemetery in Bell Road. The family by then had increased to seven children, with George (born 1882), Lily Ethel (born 1884), William Edward (born 1886), and Arthur Harold (born 1888).

Their last child, Catherine May, was born in early 1892. Though shortly after, the family suffered its first tragedy, with her death on 13th February 1892. Sadly, just five short days after Catherine's death, their eldest child, Ellen, also died, aged 16.

The next tragedy to hit the family was eight years later when the boys' mother Agnes died in 1900, aged 52. Their father George continued caring for Sittingbourne Cemetery, rising to Superintendent, until his death on 5th February 1928, aged 82.

George and Agnes' first-born son, 32-year-old George, was the first to lose his life in the war, in Gallipoli, on 3rd May 1915. The second son, 32-year-old William was next on 6th October 1918, in France, and just seven weeks later, the day after Armistice, on 12th November 1918, Arthur lost his life in Germany.

The family lived next door to another Avenue man, 24-year-old Frank Pankhurst who died in France on 22nd September 1918 (see page 224). The Pankhursts were recorded as living at Little Glovers Cottage in the 1891, 1901, and 1911 censuses.

KEMSLEY, Arthur Harold

18933, Private, 6th Battalion, Queen's Own (Royal West Kent Regiment).

Arthur was born in Sittingbourne in 1888. He worked for the East Kent Gazette as a printer, before moving to Northampton to work for the *Chronicle*. He married Eliza Brown Tompkins, known as Elsie, on 11th May 1913 in Aylesbury, Buckinghamshire. On 3rd October 1913 that year their first daughter, Elsie Lauretta Grace was born, followed by Arthur George on 21st February 1915.

When Arthur enlisted in Northampton on 15th November 1915, he was living at 33 St Pauls Road, Northampton. He served as a Private in the 6th Battalion of the Queen's Own Royal West Kent Regiment and went to France on 11th October 1916.

At the beginning of November 1917 his battalion's War Diary[83] shows they were positioned at Noeux, just south of Béthune, France. They remained there until the 16th when they travelled by train to Heudicourt, 70km to the south. Three days later they assembled at Gonnelieu with the support of creeping artillery and in conjunction with tanks, on 20th November, they attacked Latteau Wood and Le Quennet Farm. These were classed as extremely important positions and the enemy were taken completely by surprise. This initial advance was a success, with many prisoners being captured, together with a 5.6inch Howitzer and several machine guns.

For the next week the battalion consolidated its position in Latteau Wood (pictured left), despite German artillery action each day. Through the night of 29th November 1917, the enemy artillery fire continued, until at 7am the following day an enemy barrage began, which lasted for 45 minutes, before the Germans attacked.

Arthur's battalion was forced to retire to Gouzeaucourt, where they continued to fight, until the few who remained were forced to withdraw to the Hindenburg Line. Arthur was reported as missing in action on 30th November 1917, but it was not until February 1918 that it was known that he was a prisoner of war.

He was taken to Germany where he wrote to his wife from Altdamm Camp, now in Poland. By 1918 there were thousands of prisoners there, including nearly 2,000 British soldiers. Many, including Arthur, worked on farms in the area. Even before the Armistice in November 1918 many Prisoners of War had been sent back to England, but Arthur did not return.

---

[83] War Diary: 6 Battalion Queen's Own (Royal West Kent Regiment). WO-95-1861-5. July 1917-December 1917. The National Archives (UK), Kew, England.

In early 1919 Arthur's widow, Eliza, wrote to enquire about him:

Sir

In reply to your letter, I regret to say my Husband, 18933 Private A.H. Kemsley. 6th. Royal West Kents has not yet reached home.

I am getting very worried about him the last letter I received from him left Altdamm Camp (Pomerania, now in Poland) Nov. 9. 1918. He was there working many miles in the Country. He was the only Englishman in the district, I think he must be over looked.

Will you kindly do what you can for me getting news of him.

Will enclose the name of the farmer & farm which has been sent to me by an Ex-prisoner of War who was once working on the same farm with him.

Yours respectfully

E. Kemsley

In fact, Arthur had contracted Spanish influenza and died, aged 29, on 12th November 1918, at the camp and was buried there. He was moved to his final resting place in Berlin South-Western Cemetery, as the cemetery was chosen, as one of four, to be the final resting place for all those who were buried across Germany. In 1924-25 graves from 146 burial grounds were moved, to include 1,176 servicemen. It is understood that Arthur was brought from Altdamm Prisoners of War Cemetery with 45 others.

His headstone is inscribed with the words "AT THE GOING DOWN OF THE SUN AND IN THE MORNING WE REMEMBER HIM" which is taken from the poem For the Fallen, written by Robert Laurence Binyon (see page 319). The line is from the fourth stanza, which has been adopted by the British Royal Legion as an Exhortation for Remembrance ceremonies. The stanza reads:

> They shall grow not old, as we that are left grow old:
> Age shall not weary them, nor the years condemn.
> At the going down of the sun and in the morning
> We will remember them.

Arthur, like his older brothers, George, and William, was awarded the Victory and British War Medals. He too, is remembered on Sittingbourne War Memorial and the Baptist Church Memorial.

The memorial in the Baptist Church, a marble table on which 34 names are inscribed, was unveiled on 3rd December 1919. According to a report in 6th December 1919 edition of the East Kent Gazette it was an:

"IMPRESSIVE SERVICE". The evening service was completed in front of a large congregation and the communion table was adorned with a bowl of white chrysanthemums. The service was conducted by the Reverend John Doubleday, where he read out the 34 names, including those of his own son, George (see page 116).

The unveiling was made by the pulling of a cord to remove the Union Jack that covered the memorial. That honour was given to George Kemsley, father of the three brothers. As he revealed the memorial he said, "In the name of Almighty God, and in the honour of our fallen boys, I now unveil this tablet."

KEMSLEY, George

628, Private, 13th Battalion, Australian Infantry, Australian Imperial Force.

George emigrated to Australia before the war, where he worked as a draper. He enlisted in Roseberry Park, New South Wales, on 14th September 1914, and served as a Private in the Australian Infantry. His records show he was 29 years and one month old when he joined up, and 5ft, 9in tall, with dark eyes and light brown hair.

He sailed from Melbourne in the December of 1914, joining the Mediterranean Expeditionary Force in Gallipoli on 12th April 1915, just three weeks later, on 3rd May, he was reported wounded and missing.

His battalion's War Diary[84] records that the battalion left Alexandria, Egypt on HMT *Derfflinger* on 4th April 1915, arriving at the Greek island of Limnos four days later. They remained on Limnos until 24th April, when they then embarked for Gallipoli, arriving at 4am the next day. They were immediately under enemy fire, from trenches on the steep headland, and by nightfall the battalions had taken some of the trenches. The diary entry ended the day saying, "Altogether the day's battle was in favour of the Allies."

The diary records that the battalion was involved in battle every day, until 28th April 1915 when they were relieved by the Royal Marines Light Infantry, and they moved to the beach, where they were housed in bivouacs. On 1st May, the battalion returned to the trenches, to find they were in a bad state and open to enemy fire, so they spent the initial time digging temporary trenches. The diary entry for the 2nd May began "The day was one of extreme quietness as compared to previous experiences" and added that a night attack was suspected, which occurred at 7pm and was repelled.

---

[84] Australian War Memorial. Collection: Australian Imperial Force unit war diaries, 1914-1918, AWM4 Subclass 23/20-3rd Infantry Battalion, AWM4 23/20/2-April 1915.

The next day, 3rd May 1915, the battalion was subjected to heavy shrapnel fire throughout the day. The diary recorded eight men killed and 14 wounded. The 4th May was recorded, once again, as extremely quiet.

The records show that George's father had been informed by his Commanding Officer that George had been wounded and sent back to Australia. As a result, George's father wrote, on 25th October 1915, to No. 5 Australian Hospital enquiring after George. He said: 'I should be greatly obliged for any news of him. If you cannot send me any, would you be kind enough to hand this letter on to anybody who could send me news.' A reply was sent on 11th December 1915, saying that he was now listed as 'wounded and missing' and no further information was available. The response concluded that a soldier from the same battalion, in the hospital, had no knowledge of George.

A Court of Inquiry[85] was held on 28th April 1918 at Serapeum, Egypt, which officially declared George as Killed in Action on 3rd May 1915. The court was informed that orders were made at 4pm, on 3rd May 1915, for the troops to retire from their position, which they carried out between 8pm and 9pm. Before the retirement a search was made for all the wounded to ensure none were left behind, and for this reason it was stated that it was extremely unlikely that George and another soldier had been left behind or were prisoners. The other soldier referred to was named as 21-year-old Lieutenant Francis Horatio Faddy, from Sydney.

George's personal effects were sent to his father, and consisted of his Bible, a letter, and a purse.

George and Francis Faddy are commemorated on the Lone Pine Memorial, Turkey (pictured right). The memorial overlooks the front line as it was in May 1917 and stands on the site of the fiercest fighting. It commemorates over 4,900 Australian and New Zealand casualties.

Locally, George is remembered on Sittingbourne War Memorial and the Baptist Church Memorial.

Credit: New Zealand War Graves Project

85 Service Record. KEMSLEY George : Service Number – 628. Series B2455. Item 7363445. National Archives of Australia.

196

William was born in 1886 and baptised at St Michael's Church on 2nd May 1886. On 30th September 1912 he married Grace Lilian Fulher at her home parish church, St Philip and St James, Upnor. At the time of his marriage William was employed by the town council in Abertillery, Monmouthshire. Prior to enlisting he was employed as a gardener at Bourneville Park, Birmingham, which was created and owned by the Cadbury family.

William enlisted in Birmingham and joined the Worcestershire Regiment. In mid-September 1918 his battalion's War Diary[86] records that they were stationed at Agenvillers, 90km south of Calais. The next two weeks was spent training and moving east, until on 4th October they arrived at Quennemont Farm, near the village of Bony, 145km away. The next day, at 6pm, they attacked the town of Beaurevoir. Although under a heavy barrage and machine gun fire they captured the village.

The diary entry for 6th October 1918 read "Battalion held outskirts of BEAUREVOIR." The following day they were replaced and moved to Ponchaux. On the 8th they continued to advance to Honnechy and on the 11th they were relieved.

William is recorded as dying of wounds at No. 55 Casualty Clearing Station, based at Doingt, on 6th October 1918, where it had been since moving there on 17th September 1918. He was buried, aged 32, in Doingt Communal Cemetery Extension, with his headstone inscribed "FOR EVER WITH THE LORD."

Doingt was completely destroyed in the war and was in German hands until 5th September 1918, when the 5th Australian Division captured it. It then became home to Nos. 20, 41 and 55 Casualty Clearing Stations.

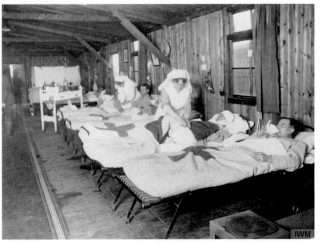

William's death was announced in the East Kent Gazette edition dated 26th October 1918. William is remembered on Sittingbourne War Memorial and the Baptist Church Memorial. He was awarded the Victory and British War Medals.

A ward of the 2nd Australian Casualty Clearing Station at Steenwerke, November 1917. IWM EAUS4623

[86] War Diary: 1/8 Battalion Worcestershire Regiment. WO-95-2251-2. September 1918-February 1919. The National Archives (UK), Kew, England.

KIDSON, Charles Wilfred

Lieutenant, 5th Battalion (attached to 2nd Battalion), Royal Dublin Fusiliers.

Credit: Queens College
Cambridge

Charles was born in Upper Norwood, Surrey, on 16th January 1894, and was baptised at the parish church of All Saints with St Margaret on 28th March 1894, by his own father, who was curate at the time. The Reverend Joseph Charles Eyre Kidson and his wife Annie Marian (née Hinnell) had five children, of which Charles was the fourth. The other children were Gladys Muriel, Ernest Jack, Frank Victor, and Edith Marian (who was awarded an MBE in 1920, for her role as Honorary Secretary of the Sittingbourne and Milton Regis District War Hospitals Supply Depot, which supplied dressings, blankets, and other essential supplies to the local war hospitals).

The Reverend Kidson was appointed the vicar of Holy Trinity Church, Sittingbourne, in 1904 and served until 1924. Charles attended Britain's oldest public school in Canterbury, King's School (pictured below), from September 1907 to July 1913, being granted a Junior Scholarship in December 1907. Three years later, he gained a Senior Scholarship in July 1910. Whilst there he was the editor of the school magazine, Cantuarian, from September 1911, and in the same year served on the committee of the Harvey Society.

In September 1912 he became the Captain of the School, a sports committee member, and President of the Debating Society, and was also promoted to Sergeant in the Officer Training Corps.

Credit: Kings
School, Canterbury

In January the following year he attained the rank of Officer Cadet, later he was awarded his first XI Cricket Colours, and in the August, Charles earned entry to Cambridge's Queens' College, through an Open Classical Scholarship.

Kind permission of © King's School, Canterbury

At Cambridge he joined the Cambridge University Officer Training Corps, as a Private. On 15th September 1914 he enlisted at Maidstone, joining the Royal Fusiliers (Public Schools Battalion). At that time, he was just over six feet tall, with a sallow complexion, brown hair, and brown eyes. He was posted for training to Woodcote Camp at Epsom. Within five months he had been promoted twice, to Lance Corporal on 8th December 1914 and to Corporal on 27th January 1915.

On 4th May 1915 Charles applied for a commission in the 5th (Extra Reserve) Battalion of the Royal Dublin Fusiliers (Special Reserve of Officers), after reverting to the rank of Private a week earlier on 30th April. By the end of May he gained his commission as a Second Lieutenant in the 5th Battalion of the Royal Dublin Fusiliers and joined them at Glengorse Camp, Milton Bridge in Midlothian. On 31st October 1916 he joined the 1st Battalion in the field in Corbie, France.

Charles' battalion's War Diary[87] records that on 19th April 1917, they were serving on the firing line in the village of Monchy. At that time, it was extremely dangerous to move about above ground because there were an extraordinary number of dead cavalry horses and men in the streets which were impossible to bury. That day, Charles and six soldiers were wounded during the heavy shelling.

Charles was evacuated and admitted to No. 14 General Hospital in Boulogne, before being transferred, via the hospital ship *Princess Elizabeth* (pictured above) to Dover, and onto No. 1 War Hospital in Reading. On 8th May 1917 the little finger on his left hand was amputated, causing much inconvenience to him, as he was left-handed.

Charles was posted to the 5th Battalion on 19th July 1917 at Curragh, County Kildare, where the following week on the 27th, he was declared fit by the medical board. On his return to France, he was attached to the 2nd Battalion.

On 1st October 1917 he was with the battalion, at Nurlu, France, where they were awaiting orders. The next few days were spent sending patrols out to the Hindenburg Line and an attack on Malincourt. By 7th October the battalion had marched to La Pannerie, then, travelling by bus and marching, they arrived in Honnechy, on the 12th. The battalion then prepared their kit and supplies to relieve the 2nd Battalion Munster Fusiliers on 16th October and attack the River Selle in Saint-Benin.

At 5.20am on 17th October 1918 the allied bombardment started and at 6.30am, in heavy fog and machine gun fire, they crossed the Selle river by bridge. Charles was killed in action whilst leading his company across the river, to rush a machine gun nest. He was buried where he fell then later his body was re-interred in Highland Cemetery, Le Cateau in France, with his headstone inscribed "A FAITHFUL SOLDIER OF THE CROSS & OF HIS COUNTRY."

His father received a telegram dated 26th October 1918, informing him of his son's death:

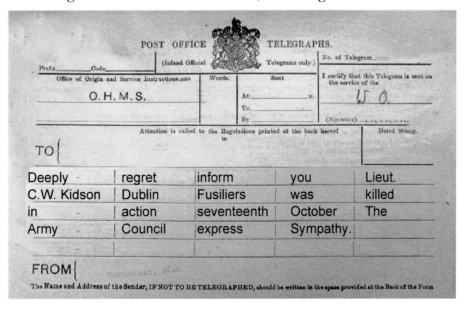

---

87 War Diary: 1 Battalion Royal Dublin Fusiliers. WO-95-2301-1. March 1916-September 1917. The National Archives (UK), Kew, England.

Charles' Commanding Officer wrote of him, 'He was a splendid officer, absolutely fearless; his men loved him, he always took such a keen interest in their welfare.'

His Captain wrote, 'He was invaluable to me, and volunteered for everything.' A Chaplain said he was, 'one of the most God-fearing, noble and sweet characters that I shall ever meet in the world ...His character and life will ever be an inspiration to me.'

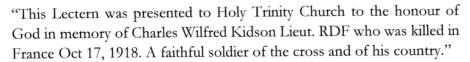

Charles is remembered on Sittingbourne War Memorial, Sittingbourne Holy Trinity Church, King's School Undercroft (pictured left), and Queen's College Cambridge Chapel. There is a Golden Eagle lectern dedicated to him in Holy Trinity Church, inscribed:

"This Lectern was presented to Holy Trinity Church to the honour of God in memory of Charles Wilfred Kidson Lieut. RDF who was killed in France Oct 17, 1918. A faithful soldier of the cross and of his country."

KNIGHT, Bertie John

915562, Gunner, "D" Battery, 62nd Brigade, Royal Field Artillery.

Bertie was born in Frindsbury on 16th February 1893 and baptised in the parish church, All Saints, on 7th May 1893. He was the second youngest child of Henry Richard, a cement miller, and Mary Ann (née Mitchell). His siblings were Mary Elizabeth Knight Mitchell, Edith Maria Mitchell, William Henry, Albert James (1884-1884), Henry Richard, George Ernest, Rosa, and Lilian Alice. His parents were both born in Sussex and by 1881 had moved to Northfleet, then in 1911 they were living in Frindsbury.

Bertie and his brother, William, were both employed at the Smeed Dean Cement Works in Sittingbourne, with Bertie working as a cooper's labourer. By 1918 the family were living in Sittingbourne at 55 Shakespeare Road.

Bertie enlisted in Sittingbourne in early 1915 and went to France in March 1916. His brigade was attached to the Royal Naval Division and took part in the fighting in Ancre, Arras and Vimy. In late 1917, during the fighting at Passchendaele, he was injured by shrapnel in the left shoulder and was transferred to Catterick Military Hospital, arriving on 3rd December 1917 and was discharged seven weeks later on 15th January 1918, when he returned to his unit in France.

A few months later Bertie was fatally injured and the brigade War Diary for the period when he was injured is transcribed here:

Instructions regarding War Diaries and Intelligence Summaries are contained in F.S. Regs., Part II, and the Staff Manual respectively. Title pages will be prepared in manuscript.	**WAR DIARY** [88] or **INTELLIGENCE SUMMARY.** (Erase heading not required.)	Army Form C. 2118.
Date	Summary of Events and Information	Remarks and References to Appendices
16-9-1918	Brigade arrived in HEUDICOURT.	
17-9-1918	Wagon Line areas heavily bombed, continued nightly up to the end of the month.	
18-9-1918	Brigade supported successful attack on CHAPEL HILL and GAUCHE WOOD. Many prisoners taken and guns captured.	
21-9-1918	Provided creeping barrage in support of 33RD DIVISION.	
23-9-1918	Brigade moved 2,000 feet south-east.	
24-9-1918	Carried out harassing fire.	
25-9-1918	Constant demand supporting local trench fighting.	
26-9-1918	Brigade used four captured German 77mm guns and shells on the enemy.	
27-9-1918	400 77mm mustard gas shells were fired into enemy lines.	
29-9-1918	Batteries heavily engaged in attack on VILLERS-GUISLAIN.	

On 28th September 1918 Bertie's gun burst, and he lost both legs. He was transferred to No. 4 General Hospital in Camiers. The diary does not record this incident.

Bertie's brother CSM Knight, The Buffs, managed to visit him, and said later that Bertie had spoken of home in a cheerful manner, but soon after septic poisoning set in.

After his mother was informed by telegram, she then travelled to France and managed to be by his side, with his brother, when he died, aged 25, on 23rd October 1918.

Bertie was buried the next day, in the presence of his mother and brother in Étaples Military Cemetery, and his mother returned later the same day. Bertie's headstone carries the words "HE PUT DUTY BEFORE LIFE ITSELF."

On reporting his death, the East Kent Gazette dated 16th November 1918, mentioned that he took part in the fighting on the Ancre, Arras and Vimy. Bertie is remembered on Sittingbourne War Memorial and St Michael's Church WW1 Memorial Window. His mother received his pay and gratuity, as well as his Victory and British War Medals.

---

[88] War Diary: 162 Brigade Royal Field Artillery. WO-95-2413-4. December 1915-June 1919. The National Archives (UK), Kew, England.

The East Kent Gazette

SATURDAY, OCTOBER 25, 1919

IN MEMORIAM

KNIGHT – In ever loving memory of our son and brother Bertie John Knight, R.F.A., who died of wounds in France, on October 23rd, 1918, aged 25 years.

One year has passed,
Our hearts still sore,
As time rolls on we miss him more;
Days of sadness still come ov'er us,
Although it is a year ago.
We often sit and think of him
when we are all alone,
For memory is the only friend
That grief can call its own.
Sad and sudden was the call,
Of him so dearly loved by all.
From his loving Mother, Father & Sister Lily.

The East Kent Gazette

SATURDAY, OCTOBER 25, 1919

IN MEMORIAM

KNIGHT – In ever loving memory of our dear brother Gunner B. J. Knight, R.F.A., died of wounds in France, on October 23rd, 1918.

We often sit and think of him,
And think how brave he died,
And, oh! how very hard to think,
We could not say "Good-bye."
From his loving Brother and Sister (Bill and Hilda), and little Niece Ivy.
There is a link death cannot sever,
Love and Remembrance last for ever.
Rest in Peace.
From his loving Brother and Sister, Henry, and Emily.

LONGFIELD, George Frederick William

260265, Corporal, 1st/6th Battalion, Royal Warwickshire Regiment.

George was born in Sittingbourne in 1896, the son of George Banks, a journeyman baker, and Elizabeth Jane (née Lockyer). He had an older brother, Henry George Banks, and younger sister Daisy Rose Mary. In 1911 the family were living at 49 East Street; George was working as a house boy and his brother was a journeyman baker. By 1917 the family had moved to St Michael's School House.

George's brother served with the Royal West Surrey Regiment in India from March to June 1917 and the Rifle Brigade until being demobilised in May 1919.

George joined the Buffs Territorials in November 1914, then in September 1917 he was drafted to the Royal Warwickshire Regiment. His battalion spent the 1st to 17th September 1917 training in Sint-Jan-ter-Biezen, Belgium, 4km west of Poperinge, before travelling by train 58km west to Louches, France. On the 30th, they returned east to Vlamertinge, between Poperinge and Ypres.

On 3rd October 1917, his battalion's War Diary[89] records that they had moved to the trenches and relieved the 4th Oxford-Bucks Light Infantry. The following day they successfully attacked the area

---

[89] War Diary: 1/6 Battalion Royal Warwickshire Regiment. WO-95-2755-2. March 1915-October 1917. The National Archives (UK), Kew, England.

around Vacher Farm, though they did not manage to take the farm. During the attack they captured 350 Germans, ten machine guns and two anti-tank guns.

The 5th October entry read "Held the line." That was the day George was wounded in the stomach. Sadly, he died a few hours later at a casualty clearing station, just three weeks after he first served abroad and his 21st birthday. He was buried in the Dozinghem Military Cemetery with "HE GAVE HIS LIFE TO SAVE OTHERS" adorning his headstone.

The East Kent Gazette

SATURDAY, OCTOBER 5, 1918

IN MEMORIAM

LONGFIELD - In loving memory of our dear son, Corpl. George Longfield, who died of wounds in France, Oct. 6th, 1917, aged 21 years.

If we could have clasped his dying hand,
And heard his last farewell;
It would not have been so hard to part,
With one we loved so well.
From Mum, Dad, Sister, and Brother.

Locally, George is remembered on Sittingbourne War Memorial and St Michael's Church WW1 Memorial Window, He is also Remembered by Milton Regis on their War Memorial, St Paul's Church Memorial, and the Old Boys Milton Council Schools Memorial. His pay and gratuity were paid to his mother.

The East Kent Gazette dated 20th October 1917, reported George's death. A year later they printed a poignant "In Memoriam".

The East Kent Gazette edition 24th June 1955, under the heading "SOLE SURVIVOR" reported that George's father, then 89 years old, was believed to be the sole survivor of the Nil Desperandum Football Club, which formed the embryo of Sittingbourne Football Club.

LUCIA, William Benjamin

269277, Chief Engine Room Artificer 2nd Class. Royal Navy, HMS Queen Mary.

William was born in Sittingbourne on 23rd December 1873, the son of Arthur and Dinah (née Willson). He was their second child, and his siblings were Arthur (1871-1885), Thomas, Frederick, Carry Althea, and Sidney Willson (1889-1916). In 1911 the family were living at 13 Dover Street; his father Arthur was employed as a master engineer and his brothers Frederick and Sidney were general engineers.

As a child, William attended the Wesleyan Day School and in January 1885, he won a certificate in freehand drawing at the annual drawing examination. After he left school, he worked as a fitter for Messrs Chittenden and Knight's Engineering Yard at Crescent Street, Sittingbourne.

He joined the Navy on 18th January 1898 for 12 years and then extended his service for the full 22-year term. His service record shows that he served on over 25 ships before the start of the war. On 14th January 1901 he married Winifred Mary Padfield in Portsmouth, where they made their home. On 31st May 1916, aged 43, William was killed whilst serving on the battlecruiser *HMS Queen Mary* (pictured right). She was part of the British fleet sent to intercept the German Navy and took part in the Battle of Jutland. At 3.50pm the *Queen Mary* opened fire on SMS *Seydlitz*

and scored two hits disabling one of her turrets. At 4.15pm *HMS Lion* came under intense fire, with the resulting smoke obscuring *HMS Princess Royal*. This forced *SMS Derfflinger* to target the *Queen Mary*.

At 4.26pm, the *Queen Mary's* forward magazine was hit and detonated by *Derfflinger*. This caused the ship to break in two at the foremast, and as the aft section of the ship began to roll, a large explosion occurred and sank the *Queen Mary*. Of her 1,286 crew, only 20 were rescued. The battle itself was seen as a British strategic victory, despite the loss of the *Queen Mary* and *HMS Indefatigable*.

William is remembered on the Portsmouth Naval Memorial (pictured left), the Sittingbourne War Memorial and Sittingbourne Holy Trinity Church WW1 Memorial.

His death was reported in the 8th July 1916 edition of the East Kent Gazette, and the 19th August edition carried a vivid first-hand account of the battle, given by a local man serving on another ship.

William's brother Frederick was an engine room artificer and was serving somewhere in the North Sea. Frederick's service record shows he was at *HMS Pembroke II*, a Royal Naval Air Station at Eastchurch on the Isle of Sheppey, just a few miles away, and he survived the war.

William's youngest brother Sidney died on 30th November 1916 at Charing Cross Hospital, London. He had been employed as an electrician in Chatham Dockyard. The East Kent Gazette, of 9th December 1916, reported that he had been working on submarines, in confined spaces, which affected his health. He had visited the doctor, who diagnosed pernicious anaemia. He saw a specialist two weeks before his death and was admitted to the hospital, where he died from exhaustion and heart failure.

The LUCKHURST Brothers

The Luckhurst brothers, Clarence, and William, both served as Stoker 1st Class in the Royal Navy, on *HMS Vanguard* (pictured left), which had been involved in the Battle of Jutland (see previous story).

The year after Jutland their ship was at Scapa Flow, Scotland, and the morning of 9th July 1917 was spent exercising and practising abandoning ship, with the captain making a speech stating that under present conditions a ship could blow up in a matter of seconds or take several hours to sink. Tragically, a few short hours later at 11.20pm his words came true, when a detonation occurred.

There was no time for the crew to abandon ship as it sank instantly with the loss of 843 crew and only three survivors.

A Board of Inquiry heard there was a small explosion, followed by two larger explosions. The Board concluded the cause of the explosion was unclear, and it was the result of a detonation of cordite charges.

The 21st July 1917 edition of the East Kent Gazette reported on their deaths. The report mentioned that both Clarence and William had on the night before the explosion, said they were looking forward to leave in August. The report added that they had both worked for Messrs Wills and Packham Ltd.

Albert John headed the Luckhurst family, a brickmaker, and Celia (née Monk). In 1911 they were living in Church Road, Brents, Faversham. They had eight children, Rhoda (1893-1893), Albert Henry John, Clarence Victor, William, Celia Victoria (1900-1919), Walter, Constance May, and Stanley Edward.

LUCKHURST, Clarence Victor

K/23208, Stoker 1st Class, Royal Navy, HMS Vanguard.

Clarence was born in Faversham in the spring of 1897 and baptised on 7th April 1897 in the church of St Mary of Charity. When he enlisted, on 24th September 1914, he was 5ft 7in tall with dark hair and blue eyes, and he had been working as a brickmaker. Although he was 17 years old, he added a year to his age, as he gave his date of birth as 13th March 1896. After training he was posted to *HMS Vanguard* on 23rd January 1915, when she was mainly patrolling the North Sea.

On 31st May 1916, *Vanguard* joined in the Battle of Jutland. She was the eighteenth ship in the battle line and at 6.32pm she fired at the cruiser SMS *Wiesbaden*, scoring several hits. At 7.20pm she engaged with several destroyers, without result. Poor visibility stopped her firing, and she is recorded as firing 65 high-explosive and 15 12-inch shells, and ten shells from her four-inch guns.

Clarence is remembered on Chatham Naval Memorial, Sittingbourne War Memorial and St Michael's Church WW1 Memorial Window. He was awarded the 1914 Star, and Victory, and British War Medals.

LUCKHURST, William

K/28536, Stoker 1st Class, Royal Navy, HMS Vanguard.

William was born in Faversham on 12th July 1898 and baptised in the parish church on 29th July 1898. Like his brother, William lied about his age when he enlisted on 27th October 1915, by adding a year to his date of birth, so he was actually underage at 17. He was 5ft 11in tall and had dark brown hair and eyes, and he had been working as a cement labourer. After his training he served on the depot ship *HMS Gibraltar* from 31st January 1916 to 5th June 1916, before returning to training at Pembroke II.

He was then posted to *Vanguard* on 24th July 1916 (after the Battle of Jutland) until 13th March 1917 when he returned to *Pembroke II*. A week later, on 22nd March 1917, he returned to *Vanguard*, where he died three days before his 20th birthday.

William is remembered on the Chatham Naval Memorial, Sittingbourne War Memorial, and St Michael's Church WW1 Memorial Window. He was awarded the Victory and British War Medals.

Clarence and William's brother, Albert, also joined the Royal Navy as a Stoker 1st Class, on 29th November 1915, and like them added a year to his age. Albert served for the rest of the war until his discharge on 4th March 1919. For the first eighteen months he served on the depot ships *Gibraltar* and *Dido*, before being based at *Attentive II*, the Dover Patrol shore base, for 14 months. He completed his service at Columbine depot on the Firth of Forth.

HMS Vanguard

The Luckhurst brothers were just two of the district's men whose lives were lost whilst serving on the *Vanguard*. An additional 15 from Swale were also lost on the same day. Their names are:

- Chief Stoker William Harvey, aged 39. William enlisted at Chatham on 22nd July 1897, and was married to Mary. He is buried in Lyness Royal Naval Cemetery, in the Orkney Islands, and commemorated in St Laurence Church, Bapchild.
- Chief Petty Officer Percy Garnet Browning, aged 38. Percy joined the Navy as a 15-year-old 'boy' on 20th September 1893, and received Long Service and Good Conduct medals, as well as the Queen's South African Medal, before retiring on 12th September 1913. He was recalled at the outbreak of war and lived in Faversham.
- Able Seaman Robert John Gamble, aged 37, of Faversham.
- Stoker 1st Class John Madams, aged 30. His wife was Ada and they lived in Faversham.
- Stoker 1st Class Albert Omans, aged 35. His wife was Harriett Ellen and they lived in Blackheath, London. He was born in Faversham, and remembered on the Faversham memorial.
- Stoker 1st Class Frank John Payne, aged 23, of Faversham.
- Stoker John Cutter, aged 32. His wife was Winifred and they lived in Sittingbourne.
- Private Harry Edwin Styles, aged 25. Harry was in the Royal Marines Light Infantry and lived in Murston.
- Leading Stoker Ernest Bolton Atkins, aged 21. Ernest joined the Navy on 5th November 1913, aged 18. He is commemorated on the Newnham and Doddington War Memorial.
- Chief Stoker William Spooner Clarke, aged 44. He was married to Amelia Jewis, they had two daughters, Elsie and Lily and lived in Rainham.
- Engine Room Artificer 3rd Class Frank Valentine Lamb, aged 27. Frank joined the Navy at Chatham on 27th December 1911 and lived in Sheerness.
- Chief Petty Officer Robert William Thorpe, aged 38. He joined the Navy aged 15, at Chatham on 3rd August 1894. He married Annie Novelle in 1903 and they had two children, Robert, and Clara, and they lived in Sheerness.
- Chief Stoker Alfred Henry Tidmarsh, aged 47. He joined the Navy at Chatham on 1st December 1887. He was married to Violet Whitely, and they had two children, Olgar and Nicholas, and a son, Charles, from his first marriage. He was a licensed victualler at The Grapes in Blue Town, Sheerness. He was recalled to service on 5th August 1914 and was buried in the Lyness Royal Naval Cemetery.
- Stoker 1st Class Frederick Chapman, aged 39, of Sittingbourne.
- Stoker 1st Class Walter Hatton, aged 20. He joined the Navy in Chatham in April 1915 and lived in Upchurch.

A memorial to the *Vanguard* stands at Lyness Royal Naval Cemetery, Isle of Hoy, Scotland, where 18 of the crew are buried, only four other crew were buried in churchyards near where they lived. The remaining crew are named on the CWGC Royal Naval memorials at Chatham, Plymouth and Portsmouth

The memorial plinth faces are inscribed "Erected by relatives and Squadron Mates" and "Traditions never die."

Credit: Martin Briscoe, IWM War Memorials Register

MALNICK, George

L/10154, Lance Corporal, 2nd Battalion, The Buffs (East Kent Regiment).

George was born in Warsaw, Poland, in 1897, however his family were originally from Grodno, Belarus. At that time, both Belarus and Warsaw were part of the Russian Empire. He was the son of Morris and Rose, and they had ten children, although by 1911 three had died. His siblings, John, Jack, Dora, Charlie, and Elijah were all born in Russia, except his youngest brother, Samuel, born in Tendring District, Essex in 1902.

At that time the family were living at 64 High Street, Whitstable, where George's father was a Toy and Fancy shop dealer, with his wife and children, John, Dora, and George assisting in the business.

When he joined the 5th Lancers of the Line in Chatham on 26th November 1913, George was 5ft 6in tall and claimed to be 18 years old, although he was only 16 at that time. He also said that he had been born in Clacton, Essex, which is where he had lived as a child, and that he was British. Just 80 days later on 13th February 1914, he bought himself out of the army for £10 (£450 today).

Five months later on 29th April 1914, George re-joined the army in Canterbury. This time he joined The Buffs, and he was refunded £5 of his buy out money. George arrived in France on 17th January 1915, and four months later, on the 6th May, he was promoted to the rank of Lance Corporal.

His battalion's War Diary[90] records that they were in Ypres from January 1915 until 20th February when they moved to Locre. At the end of March, they had moved back towards Ypres to Dickebusch, then on 13th April 1915 they arrived at Zonnebeke, near Passchendaele.

---

[90] War Diary: 2 Battalion Buffs (East Kent Regiment). WO-95-2279-2. December 1914-October 1915. The National Archives (UK), Kew, England.

On 28th April 1915 the battalion relieved the 3rd Royal Fusiliers in Zonnebeke, in an area named Gravenstafel (pictured right), where they had had "a trying time with many casualties." The 29th and 30th were recorded as quiet days, due to the enemy being occupied with a French attack. During the first three days of May they were under enemy shelling of the trenches and on the 4th May the battalion moved to a wood near Poperinge, where it bivouacked.

On the morning of the 9th the battalion marched to Potijze, east of Ypres. The next day they joined the 'remnants' of the Yorks and Lancasters in the trenches south of the Verlorenhoek-Ypres road. The trenches were in poor condition with the parapets demolished by heavy shell fire. They were ordered to hold the trenches at all costs. For the next two days, the 11th and 12th May, the trenches were subjected to heavy shelling all day. Late on the 12th they were relieved by the 2nd Life Guards.

No. 2 Casualty Clearing Station. Oultersteene (Bailleul). IWM Q437.

George was injured on 11th May and moved to No. 2 Casualty Clearing Hospital in Bailleul. He succumbed to his wounds and died on 16th May 1915. He was buried in the Bailleul Communal Cemetery Extension, close to the Franco-Belgian border.

Locally, George is remembered on Sittingbourne War Memorial and St Michael's Church WW1 Memorial Window.

His father received his pay and gratuity, 1914-15 Star, Victory, and British War Medals.

MEAD, Frederick Charles

L/8600, Private, 1st Battalion, The Buffs (East Kent Regiment).

Credit: Trevor, (great-nephew) and Sonia Young

Frederick was born in 1889 in Milton Regis, the fifth of the eight children of William Henry and Elizabeth Ann (née Hibben). His siblings were William Alfred, Charlotte Ann, George, Alfred, Elizabeth Marian, Alice May, and Albert Edward. The family were living at 14 Terrace Road, Sittingbourne, in 1911, next door to another Avenue man, Thomas Mears (see page 212) and Frederick's father was employed by Messrs Wills and Packham Ltd as a blacksmith's striker.

After leaving school, Frederick worked for the Sittingbourne Post Office. He joined The Buffs in August 1907 and on leaving in 1912 was posted to the Army Reserves. At the outbreak of war, he was recalled from the reserves, re-joining The Buffs leaving for France on 7th September 1914, where he served with his regiment in Flanders.

In late November 1915 his battalion had been relieved and had moved to Camp 'C', near Poperinge. The entry in their War Diary[91] for 2nd December 1915 noted that the battalion marched past the Army Commander Lieutenant-General Sir Herbert Plumer, with the battalion drums playing.

On the 4th December they marched to Houtkerque (pictured right) to relieve the 2nd Durham Light Infantry and were housed in scattered farmhouses.

The diary entries up to the 14th simply read "At Houtkerque", with the exception of the 9th, when they marched past the Divisional Commander Major-General Charles Ross. It also noted that the intention to create an outpost scheme was cancelled due to bad weather.

On 15th December 1915 the diary recorded that the time at Houtkerque for training was hampered by frequent rain, though they had fitted in some cross country runs to the benefit of the men's health. The next day they marched back to Camp 'C'. Early in the morning of the 19th December they were subjected to a gas attack and heavy shelling was noted from both sides.

On 20th December 1915 they moved to Forward Cottage trenches, near Ypres, where they relieved the Bedfordshire Regiment. Part of the day's entry reads "Country in terrible condition owing to rain and heavy shelling. Many trenches unoccupiable and the line held by isolated posts." The day ended with heavy howitzer fire for most of the night, with three other ranks killed and 19 wounded.

---

[91] War Diary: 1 Battalion The Buffs (East Kent Regiment). WO-95-1608-1. August 1914-December 1915. The National Archives (UK), Kew, England.

Over the next three days the battalion suffered more casualties from the heavy shelling and returned to Camp 'C' on Christmas Eve. The diary entry for the 25th was headed "Christmas Day" and added that many of the battalion spent the day in the trenches, in the wood and in billets.

Frederick was killed a few days before Christmas Day on the 20th. He was buried, aged 26, next to Ypres Canal in the Watermolenbrug area, 2.5km south-west of Forward Cottage trenches. Buried with him was another local man, 26-year-old Walter William Richard Sears, whose parents ran the Old Oak Inn in Newnham. Walter is remembered on the Newnham and Doddington Memorial Cross.

In February 1919, Frederick and Walter were moved to their final resting place at Duhallow A.D.S. Cemetery. (ADS - Advanced Dressing Station)

A report in the 1916 New Year's Day edition of the East Kent Gazette, reported that Frederick had been a postman for three years in Lynsted and Newnham districts. It also mentioned that Frederick played centre forward for Sittingbourne Wednesday Football Club. The report concluded "The young soldier was a general favourite with the postal staff, and in his postal district, and his death will be genuinely mourned."

Frederick's father received his son's pay and gratuity, as well as his 1914-15 Star, and Victory and British War Medals. He is remembered on a plaque in Sittingbourne Post Office, on Sittingbourne War Memorial, and on St Michael's Church WW1 Memorial Window.

Two of Fredericks' Post Office colleagues were also killed in the war. Lance Corporal Edward Burley, 15th Division Signal Coy, Royal Engineers, died of wounds after being gassed, aged 30, on 30th July 1918 at the 63rd Casualty Clearing Station, Senlis, France. Edward is also commemorated on the Avenue (see page 92). Private Barnard Gray, The Buffs (East Kent Regiment), was 33 years old when he died on 27th March 1918 and is commemorated on the Pozieres Memorial to the Missing and the Bobbing Church WW1 Memorial.

210

MEARS, Lawrence

11126, Serjeant, Royal Flying Corps.

Lawrence was the youngest of eleven children of James, a brick-temperer, and Jane (née Smith). Lawrence was born on 22nd June 1896 in Sittingbourne. His siblings were Henry, Lily, Ada, George, Ernest James, Edward, Norris, May, David Richard, and Hilda Jane. His parents came from Stoke in Suffolk, which was where Henry and Lily were born, but by 1877 they had moved to Sittingbourne as Ada was born in Sittingbourne that year. In 1911 the family were living at 7 Cowper Road, Sittingbourne. In 1907 Lawrence's brother Henry emigrated to Virginia, USA, and in 1924 his siblings Ada and David emigrated to Ontario, Canada.

Lawrence joined the Royal Flying Corps in the autumn of 1915 and trained in England and Scotland, before gaining his Aviator's Certificate[92] on 26th September 1917 at the Military School in Montrose, Scotland, flying a B.E.2e biplane. He was posted as an instructor to No. 1 School, Navigation and Bomb Dropping, stationed at Stonehenge, Wiltshire.

On 7th March 1918, Lawrence was instructing 27-year-old Lieutenant William Henry Collins, in a DH4 biplane (pictured right). They were flying over Salisbury Plain and had been up for an hour, when coming into land, the aircraft plunged 70 feet (21 metres) to the ground and caught fire, killing them both.

Credit: National Museum of the U.S. Air Force

Lieutenant William Collins, Royal Flying Corps, was born in Muttra, India, the son of Major William Henry and Elizabeth Collins. He was buried in Durrington Cemetery, Worthing and was formerly in the Yorkshire Hussars Yeomanry.

The Captain and Adjutant of the school wrote to Lawrence's father to say:

> "Will you allow me to convey on behalf of the officers, warrant officers, N.C.O.'s, and men of this station our deepest sympathy in this your sad bereavement and believe me your son was held in the greatest respect by all the officers and comrades in this station."

The station chaplain, Reverend P C Barber also wrote to the family expressing his sympathy and added that both men had died instantaneously.

The East Kent Gazette of 16th March 1918 included an article about Lawrence. They reported that before the war he had worked on the clerical staff of Messrs Smeed, Dean and Co. They added that Lawrence attended the Primitive Methodist Church in Shakespeare Road, where he was also a preacher. He associated himself with chapels wherever he trained and gave sermons. A letter from the Wesleyan Minister at Richmond, Yorkshire, Reverend H Tregoning, mentioned they were to hold a memorial service, as Lawrence had preached several times at Catterick Wesleyan Chapel.

[92] Royal Aero Club. Royal Aero Club index cards. Royal Air Force Museum, Hendon, London.

Lawrence was 21 years old when he died and he was buried in Sittingbourne Cemetery, with full military honours. His pall bearers were eight flight sergeants from a Kentish station and the 3rd Battalion Wiltshire Regiment formed a firing party. Lawrence's funeral was conducted by the Reverend A E Noble, minister of the Primitive Methodist Church.

He is remembered on St Michael's Church WW1 Memorial Window and Sittingbourne War Memorial.

Lawrence's father received his pay and gratuity.

MEARS, Thomas

6159, Rifleman, 1st/18th Battalion, London Regiment (London Irish Rifles).

Thomas was born in Sittingbourne in 1890, the son of John, a brickfield labourer, and Martha (née Gibbons). He was the second youngest of eight, and his siblings were Lillie Margaret, William, Ernest John, Gertrude, Sarah, Esther (1886-1889), and Leslie. In 1911 Thomas was working as a brickfield labourer and the family was living at 13 Terrace Road, next door to another Avenue man, Frederick Charles Mead (see page 209).

In late 1915 he married 23-year-old Hannah Batchelor, from Snodland, and on 8th January 1916 their daughter Dorothy May was born in Faversham, where they lived at 50 Westgate Road.

Before the war he had been a fitter's labourer in the paper mill and attended Sittingbourne's Baptist Church.

Thomas enlisted in the 4th Battalion, The Buffs in Canterbury early in 1916, but later transferred to the London Regiment where he served as a Rifleman. He arrived in France on 21st August 1916. His battalion's War Diary[93] records that at that time they were in the trenches, 5km south of Albert. They were heavily engaged with the enemy and on the 25th August 204 had been killed or wounded. The diary entry for the 29th August shows they had moved to Faviere Wood, near Albert, and that they had received a draft of 200 Other Ranks. It is probable that Thomas was one of these drafts.

Over the next few days, the battalion made its way to Needle Wood, encountering the enemy and shelling on the way. They arrived on the last day of August. On the 1st and 2nd of September 1916 they successfully attacked nearby Moislains Wood. Late on the 2nd they were relieved by a company of

Biaches and Péronne in the middle and Moislains ridge on the horizon.

[93] War Diary: 1/18 Battalion London Regiment (London Irish Rifles). WO-95-2737-2. March 1915-February 1919. The National Archives (UK), Kew, England.

Troops at rest in Bivouacs, June 1915.
IWM (Q 49356)

machine gunners and moved to Hospital Farm, where they spent the next two days resting. On the 5th and 6th September 1916, they returned to Moislains and attacked an area north and east of the village. The next day they moved to Corbie and remained here resting for four days before entraining 100km north to Raimbert, just south of Béthune. They arrived on 11th September 1916, and spent the rest of the month training there. At the end of September, they marched 30km south-west to Pierremont.

On 1st October 1916 they travelled by train the 50km north-east to the Estaires Area, where they were in bivouacs in a field. The following day they moved to Fromelles, which was noted to be under "hostile machine gun fire and snipers very active," sustaining 30 casualties.

On 4th October 1916 Thomas was killed. His battalion had moved to support 19th and 20th Battalions, who were held up near the railway north of Radinghem. He had been in France for just six weeks.

Thomas' death was announced in the East Kent Gazette in the 28th October 1916 issue.

He is remembered on the Thiepval Memorial to the Missing, Sittingbourne War Memorial and Baptist Church Memorial. Thomas was awarded the Victory and British War Medals, and his pay and gratuity were paid to his wife.

> ## The East Kent Gazette
>
> ### SATURDAY, OCTOBER 5, 1918
>
> ### IN MEMORIAM
>
> **MEARS** – In loving memory of my dear husband, Thomas Mears killed in action Oct 4th, 1916, somewhere in France.
> Not dead to us, but still we miss you,
> Not lost, but gone before;
> You live with us in memory still,
> And will for evermore.
> From his loving Wife and Baby Dorothy.

MILGATE, Henry Sidney George

T/328740, Private, 23rd Lines of Communication Coy, Royal Army Service Corps.

Henry was born in Sittingbourne at the beginning of 1889 and was baptised at Holy Trinity Church, Sittingbourne, on 17th February 1889. He was the third child and eldest son of George, a bricklayer's labourer, and Emma Elizabeth (née Houghting). His siblings were Florence Eliza (1885-1886), Maude Mary (1887-1900), Albert Edward (1891-1899), William Charles, Emily Elizabeth, Lilian Ivy Victoria, Edith May, Ernest Alfred, Amos John, and Dorcas Eva (1906-1930). In 1911 the family were living at No.2 Grafton Cottages, The Butts (now St Michael's Road) and Henry was working as a carman. He married 22-year-old Ellen Mary Baker at Faversham on 12th June 1915.

When Henry enlisted on 16th April 1917 in Herne Bay, he was living at 32 Crown Road, Sittingbourne. He was 5ft 2in tall and had been working as an engine driver. Henry was posted to the Egyptian

Expeditionary Force and, travelling via France, arrived in Egypt on 26th September 1917. However, he returned three weeks later due to illness, on 19th October 1917. It seems likely that he became ill whilst in Egypt as he was admitted, semi-conscious, to Fort Pitt Military Hospital, Chatham, on Christmas Eve 1919.

Henry was diagnosed as suffering from enteric fever, recorded as contracted whilst on active service. His wife was with him when he died three days later, aged 30, on 27th December 1919. A post-mortem was carried out and evidence of typhoid was found. His wife received his pay and gratuity, together with his Victory and British War Medals.

Henry was buried in Sittingbourne Cemetery and is remembered on Sittingbourne War Memorial and St Michael's Church WW1 Memorial Window.

MILLEN, Wilfrid

11266, Private, 4th Battalion, Canadian Infantry.

Wilfred was born in Sittingbourne on 26th November 1887 and was baptised on 29th April 1888. He was the youngest of the eight children of Alfred, a master butcher, and Sarah Anne (née Pigrum). His siblings were Seymour Alfred, Frank, Harry, Sarah Ann, Leonard, Alfred Dyson, and Emily Mary.

In 1901 Wilfred was a boarder at King's School, Rochester. The school is the second oldest in the world and the oldest choir school. After leaving the school he worked as a solicitor's clerk, before emigrating to Canada in 1913 where he was employed at the Home Bank, Toronto.

Wilfred enlisted in the 36th Regiment, Canadian Infantry on 22nd September 1914 and on his Attestation Papers he recorded he had previously served in The Buffs (East Kent Regiment), for one year. He gave his height as 5ft 7½in and his date of birth as 1888 instead of 1887. There is no reason for him to have done that deliberately as the upper age limit to enlist was 41 and he was only 26.

Wilfrid's battalion set sail from Canada on 3rd October 1914 and served on the Western Front. They spent April 1915 training at Steenvoorde (pictured right), on the Franco-Belgian border, near Ypres. On the 19th they had moved to Proven, and the battalion

STEENVOORDE.- Grand'Place

214

diary[94] noted that they received a sanitation lecture. Two days later they moved to billets in Vlamertinghe, where they carried out more training. On 23rd April 1915, they moved to a farmhouse at Picklen where the enemy was entrenched, and attacked their position until 9pm, when they were relieved. The diary reported 505 casualties. The following day they rested, then on 25th April they occupied trenches in Fortuen. During that day Wilfrid was wounded in the scalp and left arm.

On the 4th May 1915, Wilfrid was transferred to the Southern General Hospital in Bristol. A month later on 7th June 1915 he was admitted for a second time, again from wounds. After this occasion he was placed on sick furlough and attended the Canadian Convalescence Hospital in Monks Horton near Ashford, Kent.

He was then posted to Shorncliffe on 17th July 1915, joining the 12th Battalion, and in October he was assigned to Moore Barracks Canadian Hospital (pictured above). He remained at Shorncliffe until 25th April 1916 when he was returned to his unit.

However, a month later on 16th May 1916 he was again admitted to the Moore Barracks with a condition that required an operation. On the 30th he went to Woodcote Park Military Convalescent Hospital, Epsom, from where he was discharged a week later on 5th June 1916. In January 1917 he was posted to the 3rd Reserve Battalion at West Sandling, Hythe.

At the start of 1917, Wilfrid married Beatrice Eastwood in St Michael's Church, Sittingbourne.

Wilfrid was admitted to the Red Cross Hospital in Sittingbourne on 21st March 1917 and discharged to West Sandling eight months later on 20th November 1917. He returned to France the following year on 29th March 1918, and re-joined his unit on 13th April.

His battalion's War Diary[95] records that at the start of August 1918 they were in reserve at Grand-Rullecourt, near Arras. On 4th August the battalion moved by marching and train 65km south-west to Saint-Maulvis. Then on the 5th they moved 50km east just past Amiens, in a column of 270 buses, to prepare for an attack on the 8th.

---

[94] Government of Canada. War diaries-4th Canadian Infantry Battalion. Date: 1914/09/24-1916/08/31. Reference: RG9-III-D-3, Volume number: 4915, Microfilm reel number: T-10707.

[95] Government of Canada. War diaries-4th Canadian Infantry Battalion. Date: 1918/0/01-1919/04/24. Reference: RG9-III-D-3, Volume number: 4916, Microfilm reel number: T-10708.

On arriving at Boves Wood, the diary read 'bivouacked in the wood without shelter'. The next day when the battalion assembled at Gentelles Wood, near Amiens, visibility was poor.

On 8th August 1917 the battalion attack started at 4.30am in thick mist, in the area of Aubercourt and Cayeux, near Amiens, and seven hours later the objectives had been reached. The diary recorded about 125 casualties. One of these was Wilfrid who had been wounded.

The Canadian War Grave Registers[96] record that Wilfrid 'shortly after reaching the objective near Ruisseau Wood at about 4pm, was shot, by enemy rifle fire, in the left shoulder and back. After being given First Aid he was taken to a Field Ambulance and evacuated to No. 10 General Hospital, Rouen.'

Wilfrid died two days later on 10th August 1918. He was 29 years old and was buried in St Sever Cemetery Extension, Rouen. His headstone was inscribed with the words chosen by his family "FAITHFUL UNTO DEATH."

An officer wrote of him, 'He proved himself a real gentleman in the face of great danger ... Set a wonderful example by his willingness and bravery in battle'.

He is remembered on Sittingbourne War Memorial, St Michael's Church WW1 Memorial Window and King's School Memorial, Rochester (below). He is also listed in De Ruvigny's Roll of Honour 1914-1918.

Credit: Susan Featherstone, IWM War Memorial Registers

The MILLS Brothers

Ernest William Cornelius and Frank Edward were both born and baptised in Snodland and were the two eldest of five children of William Mills and Emily Mary Over. Their three siblings were Alice Lilian Nellie, Kate Julia, and Frederick Robert, who were all born in Sittingbourne.

Their father, William, was a reelerman in the paper mill and the family lived in Snodland until about 1893 when they moved to 8 Burley Road in Sittingbourne.

All Saints Church, Snodland

96 War Graves Ledger Books. RG 150, 1992-93/314, vols. 239–302. Library and Archives Canada, Ottawa, Ontario, Canada.

MILLS, Ernest William Cornelius

14263, Sergeant, Grenadier Guards.

Ernest was born in Snodland in 1890 and was baptised there, at All Saints Church, on 13th April 1890. He enlisted before the war started with the 3rd Battalion Grenadier Guards, at Canterbury on 15th February 1909. His Attestation Papers record he stood 5ft 11in tall with blue eyes and brown hair and had been working as a papermaker.

A report in the East Kent Gazette dated 3rd September 1910 recorded that Corporal Mills was one of the bearer party at the funeral of Florence Nightingale on 20th August 1910, at St Margaret of Antioch Church, East Wellow, Hampshire (pictured below). The bearer party of Grenadier, Coldstream, and Scots Guards represented the battalions that had fought in the Crimean War.

On 25th October 1910 he extended his service to complete seven years and on the same day he was promoted to Lance Corporal. In 1911 he had been posted to the 1st Battalion, Grenadier Guards and stationed at Wellington Barracks, St James Park, Westminster, London.

Ernest married Ellen Selina Vincent at the Baptist Tabernacle in Aldershot on Christmas Day 1911, where Ellen's sister Elsie and a James McKenzie were witnesses. Elsie married fellow Grenadier Guard, Corporal Thomas William Dixon in 1915, when James McKenzie was also a witness. Thomas served in the war but was discharged due to Consumption and died in 1923.

Ernest was promoted a number of times, rising to Orderly Regimental Sergeant on 6th March 1915, and a month later on 26th April 1915 he further extended his service to complete twelve years.

On 1st February 1916 he reverted to the rank of Sergeant and a Court of Inquiry, held on 25th February, recorded that he had deserted on 2nd February. A report published in the East Kent Gazette, dated 11th May 1918, said Mr and Mrs William Mills of 8 Burley Road had received the news that Ernest had been killed in action. According to the report:

"On April 8th he was "up in the line", when he was shot through the heart, and died instantaneously."

It is not clear as to whether or not this news came from the military authorities or a letter from someone serving with him, as the report unusually included how Ernest died. He is remembered on Sittingbourne War Memorial, Sittingbourne Holy Trinity Church WW1 Memorial and Snodland's War Memorial.

What happened between the time Ernest deserted and the report of his death two years later is a mystery, as there are no further entries in his service record. The question remains though as to why there are no military records of his death.

The Commonwealth War Graves Commission database has no entry for Ernest and research has not identified his final resting place. Although Ernest's place of death and where he was buried are at present unknown, research will continue in an attempt to identify this information.

MILLS, Frank Edward

2783, Trooper, 2nd Life Guards.

Frank was born in Snodland in 1892 and was baptised on the 3rd February 1892 in All Saints Church (pictured right). In 1911, he was working as a clerk in the paper mill.

Frank served in the Life Guards, Household Cavalry and arrived in Zeebrugge on 8th October 1914, and their War Diary[97] records that they marched to bivouacs just outside the town. The next day they marched the 13km south to Bruges and took six Germans prisoner on the way. The diary for the 10th noted that the 'small ration biscuit' was more palatable, and 'can be eaten by men whose teeth are faulty.'

Ruins of Zandvoorde Church. February 1917

Over the next few days, the Life Guards marched their way down to Ypres. On 14th October 1914 there was much excitement at the sight of a German aeroplane, which the diary recorded was 'brought down at the expense of about 100 rounds', with both wounded airmen being taken prisoner.

By the 16th Frank's regiment had marched through Ypres to billets in Westroozebeke, encountering some enemy action on the way. For the next three days they were in the trenches from which they sent out patrols and encountered some enemy action.

On 26th October 1914 they had moved back towards Ypres and into billets at Zillebeke. The following day they were in trenches to the north-west and south-east of Zandvoorde and, whilst they were there, they were met with shell fire and sniping. On 30th October 1914 they were forced to retire, as they were being surrounded, to Zillebeke Ridge. By the end of the day the regiment eventually moved into nearby billets at Verbranden-Molen.

During this action and withdrawal on 30th October 1914, Frank was killed, aged 23. He is remembered on the Ypres (Menin Gate) Memorial, Sittingbourne War Memorial, Sittingbourne Holy Trinity Church WW1 Memorial (pictured right), and the Congregational Church Memorial.

Frank's pay and gratuity were paid out to his father. He was also awarded his Victory and British War Medals.

---

[97] War Diary: 2 Life Guards. WO-95-1155-2. August 1914-March 1918. The National Archives (UK), Kew, England.

Edward was the second youngest of a large family of 14 children, whose parents were Alfred James and Elizabeth (née Thomas). The children were Sarah Ann Matilda (1870-1871), Alfred James John, Elizabeth Harriett, Alice Maud Mary, William Charles George, Clara Lilian Beatrice, Beatrice Jane Amelia, Emily Mary Ann, Elsie Mildred (1885-1889), Albert John, Frederick Walter, Sidney Edward (1892-1893), and Daisy May.

Edward was born in the summer of 1894 and baptised at the age of eight on 16th November 1902 in St Michael's Church, Sittingbourne. The family lived at 18 Shortlands Road from at least 1901, and by 1911 Edward, his father and brothers William and Frederick were working as brickfield labourers at Messrs Wills and Packham Ltd.

In the summer of 1915 Edward married local girl Alice Ann Houghton, aged 23. He enlisted in Sittingbourne at some point before 29th March 1917, joining the London Rifles. He served with them until 14th April 1917 when he was posted to the Royal Fusiliers.

Edward's father died the day before his 70th birthday on 21st January 1918, as reported in the East Kent Gazette edition of 2nd February. The newspaper reported that besides Edward, his brothers William and Frederick were also serving; William was in the Royal Navy and Frederick in the Household Battalion and in hospital wounded. All three sons attended their father's funeral.

Afterwards Edward returned to the Western Front. The last main action in his battalion's War Diary[98], before Edward's death, occurred in the last week of August 1918 when the battalion attacked the village of Ablainzevelle. They were supported by tanks, with the attack starting in the early morning of 21st August 1918. There was a heavy mist which caused problems as it made it difficult for the men to find

their way. However, the attack was successful and all objectives achieved by late morning. In the afternoon they attacked Achiet-Le-Grand, only to find a large German Garrison was holding the village, which offered quite a lot of resistance. The Germans were overcome, and the diary reported that a platoon of 19 men had captured 119 Germans. The fighting continued for a few more days. September was spent in Logeast Wood, where they carried out training.

It is likely that Edward had been wounded during the action in August. He was 24 years old when he died of wounds on 26th September 1918 in No. 32 Stationary Hospital, Wimereux. He was buried in Terlincthun British Cemetery, Wimille. The cemetery is located in the north of Boulogne and was used mainly for those that had died in the base hospitals in Boulogne and Wimereux, just north of the town.

Locally he is remembered on Sittingbourne War Memorial and St Michael's Church WW1 Memorial Window.

[98] War Diary: 10 Battalion Royal Fusiliers. WO-95-2532-1. August 1915-March 1919. The National Archives (UK), Kew, England.

Edward was awarded the Victory and British War Medals, and his wife, who was living at 37 Bayford Road, Sittingbourne, received his pay and gratuity.

Edward was loved and missed by his wife and family; for several years after his death, poignant and emotional "In Memoriam" were published on his anniversary. Those published on 25th September 1920 in the East Kent Gazette were very emotional and are reflective of the feelings and emotions felt by all those who lost loved ones during the war. From the wording of that from his wife, and the time between the fighting in August and his death in September, it is possible that she may have been able to be with him when he died.

<table>
<tr>
<td>

The East Kent Gazette

SATURDAY, SEPTEMBER 25, 1920

IN MEMORIAM

MOORE – In ever-loving memory of our dear boy, Edward Thomas Moore, aged 24 years, died of wounds in hospital, in France, 26th Sept., 1918.

We pictured his face returning,
We longed to clasp his hand;
But God has postponed the meeting,
Till we meet in the Better Land.
From his loving Mother, Sister and Brothers.

</td>
<td>

The East Kent Gazette

SATURDAY, SEPTEMBER 25, 1920

IN MEMORIAM

MOORE – In ever-loving memory of my dear husband, Edward Thomas Henry Moore, who died of wounds in France, 26th Sept., 1918, aged 24 years.

He suffered long, he murmured not,
I watched him day by day,
With aching heart, grow less and less,
Until he passed away.
From his loving Wife, Alice.

</td>
</tr>
</table>

NORRIDGE, Walter Henry

5646, Private, 1st/23rd Battalion, London Regiment.

Walter was born in Milton Regis in 1893, the eldest of the five children of Walter, a pedlar, and Maria Jane (née Hopkins). His siblings were Beatrice May, Percy Fortred, Florence Gladys, and Bertie Reginald. In 1911 the family were living at 8 Laburnum Place, Sittingbourne, and Walter junior was working as a mill-hand in the paper mill.

Walter's brother Lance Corporal Percy had served with the 1/4th Battalion, The Buffs (East Kent Regiment) and went with them to India on 29th September 1914, where he remained for the duration of the war. He also served in Bombay, Aden, Karachi, Barielly, and Mumbai.

Walter worked at Sittingbourne Paper Mill for seven and a half years. He made two failed attempts to enlist, being rejected both times on medical grounds. However, he didn't give up and when he was employed at a munition works in Erith he applied to join at Bexleyheath. That time he was successful, joining the Kings Royal Rifle Corps before being transferred to the London Regiment.

From the start of August 1916 until mid-September Walter's battalion was in training on bayonet, musketry, and gas attacks, together with physical training. Its War Diary[99] records they billeted at Saint Riquier and Lahoussoyne, near Amiens, before they marched, on 10th September, to the town of Albert.

Over the next few days, they marched to High Wood (pictured right), via Mametz Wood and Bazentin le Petit arriving on the 15th. At 9.25am the next day they moved to attack Cough Drop. The report for 16th September 1916 said they had not received any casualties before. At the east of High Wood, they came under heavy barrage fire and machine gun fire. The next entry, an hour later, said the attack was going well, though casualties were heavy. After dark, patrols were sent out and German prisoners taken, including an officer.

On the 17th the attack proceeded in good order moving around Cough Drop, finding the trenches obliterated. The diary noted that the battalion was exposed to heavy fire and comments 'must also have suffered from our own artillery.'

It was during the action on 16th September 1916, after tanks had been mobilised in the area, that 23-year-old Walter was killed, three months to the day from when he arrived in France. He is remembered on the Thiepval Memorial to the Missing in France, as well as locally on the Congregational Church Memorial, Sittingbourne and Milton Regis War Memorials, St Paul's Church Memorial and Old Boys Milton Council Schools Memorial.

On reporting his death, the 4th November 1916 edition of the East Kent Gazette mentioned that Walter was carrying a photo of his sweetheart, with instructions to his comrades that if he was killed, they were to communicate with the young girl. This was duly carried out with his comrade saying he died a brave soldier, and they were mourning his death.

Walter was awarded the Victory and British War Medals, which his mother received, along with his pay and gratuity.

The PAGE Brothers

The Page family lost brothers Stephen John and Alfred George, in 1915 and 1917.

The brothers came from a large family of 13 children, and unusually for the period they all survived to adulthood. Their parents, James William, and Frances Harriett (née Lawrence) lived in Preston-next-Faversham until at least 1902. James was a brick making labourer, as were his first five sons.

The children were named Thomas, James William, Louisa, Charles Edward, Beatrice Frances, Stephen John, Maud, Alfred George, Frank Henry, Ethel Maria, Ernest Arthur, Harry, and May Elizabeth.

---

[99] War Diary: 1/23 Battalion London Regiment. WO-95-2744-1. March 1915-May 1919. The National Archives (UK), Kew, England.

With the exception of Louisa and Stephen, who had emigrated to Canada, all of James and Frances' children were living at home in 1911, at No.1 Admiralty House, Admiralty Terrace, Sittingbourne, together with Frances' 85-year-old widowed father, James, and a 20-year-old boarder, Walter Smith, who was also a labourer in the brickworks and married Maud Page in 1916. Walter enlisted in December 1915 in the 40th Battalion, Warwickshire Regiment, and gave No. 1 Admiralty House as his residence.

In May 1916 he was posted to The Buffs and went to France in September 1917, where a month later he was shot in the left foot. He returned to France in April 1918 and survived the war. Other family members were touched by the tragedy of war, as Ethel had married into the Luckhurst family, through her husband Albert Henry Luckhurst, who also lost two sons, Clarence and William, on the same day on *HMS Vanguard* (see page 206).

PAGE, Stephen John

L/8660, Lance Corporal, 1st Battalion, The Buffs (East Kent Regiment).

Stephen was born in 1889 and baptised a few days before Christmas on 22nd December 1889 in St Mary of Charity Church, Faversham. When he joined The Buffs at Sittingbourne on 17th October 1907, he was 5ft 5¼in tall. He had been working as a labourer, and gave his age as 18 years 1 month, even though he was still only 17.

He joined as a Private and went to Ireland where he was stationed in Dublin, Kilbride, and Fermoy. He was appointed Lance-Corporal in 1910 but had the Lance stripe removed for misconduct, through being drunk, in March 1913. He joined the British Expeditionary Force on 7th September 1914 and fought that November, he was reinstated to Lance Corporal in March 1915.

The War Diary for Stephen's battalion during the period leading up to his death is shown here:

| Instructions regarding War Diaries and Intelligence Summaries are contained in F.S. Regs., Part II, and the Staff Manual respectively. Title pages will be prepared in manuscript. | WAR DIARY [100] or INTELLIGENCE SUMMARY. *(Erase heading not required.)* | Army Form C. 2118. |

Date	Summary of Events and Information	Remarks and References to Appendices
11-7-1915	Battalion were in trenches near LA BRIQUE. Trenches little more than waist high and sandbags few. Suffering more from rifle grenades.	
12-7-1915 to 26-7-1915	Parties working on improving the trenches. Few casualties each day.	
27-7-1915	Relieved by 3RD RIFLE BRIGADE. Marched to huts midway between POPERINGE and YPRES.	
5-8-1915	Battalion visited by Major-General Congreve V.C., Commander 6th Division. He pointed out the need to take back the trenches at Hooge and said that 6TH DIVISION had been selected for the task, as they were considered the best, and he did not understate the difficulty of the task.	

---

[100] War Diary: 1 Battalion The Buffs (East Kent Regiment). WO-95-1608-1. August 1914-December 1915. The National Archives (UK), Kew, England.

6 to 7-8-1915	In billets.
8-8-1915	6.30pm - Marched to attack HOOGE from crater on the east side. Support from the YORKS and LANCS on the left and the KING'S SHROPSHIRE LIGHT INFANTRY on the right.
9-8-1915	2.45am - Bombardment started. A terrific fire was directed on the hostile lines. 3.15am - Attack commenced and completed successfully. Heavy losses incurred. During the night attacking troops relieved. Expected German counterattack did not materialise.
10-8-1915	Trenches and Crater full of dead and wounded from both sides. This fact impeded free movement. Continuous shell fire was heavy and annoying. Night spent consolidating trenches. CASUALTIES - 25 killed, 162 wounded, 5 missing.

One of those missing on 10th August 1915 was Stephen, who was later presumed to have been killed in action, aged 25, on 9th August 1915, and as such is commemorated on the Ypres (Menin Gate) Memorial to those who have no known grave. Stephen is also commemorated on Sittingbourne War Memorial and Sittingbourne Holy Trinity Church WW1 Memorial.

Stephen's pay and gratuity were paid to his father, who would also have received Stephen's 1914 Star with clasp, together with the Victory and British War Medals.

PAGE, Alfred George

G/40121, Corporal, 6th Battalion, The Queen's (Royal West Surrey Regiment).

Alfred was born in Faversham in 1893 and was baptised there in St Mary the Charity Church on 13th October that year. Like his brother Stephen, Alfred enlisted with The Buffs (East Kent Regiment) in Sittingbourne and then transferred to The Queen's (Royal West Surrey Regiment).

On 1st May 1917 Alfred's battalion was to position north of Rifle Farm, near east Arras, on what was designated the Brown Line. Early the next day they moved up to the Orange Line, 1.5km further east. His battalion's War Diary[101] records that on 3rd May the brigade attacked nearby Scabbard Trench, with the 6th The Buffs and the 7th East Surrey Regiment to the right and left. The 6th Royal West Kents were in support and The Queens in reserve.

The attack started at 3.45am and was initially repulsed. Reinforcements were brought forward to the front line, moving to nearby Gun Pits and they held this position for the remainder of the day. The diary recorded the casualties as three killed and 32 wounded. This period became known as the Third Battle of Scarpe. Alfred went missing during the battle and in October 1917 he was officially recorded as missing in action presumed killed on 3rd May 1917.

[101] War Diary: 6 Battalion Queen's (Royal West Surrey Regiment). WO-95-1863-1. June 1915-October 1919. The National Archives (UK), Kew, England.

Alfred is commemorated on the Arras Memorial to the Missing, Sittingbourne War Memorial and Sittingbourne Holy Trinity Church WW1 Memorial. His father received his pay and gratuity, and he also received Alfred's Victory and British War Medals.

A poem was printed in the East Kent Gazette in Alfred's honour, reproduced here:

The East Kent Gazette

SATURDAY, NOVEMBER 3, 1917
ROLL OF HONOUR

PAGE – On May 3rd, in France, Lance Corpl. Alfred George Page, who was reported missing, now killed, this being the second son of Mr. and Mrs. James William Page, Admiralty house, Sittingbourne, who has been killed in action, aged 24 years. "Rest in the Lord."

He marched away so bravely
His young head proudly held;
His footsteps never faltered,
His courage never failed.
Then on the field of battle,
He calmly took his place;
He fought and died for Britain,
And the honour of his race.
Sleep on, oh dear Alfred in a far off grave,
A grave we shall never see;
But as long as life and memory last,
We shall always remember thee.
From his sorrowful Mother, Father, Sisters, and
Brothers.

PANKHURST, Frank

270492, Private, 10th (Royal East Kent and West Kent Yeomanry) Battalion,
The Buffs (East Kent Regiment).

Frank was born in Sittingbourne in 1894, the son of William Arthur, a life insurance agent, and Louisa (née Hunt). He was the second of seven children, and his siblings were Madeline, Sidney, Elsie, Louie, Annie, and Gladys. Frank's grandfather was also a life insurance agent and was working for Prudential Assurance Company.

By 1901 the family were living apart as Frank' eldest sister Madeline was living at 46 William Street, with her uncle Horace Hunt and grandmother Elizabeth Hunt. Frank was living with his paternal grandparents, William, and Emma Pankhurst, at Little Glovers Cottages, next door to Cemetery Lodge, the home of the Kemsley family, who lost three sons in the war (see page 192). His parents and other siblings were living in Bexley, Kent.

His grandmother died in 1909, and in 1911 Frank was living with his grandfather, his mother and all his siblings except for Madeline who was away from home working as a servant nurse. His father was not living with the family and may have emigrated to America. He was recorded on a Passenger List[102] as arriving in New York on 11th June 1908 and also 4th June 1921[103], where Frank states his residence as Pittsburgh, USA. Frank's mother died in the spring of 1912 in the Sittingbourne area.

Templeux-le-Guerard and Hargicourt on 11th September 1918

Frank enlisted in Sittingbourne and joined the 3/1st Battalion, East Kent Yeomanry, but he later transferred to The Buffs.

His battalion's War Diary[104] records that on 16th September 1918 they had moved to Faustine Quarry, near the village of Villers-Faucon, near Cambrai. The next day they replaced the 15th Suffolks in the front line. At 8.30am on the 18th, the barrage started to support the advance on Sunken Road and Connor Post, just to the north of Hargicourt. In the evening they were forced to withdraw a short distance due to the 'barrage coming down on us.'

The diary entry for 19th September 1918 started 'Considerable artillery activity' and said they had taken up position in trenches to the north-east of the village and remained there for the following day. On the 21st they advanced on nearby Zoo Trench, under a barrage, and were met by 'tremendous' machine gun

[102] New York, Passenger and Crew Lists (including Castle Garden and Ellis Island), 1820-1957. Year: 1908; Arrival: New York, New York, USA; Microfilm Serial: T715, 1897-1957; Line: 16; Page Number: 46. Ancestry.co.uk.

[103] New York, Passenger and Crew Lists (including Castle Garden and Ellis Island), 1820-1957. Year: 1921; Arrival: New York, New York, USA; Microfilm Serial: T715, 1897-1957; Line: 3; Page Number: 30. Ancestry.co.uk.

[104] War Diary: 10 Battalion East Kent Regiment (Buffs). WO-95-3153-2. May 1918-May 1919. The National Archives (UK), Kew, England.

fire, necessitating a withdrawal, though some troops did not manage to get back until early the following morning. That evening the battalion was relieved by 15th Battalion, Suffolk Regiment and withdrew to Sherwood Trench, in Ronssoy.

On 22nd September 1918 the battalion returned to Connor Post in the front trenches and the next day returned to Sherwood Trench after being relieved by 8th Battalion, London Regiment. Frank was reported to have died from wounds on that day.

Frank was buried in the Doingt Communal Cemetery Extension and his headstone is inscribed with a line from the Bible in Revelation 2:10 "BE THOU FAITHFUL UNTO DEATH AND I WILL GIVE THEE A CROWN OF LIFE."

The village of Doingt (pictured left) was completely destroyed in the fighting to capture it, involving the 5th Australian Division, on 5th September 1918. Shortly after the 20th, 41st and 55th Casualty Clearing Stations arrived, remaining until October, when the cemetery was closed. There are 417 Commonwealth burials, of which one is unidentified. The cemetery was designed by Sir Herbert Baker.

Frank is remembered on the Sittingbourne War Memorial and St Michael's Church WW1 Memorial Window. His sister Madeline Brett, who lived at 60 Ufton Lane, received his personal effects, medals and his pay and gratuity. His brother Sidney served as an Able Seaman in the Royal Navy, for five years, from January 1915 to January 1920.

PARKS, Arthur Wallace

14380, Gunner, "C" Battery, 162nd Brigade, Royal Field Artillery.

Arthur was born in Faversham in the spring of 1895 and was baptised there in St Mary of Charity Church on 30th June 1895. He was the son of Wallace John, a brickfield labourer, and Lydia Jane (née Brigden). Arthur had one sister, who died in infancy, Emily Gertrude (1898-1898), and his mother died when he was five years old.

In 1902 his father married Lucy Ann Norrington in Faversham, and they had three children Harold William, Ernest Stanley, and Ethel Mildred. The family moved to Sittingbourne and Arthur attended Sittingbourne Council School. In 1911 the family were living at 37 Cowper Road, Sittingbourne and Arthur was employed by Mr C J Trowell, as a market garden labourer.

Arthur enlisted in Chatham and went to France in August 1914 as part of the British Expeditionary Force.

The report of his death in the 11th May 1918 edition of the East Kent Gazette records that he had been in the Special Reserve before enlisting and had been in the retreat from Mons. He had also been badly gassed and had served throughout the war on the Western Front.

On 17th April 1918, Arthur's battery moved to Devonshire Camp, near Bussebomb, near Poperinge, though the next day they had to move to nearby Hallbast Corner, due to infantry moving in. The War Diary[105] recorded that the battery HQ had been shelled consistently all night and incurred a direct hit. On the 19th they and the battery moved near to the windmill at Reningelst (pictured right), into bivouacs. On the 20th it was recorded that the wagon lines had been shelled incurring casualties.

Credit: westhoekverbeeldt.be HEU004500896

The battery remained near the windmill and on 25th April 1918, the enemy attacked, though the diary provides no more details. On the 27th the battery moved to Ouderdom. Their diary recorded the number of casualties for April as 22 killed and 77 wounded, with 17 admitted to hospital.

Arthur was wounded by a shell burst, which injured his left leg and both shoulders, on 25th April 1918, at a place called Kemmel Hill. He was not admitted to a base hospital until three days later. On 30th April he was transferred to Edmonton Military Hospital in England, where he developed tetanus poisoning and died on 3rd May 1918, aged 23.

On 8th May 1918, he was buried with military honours in Sittingbourne Cemetery, where "HIS LABOUR O'ER A REST WELL EARNED" adorns his headstone. He is remembered on Sittingbourne War Memorial and St Michael's Church WW1 Memorial Window.

Arthur was awarded the Victory and British War Medals, and his father received his pay and gratuity.

PASHBY, Frederick Thomas

G/5546, Private, 8th Battalion, The Buffs (East Kent Regiment).

Frederick was born in 1888 in Sittingbourne and was baptised in the parish church of St Michael on 10th June 1888. He was the fifth of the eight children of Henry, a mariner, and Lydia Sophia (née Redwood). The names of his siblings were Ellen Jane, Lydia Sophia, Henry Alfred, William, Eliza Caroline, Sydney Edward, and Stephen Thomas. The family were originally from Blean and had moved to Milton in 1881.

Frederick's mother died in 1902, and in 1911 he was working as a brickfield labourer and living at 41 Milton Road, Sittingbourne with his sister Eliza and her husband Percy Hodges.

[105] War Diary: 162 Brigade Royal Field Artillery. WO-95-2413-4. December 1915-June 1919. The National Archives (UK), Kew, England.

Frederick's brother William joined The Buffs, East Kent Regiment on 17th November 1915, aged 34. He was transferred to the Machine Gun Corps on 1st January 1916 and discharged on 10th October 1917 as no longer physically fit for active duty because of kidney disease.

When Frederick enlisted in Canterbury, on 20th January 1915, he was 5ft 4in tall and had been working as a waterman. He was posted to France on 24th September 1915, and just four months later, on 22nd January 1916, Frederick was treated for a week for shell shock, by No. 73 Field Ambulance.

In the week leading up to this his battalion was on the Ramparts in Ypres and had sustained heavy artillery and rifle grenades for four of the seven days.

Advanced Dressing Station near Pozieres Ridge

When Frederick returned to his unit they were based in the trenches at Belgian Chateau, on the south-western outskirts of Ypres. Their War Diary[106] records his first days as quiet. On 3rd February 1916 the diary recorded great aeroplane activity, despite strong winds, and the following day some artillery activity.

For the following week, the entries noted artillery fire almost every day, mainly whizz bangs. The 11th and 12th February recorded 'Intense artillery fire on our trenches all day. They are beginning to look considerably the worse for wear.'

The diary noted one killed and 14 wounded on 12th February 1916. One of these was Frederick, who received a gunshot wound which fractured his right leg. He was treated at No. 10 Casualty Clearing Station and on No 14 Ambulance Train. On 21st February he was admitted to General Clearing No 8 Stationary Hospital, in Rouen, where he died the same day, aged 28.

Frederick was buried in Wimereux Communal Cemetery (pictured right) and the words "IN LOVING MEMORY OF OUR DEAR BROTHER FRED NEVER FORGOTTEN BY ELIZA & PERCE" are inscribed on his headstone. The cemetery was used by the town's medical units, as Wimereux and nearby Boulogne formed a hospital centre.

He is remembered on Sittingbourne War Memorial and St Michael's Church WW1 Memorial Window. His pay and gratuity went to his sister Eliza. He was also awarded the 1915 Star, and Victory and British War Medals.

Credit: ww1cemteries.com

[106] War Diary: 2 Battalion The Buffs (East Kent Regiment). WO-95-2207-1. August 1915-January 1918. The National Archives (UK), Kew, England.

228

PAYNE, Frank

24849, Private, 11th Battalion, Machine Gun Corps (Infantry).

Frank was born in Stone, Greenhithe in 1896, the fourth child of Erasmus Eli, a brewer's storekeeper, and Elizabeth (née Clark). By 1911 they had eight children, with three of them having died, and despite research two of the children are unnamed. The other children were named as Elizabeth Frances (1885-1901), Erasmus Ernest, Ethel May, Edward, and Nellie. In 1911 Frank was living with his family at 110 High Street, Milton Regis and working as a butcher's errand boy, for Fletcher and Co. who had shops in Milton and Margate.

Frank enlisted in Margate with the East Kent Regiment before transferring to the Machine Gun Corps. He arrived in France on 1st June 1915 and served all his time there.

His battalion was stationed in the area of Arras and its War Diary[107] from the 1st September provides no detail on the actual location of the battalion. Most daily entries recorded that Arras was shelled.

On 16th September 1918, Frank was injured by a burst enemy shell. Sadly, he died two hours after being admitted to the 1st Canadian Clearing Station, aged 22. He was buried in the Duisans British Cemetery, Etrun, in France.

In the report of Frank's death, the East Kent Gazette of 26th October 1918, included these words from a letter sent to his mother by his captain:

> "He was a splendid soldier and a thorough gentleman. All his comrades join me in expressing our deepest sympathy for you in your great bereavement, and hope that at least you will find a little consolation in the knowledge that he died doing his duty."

Credit: New Zealand War Graves Project

Duisans Cemetery, designed by Sir Reginald Blomfield, was primarily used by the Casualty Clearing Stations, though some bodies were brought in from the front lines. At the time of Frank's death, the 1st, 4th and 23rd Canadian Clearing Stations were in operation. There are 3,206 Commonwealth war graves at the cemetery.

Frank is remembered locally on the Sittingbourne War Memorial and the St Michael's Church WW1 Memorial Window. His pay went to his mother, who died in 1919, and his war gratuity to his father. He was also awarded the 1915 Star, and Victory and British War Medals.

---

[107] War Diary: 11 Battalion Machine Gun Corps. WO-95-1804-3. March 1918-June 1919. The National Archives (UK), Kew, England.

PAYNE, William Stephen

235, Sergeant, Natal Light Horse.

The youngest of the five children of George Henry and Sarah Ann (née Bottle) William was born in Tonge in 1883. His siblings were Elizabeth Ann, George William Henry, Ellen Mary, and Robert Arthur. His father was a farm labourer, and his parents were living at 8 West Lane, Sittingbourne in 1911.

William's brother Robert emigrated to Australia and on 2nd March 1917 he enlisted with 16th Battalion, Australian Imperial Force. He joined the forces in France in January 1918 and left to return to Australia on 12th July 1919, with his discharge on 16th September 1919.

WW1 pension records indicate that William's other brother George had also served during the war.

William was 5ft 7in tall and had been working as a brickfield labourer when he enlisted in Chatham, on 9th June 1902. He joined the Army Ordnance Corps at Woolwich, and on 16th March 1906, he was posted to South Africa. On 9th June 1910 he was transferred to the Army Reserve in South Africa, and settled there. He was discharged on 8th June 1914, but at the outbreak of war was recalled and joined the Natal Light Horse Unit of South Africa.

The Natal Light Horse was formed in August 1914. Their first action was to quell a rebellion of the Boers, who were recruiting men to the German cause. The action at Khels Drift prevented the Boer commandos from crossing into German South-west Africa. The Natal Light Horse then went by train to Cape Town where they spent Christmas.

On 25th April 1915 the Natal Light Infantry moved to Gibeon, South West Africa (now Namibia) to confront the German army. Over the next month they successfully cleared the area of Germans, reducing the threat. This success was the last action seen by the Natal Light Horse, and they were disbanded in June 1915.

Sadly though, William was shot and wounded during this action, and he died at Gibeon Hospital on 19th May 1915, aged 31. He was buried at Gibeon Station Cemetery, Namibia. The cemetery is the final resting place of 39 men, 29 of whom were killed on 27th April 1915. Six of the burials are of men from the German Army.

William is remembered on the Sittingbourne War Memorial, though his name is spelt 'Payn'.

The 12th June and 3rd July 1915 editions of the East Kent Gazette, reported on the death of William. They mentioned that William spent many years in Maritzburg, Natal and was a well-known footballer there, playing full back for the Etcetera's Club.

William's service record shows he strained his right knee playing football on 2nd October 1911, in Durban, South Africa. The newspaper also reported he had been the manager of the Phoenix Bar and Billiard Saloon for the previous two years and was formerly in the butchery business.

Credit: South Africa
War Graves Project

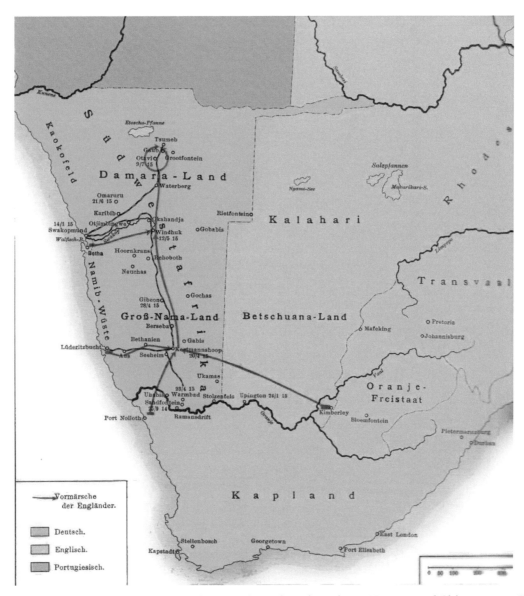

Map of the South-West Africa Campaign in 1915 by Eduard Rothert, Karten und Skizzen zum Weltkrieg, Druck und Verlag von A. Bagel, Düsseldorf, 1916.

PELVIN, G W

Amongst the names on St Michael's Church WW1 Memorial Window is G W Pelvin, under Army. A report of the window's dedication in the East Kent Gazette on 7th January 1992 list the names with ranks, though G W Pelvin was not listed.

His name is also recorded on Sittingbourne War Memorial.

Research into this individual at the time of printing, had not provided an identity, and it continues in order to enable his story to be told.

We remember him, as did those who knew him.

PETTETT, John Thomas Richard

3858/SD, Deck Hand, H.M. Trawler Aiglon, Royal Naval Reserve.

John was the first son and second child of Thomas and Emily Jane (née Gawler) and his surname at birth was registered as Petitt. He was born in Murston, on 5th November 1888, and was baptised in Sittingbourne's St Michael's Church on 6th January 1890.

He had seven siblings, Esther Victoria (1887-1888), Florence Emily Louisa (1891-1899), Beatrice Victoria Matilda, Lilian Agnes Deborah (1896-1902), Dorothy Rosalette, Alice Pretoria, and Edward Frederick George.

Since at least 1901 the family lived at The Wall, Sittingbourne and John's father was employed as a brickfield labourer. John attended Milton Council School then worked as a bargeman's mate. In 1911 he was aboard the sailing barge *Hambrook*, moored at the Town Quay, Barking Creek, Essex. After working for Smeed Dean and Co. he was a barge mate for Messrs E Lloyd Limited.

He enlisted on 31st December 1915 and served in the Royal Naval Reserve. He was assigned to the trawler HMT *Aiglon*, though he also served on the trawlers *Research* and *Actaeon*. This was because HM Trawlers were designated as military assets and enabled maintenance of control to the seaward approaches to major harbours.

John, aged 30, died of influenza in Haslar Royal Naval Hospital, Gosport (pictured right), on 20th February 1919. His body was brought back and buried in Sittingbourne Cemetery. He is remembered on Sittingbourne War Memorial and Sittingbourne Holy Trinity Church WW1 Memorial. He was awarded the Victory and British War Medals.

PHILPOTT, Harold James

3/4228, Private, 10th Battalion, Hampshire Regiment.

Harold was born in Sittingbourne in 1897, the son of Edward Albert, a postman, and Rosa Elizabeth (née Hill). He had a younger brother, Stanley Edward. The family lived at 59 Shortlands Road, Sittingbourne, in 1911 and later moved to Railway Terrace.

At fifteen years of age, Harold enlisted with The Buffs at Sittingbourne on 14th August 1912, claiming he was 17 years and 5 months old and employed as a grocer's assistant. He had hazel eyes and brown hair, and at 5ft 7in tall he may well have appeared older than he actually was.

Harold left the Buffs to join the 3rd Hussars in July 1913 and was discharged on 19th January 1914. Six months later, Harold enlisted at Woolwich, joining the Hampshire Regiment. His battalion arrived in Gallipoli, on *TSS Transylvania* (pictured right), on 5th August 1915. They landed at Anzac Cove, 30km north of Helles, and went straight into action at the Sari Bair Range. This was a ridge of high ground that dominated the middle of the Gallipoli peninsula.

Harold, by then being 18 years old, was reported as 'missing in action' on 10th August 1915. However, it was fourteen months before he was officially reported as 'killed in action'. This was reported in the East Kent Gazette published on 4th November 1916.

Harold is commemorated on the Helles Memorial to the Missing, which lists 20,960 names of those with no known grave who were killed during the Gallipoli campaign, and also serves as a battle memorial. It was designed by John James Burnet and was unveiled in 1924.

He is also remembered on Sittingbourne War Memorial and St Michael's Church WW1 Memorial Window. His pay and gratuity were paid to his father.

PILBEAM, George William

64145, Lance Bombardier, 216th Siege Battery, Royal Garrison Artillery.

The Avenue plaque records an Ordinary Seaman A W Pilbeam, though no record of a navy serviceman with this name and rank was identified. The Roll of Honour in the East Kent Gazette dated 28th May 1921, reporting the unveiling of the War Memorial, records the name, G W Pilbeam. It is assumed this is the correct name and the plaque is in error.

George was born in 1894 in Ashford and was baptised at St Mary the Virgin Church there on 20th September 1894. He was the son of Richard Ernest, a boiler maker for the South-East and Chatham Railway, and Rosa (née Caspall). He was their second child, and his siblings were Arthur James, Millicent Rosa, and Louisa Celia.

George's brother Arthur was a Private in the 1st/5th Battalion, The Buffs, East Kent Regiment and died on 27th July 1916, aged 23. He was buried in Amara War Cemetery, Iraq. As he was living in Ashford he is not commemorated on the Avenue of Remembrance or Sittingbourne War Memorial.

George was working as a grocer's apprentice in Ashford in 1911, however, he moved to Sittingbourne shortly after, where he worked in the grocery department of Sittingbourne Co-operative Society Limited for four years. He lodged with Mr. and Mrs. Edwards at 21 Canterbury Road, Sittingbourne, where he met his fiancée, Edith.

He was 5ft 11in tall when he joined up on 27th October 1915 in Sittingbourne and he spent his first year at Trench School. He went to France in February 1916, then on 14th May 1916 he was admitted wounded to hospital, in the field, and four days later discharged. He returned to Trench School in August 1916 for three months, going back to his unit on 29th November.

George was killed in action, aged 23, on 24th April 1918. He was initially buried on the east of the village of Franvillers, near Albert, with a number of other casualties, who were mainly Australian forces. His body was reinterred on 8th August 1919 in the Ribemont Communal Cemetery Extension in France.

He is remembered on Sittingbourne War Memorial and after his death his pay and his war gratuity went to his mother. He was awarded the British War and Victory Medals on 19th August 1921.

Credit: New Zealand War Graves Project

Unfortunately, news of his death did not immediately reach his fiancée and on 7th May 1918, Edith wrote to his commanding officer asking for any news of George. She said that her last letter to him, dated 16th April, had been returned and that her last letter from George was received on 22nd April.

The East Kent Gazette of 25th May 1918 reported that George's fiancée, Edith had finally received the sad news of his death. George's commanding officer wrote to her to say:

> "George Pilbeam was a great favourite with the Battery, and all feel the loss of such a cheerful N.C.O. very keenly. His death was instantaneous, and he suffered no agony. Death was caused by an unfortunate splinter. Careful hands attended to him, but all efforts were unavailing, the wound being too serious."

QUAIFE, Thomas

T/270324, Private, "B" Company, 10th (Royal East Kent and West Kent Yeomanry) Battalion, The Buffs (East Kent Regiment)

Thomas was born on 28th June 1891 in Cranbrook and was christened there on 28th June 1891. He was the youngest son of Thomas, a maltster, and Mary Ann (née Hatcher) and his siblings were Ernest Henry (1874-1901), Frank William, and Ada Elizabeth. In 1911 the family were living at 36 Unity Street, his mother was widowed, as his father died on 9th January 1904 in Cranbrook. Thomas was working in the book department of the Co-operative Society in East Street.

His brother Private Frank William, a postal worker, served in the Labour Company, Essex Regiment and was billeted in Maidstone. He continued to live there and was recorded in the 1939 Register as a retired postman.

Thomas enlisted in Canterbury and joined the 3/1st Royal East Kent Yeomanry, (The Duke of Connaught's Own) (Mounted Rifles). In April 1916 he was posted with the Egyptian Expeditionary Forces, by which time the regiment had become an infantry one due to a lack of horses. On 1st February the 10th (Royal East Kent and West Kent Yeomanry) Battalion was formed from two dismounted Yeomanry Regiments, and so Thomas became a part of them.

In March 1917 they sailed from Sollum, Egypt, for Sidi Bishr, Alexandria, Egypt. The following month, on 11th April 1917 they moved 400 km to the east to Deir el Belah, Israel, and provided outpost duty just north of the Wadi Ghuzze. Two weeks later his battalion were on trench digging duty in the area of Tel-el-Jemmi. On 9th July 1917, the Buffs marched to Dorset House, where they undertook day and night attacks.

On 7th August 1917 they marched to Deir el Belah to practise field firing and returned to Wadi Ghuzze (pictured right) on the 5th September for more trench digging. As they were next to the sea, they took an opportunity for bathing, something that was very welcome because of the heat.

AUSTRALIAN WAR MEMORIAL   B00972

The night of 25th October 1917 saw them march south-east to El Khasif, near Gaza. On 31st October 1917 the Battle of Beersheba began, with the British attacking and capturing the garrison in Beersheba (now known as Be'er Sheva) (pictured left). The casualties for the day were recorded as nine killed, 104 wounded and two missing.

Thomas died from his wounds on 4th November 1917, and as he was in action in Beersheba on October 31st, it is presumed he received his wounds there. He was buried in the Kantara War Memorial Cemetery,

Egypt. The cemetery is located 160km south of Cairo, on the east side of the Suez Canal. It was started in February 1916 to serve the various hospitals in the town. After the Armistice it was used to consolidate the scattered battlefield graves and other cemeteries. It is the final resting place for 1,562 Commonwealth WW1 burials.

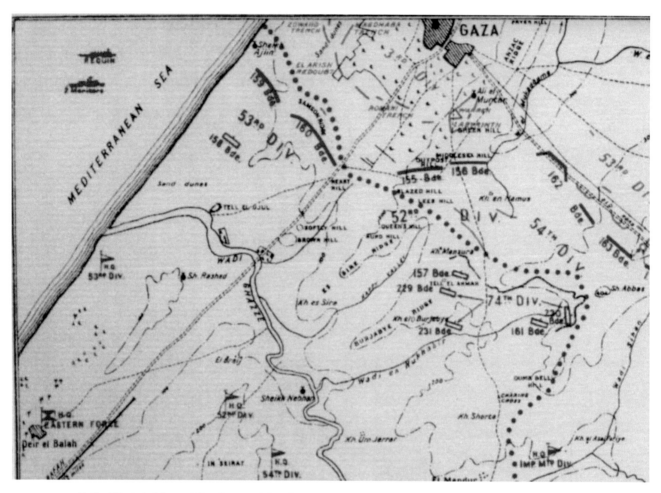

Falls Sketch Map of the Second Battle of Gaza western section of the battlefield, 1930.
Source: Official History of the Great War Based on Official Documents by Direction of the Historical Section of the Committee of Imperial Defence Military Operations Egypt & Palestine from the outbreak of war with Germany to June 1917. Author: Cyril Falls and G. MacMunn.

The East Kent Gazette of 24th November 1917, reported Thomas' death under the headline "SITTINGBOURNE CO-OPERATIVE EMPLOYEE DIES IN PALESTINE - PRIVATE THOMAS QUAIFE, THE BUFFS." The article mentioned that he was yet another Co-op employee to have nobly laid down his life for King and Country.

Thomas is remembered on Sittingbourne War Memorial and Lynsted Church Memorial. After his death his brother, Frank, received his pay and war gratuity. Thomas was awarded the British War and Victory medals.

Although Thomas is commemorated on Lynsted Church Memorial, no clear connection to the village has been identified. However, as he was employed by the Co-operative Society, he may have worked at their Greenstreet store[108].

---

[108] Lynsted with Kingsdown Society. First World War. Roll of Honour. www.lynsted-society.co.uk/research_ww1_casualties.html

RALPH, James Daniel

110395, Private, 1st Battalion, Queen's Own (Royal West Kent Regiment).

James was born in 1895 in Faversham and was baptised there, in the parish church of St Mary of Charity, on 24th July 1895. He was the second of the ten children of Daniel, a brickfield labourer, and Florence May (née Clements). His siblings were William Thomas (1893-1915), Thomas John, Emmeline Blanch, Florence Frances May, Daniel Sidney (1903-1904), Daniel Sidney (born 1905), Walter Leonard, Annie Marie, and Gladys May.

The family were living in Preston-next-Faversham in 1901, but by 1911 they had moved to 14 Black Houses, Grovehurst, Milton Regis, where James was working on a farm.

When James joined the 4th Battalion, The Buffs, on 8th December 1913, he had been working as a groom. At that time, he was 5ft 5in tall with blue eyes and brown hair. He transferred to the Royal West Kent Regiment on 7th July 1914. In September 1914 he spent 42 days in detention after being discovered sleeping on his post. The next year he was posted to the Western Front and arrived in France on 13th January 1915.

BRAY-SUR-SOMME — Les Rives de la Somme

In August 1915, his battalion spent the first two weeks in the trenches at Carnoy, near Albert. On 15th August 1915 they were relieved by the 2nd Kings Own Yorkshire Light infantry, as recorded in the battalion War Diary[109]. By midnight they had moved to billets in Bray-sur-Somme (pictured left). The diary records that they spent the 16th cleaning up and bathing in the canal 'which they much enjoyed'. The entry for the 20th read 'Nothing of importance happened.'

Late on 24th August 1915 the battalion returned to Carnoy and relieved the 2nd Kings Own, who had relieved them previously. 'It was a very fine moonlight night' read the diary for that day, and for the 25th and 26th each was recorded as 'A fine warm day. Nothing of importance happened, the enemy being very quiet.' The 28th was again recorded as a quiet but hot day, with thunderstorms at night, and one man killed. The next three days record no casualties.

In all the official documents James' death is recorded as killed in action on 29th August 1915. He was also the only man from that battalion to be recorded as having died during this period, so it can be assumed that he was the casualty mentioned in the War Diary for 28th August.

---

[109] War Diary: 1 Battalion Queens Own. WO-95-1553-4. June 1915-September 1915. The National Archives (UK), Kew, England.

James was 20 years old when he died and was buried in Carnoy Cemetery, which is home to over 850 burials. The cemetery was started by the 2nd Kings Own Yorkshire Light Infantry and 2nd Kings Own Scottish Borderers at the beginning of August 1915.

7. CARNOY Cemetery

Locally, James is remembered on Sittingbourne and Milton Regis War Memorials, Sittingbourne's Holy Trinity Church, and St Paul's Church Memorial (which is now located in Holy Trinity Church, Milton Regis).

James was awarded the 1914-1915 Star, as well as the British War and Victory Medals, and his father received his pay and gratuity.

James' brother William (21) was working as a barge-mate with captain George Charles Houghton (35) when their barge *Ada Mary* foundered during a great gale on 28th December 1914. Sadly, his body was not found for five months, and George's a few weeks after. The barge was laden with flint and owned by Messrs Smeed, Dean and Co. Ltd., and was found between Thames Haven and Hole Haven, just to the east of Canvey Island. William was buried in Sittingbourne Cemetery.

James and his brother William were sadly missed by their family as these emotive "In Memoriams" show.

The East Kent Gazette

SATURDAY, SEPTEMBER 25, 1915

IN MEMORIAM

RALPH – In loving Memory of our Son, James Daniel Ralph, who was killed in action on the 28th of August, 1915, aged 20 years.

No mother's care did him attend
Nor o'er him did a father bend,
No sister by to shed a tear,
No brother his last word to hear.
True to his duty did he stand,
On the battlefield he fought and died;
No mother near to close his eyes,
Far from his native land he lies.
From his Sorrowing Father, Mother, Brother, and
Sisters.

The East Kent Gazette

SATURDAY, SEPTEMBER 25, 1915

IN MEMORIAM

RALPH – In loving memory of our Son, William Thomas Ralph, who was drowned off the barge Ada Mary, Dec. 28th, 1914, aged 21 years.

Gone, but will never be forgotten.

RANSOM, Walter Frederick

G/18490, Lance Corporal, 11th Battalion, Queen's Own (Royal West Kent Regiment).

Walter was born on 14th May 1896 in Wormshill, the oldest of the four children of Walter, an agricultural labourer, and Ellen Eliza (née Smith). His siblings were Dora Olive Emily, Clarence Alfred, and Harry Thomas. Walter was educated at Rodmersham Green School.

In 1911 the family were living at New Cottages, Highsted, Sittingbourne and Walter was working as an errand boy.

When Walter enlisted on 12th October 1914, he was 5ft 8in tall and had been working as a butcher. He joined the Royal East Kent Mounted Rifles and on 21st September 1916 was posted to the Expeditionary Force in France. Then on 11th October 1916 he was transferred to the 11th Battalion, Royal West Kent Regiment.

His battalion's War Diary for August 1917 is reproduced below:

	WAR DIARY [110] or **INTELLIGENCE SUMMARY.** (Erase heading not required.)	Army Form C. 2118.
Instructions regarding War Diaries and Intelligence Summaries are contained in F.S. Regs., Part II, and the Staff Manual respectively. Title pages will be prepared in manuscript.		
Date	Summary of Events and Information	Remarks and References to Appendices
4-8-1917	In the trenches at HOLLEBEKE.	
5-8-1917 to 9-8-1917	Relieved by 18th KING'S ROYAL RIFLE CORPS, and moved to WOOD CAMP, RENINGHELST. Resting and re-organising.	
10-8-1917	In the trenches at HOLLEBEKE.	
13-8-1917	Moved to camp at ELZENWALLE.	
14-8-1917 to 19-8-1917	Travelled by lorry to billets at ROUKLOSHILLE. Time spent resting, bathing and being inspected.	
20-8-1917 to 13-9-1917	Marched and travelled by bus to BOISDINGHEM. Training.	
14-9-1917 to 16-9-1917	Marched (60km) to RIDGE WOOD (near YPRES).	
18-9-1917	Midnight – Proceeded to trenches at LARCH WOOD. Throughout the day on receiving end of gas and shell attack. 43 Casualties.	
19-9-1917	Battalion moved to BODMIN COPSE, via a pre-marked path, to attack TOWER HAMLETS. Battalion laid up in shell holes.	

---

[110] War Diary: 11 Battalion Queen's Own (Royal West Kent Regiment). WO-95-2634-4. May 1916 - October 1917. The National Archives (UK), Kew, England.

20-9-1917	5.40am - Magnificent barrage started and battalion moved forward behind 15th HAMPSHIRE REGIMENT, who incurred many casualties.
	With the 15th HANTS rushed a strong point, hampering our advance.
	6.15am - reached first objective, the RED LINE. By 7.15am moved forward and captured next objective, the BLUE LINE.
	Just before 10am - advanced again with barrage support to GREEN LINE, met some machine gun fire, though successfully reached GREEN LINE.
	40 to 50 prisoners taken, including three officers.
	2pm - Enemy seen preparing for counterattack but was smashed up by artillery fire.
21-9-1917	Remained on the line, subjected to artillery shelling.
23-9-1917	Relieved
	CASUALTIES
	28 killed, 179 wounded, 53 missing

Walter was reported 'Missing in action presumed killed' on the first day of the attack. He was 21 years old and his death is recorded as occurring on 20th September 1917. He is commemorated on the Tyne Cot Memorial to the Missing, Sittingbourne War Memorial, and Rodmersham Church Memorial.

His personal effects, which were returned to his family, included a flash lamp, canvas wallet, souvenir cards, and pegs. Walter was awarded the Victory and British War Medals.

REEVES, William John

S/7942, Private, 1st Battalion, The Buffs (East Kent Regiment).

William was the oldest son and second child of William and Emily Margaret Field (née Terry). He was born in East Sutton, Kent, in 1884 and was baptised there at the parish church of St Mary the Virgin on the 1st February 1885. His siblings were Jane Eliza, George Henry, Walter James, Albert Edward (1893-1894), Ernest Edwin (1895-1916), Reginald Thomas (1899-1899), and Bertha Emily.

His family moved to 173 Shortlands Road, Sittingbourne between 1891 and 1901. In 1901 William's father was working as a labourer in the paper mill, but by 1911 he was a carman for an ironmonger.

William married Elizabeth Ellen Sharp in St Stephen's Church, Rashcliffe, Yorkshire (pictured right) on 2nd August 1913. Their marriage certificate records they were living at Somerville, 37 Perseverance Street, Primrose Hill, Huddersfield, and William was working as a policeman.

Credit: Stephen Armstrong CC BY-SA 2.0

Though William's brother Ernest was in the age range for service, there is no evidence that he served. An "In Memoriam" in the East Kent Gazette dated 17th September 1917, a year after William's death, records that he 'passed away peacefully.'

William enlisted in Sittingbourne and was sent to France on 31st August 1915. By the beginning of September 1918 his battalion had arrived in Arques, 45km south-east of Calais, after several moves during August, where their War Diary[111] noted they travelled by train 100km south to Heilly, near Amiens. They arrived billeted in the ruins of Bonnay 3km to the south-west, then on 4th September they marched back to Heilly, where they stayed in dug outs and shelters for the next week. Then on the 11th they returned to Bonnay and continued on to Fouilloy, where they stayed for three days.

Street remains in Fresnoy-le-Grand, France. June 1917

The 14th September 1918 brought them to Trefcon, near Saint-Quentin. They had now been moving from place to place for five weeks. Three days later, on the 17th, they moved to battle lines at Saint-Quentin Wood, to attack a line from Gricourt to Fresnoy-le-Petit. At 5.20am the next day the barrage started, and the 2nd Yorks and Lancs advanced at 6.40am, soon reaching their objective. The Buffs then followed, but they became disorientated due to the smoke and darkness and lost direction. They reached Fresnoy-le-Petit but were forced to withdraw due to machine gun fire, which was completed by 3am the next morning. The next few days were spent attacking Fresnoy-le-Petit, but each time they were forced to withdraw, and the battalion remained in the area and woods for the rest of the month, sustaining casualties every day.

William's battalion diary records, on 19th September 1918, 'Congratulations Received' from the Divisional Commander, for the 'gallantry and devotion to duty in extremely difficult and trying circumstances.' The diary also recorded for the 18th and 19th September 30 killed, 136 wounded, one missing and four gassed.

William, aged 33 years, was killed in action on the first day of the attack on 18th September 1918. He was buried in Trefcon British Cemetery, Caulaincourt, France. The cemetery was started in September 1918 by the IX Corps (6th and 32nd Divisions) and was originally called Caulaincourt Military Cemetery. The cemetery is the final resting place for 276 First World War burials, of which all but six were killed in a three-week period from 11th September 1918 to 1st October 1918.

Locally, William is remembered on Sittingbourne War Memorial, St Michael's Church WW1 Memorial Window and Tonge Church Memorial (pictured right). William was awarded the 1915 Star, and the Victory and British War Medals.

111 War Diary: 1 Battalion, The Buffs (East Kent Regiment). WO-95-1608-4. January 1918-May 1919. The National Archives (UK), Kew, England.

Sadly, William's wife, Elizabeth, died within a week of him, on 24th September 1918, at the home of her parents at 31 Gladstone Road, Ware, Hertfordshire. Her death certificate records that her mother, Clara, was present and that she died from cancer and exhaustion, aged 32.

RICHARDS, John Martin

304400, Stoker 1st Class, Royal Navy, HMS Pathfinder.

Petty Officer Stoker
Dress Insignia

John was the first of the Avenue men to lose his life, just a month after the war started. John was born in Sittingbourne on 4th June 1885 and was baptised at St Michael's Church on 1st November 1885. He was the sixth of the nine children of Henry William, a brickfield labourer, and Harriett (née Scoones). His siblings were William David (1876-1903), Frederick Martin (1877-1877), Frederick John, Henry Martin (1880-1905), Albert, Mary Ann, Sarah (1889-1889) and Frank.

When John joined the Navy, on 16th June 1903, he was 5ft 5½in tall and had been working in the brickfields of Messrs C Burley Ltd. He was promoted to Stoker 1st Class three years later on 1st July 1906 and his longest period of service was on the repair ship *HMS Cyclops*, from October 1907, shortly before she was commissioned the following month, to May 1911. In 1911 the *Cyclops* was docked at Chatham Dockyard. He joined the *Pathfinder* on 10th April 1914.

John was a crew mate of the scout cruiser *HMS Pathfinder* (pictured left), when she was sunk on 5th September 1914 by German U-boat *SM U-21*, in the North Sea 340km east of Edinburgh. Earlier in the month, the periscope of the U-boat had been spotted in the Firth of Forth, near the Forth Bridge.

At 3.43pm on 5th September 1914, *SM U-21* spotted *Pathfinder* while she was on patrol and fired a single torpedo. The *Pathfinder* spotted this, and she tried to take evasive action, but was hit below the bridge, detonating cordite charges in one of the magazines, which caused a second explosion that broke the ship in two. Records show that there were 20 survivors from a crew of 270. The *Pathfinder* was the first ship to be sunk by a self-propelled torpedo.

John is remembered on the Chatham Naval Memorial to the Missing, Sittingbourne War Memorial and the Sittingbourne Holy Trinity Church WW1 Memorial.

Launched in 1913, German U-boat *SM U-21* was assigned to the North Sea at the outbreak of war. In April 1915 she moved to the Mediterranean, serving off Gallipoli and in the Black Sea.

U-Boat U21 sinks two English steamships 1915
Credit: Thomas Quine CC-BY-2.0

242

U-boat *SM U-21* returned to the North Sea in early 1917 until the end of the war. She accidentally sank on 22nd February 1919 in the North Sea whilst under tow to Britain to formally surrender.

HMS Pathfinder was the first ship *SM U-21* sank and she went on to sink a further 39 ships, 12 of which were British merchant vessels. Two of the ships sunk were Royal Navy, *HMS Triumph* (25th May 1915) and *HMS Majestic* (27th May 1915), and a French naval vessel *Admiral Charner* (8th February 1916).

RICHARDSON, Percy Anthony

243012, Lance Corporal, 1st/5th Battalion, The Buffs (East Kent Regiment).

Percy was born in Sittingbourne in 1898, the third son of Joseph Frederick and Florence Annie (née Pay). His siblings were Frank Joseph, Leonard George (1893-1893), Lewis Daniel, Alfred Walter Thomas, and Cecil John.

In 1911 the family were living at 14 Laburnum Place, Sittingbourne, Percy's father was employed as a boiler stoker in the paper mill and his brother Frank was a reeler's assistant in the mill.

Percy's father enlisted a year after him on 30th August 1915, joining the Army Service Corps. He was posted to France, and just three weeks later on 24th September 1915, he was transferred to the Labour Corps. He served for the duration of the war and discharged in January 1919.

Before Percy enlisted, aged about 16, in August 1914, he had been working in the paper mill, and was one of the 'papermakers' who all served together in the Buffs, and he was originally posted to 1/4th Battalion. By 1917 his battalion, also known as 35 Indian Infantry Brigade, were in Iraq as part of the Mesopotamia Expeditionary Force and were in the region of Besouia (now known as Imam Sayyid Mansur).

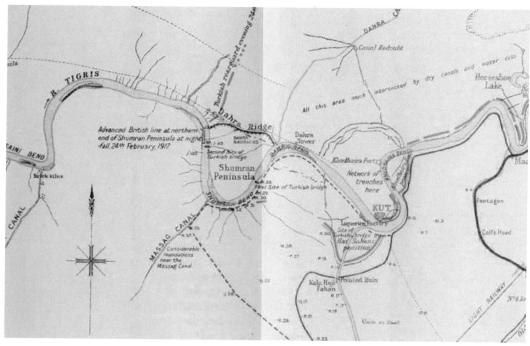

The War in the Air (vol 5) by HA Jones, 1935

Percy and his battalion were involved in the Battles of the Hai salient, Dahra Bend and the Shumran Peninsula (11th January - 24th February 1917). An extract from the battalion War Diary for this period is reproduced here:

	WAR DIARY [112] or INTELLIGENCE SUMMARY. (Erase heading not required.)	
Instructions regarding War Diaries and Intelligence Summaries are contained in F.S. Regs., Part II, and the Staff Manual respectively. Title pages will be prepared in manuscript.		Army Form C. 2118.
Date	Summary of Events and Information	Remarks and References to Appendices
1-1-1917 to 3-1-1917	Battalion west of HAI, south of RIVER TIGRIS, opposite Kut el Amara. Creating new defence lines. Working parties 130 men on new defensive line.	
4 to 10-1-1917	Musketry, bombing and Lewis Gun classes	
11 to 21-1-1917	Consolidating trenches. Dug Communication Trench.	
22-1-1917	Occupied ANDREW, FISHER, and trench from PIONEER TRENCH to BUFF STREET. Casualties 3 men killed.	
25-1-1917	39TH BRIGADE attacked on right, but not successful. 1 OR killed, 1 officer and 8 ORs wounded.	
26-1-1917	36TH BRIGADE attacked the lines, most successful.	
27-1-1917 to 31-1-1917	STAFFORD STREET TRENCH connected to new fire trench P21B-P12B. Fire trench P19A-P16B dug and meet BUFF STREET and PIONEER TRENCH.	
1-2-1917 to 4-2-1917	Occupied ANDREW, MATTHEW and BIGNALL TRENCH. Attack parties sent out and emplacements and piquets dug for French Howitzers.	
5-2-1917	As consequence of shell fire Battalion moved back behind line of batteries. Party of 75 men furnished for clearing the battlefield.	
6-2-1917	52 Turks buried. and continued clearing. Party of 75 men furnished for clearing the battlefield. 100 men for digging.	
7 to 8-2-1917	In bivouacs KALA HAJI FAHAN.	
9-2-1917	Moved to HARVEY ROAD at 9.30, preparation for attack on 10th.	
10-2-1917	Attacked from line N20G-N41A with 2/4 GURKHA RIFLES on right. Attack successful as enemy already vacated line. Patrols and bombing parties pushed on.	
11-2-1917	Patrols and bombing parties reached line M13C-M13B-M13A.	
12-2-1917	Creating and consolidating trenches. Patrols sent out.	
15-2-1917	1.30pm Attacked in 8 lines, very successful reaching K41H-J62. 600 prisoners taken. 12 ORs killed. 1 officer and 67 ORs wounded.	
16-2-1917	Following picquet line along riverbank. Very heavy rain. 2 OR wounded. 1 OR killed.	
17-2-1917	Following picquet line along riverbank. Trenches all flooded. Impossible to clear battlefield.	

The CWGC database records the only OR (Other Rank) killed on 16th February 1917 was 18-year-old Percy.

[112] War Diary: 35 Indian Infantry Brigade: 1/5 Battalion Buffs (East Kent Regiment), WO-95-5175-2. December 1915 – December 1917. The National Archives (UK), Kew, England.

According to official records Percy was buried in Amara War Cemetery, Iraq, and his memorial headstone is inscribed with the words: "BELIEVED TO BE BURIED IN THIS CEMETERY."

Amara became a hospital centre in June 1915 and by 1916 there were seven general hospitals and some smaller units. The cemetery holds 4,621 burials, 3,000 of which were brought in after the Armistice. At the time of printing the cemetery was in a poor state as a result of the Iraq War (2003-2011) and the Commonwealth War Graves Commission are planning a major rehabilitation project, when the situation allows.

Locally, Percy is remembered on a number of memorials including Sittingbourne War Memorial, Sittingbourne's Holy Trinity Church, Milton Regis War Memorial, St Paul's Church, and Old Boys Milton Council Schools Memorials. His mother received his pay as well as his Victory and British War Medals.

RICKARD, William John

243696, Private, 1st/5th Battalion, The Queen's (Royal West Surrey Regiment).

William was born in Catmere End, Essex in 1884. He was the eleventh of the thirteen children of Thomas, an agricultural labourer, and Emma (née Camp). His siblings were Walter Thomas, Charles John (1868-1884), Albert James, William Henry (1872-1874), Frederick George, Emily Jane, Herbert, Margaret Ellen, Rose, Maria, Eliza (1886-1886), and Charles Henry.

On 15th April 1911, William married local girl Mary Ann Sedge, in St Mary Magdalene Church, Stockbury. Shortly after their marriage, they moved to William's hometown of Littlebury in Essex, where they had two daughters Winifred Helen (born 21st January 1912) and Dorothy Mary (born 13th July 1913).

The family later moved to Sittingbourne and when William enlisted on 24th October 1916, he was working at Sittingbourne Paper Mill. He left for service abroad on Christmas Eve the same year, and served in India, Mesopotamia, and Salonika. He served in the Queen's (Royal West Surrey Regiment), 1st/5th Battalion. William was discharged aged 35 and returned to England on 25th May 1919 and returned home three days later. Shortly after his return he complained of stomach pains and was admitted to Fort Pitt Military Hospital (pictured right) on 7th June 1919.

245

It was found that William was suffering from an appendix abscess, which was operated on, on 16th June 1919. A month later, on 25th July, he had another operation for an intestinal obstruction, which appeared to provide some relief. A third exploratory operation was undertaken on 8th September and the doctors concluded that 'the case was considered hopeless from that date.'

On 18th September 1919, his wife visited him in hospital during the morning, but in the afternoon, William took his own life.

An inquest was held on 20th September 1919 and was reported upon in the East Kent Gazette, the following week on 27th September, under the headline "SOLDIER'S SAD END." The inquest heard from the hospital orderlies, nurses and doctors concerning his treatment. One of the witnesses, Major Alan Cunliffe Vidal, Royal Army Medical Corps, explained that on the morning of the 18th, William had asked point blank about his condition, and he responded that there was nothing further that could be done. The witness added that he was called to see the patient, and found an abdominal wound, which he established, due to his condition, that he would not survive.

The coroner returned the verdict that William had taken his own life and was not in a sane state of mind at the time. He added 'that it was evident that the countries in which he had served his King and country during hostilities did not possess the healthiest of climates.' All this had, in the coroner's opinion, contributed towards William's state of health.

William was buried in the Fort Pitt Military Cemetery, Chatham, with the words "GONE BUT NOT FORGOTTEN" inscribed on his headstone. Locally he is remembered on Sittingbourne War Memorial and Lloyd's Paper Mill Memorial. His wife, Mary Ann, received his pay. She remarried in 1921 to James Turner in Milton Regis district.

ROCKLIFFE, George Henry

64090, Corporal, 26th Battalion, Royal Fusiliers.

George was born in Sittingbourne in 1892, the fourth of the eight children of William Edward, a barge captain, and Sarah Louisa (née Clayton). His brothers and sisters were Alice Maud, Ellen Annie, William Edward, Dorothy Jane, Grace Emily, Laura (1901-1909) and Albert Edwin.

George's father, William, was found drowned in Conyer on 11th November 1904, where his barge the *John and Sarah* was moored. An inquest was held the following week at the Ship Inn, Conyer, which heard that on the evening of the 10th William had been at the Ship Inn and left with a friend for the walk to Teynham to get a train, when it started to rain. William decided to go to the barge instead and it was noted that it was very rough and very dark. William was found the next morning by the barge lying in the mud. The coroner passed a verdict of "Accidental death."

In 1911 George was living with his widowed mother at 12 Princes Street, Milton Regis, across the road from the paper mill where he, his mother and his brother William all worked as labourers. He married 19-year-old Fanny Wildish on 6th September 1913 at All Saints Church, Murston, and they had a daughter, Ena Ivy, who was born on 14th November 1914.

George enlisted in Sittingbourne, joining the 32nd Battalion, Royal Engineers, and arrived in France on 23rd September 1917. He was transferred to the 26th Battalion on 16th March 1918.

The War Diary for his battalion in September of 1918 is reproduced here:

Instructions regarding War Diaries and Intelligence Summaries are contained in F.S. Regs., Part II, and the Staff Manual respectively. Title pages will be prepared in manuscript.

WAR DIARY [113]
or
INTELLIGENCE SUMMARY.
(Erase heading not required.)

Army Form C. 2118.

Date	Summary of Events and Information	Remarks and References to Appendices
1-9-1918	Battalion spent the night travelling to DICKEBUSCH.	
2-9-1918	Relieved 2nd BATTALION, 105TH REGIMENT, 27TH AMERICAN DIVISION in reserve.	
4-9-1918	Moved to VIERSTRAAT to relieve 20th BATTALION DURHAM AND LIGHT INFANTRY.	
5-9-1918 to 8-9-1918	Ordered to restore the front line and push forward.	
9-9-1918	2am - Relieved by 10th BATTALION ROYAL WEST KENT REGIMENT and moved back from DICKEBUSCH to the lake. Remained in support.	
11-9-1918	Moved into reserve at DOMINION CAMP, (near OUDERDOM).	
15-9-1918 to 26-9-1918	Battalion entrained and marched to RECQUES training area,	
27-9-1918	Entrained and marched to TORONTO CAMP, (located halfway between YPRES and POPERINGE. Arriving at 9pm.	
28-9-1918	Relocated to SWAN CHATEAU. 3pm - Started advance south-east on the enemy, met by machine gun fire. Managed to outflank and surround them. Advance continued and final objective achieved at 6.30pm. Enemy counterattack quickly suppressed. Battalion established and consolidated the line at COMINES-WARENTON. On right 10TH BATTALION QUEENS and 35TH DIVISION to the left.	
29-9-1918	7am - Advance continued from HELL'S DELIGHT and DELESEQUE FARM. More resistance met than previous day from machine guns and snipers. Soon dealt with. 8.30am - Objective achieved. 10TH ROYAL WEST KENT proceeded through the line and attempted to advance to RIVER LYS (now known as RIVER LEIE) but forced to withdraw.	
30-9-1918	5.30am - Battalion moved off. Rapidly managed to clear ground forcing enemy machine gun teams to withdraw. 8.30am - Reached RIVER LYS and watched enemy withdraw rapidly on the other side of the river. Operational CASUALTIES - 11 killed, 43 wounded, 7 missing.	

George was killed in action on the second day of the operation on 29th September 1918, aged 23.

[113] War Diary: 26 Battalion Royal Fusiliers. WO-95-2644-2. March 1918-September 1919. The National Archives (UK), Kew, England.

Initially, George was buried 200m north of the main road through Klein Zillebeke and 600m from the Cavalry Church Memorial, with a number of other casualties. Later, his body was moved and buried in Menin Road South Military Cemetery in West-Vlaanderen, Belgium.

Locally he is remembered on Sittingbourne War Memorial, as well as Sittingbourne Holy Trinity Church WW1 Memorial and Lloyd's Paper Mill Memorial. On the latter and the Avenue of Remembrance, his name is incorrectly spelt 'Rockcliffe'.

George was awarded the Victory and British War Medals. Unusually his pay and gratuity were to be paid to his daughter Ena Ivy on her sixteenth birthday. Ena was living with her paternal grandmother, Sarah, in Princes Street as her mother (George's wife Fanny) had passed away on the 27th March 1916 at Keycol Hill Hospital, Bobbing.

ROSSITER, Henry

40111, Private, 9th Battalion, Lancashire Fusiliers.

Henry was born in Sittingbourne in 1884 and was the oldest of the five children of Ernest and Sarah (née Allright). His siblings were William, Albert, Annie, and Doris May. In 1901 the family were living at 21 Hythe Road, Sittingbourne and Henry, his father and brother William were all employed at the paper mill as labourers, and Albert as a shop errand boy.

In the spring of 1909, Henry married local girl Daisy Tyler in the Milton Regis district. In 1911 they were living at Hill Side, Horns Cross, London Road, Stone, Kent, and he was working as a dryerman for a wallpaper manufacturer. Daisy's 14-year-old brother, Leslie, was living with them and he was also employed by the wallpaper manufacturer, as a winder boy.

The previous year, on 22nd April 1908, all of Henry's family emigrated to Oswego, New York, USA (pictured below), as did many from the Sittingbourne area. His father obtained employment in a starch factory as a labourer, but sadly died just four years later aged 53.

Henry enlisted with the East Lancashire Regiment in Darwen, Lancashire before he was transferred to the Fusiliers.

At the start of July 1917, his battalion were in training in Mentque, where they remained until 26th July when they moved to Wormhoudt (now Wormhout). Then on the last day of July their War Diary[114] records that they were subject to an inspection, after arriving the previous day at Windmill Camp, near Ypres, just outside the village of Millekruisse.

Henry's battalion continued training, which included short route marches, physical training and bayonet

---

[114] War Diary: 9 Battalion Lancashire Fusiliers. WO-95-1820-2. July 1916-February 1918. The National Archives (UK), Kew, England.

fighting, at Windmill Camp for the first week of August 1917 and then on the 8th they moved to Siege Camp, near Ypres. The diary records that the battalion spent the 8th to 14th August training, with 'special attention paid to following up on a tape both by day and night'. On 15th August the battalion was positioned north of Ypres, next to the canal.

The formal War Diary entry for the 16th/17th August 1917 reads "The battalion took part in the Fifth Army offensive operations." The diary held by the National Archives includes a report of the offensive. The report stated the objective was an attack on Pheasant Trench, Pheasant Farm and White House, near Langemarck.

At 4.45am on the morning of 16th August 1917 the battalion was formed up behind the 5th Dorset Regiment and to the left of the 11th Manchester Regiment, along 600m of the Langemarck-Zonnebeke road, just on the edge of Langemarck (above). At this time the barrage started, the forces advanced and the first objective of White House, 600m ahead, was taken.

The battalion was about 300m short of Pheasant Trench and was held up as the Manchesters had been exposed to heavy fire and the line had halted at Rat House, situated on the right flank about 300m from the trench. The delay was compounded by the work of German snipers in woods to the east of Rat House. The following afternoon, orders were given to clear the woods, the battalion advanced and located eight snipers in 'improved shell holes', which they dealt with. After this the line advanced 150m.

That night on 16th August 1917, the battalion was relieved by the 9th Notts and Derbys. Their diary recorded that 50 prisoners had been taken and the casualty list was 34 killed, 191 wounded and 24 missing. After the battle the battalion returned to Siege Camp to re-organise and re-equip.

Henry was reported missing in action and was last seen on the first day of the battle. He was officially declared as "Missing in action presumed killed" on 16th August 1917, aged 35.

He is remembered on the Tyne Cot Memorial to the Missing and on Sittingbourne War Memorial. He was awarded the Victory and British War Medals. Henry's wife received his pay and gratuity.

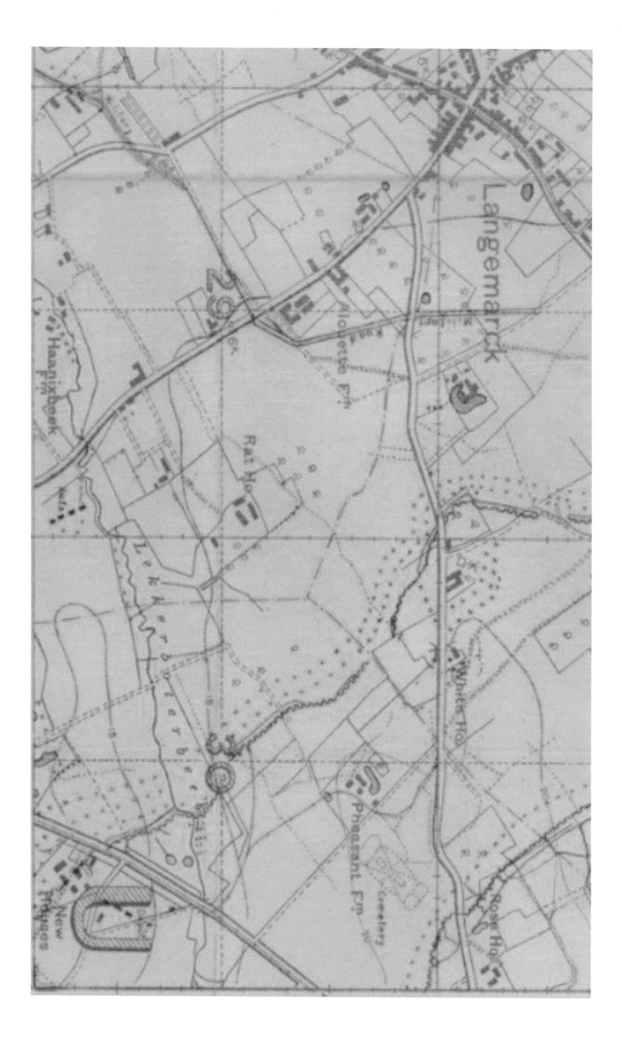

Trench Map Sheet 20.SW.4 -May 1917. Reproduced with the permission of the National Library of Scotland

RUSSELL, Alfred Warren

282398, Private, 2nd/4th Battalion, London Regiment (Royal Fusiliers).

Alfred was born in Sittingbourne in 1878 and was baptised at St Michael's Church on 4th May 1879. He was the seventh of eleven children of John James and Matilda (née Lucas). His siblings were Minnie, Frank John (1870-1870), Mary Ann, John James, William (1875-1876), Bessie, Alice Eliza, Flossy, George Claude (1883-1884), and Lily Emily. He also had an older half-sister, Kate Matilda Lucas, on his mother's side.

Alfred's father was a tailor and the family lived at 115 East Street, Sittingbourne, during the last three decades

of the 19th century. Alfred's father died in 1894 and his mother in 1908. By 1911 Alfred was boarding, with his brother-in-law Walter and his sister Mary Ann Lawrence, and their four children at 5 Terrace Road, Sittingbourne. Both Alfred and Walter were employed as paper makers.

Alfred's two youngest sisters emigrated to Toronto, Ontario, Canada, (pictured right) with Lily moving in 1909 and Alice in 1913.

Alfred enlisted in London in February 1916 and spent eleven months training before embarking for France on 23rd January 1917 from Southampton. On arrival at Le Havre his battalion embarked on a train journey 200km to the north-east to Fortel-en-Artois, near Arras. The battalion's first time in the trenches was on 10th February 1917 at Sus-Saint-Léger (below), for five days. Their War Diary[115] entries throughout that time recorded 'A quiet day.'

SUS-SAINT-LÉGER (P.-d.-C.) – Grande Rue

Following their arrival in France until the end of May 1917 his battalion spent 27 days out of 128 days in the trenches. From mid-April to mid-May they were part of working parties repairing the roads and railway in Achiet-le-Grand.

At the beginning of June 1917, they were billeted at Mory near Achiet-le-Grand. On 3rd June 1917 they relieved the 2/2nd London Regiment east of Croiselles. For the next week, their diary records heavy shelling as well as the British shelling the enemy trenches and wire, and that they were clearing trenches to link up isolated posts.

---

[115] War Diary: 2/4 Battalion London Regiment. WO-95-3001-9. January 1917-September 1918. The National Archives (UK), Kew, England.

On 12th June 1917 Alfred's battalion moved to nearby Saint-Léger to prepare for an attack on the Hindenburg Line at Bullecourt (pictured below). Three days later, on the 15th, the attack on the front-line German trenches on the Hindenburg Line was completed successfully. The next day, they attacked the support trenches and B and D Companies of the battalion entered the trenches, but divisional support on the left failed to reach their objectives. As a result, the Companies were surrounded, and no news had been received.

It was learned from a German communique that they had taken 70 prisoners, who were assumed to be B and D Companies. The next day the battalion was relieved and returned to Mory Camp. The casualty figures recorded in the diary for the two days was 14 killed, 93 wounded and 2116 missing, the latter were assumed to be primarily missing due to being captured and becoming prisoners of war as opposed to being 'missing in action presumed killed'.

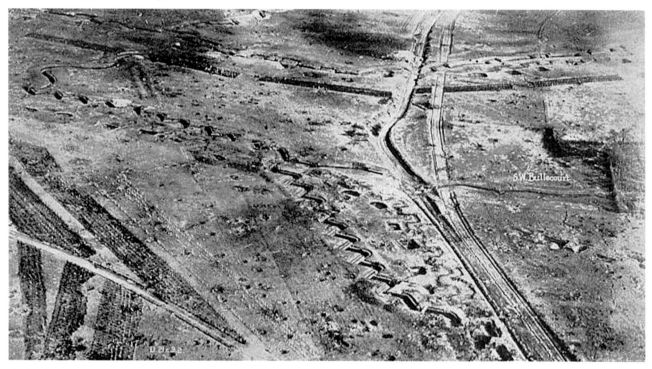

Alfred, aged 38 years, was initially posted as missing and later confirmed as killed in action on the first day of the attack, on 15th June 1917.

Alfred's death was reported on in the East Kent Gazette edition dated 16th February 1918. It reported that his family had just received official confirmation that he had been declared "Missing in action presumed killed." The report mentioned that he had a large circle of friends and had worked at the paper mill for twenty-three years, having started at the age of 14 years. Before enlisting he had been a reelerman and was a member of the Mill's cricket and football teams.

He is remembered on the Arras Memorial to the Missing, and locally on Sittingbourne War Memorial and St Michael's Church WW1 Memorial Window. His pay and gratuity were paid to his brother John, and he was awarded the Victory and British War Medals.

Credit: ww1cemeteries.com © Werner Van Caneghem

SAGE, Sidney

6333, Private, 10th (Prince of Wales's Own Royal) Hussars.

Sidney was born in Sittingbourne in 1890, the son of Alfred Robert and Louisa Jane (née Denne). He was the fifth of their nine children and his siblings were Alfred Thomas, Edwin George, Flossy Emma Louisa, George Coleman, Ellen Mercy, Gertrude (1893-1893), Mabel, and Percy (1896-1896).

Sidney's father had a variety of jobs, in 1882 he was a publican running the Old Oak Inn and in 1891 he was running the Plough Inn, both in East Street, Sittingbourne. He then worked in the paper mill and by 1911 he was a dealer in fireworks. Two years later, he died after a long illness and four years later his wife Louisa also died.

Sidney's eldest brother, Alfred, served in the same regiment as him. Alfred was in France from August 1914 and was a batman for his commanding officer Colonel W. Llewellyn, with whom Alfred went to work as a stud groom after he left the army. The report of Alfred's death in the East Kent Gazette dated 8th March 1947 said that he was born in the Old Oak Inn, in 1882, and had served in South Africa's Boer War.

Sidney had enlisted before 1911 as the census for that year records him at Aliwal Military Barracks (pictured right) in South Tidworth, Hampshire.

Sidney's battalion War Diary[116] records they left Tidworth on 6th October 1914 and arrived in Ostend on 10th October 1914. They then moved to billets at Rollegem-Kapelle, near Ypres, on the 13th. The next day, on the 25km march south-west to Wytschaete, they shot down a German aeroplane, and then on the 15th they were fired upon by the Germans.

By 18th October 1914 his regiment had arrived in Passchendaele, and the following day they moved to Ledegem (pictured left) and drove out the German troops situated in the south of the village. For the rest of the month, they moved around the outer area of Ypres engaging with the enemy, reporting occasions of shelling and sniper action.

During this time, they had little rest or time away from the action. They spent odd days in billets, 28th October, 4th and 5th November 1914. On the 7th they moved to Halte, near Ledegem. Three days later they moved east to the trenches in Zillebeke, on the outskirts of Ypres.

---

[116] War Diary: 10 (Prince of Wales) Hussars. WO-95-1156-4. October 1914-February 1918. The National Archives (UK), Kew, England.

The 11th November 1914 was recorded to be heavy rain and heavy shelling. The following day they were forced to move back 100m out of the trenches due to them being washed out. During the fallback they were subjected to sniper attack. Then on 14th November they moved out to billets at Vlamertinge, near Ypres. A day later at 4am, they travelled to the opposite side of Ypres to Hooge, to support the 3rd Infantry Division, and their diary noted that the day 'Remained in snow until 10am' when they returned to billets, though later in the day they returned to the east to trenches between Hooge and Zillebeke.

In the afternoon of 17th November 1914, the Germans attacked, getting within a few yards of the trenches, before 'grazing fire was put down'. The diary noted about 200 German casualties. The Germans also shelled their positions. The casualty numbers were recorded as 12 killed and wounded. The next few days were spent resting in billets, whilst it was snowing. Following the action, General Sir Douglas Haig sent a congratulatory telegram concerning the 'excellent fight.'

Credit: ww1cemeteries.com

Sidney was killed during the German attack on 17th November 1914, aged 23. He is remembered on the Ypres Menin Gate Memorial (pictured left) to those who have no known grave.

Locally, he is remembered on Sittingbourne War Memorial. His pay was paid to his mother and his sister, Flossie, received his war gratuity as their mother had died by the time it was issued. Sidney was awarded the Victory and British War Medals.

SAWYER, Herbert William

613115, Private, 19th Battalion, London Regiment.

Herbert was born in Murston in 1896 and was the middle child of nine. His parents were William, a mariner, and Mary (née Hyland). His siblings were William Richard (1886-1886), Nellie Maude, Annie Elizabeth, Charlie, James Henry, Polly, and Lizzie. Sadly, he also had one sister who died in infancy and was registered unnamed in 1890.

Herbert's father died between 1906 and 1911, and his mother died four years later in December 1915. In 1911 the family were living at 123 Shortlands Road, Sittingbourne, and Herbert was employed as a labourer at the brickfields.

Herbert enlisted in Canterbury and joined the 4th Battalion, The Buffs (East Kent Regiment). He later transferred to the London Regiment and was serving with them as a Private in France when he was badly gassed.

From 24th November 1917 Herbert's battalion was in billets at Marœuil, near Arras, refitting and resting. Then on the 25th they moved out and spent the next four days travelling by marching and motor lorry, a 60km route to Rocquigny. Two days after that they moved to the Hindenburg Support Line at Havrincourt.

His battalion's War Diary[117] recorded on 28th November 1917 they had moved to Bourlon Wood (pictured right), near Cambrai, and it added that night the woods were bombarded. Then at 11.30pm the 'enemy sent over gas shells of the tear variety', which lasted until 2.15am. The 29th saw more shelling and enemy planes fly over, and in the evening more gas shells, which were different to the tear ones and the 'men were sick and their eyes affected.' The shelling stopped at 3.15am on the 30th and in the morning a visit by the medical officer determined that 50% of the men were affected and to be evacuated.

BOURLON WOOD FROM THE SOUTH-WEST.

On 1st December 1917 Herbert's battalion remained in the woods and the next day returned to the Hindenburg Support Line. The following day more men had to be evacuated due to gas and the remainder of the battalion moved to Hermies. Their diary noted that the 4th was a quiet day spent re-organising. The diary entry for 4th December started 'Moved again', this time 52km south-east to Berthenicourt, where they remained cleaning and further re-organisation taking place until 16th December.

Herbert died on 9th December 1917 at No. 3 Casualty Clearing Station, Grévillers, after having been gassed. The records do not show exactly when Herbert was gassed, but it was probably during his time in Bourlon Wood.

Credit: ww1cemeteries.com © Werner Van Caneghem

He was buried in Grévillers British Cemetery, which was designed by Sir Edwin Lutyens. Grévillers was the base for a number of Casualty Clearing Stations, after it was taken by the New Zealanders on 24th August 1917. Within the cemetery is the Grévillers (New Zealand) Memorial to 450 officers and men from New Zealand who have no known grave.

Herbert is remembered on the Murston and the Sittingbourne War Memorials, as well as on St Michael's Church WW1 Memorial Window. His sister, Nellie, received his pay and gratuity, and he was awarded the Victory and British War Medals.

[117] War Diary: 1/19 Battalion London Regiment (St. Pancras). WO-95-2738-1. March 1915-May 1919. The National Archives (UK), Kew, England.

Sadly, just two months before Herbert's death, his sister Nellie's husband, Francis Lucas Stapley was killed on 16th September 1917 in France. Francis was a Sapper in the 345th Road Construction Company, Royal Engineers. He was killed when an enemy aircraft dropped a bomb as he and a colleague were leading horses and a wagon along a road in France on 14th August 1917. He was taken to a base hospital and then moved to Cosham Military Hospital in Wiltshire, where he passed away with Nellie present.

Herbert left an eight-year-old daughter, Margaret Elizabeth. Like Herbert, Francis is commemorated on Murston's War Memorial, and he was buried in Sittingbourne Cemetery with his headstone inscribed with one word "MEMORIES."

The East Kent Gazette

SATURDAY, DECEMBER 7, 1918

IN MEMORIAM

SAWYER. – In loving memory of our dear brother, Pte. Herbert William Sawyer, who was killed in action, December 9th, 1917; also of our dear mother, Mary Sawyer, who passed away, Oct. 31st, 1915.

When alone in our sorrow and bitter tears flow,
There stealeth a dream of a sweet long ago;
And unknown to the world, they stand by our side,
And whisper these words "Death cannot divide."
From loving Sons, Daughters, Brothers, and Sisters.

SCOTT, Percy George

Lance Corporal, 7th Royal Fusiliers.

An Avenue tablet records a L/Cpl P. G. Scott and St Michael's Church WW1 Memorial Window records a P. G. Scott, H. M. Army.

A report of the unveiling of the memorial window in the East Kent Gazette edition dated 7th January 1922 provides additional information for the names on the window. One entry records:

Percy George Scott, 7th Royal Fusiliers (died of wounds in France)

The CWGC database has no matching or close matches for a Percy George Scott or a match to a member of the 7th Royal Fusiliers.

Research to identify Percy and tell his story will continue.

His name is also recorded on Sittingbourne War Memorial.

Though Percy's story cannot be told at this time,

We remember him, as did those who knew him.

SHAW, Frederick James

27716, Serjeant, 9th Battalion, Essex Regiment.

Frederick was born on Christmas Day 1884 in Lancaster, Lancashire, and was baptised there in the parish church of St Anne's on 19th April 1885. He was the son of John and Eleanor (née Gardner) who had eight children, though sadly four died in infancy, Frederick (1882-1882), John (1887-1887), Agnes (1888-1893) and Alfred (1895-1895). Their other children were Elizabeth Ann (born 1881), John (born 1890) and Francis Henry (born 1893). Tragically, Frederick's mother, Eleanor, died in 1895.

The family had lived in Lancaster until at least 1895 but by 1901 had moved to Bromley, Kent. Frederick in 1901 was recorded as an iron moulder, the same occupation as his father. Frederick's father married Margaret Holmes, who was his housekeeper in Bromley, and they had a daughter Lily who was born in 1903. Margaret already had a daughter, Violet, born in 1895, who was already using the surname Shaw in 1901. By 1911 Frederick's family had returned to Lancaster.

When Frederick joined the Essex Regiment on 10th October 1902, he was 5ft 2in tall. He served in Malta from 19th April to 19th October 1904 and was promoted to Lance Corporal on 25th November 1904. Eleven months later, on 9th October 1905, he transferred to the Army Reserve.

On 19th January 1907, Frederick married Edith Janette Ellis. They had five children, Edith Eleanor (born 1907, West Ham), Frederick William (born 1909, Lancaster), Ethel (born 1912, Sittingbourne), Agnes May (born 1914, Sittingbourne) and James Victor (born 1916, Sittingbourne). In 1911 they lived at Pitstock Farm, Rodmersham and they later moved to 10 Pembury Street, Sittingbourne.

The day after Great Britain declared war on Germany, 4th August 1914, Frederick was mobilised to Warley, Essex, and three days later was posted to 3rd Battalion, Essex Regiment. He was transferred to the 2nd Battalion when they were sent to France on 9th February 1915. Three months later, on 30th April 1915, he was wounded by a gunshot to the right shoulder.

Initially he was treated at No. 84 Field Ambulance on 2nd May 1915, before being admitted, the same day, to No. 11 General Hospital in Boulogne. He was then moved on the 7th, to No. 6 General Hospital in Rouen. Two weeks later, on 21st May 1915, he returned to his unit in the field.

Frederick returned home to England on 30th September 1915 and nine days later he was discharged, with his record recording the reason as 'time expired'.

Credit: World War One: Rouen, France: a general view of hospital tents. Photograph, 1916. Wellcome Collection.

However, Frederick re-enlisted in Sittingbourne, this time joining the Essex Regiment, and again found himself fighting in France. On 1st July 1916 his battalion moved to Henencourt Wood, near Albert and early the next morning, its War Diary[118] records that they relieved 23rd Brigade in Ribble Street, west of the village of Ovillers. In the early afternoon of the same day, they were moved again to Marmont Bridge, on the northern outskirts of Albert, with orders to hold back the enemy. At 7.30pm the battalion returned to Ribble Street.

British communication trench, Ovillers, July 1916. IWM (Q 889)

At 2.15am on 3rd July 1916 the British artillery started a bombardment of Ovillers, to which the Germans retaliated. At 3.20am the Berks and Suffolk's left the line and advanced on the German front and support lines, as well as the village, with Frederick's battalion following up behind. Their diary records that they 'suffered severely' owing to the open country and enemy machine gun fire from the flank and village. By 4.30pm the remainder of the battalion withdrew back to Ribble Street and the Norfolk's took over at the front.

Attacks continued on the village of La Boisselle, south of Ovillers, with the Royal Welch Fusiliers and Glosters meeting up with the Norfolks. Together they managed to capture the north-east area, taking 177 prisoners. Frederick's battalion remained in Ribble Street on the 4th and 5th July 1916, they relocated to Albert. The diary listed their casualty numbers as 398 wounded, missing or killed.

Frederick was presumed to have been killed during the attack on 3rd July 1916, aged 32. He is remembered on the Thiepval Memorial to the Missing.

Locally, he is remembered on Sittingbourne War Memorial and Sittingbourne Holy Trinity Church WW1 Memorial. He was awarded the 1914-15 Star, Victory, and British War Medals.

Frederick's wife, Edith, received his pay. In 1920 Edith married John Edward Milway in Milton Regis and the following year they had a daughter, Eileen Mildred. However, Edith suffered the death of her second husband in 1922, when John died after being run over by a lorry in Keycol Hill, Sittingbourne. Their daughter, Eileen, died in 1938 and later that year Edith married Henry Robert Abbott.

[118] War Diary: 9 Battalion Essex Regiment. WO-95-1851-2. July 1916-November 1916. The National Archives (UK), Kew, England.

SHILLING, Charles Edward

124135, Private, 50th Battalion, Machine Gun Corps (Infantry).

Charles was born in Sittingbourne in 1898, the fourth of eleven children to Charles, a brickmaker's labourer, and Lizzie Virginia (née Attwood). His siblings were Mabel (1894-1915), George, Jesse, Lizzie Virginia (1899-1902), Ernest, Clara, Mary Ann, Frederick, Albert and Elsie.

The family were living at 1 Thomas Road, Sittingbourne in 1911, with Charles' grandfather, Jesse Attwood, a hay-cutter. Charles attended St Michael's School and the Salvation Army Sunday School. On leaving school he worked for Messrs Smeed, Dean and Co. Ltd. On Christmas Day 1917 Charles married Edith May Sharp (who already had a two-year-old son, Ryland) at All Saints Church, Murston.

Charles enlisted in Sittingbourne, in November 1914, when he was still sixteen years old. He joined The Buffs (East Kent Regiment) but was transferred to the Machine Gun Corps when he was sent to France in January 1917.

The East Kent Gazette dated 6th April 1918, reported that Charles had been gassed and was in hospital. The report added that his two older brothers were also serving, George was a Rifleman in the King's Royal Rifles and was in Salonika, and Jesse was a Private in Palestine with the Queen's (Royal West Surrey) Regiment. Both his brothers survived the war.

On 28th September 1918 Charles' battalion arrived at Poulainville, just north of Amiens, for rest in the line. Their War Diary[119] records that during the October they were suffering casualties almost every day, whilst they were in the line and that the weather was unsettled, being fine one day and showery the next. The diary does not record how the casualties occurred.

Charles was killed on 17th October 1918, when he was 20 years old. The report of Charles' death in the East Kent Gazette dated 23rd November 1918 said that Charles' section officer, Second Lieutenant E. A. Deacon had informed his mother that he was killed by a piece of flying shell and had been buried at a farmhouse on cross-roads three miles from Le Cateau, on the main road between Le Cateau and Honnechy.

Despite details of his burial, Charles is commemorated on the Vis-en-Artois Memorial to the Missing, France, so it is assumed that his burial place was not found or had been destroyed.

Locally, Charles is remembered on Sittingbourne War Memorial and St Michael's Church WW1 Memorial Window.

His widow, Edith, received his pay and war gratuity, and his Victory and British War Medals. In 1922 she married David Higgins.

The East Kent Gazette

SATURDAY, OCTOBER 18, 1919

IN MEMORIAM

SHILLING. – In ever-loving memory of Pte. Charles Shilling, 50th Batt., M.G.C., who was killed in action Oct. 17th, 1918.

The happy hours we once enjoyed
How sweet their memory still;
But death has left a vacant place
This world can never fill.
His memory still is very dear,
And oft' we shed a silent tear:
The far-off grave is the bitterest blow
None but aching hearts can know.

From his loving Wife and Child.

---

[119] War Diary: 50 Battalion Machine Gun Corps. WO-95-2823-3. April 1918-April 1919. The National Archives (UK), Kew, England.

The SHRUBSALL Brothers

Paul Shrubsall, a fisherman, married Mary Ann Goldfinch on 13th May 1882. She already had a son, Frederick William, who was born on 18th August 1881. As a child he took the surname Shrubsall, however when he married Elizabeth Pettett in 1904, he used the surname Goldfinch. He served in India with The Buffs throughout the war.

Paul and Mary Ann had three children of their own, Strains, Muriel Dorothy (1895-1977) and Edward Paul. Their father, Paul, died in 1910, and in 1911 Mary Ann married William Barratt, a fisherman.

SHRUBSALL, Strains Blacketer

5175, Private, 8th Battalion, The Buffs (East Kent Regiment).

Registered at birth as Strains, he is recorded on the CWGC database and some documents as Sham, and his pension card as Strains Blackaton, though his name is likely to be Strains Blacketer as this was a family name, after his uncle Strains Blacketer Shrubsall and his grand-father George Blacketer Shrubsall.

Strains was born in Sittingbourne in 1888 the second son of Mary Ann (née Goldfinch) and eldest son of Paul. Strains had an older brother Frederick William Goldfinch, a younger brother Edward Paul (1899-1918), who also died in the war, and a younger sister Muriel (1895-1977). In 1901 the family were living at 1 Short Street, Sittingbourne. Strains was 13, and his father and older brother Frederick were both registered as fishermen, so it is likely that Strains followed in their footsteps. His father died in 1910, when Strains was 21 years old.

He enlisted in Sittingbourne in late 1914 and arrived in France on 7th October 1915. Strains battalion's War Diary[120] records at the beginning of August 1916 they were at the Sandpits, north-east of Cambrai and on 8th August moved to Waterlot Farm, Trones Wood and Barnafay Wood, to the south-east of Guillemont. On 18th August they attacked near Guillemont. German author Ernst Junger later said:

> "From nine till ten, the shelling acquired a demented fury. The earth shook, the sky seemed like a boiling cauldron. Hundreds of heavy batteries were crashing away at and around Combles, innumerable shells criss-crossed hissing and howling over our heads. All was swathed in black smoke, which was in the ominous under lighting of coloured flares. Because of racking pains in our heads and ears, communication was possible only by odd, shouted words... When day dawned we were astonished to see, by degrees, what a sight surrounded us. The sunken road now appeared as nothing but a series of enormous shell holes filled with pieces of uniform, weapons, and dead bodies. The ground all round, as far as the eye could see, was ploughed by shells. You could search in vain for one wretched blade of grass. This churned-up battlefield was ghastly. Among the living lay the dead."

---

[120] War Diary: 2 Battalion, The Buffs (East Kent Regiment). WO-95-2207-1. August 1915-January 1918. The National Archives (UK), Kew, England.

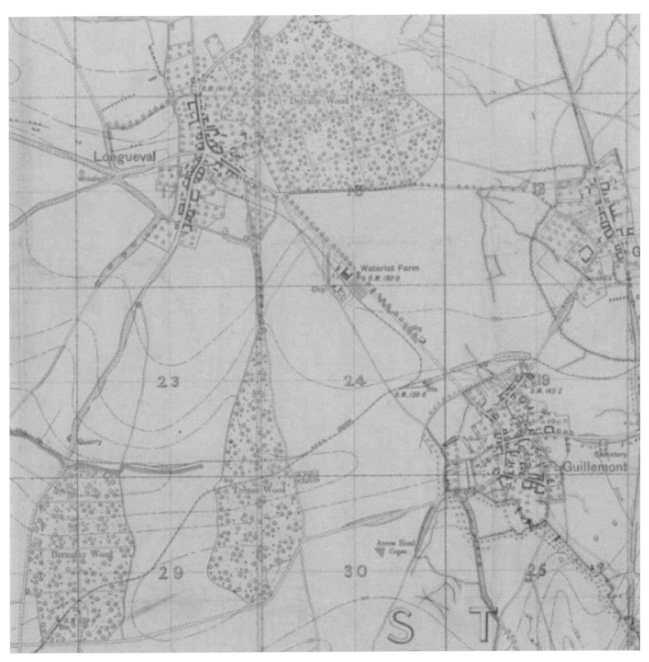

Trench Map 57C.SW.3 September 1916.
Reproduced with the permission of the National Library of Scotland

On 17th August 1916 the battalion had taken the line between Delville Wood and Guillemont. The fighting and bombardments continued on the 18th and the War Diary records 1 officer killed and 6 wounded, and of the Other Ranks 39 killed, 297 wounded and 16 missing.

The 19th August 1916 orders were "that no assault would take place today" and the diary noted "the morning was quiet."

Strains died of wounds, aged 27, on 28th August 1916, at No. 21 Casualty Clearing Station, La Neuville de Corbie. It is probable these were sustained during the attacks of the previous weeks, as the battalion had been relieved from the front line by the 22nd and had moved to Happy Valley.

He was buried at La Neuville British Cemetery, Corbie, with the words "THOUGH LOST TO SIGHT TO MEMORY DEAR" adorning his headstone. The cemetery was designed by Sir Edwin Lutyens and contains 866 Commonwealth burials.

164 Crown Copyright reserved   THE HIGH STREET OF GUILLEMONT (captured September 3rd, 1916)   "Daily Mail" Official Photograph

According to the 2nd September 1916 edition of the East Kent Gazette, Strains had died before his mother had even been told that he was wounded.

Locally, Strains is remembered on a number of memorials which include Sittingbourne War Memorial, Sittingbourne Holy Trinity Church WW1 Memorial, Milton Regis War Memorial, St Paul's Church Memorial (now in Milton Parish Church) and the Old Boys Milton Council Schools Memorial. He was awarded the 1915 Star, Victory and British War Medals, and his mother received his pay and gratuity.

SHRUBSALL, Edward Paul

K/44341 (CH), Stoker 2nd Class, Royal Navy, HMS Racoon.

Edward was born in Sittingbourne on 4th July 1899 and was baptised at Milton Regis's Holy Trinity Church with St Paul's Church on 23rd July 1899. Edward was the youngest son of Paul and Mary Ann (née Goldfinch). He had three elder siblings, Frederick William Goldfinch (his half-brother), Strains Blacketer, and Muriel. In 1901 the family were living at 1 Short Street, Sittingbourne.

Edward had attended the Holy Trinity Day School and Milton Congregational Sunday School. He had been employed as a reeler's assistant at Sittingbourne Paper Mill for three years before enlisting.

When Edward joined the Royal Navy on 19th July 1917, he was 5ft 4in tall with brown hair and blue eyes. He joined the destroyer *HMS Raccoon* on 10th October 1917.

On 9th January 1918 *Racoon* was en-route from Liverpool to Lough Swilly, in the north of Ireland, to take up anti-submarine duties. She was caught in a snowstorm and struck rocks at about 2am off Malin Head, the most northerly point of Ireland in County Donegal. She was lost with all 91 crew.

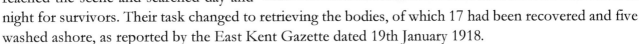

Despite the dangerous coast and the severe weather, a number of boats reached the scene and searched day and night for survivors. Their task changed to retrieving the bodies, of which 17 had been recovered and five washed ashore, as reported by the East Kent Gazette dated 19th January 1918.

Edward, aged 18 years, was one of the 32 bodies that were eventually found and buried in the churchyard of St Colomb Church, Rathmullan, County Donegal. He was buried with 15 fellow crew members in a single grave, which is marked by a single headstone. Rathmullan is located on the western shore of Lough Swilly, 50km to the south-west of Malin Head.

Together with Edward were four other Swale men, two of whom are buried alongside him. They were both from Faversham and are:

Stoker 1st Class Charles Alfred Harris, age 36. He was married to Amy Annie (née Hopkins) and they had three children; Percy (born 1906), Annie (born 1909) and Jessie (born.1913), and resided at 8 Union Street, Faversham.

Stoker 2nd Class Charles Mannouch, age 23. He was married to Alice (née Partridge) and they had a son Charles (born 1915) who tragically died a week after his father due to a fire in the home.

The other two men were:

Ship's Cook Walter Griffin, age 31. He was married to Rose Eliza (née Jarvis) and they lived in Higham. He was buried in Ballintoy Churchyard, County Antrim, Ireland.

Petty Officer Stoker Henry William Taylor, age 40, who was married to Elizabeth Alice (née Breadmore) and they had four children, whose names were Elizabeth May (born 1910), Harry Edwin Dennett (born 1912), Emily Louisa Clara (born 1913) and Vera Winifred Joyce (born 1917). They lived in Rainham. He was not found and is commemorated on Chatham Naval Memorial.

Locally, Edward is remembered on Sittingbourne War Memorial, Sittingbourne Holy Trinity Church WW1 Memorial and Lloyd's Paper Mill Memorial (pictured right) which was originally erected in Lloyd's Leisure Club on the Avenue and is now located at Kemsley Paper Mill, Sittingbourne.

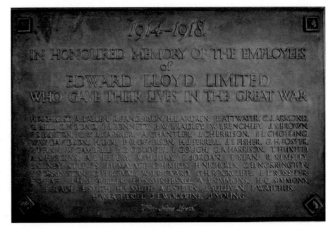

SIMMONS, Arthur James

T/201239, Serjeant, 7th Battalion, The Buffs (East Kent Regiment).

Arthur was born in the spring of 1889 in Chelsfield, Kent and was baptised there in the parish church of St Martin of Tours on 14th July 1889. He was the third of the eight children of James Edward and Mary Lydia (née Vale). His siblings were Florence, William Henry (1887-1905), Herbert John, Frederick Charles, Charles Edward, Cecil Edmond, and Hilda Mary.

Arthur's father was a police constable and they lived in Chelsfield and then Knockholt, before moving to Sittingbourne, where they were living at 13 Wellwinch Road in 1911. By then, James had retired from the police, but he re-joined when the war started and was also the County Court bailiff. Arthur and his brothers Herbert and Frederick were employed as paper makers.

Arthur had attended St Michael's School and whilst working for the paper mill (pictured right) enlisted with The Buffs (Territorials) but was not serving when war broke out. Arthur later re-enlisted in The Buffs, and qualified as a physical training and bayonet instructor, however it was not until New Year's Day 1918 that he went to France.

Two of Arthur's brothers, Herbert, and Frederick, also served in the same battalion. Frederick served for three years in France before being discharged due to illness.

The battalion War Diary for the weeks leading up to Arthur's death are reproduced below:

	WAR DIARY [121] or INTELLIGENCE SUMMARY. (Erase heading not required.)	Army Form C. 2118.
Instructions regarding War Diaries and Intelligence Summaries are contained in F.S. Regs., Part II, and the Staff Manual respectively. Title pages will be prepared in manuscript.		
Date	Summary of Events and Information	Remarks and References to Appendices
1-8-1918	On front line at MORLANCOURT.	
2-8-1918	The day passed without incident or importance.	
3-8-1918 to 9-8-1918	Battalion remained in the line, sending out night patrols, and their time remained uneventful.	
10-8-1918 to 16-8-1918	Marched to WARLOY-BAILLON, to billets. Cleaned up and re-organised.	
17-8-1918	Relieved 8TH ROYAL BERKSHIRES in LAVIÉVILLE. American platoon attached to each battalion company.	
21-8-1918	Battalion moved to MILLENCOURT. Battalion in readiness for planned attack.	

[121] io[121] War Diary: 26 Battalion Royal Fusiliers. WO-95-2644-2. March 1918-September 1919. The National Archives (UK), Kew, England.

22-8-1918	5.45am - 8TH BATTALION EAST SURREY REGIMENT moved forward east towards ALBERT, with orders to clear the town. 8.25am - Battalion moved up to the railway line on the edge of town at 8.25am and half an hour later were ordered to proceed into the town. By 4pm - Heavy casualties. 10.15pm – Battalion ordered to push forward.
23-8-1918	Morning – Battalion reached the eastern side of ALBERT and captured the town, pushing the Germans out. Midday – Battalion returned to MILLENCOURT.

This attack was to become known as the Third Battle of Albert.

Arthur sadly lost his life in the attack on 22nd August 1918, aged 29, after he was shot by a sniper. He was buried in Becourt Military Cemetery (pictured below c1920s), and "LEAD THOU ME ON" is inscribed on his headstone. The words are taken from the first verse of the hymn Lead, Kindly Light.

Credit: ww1cemeteries.com

Locally, Arthur is remembered on Lloyd's Paper Mill Memorial, Sittingbourne War Memorial, St Michael's Church WW1 Memorial Window and Milton Regis War Memorial. Arthur's mother received his pay and gratuity.

The East Kent Gazette

SATURDAY, AUGUST 23, 1919

IN MEMORIAM

SIMMONS – In loving memory of our dear son and brother. Sergt. Arthur James Simmons, 7th Buffs, killed in action, near Albert, August 22nd, 1918.

One of the first to answer the call,
He died for his loved ones, his country and all.

From his Mother, Dad, Sisters and Brothers.

On reporting his death under the heading "KILLED BY A SNIPER", the East Kent Gazette of 7th September 1918 reported that Arthur had played football for the paper mill team, as well as for Murston when they won the Sittingbourne, Milton and District League. The report added that he was an entertaining comic singer and an all-round good fellow.

The 23rd August 1919 edition of the East Kent Gazette printed an "In Memoriam" to Arthur, which echoed the sentiments of many families who lost fathers, sons, brothers, and relatives in the conflict.

SIMMONS, Harry John

70116, Private, 6th Battalion, The Queen's (Royal West Surrey Regiment).

Harry was born in Sittingbourne in 1899 and was baptised at St Michael's Church on 31st May that year. He was the only son of Henry Matthew, a mariner, and Elizabeth Charlotte (née Jarman). He had had an older sister Hilda Amy who died when she was just two years old in 1896. In 1911 the family were living at 33 Harold Road, Sittingbourne, with Harry's cousin, Arthur Jarman, who grew up with them.

Harry attended St Michaels School and then worked for three years in the Distribution Department of the Sittingbourne District Gas Company.

Harry enlisted in Sittingbourne on 26th May 1915 and arrived in France at Easter 1917, aged 18. An extract for September 1918 from the battalion's War Diary is shown below:

	WAR DIARY [122] or INTELLIGENCE SUMMARY. (Erase heading not required.)	Army Form C. 2118.
Instructions regarding War Diaries and Intelligence Summaries are contained in F.S. Regs., Part II, and the Staff Manual respectively. Title pages will be prepared in manuscript.		
Date	*Summary of Events and Information*	*Remarks and References to Appendices*
30-8-1918	Battalion left line at MAUREPAS and moved to TALUS WOOD.	
31-8-1918	Devoted to rest and cleaning.	
3-9-1918	Moved to COMBLES.	
6-9-1918	Battalion moved to RIVERSIDE WOOD.	
7-9-1918	Moved to HEUDICOURT, to support the 6TH BUFFS and 6TH ROYAL WEST KENTS. Heavy shelling forced Battalion to return to RIVERSIDE WOOD.	
8-9-1918 to 17-9-1918	Moved to VAUX WOOD. Training and resting. 13th - Bombing machines were brought down in flames.	
18-9-1918	Battalion moved to railway on the east side of ÉPEHY. Orders to await the "mopping up" of the village. Preparing to attack MOLASSES (MALASSISE) FARM.	
19-9-1918	11am - 6TH BUFFS on the right and the 35TH INFANTRY BRIGADE on the left, Battalion attacked the farm from the north. Attack successful, despite intense machine gun fire, farm captured. CASUALTIES - 21 killed, 105 wounded.	
20-9-1918	Battalion attacked No. 12 COPSE WOOD (TWELVE TREE COPSE WOOD) and HORSE POINT, met little resistance.	
21-9-1918	Battalion withdrawn to PRINCE RESERVE at dusk where it was in Brigade Reserve.	

---

[122] War Diary: 6 Battalion Queen's (Royal West Surrey Regiment). WO-95-1863-1. June 1915-October 1919. The National Archives (UK), Kew, England.

Credit: ww1cemeteries.com

Harry was killed during the initial attack on 19th September 1918, aged 19. He was buried nearby in Épehy Wood Farm Cemetery, and his headstone carries the words "GOD IS LOVE R.I.P."

The cemetery is the final resting place for 997 burials, of which 459 were identified as being lost during the battle for Épehy and the subsequent ten days, with 235 remaining "Known unto God."

Harry is remembered locally on Sittingbourne and Milton Regis War Memorials, and St Michael's Church WW1 Memorial Window.

His death was reported in the East Kent Gazette dated 12th October 1918. The same newspaper dated 2nd November 1918 reported on the Bargeman's Memorial Service, held on 27th October, at St Michael's Church, after a procession, headed by the Salvation Army band, from Station Yard. The service was held for Harry and Albert Freeborn, Albert William Port and Montague Wesley Patrick.

Just two weeks later the newspaper was reporting on the death of Harry's cousin, Lance Corporal William Thomas Jarman MM (see page 179), who died just a month after Harry on 24th October 1918. William was the son of Harry's uncle William Thomas.

The East Kent Gazette

SATURDAY, SEPTEMBER 18, 1920

IN MEMORIAM

SIMMONS – In loving memory of Harry John Simmons, son of Henry and Elizabeth Simmons killed in France, Sept. 18th, 1918, aged 19 years and 4 months.

We pictured his face returning,

We longed to clasp his hand;

But God has postponed the meeting

Till we meet in that better land.

God is Love.

From Mum, Dad, and Arthur.

For a number of years after his death Harry's family posted the above "In Memoriam" in the East Kent Gazette, with this one being especially poignant.

SKINNER, Sydney

915646, Gunner, "D" Battery, 223rd Brigade, Royal Field Artillery.

Sydney was born in Sittingbourne in 1898, the son of James, a brickfield labourer, and Alice (née Hayter). He was the middle of their five children and his siblings were Christabel, Nellie Florence, Elsie, and John Horace.

In 1911 the family were living at 42 Murston Road, Sittingbourne. Sydney had attended St Michael's Day School and the Baptist Church Sunday School.

Before Sydney enlisted in January 1915 in Sittingbourne, aged 16, he was working for Mr T Kingsmill, a local jeweller, based at 32 West Street.

At the start of March 1918 his battery and brigade were located in Trescault, near Cambrai, where their War Diary[123] records that for the first ten days they were carrying out harassment firing at night on any enemy movements. On the 11th March 1918 the diary recorded they were shelled by gas all night with Sydney's "D" Battery suffering the largest casualties of 50 other ranks.

Hauling 18 pounder at Zillebeke 1917 - IWM Q 6236

The nights of 12th and 13th March 1918 were the same as the previous night with the gas shelling, though casualties were a lot less. The battery stayed at Trescault until 22nd March when they withdrew to Havrincourt Wood, and on the 25th they moved to Courcelette Sector. The diary recorded they had to blow up three of their guns as they got stuck and were unable to be moved. As the brigade were transferring positions, they had to maintain a rear-guard action. They travelled west to Martinsart and Englebelmer the following day.

On the 27th March 1918 they remained in position and reported that firing still continued. For the rest of the month, they repositioned further west to Puchevillers to re-equip.

The East Kent Gazette dated 20th April 1918, reported Sydney's death, and said that he was wounded on 27th March 1918 and died of his wounds at No. 10 General Hospital, Rouen, aged 19, on 4th April 1918. The hospital Matron wrote to his mother saying;

> "I am so very sorry to have to tell you that your son, Gunner S. Skinner, died in hospital to-day at 5.10 a.m. I can assure you he had all done for him that was possible. He was seen by the Chaplain and will be buried in the military cemetery here. . . . May I say how very sorry I am for you in this trouble. The poor boy was not 20 I believe."

Sydney was buried in the St Sever Cemetery, Rouen. His headstone is simply inscribed with "REST IN PEACE".

In the East Kent Gazette dated 6th April 1918 under the sub-heading "GASSED AND WOUNDED", it had reported on a number of casualties, including Sydney. It mentioned that he had been shot through the abdomen and was dangerously wounded. The column also included a report that Sydney's next-door neighbour, at 43 Murston Road, 20-year-old Gunner Leonard Anderson, Howitzer Battery, was in Chichester Hospital, Sussex, after being gassed.

Sydney is remembered on Sittingbourne War Memorial and St Michael's Church WW1 Memorial Window. His mother received his pay and gratuity as well as his Victory and British War Medals.

Sydney's brother John joined the Royal Artillery on 17th December 1926, when he was 22 years old, and served with them until 16th December 1933.

---

[123] War Diary: 223 Brigade Royal Field Artillery. WO-95-3102-1. July 1916-March 1919. The National Archives (UK), Kew, England.

Sydney's brother-in-law, Private John McArdle, of the Royal Dublin Fusiliers died from his wounds on 9th July 1916 in France, aged 29 years, and was buried in Étaples Military Cemetery. John had married Sydney's sister, Christabel, just six months before he died, and never knew his son, James John Thomas, who was born in the autumn of the same year.

Chichester Hospital

SMEED MM, Frank Alfred

536144, Serjeant, Royal Army Medical Corps.

Lewisham Borough News
British Library

Frank was born in Sittingbourne in 1892, the son of Thomas Charles, a cabinet maker, and Ann Elizabeth (née Robinson). He was the fourth of their six children, and his siblings were Emily Edith, William Thomas, Annie, Minnie, and Ronald John (1898-1901).

His family lived at 72 West Street, Sittingbourne, but by 1911 Frank was living in London, at 107-111 Newington Butts, Elephant and Castle and was working as a house furnisher's assistant. In the same house were others of the same occupation, including the head of the house, Joseph East, who was also a manager, Joseph's brother, Walter East, George Robert Simmons, aged 26 from Worcester and Charles Mavor, aged 20, from Harrow, Middlesex. Also living at the house were Joseph's wife and daughter, both named Lydia, and Walter's wife Florence.

Frank was working for Chiesmans department store in Lewisham, when he enlisted at the outbreak of war in August 1914 in Woolwich, joining the Royal Army Medical Corps, though he was attached to the 12th Battalion, London Regiment (The Rangers). He arrived in France in March 1917 and two months later Frank was awarded the Military Medal for bringing in two wounded men whilst under heavy fire. This was reported in the East Kent Gazette edition of 5th May 1917. The newspaper added that he was also awarded the Médaille Militaire (the French equivalent of the Military Medal). Frank's Military Medal award was also announced in The London Gazette dated 15th June 1917, and reported in the Lewisham Borough News on 23rd February 1917. A fellow employee of Chiesmans, Corporal Heal RAMC, had written a letter describing "how Smeed climbed over the parapet of the trenches with snacks, provisions and other necessaries, to some wounded lying in No Man's Land, crawling from shell hole to shell hole, dressing their wounds until such time as they could be rescued."

On 29th July 1918 the 12th Battalion, London Regiment War Diary[124] records they were at Vaux, near the town of Albert, to attend a demonstration of a tank attack. The next day they relieved the 8th London

---

[124] War Diary: 12 Battalion London Regiment. WO-95-3009-8. February 1918-May 1919. The National Archives (UK), Kew, England.

Regiment in reserve, at St Lawrence Valley, near Bresle. They moved into tents and bivouacs. Then on the 31st they relieved the American 2nd Battalion, 132 Infantry Regiment to the south of the Amiens-Albert Road. The next three days they remained in position, sending out patrols, to previously occupied enemy lines.

Overnight on 3rd August 1918 they marched to Baizieux, where they boarded buses and at 6am travelled west to billets in Vignacourt. The next three days were spent refitting and bathing. Then on the night of the 7th his battalion were conveyed to Bois d'Escardonneuse, south of the Amiens and Albert, and midway between the two. On the 8th they were under one hour's notice and issued with battle stores.

Early in the morning of 9th August 1918 they proceeded to a point just north of the village of Sailly-Laurette, which stood on the north side of the Somme river. With the 131st American Regiment on the right and 8th London Regiment on the left, the attack started at 4.50pm. The objective was just outside the village of Morlancourt (pictured below). By 9pm the objective had been reached, with 250 prisoners taken. The battalion remained in position, sending patrols out, for the next few days.

Somme Canal near Sailly-Laurette July 1918

Frank was mortally wounded and died before he could receive medical attention, during the first day of the attack on 9th August 1918. He was 26 years old and was buried in the Beacon Cemetery, Sailly-Laurette, where his headstone is inscribed with "WE WILL REMEMBER THEM".

Frank's death was reported in the East Kent Gazette dated 24th August 1918 (pictured right). The newspaper mentioned that the award of the French Medaille Militaire was a special distinction, and that he was due to take up a commission.

His parents received a letter from Frank's old Colonel who said Frank was "the bravest man I knew". Also, a Lieutenant Bennett wrote that "the young man volunteered several times for posts of great danger, and always showed great coolness under fire."

A PROMISING SITTINGBOURNE SOLDIER KILLED.

"THE BRAVEST MAN I KNEW"

Another gallant son of Sittingbourne has laid down his life for his country in the Great War in the person of Sergeant Frank Smeed, R.A.M.C., attached to the London Regiment, the younger son of Mr. and Mrs. Thomas Charles Smeed, of 72, West Street…He was awarded our own Military Medal, and the much-prized French Medaille Militaire, which is a special distinction.

His entry in the Army Register of Soldier's Effects records that he was serving as Acting Sergeant with the 1/5 London Field Ambulance, RAMC at the time of his death. His mother received his pay and gratuity, as well as his Victory and British War Medals.

Frank is remembered locally on the Sittingbourne War Memorial and Sittingbourne Holy Trinity Church WW1 Memorial.

SMITH, Ernest Stephen

L/7936, Private, 1st Battalion, The Buffs (East Kent Regiment).

Ernest was born on 13th March 1887 at 20 Flushing Street, Milton Regis. He was the youngest of the four children of Frederick, a plasterer, and Agnes (née Goody). His siblings were Minnie, Frederick, and Rhoda, and in 1891 the children were in Faversham Workhouse, where they had been since 1889.

By 1901 Minnie had married Harry Darlow, a bargeman, and was living at 13 Short Street, Sittingbourne, with their two-year-old daughter Ellen. Rhoda was also married by then and was living in Southampton with Francis Allen Foord, who had served in the Buffs (East Kent) Regiment and the Queen's (Royal West Surrey) Regiment.

The couple had thirteen children, and their 22-year-old son Clifford Ashley Vale, was killed on 10th April 1944. He was a Private, serving in the 4th Battalion, Queen's Own Royal West Kent Regiment, in Kohima, India which is where he was buried. Clifford is commemorated with a tree and tablet in Central Avenue, Sittingbourne and on the WW2 memorial in Sittingbourne Holy Trinity Church.

Ernest, himself, was still in the Faversham Workhouse in 1901. When he joined the 3rd Battalion, The Buffs, at Canterbury on 1st March 1904 he was 5ft 3½in tall. He served with them as a Private until his period of service ended. He then worked in Lloyd's paper mill in Sittingbourne.

Ernest met Lilian May Finch and lived with her at 35 New Road, Sittingbourne. On 26th June 1914 their son Ernest John Frederick was born.

As Ernest had previously served in the army, at the outbreak of the war, he was immediately mobilised.

Ernest during his time in service kept a diary, and his first entry records he arrived at Canterbury on 5th August 1914, and was recalled to the 1st Battalion, The Buffs, and the same day the battalion went to Fermoy, Ireland. He spent August and the first week of September, training at Fermoy, Queenstown, Grantchester and Cambridge.

On the 8th September 1914, Ernest and his battalion embarked from Southampton on the *SS Minneapolis* for Saint-Nazaire, France. Later in the war, on 23rd March 1916, the *Minneapolis* was torpedoed in the Mediterranean Sea and sank with the loss of 12 of her 188 crew.

By 14th September 1914 they had travelled 490km to Jouarre. Ernest entered in his diary (pictured left), "Billeted in hotel. Irish stew and wine in abundance." The following day they marched to Château-Thierry and spent the night in the rain without shelter or cover. The next couple of days were spent travelling, and on the 18th, they had their first experience of the trenches at Rosières. Ernest noted it was raining all night and they were on guard duty over some prisoners.

Late on 19th September 1914 the battalion was on the move again, arriving in Vailly, 155km to the south-east. Ernest recorded they spent their time digging trenches up to the end of the month, noting 'Heaps of dead Germans lying about' and occasions of heavy fire from the Germans. On 2nd October, after a breakfast of pork, beef, potatoes, biscuits, plus bread and jam, they relieved the Royal Irish Regiment in the firing line, and then returned four days later on the 5th.

Ernest noted that on 6th October 1914, about 2,000 Germans had taken up position 300m in front of the trenches at a farm, and that the artillery on both sides were duelling. On that night the Germans attacked and were repelled with them sustaining heavy losses.

The last entry in Ernest's diary was on 8th October 1914, which reads:

"Attack at dawn German (trenches). Cannonade of artillery all morning onto the German trenches. German bombardment of Town all the afternoon. All the people leaving. This is the 12th time of bombardment."

Ernest died on this day, 8th October 1914, aged 27.

Ernest is remembered on the La Ferte-Sous-Jouarre Memorial to the Missing. The memorial was designed by George H. Goldsmith and commemorates 3,740 officers and men. It was unveiled on the 4th November 1928 by Sir William Pulteney, Commander of the III Corps in 1914.

He is also remembered on Sittingbourne War Memorial, Sittingbourne Holy Trinity Church WW1 Memorial, Lloyd's Paper Mill Memorial, and Milton Regis War Memorial.

Ernest's pay was paid to his sister Minnie and after the war his gratuity were paid to his unmarried wife Lilian. The status of 'unmarried wife' was acknowledged by the state in 1916, to recognise relationships and provide separation allowance and war widows pension to the named recipient.

The East Kent Gazette edition of 28th November 1914, under the headline "A MILTON BUFFS LAST LETTER", published a letter from Ernest to his wife, Lilian. Ernest wrote the letter just two days before his death. The letter (pictured on next page) read:

"I am quite well and safe at present. We are having it rather quiet out here. The Germans are all down on their luck. The poor beggars are almost starved, and I can tell you it is getting rather cold out here just now. That makes it worse, as we don't get feather beds to lay upon.

We sleep in holes dug out of the roadside in banks, and under shelter of the trees, with all our clothes and boots. I have not had a good night's rest since I left; and we don't know what it is to take our boots off, as we have not had the chance for over a month.

"It takes from nine to ten days for your letters to reach us. I like yours and baby's photograph very much and I keep taking it out of my pocket every chance I get to have a look at our darling boy. I am looking forward to the time to nurse him again, and very shortly too, as this affair can't last a month longer. It is getting nearer towards peace every day, and the sooner the better, as I am longing for a change of food. Don't be surprised if you see me eat extraordinarily when I arrive home – which I hope to, with God's help."

SMITH, Henry John

L/9285, Serjeant, 2nd Battalion, The Buffs (East Kent Regiment).

Henry was born in Sittingbourne in the summer of 1888. He was the sixth of the ten children of James, a cement mill labourer, and Frances Harriett (née Hills). His brothers and sisters were James Henry Cornelius, William John (1881-1882), Albert, Harriett (1885-1886), Ada Elizabeth, Emily Amelia, Alfred Thomas, Hilda Sophia, and Kate Annie.

In 1911 his family were living at 32 William Street, Sittingbourne, but by then Henry had enlisted.

He was 5ft 4in tall and had been working as a milkman when he enlisted on 7th April 1910. He served in Dublin before his posting to Singapore from 4th October 1911 to 31st January 1913, during which time he gained promotion to Lance Corporal on 6th December 1912.

After Singapore he was posted to India up until 15th November 1914 when he returned to England. Two months later, on 17th January 1915, he was sent to France and the following month, on 19th February, he was promoted to Corporal, followed quickly by gaining his Serjeant's stripes on 3rd May 1915, which turned out to be an exceptional day for his battalion, as can be seen below.

Instructions regarding War Diaries and Intelligence Summaries are contained in F.S. Regs., Part II, and the Staff Manual respectively. Title pages will be prepared in manuscript.	WAR DIARY [125] or INTELLIGENCE SUMMARY. *(Erase heading not required.)*	Army Form C. 2118.
Date	Summary of Events and Information	Remarks and References to Appendices
28-4-1915	Battalion in trenches in GRAVENSTAFEL.	
29-4-1915	Quiet day.	

---

[125] War Diary: 2 Battalion Queen's The Buffs (Royal East Kent Regiment). WO-95-2279-2. December 1914-October 1915. The National Archives (UK), Kew, England.

30-4-1915	GRAVENSTAFEL (pictured below) - Quiet day.
1-5-1915	Heavy shelling and in the evening the battalion moved to D4 and D5 to a new support trench.
2-5-1915	Very heavy shelling. Could not be suppressed by our artillery.
3-5-1915	Dawn - Mortaring and shelling of the trenches in a relentless and determined manner. 7.30am - Enemy amassing to the left. Enemy shelling included high explosives and whiz-bangs. Our artillery made little or no reply. It was a most nerve racking and trying period for all the troops concerned. A state of affairs existed which was almost intolerable. 3.30pm - Artillery action intensified, sounding like machine gun fire. Enemy seen entering the D5 trenches on the left, with little resistance. Appeared the 80 men that occupied it were missing and believed most had been killed or wounded. The Germans were making their way along the trenches and reached the new support trench and were within yards of the troops.
	5pm - Battalion had retired from the trenches. Enemy tried to advance beyond the trenches, held by the ROYAL FUSILIERS and some of 4TH EAST YORKS. The contest was an unequal one, with no artillery support. It was infantry against infantry and artillery. Enemy infantry lacked push and determination. Dusk - things quietened down and enemy remained in the trenches. Dark - Troops retired to woods west of POPERINGHE.
8-5-1915 to 9-5-1915	Battalion marched to camp west of YPRES and then east to POTIJZE. Placed in reserve south of the YPRES-ZONNEBEKE ROAD.
10-5-1915	Battalion took over a portion of the advanced trench line south of VERLOREN HOEK, from the YORKS AND LANCASHIRES, 3RD MIDDLESEX, and EAST YORKSHIRE REGIMENTS.
11-5-1915	Trenches shelled all day.
12-5-1915	Trenches shelled all day.
13-5-1915	Relieved by 2ND LIFE GUARDS.

Henry was reported missing, and was presumed dead on 12th May 1915, just a few days after his promotion. He was 26 years old and is remembered on the Ypres Menin Gate Memorial to the Missing, which also commemorates 161 additional soldiers of the Buffs who were killed during the same period.

Entries in the War Diary give the total 'approximate' casualty numbers, for this period, as 67 killed, 259 wounded, 13 wounded and missing and 363 missing, together with a note saying that many were buried in the trenches and retrieving identity discs was impossible.

Henry is also remembered on Sittingbourne War Memorial. He was awarded the 1914-1915 Star, Victory, and British War Medals.

STEERS, S

An Avenue of Remembrance tablet is inscribed Pte. S. Steers, and his name is also inscribed on the Sittingbourne War Memorial.

Research at the time of print has not managed to identify Private Steers. Locally in St Peter and St Paul's Churchyard, Borden lies Private Albert Edward Steers, of the Grenadier Guards, who died on 1st December 1917, though no relationship with Private Steers has been identified.

Research into Private Steers continues to enable his story to be told.

We remember him, as did those who knew him.

STICKELLS, Arthur John

6673, Private, 10th Battalion, Queen's Own (Royal West Kent Regiment).

Arthur John, known as Jack, was born in Ham Street, Tenterden, in 1885. He was the first child of George, a carpenter on a farm, and Annie Laura (née Swinyard). The 1911 census records he had eight siblings. Sadly, four of the children died before 1911, including an unnamed boy in 1896, and the names of some of the other children have not been identified. Those we can identify were named Edward George (1886-1889), Florence Alice, William Frederick, Harold Frank, and Augusta (1902-1902).

In 1911 Arthur, employed as an agricultural labourer, was living with his parents at Crouch Cottages, Boughton, Kent and later that year in Faversham, Arthur married Fanny Revell, from nearby Luddenham. They moved to 35 Shakespeare Road, Sittingbourne, and had two sons, William Frank Hughes (born 1912) and Arthur George (born 1915).

On 30th May 1917 his battalion's War Diary[126] recorded that they relieved the 4th Battalion, South African Scottish Regiment in the trenches at

Armentières 1918
Credit: WW1 Photos Centenary, Paul Read

---

[126] War Diary: 10 Battalion Queen's Own (Royal West Kent Regiment). WO-95-2638-1. May 1916-October 1917. The National Archives (UK), Kew, England.

Armentières, France, near the French-Belgium border. The entry added that 268 Other Ranks were left at Le Bizet, as the trenches were not large enough to accommodate the whole battalion.

The entries for the next day and the first five days of June read "Situation normal," though casualties had been received with one killed and 16 wounded. Late on 5th June 1917, the battalion was relieved by the 4th Battalion, Queens, and returned to billets at Le Bizet, 3km to the south-west on the border. From the 6th to 11th, they remained in billets before a return to the trenches for four days.

Credit: National Army Museum of New Zealand

Arthur was wounded and died three days later, at New Zealand Stationary Hospital in Hazebrouck (pictured left), aged 32, on 10th June 1917.

He was buried in the Hazebrouck Communal Cemetery in France, with the inscription "DEATH DIVIDES BUT MEMORY CLINGS" adorning his headstone. Hazebrouck at the time was the location for a number of Casualty Clearing Stations.

Arthur is remembered on Sittingbourne War Memorial and St Michael's Church WW1 Memorial Window. His wife received his pay and gratuity, as well as his Victory and British War Medals. Fanny did not remarry.

Arthur's brother William (who did not live in Sittingbourne) served as a Driver in the Army Service Corps, and was attached to the 162nd Brigade, Royal Field Artillery. He died from Addison's disease on 3rd November 1916, aged 25 in No 21 Casualty Clearing Station, and he was buried in La Neuville British Cemetery, Corbie, France. His headstone is inscribed "WE MISS HIM MOST WHO LOVE HIM BEST GOD'S WILL BE DONE." William is commemorated on the Dunkirk, Kent, War Memorial Cross and on the memorial in Faversham's St Mary of Charity Church.

STORR, George Percy

64122, Private, 7th Battalion, Royal Fusiliers.

George was born in 1883 in Sittingbourne, the son of William, a butcher, and Annie (née Brenchley). He was the second youngest of their nine children and his siblings were Esther Annie, William James, Stephen Heber, Anne Eliza, Ada, John Arthur, James Brenchley and Olive Gertrude.

From 1881, the family lived at 61 Goodnestone Road, Sittingbourne, and George is recorded by his middle name, Percy. In 1911 he was employed as a bricklayer and his father was recorded as infirm. George's father died six years later in 1917, aged 80.

George enlisted in Sittingbourne and joined 2/4th Battalion, The Buffs, before being posted to the Royal Fusiliers.

The War Diary for July 1917 is transcribed here describing the period in which George was killed:

Date	Summary of Events and Information	Remarks and References to Appendices
WAR DIARY [127] *or* **INTELLIGENCE SUMMARY.** (*Erase heading not required.*) *Instructions regarding War Diaries and Intelligence Summaries are contained in F.S. Regs., Part II, and the Staff Manual respectively. Title pages will be prepared in manuscript.*		*Army Form C. 2118.*
29-7-1918 to 3-8-1918	*Battalion arrived at HÉNU (near Arras). Time spent training and undergoing rifle inspections by the Armourer Staff Sergeant.*	
4-8-1918	*9.15pm - Battalion spent four hours moving towards AMIENS and on to RAINCHEVAL.*	
5-8-1918 to 7-8-1918	*Training continued.*	
8-8-1918	*7pm - Very short notice, moved to BEAUCOURT.*	
9-8-1918 to 13-8-1918	*Training.*	
14-8-1918	*2am – Moved by road to billets at THIÈVRES (near ARRAS).*	
15-8-1918 to 19-8-1918	*Training.*	
20-8-1918	*Arrived at 4am at SOUASTRE, preparing for active operations in the line. 10.20pm - Proceeded to the line west of ACHIET-LE-GRAND.*	
21-8-1918	*5.30am - ZERO HOUR. Heavy mist and heavy smoke barrage made it impossible to keep in touch between platoons. Everybody was late and lost. Tanks wandering about lost. Nightfall - Troops had consolidated with the BEDFORDS on the right, ARTISTS in the centre and FUSILIERS on the left.*	
22-8-1918 to 23-8-1918	*5.30am - Germans counter attacked unsuccessfully, tried again later in the morning, again unsuccessfully. The day was terribly hot and a serious shortage of water. Relieved at 6pm with arrival of 32 tons. Shortage of ammo. Ammo dropped by aeroplane landed in No Man's Land or the woods and could not be found. BEDFORDS lent some to FUSILIERS. All quiet and line intact at 12.30pm*	
24-8-1918	*Battalion proceed to position for attack on LE BARQUE, LIGNYTHILLOY and THILLOY.*	

George was reported killed in action, aged 35, on 21st August 1918. He was buried on the battlefield, with his grave marked with a cross, near where his final resting place would be. He was buried with at least four others who fell on the same and next day: Lance Corporal Harry Duffell MM DCM, 2nd Battalion, Royal Irish Regiment, aged 25; an Unknown soldier; Able Seaman Cyril Russell, Drake Battalion, Royal Naval Volunteer Reserve, aged 19 and Private Henry Wilkins, 7th Battalion, Royal Fusiliers, aged 19.

[127] War Diary: 7 Battalion Royal Fusiliers. WO-95-3119-1. July 1916-April 1919. The National Archives (UK), Kew, England.

George was reinterred in Achiet le-Grand Communal Cemetery Extension. "IN JESU'S KEEPING WITH LOVED ONES FAR AWAY GOD IS LOVE MOTHER" is inscribed upon George's headstone. He is remembered locally on Sittingbourne War Memorial.

George's mother received his pay and gratuity and also received his Victory and British War Medals.

Credit: ww1cemeteries.com

SUTTON, Charles

307456, Petty Officer Stoker, HMS Curacoa, Royal Navy.

Petty Officer Stoker
Dress Insignia

Charles was born in Strood on 15th June 1885, the son of Charles, a farm labourer, and Matilda (née Bolton), and his siblings were Clara Katherine, Edward Henry, and Alfred William (1888-1893). He also had two stepsiblings, Hilda, and William, after his mother remarried, following the death of his father in 1900, to John William Bolton, in 1901 in Milton. John was a machine engine driver at the brickworks.

Charles was 5ft 2in tall and had been working as a farm labourer when he joined the Navy at Chatham on 6th July 1904. In 1908 Charles married Margaret Emmeline Beatrice Baker from Milton, and in 1911 they were living at 25 Cavendish Road, Rochester. Together they had five children Charles George Lewis (born 1910), George William (born 1911), Doris Maud (born 1913), Vera Beatrice (born 1914) and Florence Margaret Beatrice (born 1917). Margaret also had a daughter, Ada Margaret (born 1907) from a previous relationship.

During the war Charles, between shore service at *HMS Pembroke II* in Chatham, served on the scout cruiser *HMS Blonde* out of Scapa Flow (Dec 1913 - May 1916); cruisers *HMS Centaur* (Aug 1917 - Dec 1917) and *HMS Curacoa* (Jan 1918 – Sep 1918) (pictured right), patrolling the Strait of Dover and the English Channel.

On 23rd September 1918, in the Royal Naval Hospital, Chatham, Charles died of pneumonia, aged 33, and was buried in the Woodlands Cemetery, Gillingham. At the time of his death his family lived at 34 Middletune Avenue, Milton Regis. Charles is remembered on Sittingbourne and Milton Regis War Memorials and Sittingbourne Holy Trinity Church WW1 Memorial.

TANTON, Leonard George

172401, Private, 2nd Battalion, Canadian Infantry.

Leonard was born in Sittingbourne on 5th October 1890. The son of William George, a bricklayer, and Fanny (née Owlett). He was the third of their six children, and his siblings were Harriett Frances, Herbert John William, Lylie May, Frank William (1899-1900) and sadly, one unnamed child. Leonard's father died in 1909 and in 1911 Leonard was working as a paper maker's assistant and living with his mother, who was an assistant caretaker for Holy Trinity Schools, Sittingbourne.

Leonard attended Holy Trinity Day School and went on to work at the paper mill in various capacities, before he emigrated to Canada in May 1913. His sister Harriet had emigrated before him in 1907 to Oswego, New York.

Leonard enlisted in Toronto on 21st December 1915, he was 5ft 5in tall, and had been working as a painter. On 24th April 1916 his battalion left Halifax, for Liverpool, on the *SS Olympic*. They spent time in West Sandling and Shorncliffe Camps, before Leonard arrived in France on 28th August 1916.

His battalion's War Diary[128] recorded the events of 8th April 1917. At 1.15pm, the battalion marched the 30km from Camblain-l'Abbé to Écoivres. On arrival they were provided with a hot meal and 24-hour rations. At 9.45pm they moved to the battle assembly area at Maison Blanche to the east. At 7.30am the next day the battalion moved out to advance on the Zwischen-Stellung trench in the village of Thélus. By 2.30pm the advance, with little resistance, had reached Bois-Carré, near Vimy. The next day was spent consolidating their positions, and they received enemy artillery fire. His battalion was positioned at Thélus and nearby Farbus Woods to relieve the 3rd and 4th Canadian Battalions.

At 3am on 11th April 1917 his battalion was relieved, and the War Diary entry read "Nothing of importance occurred." The following day they were subjected to heavy bombardment and relieved the 5th Canadians in the line, and at midnight were themselves relieved by the 8th Canadians and returned to Maison Blanche.

The ruined village of Farbus c.1917.

---

[128] Library and Archives Canada (LAC); War Diary, RG9-III-D-3, Volume 4913, Microfilm T-10705, File 354, 1917/01/01-1918/02/28.

Leonard was killed on 12th April 1917, aged 26. He was originally buried in one of the makeshift cemeteries 1.5km east of Thélus[129], before he was reinterred in Bois-Carre British Cemetery, Thélus, with the words "REST IN THE LORD" inscribed on his headstone.

The East Kent Gazette

SATURDAY, APRIL 17, 1920

IN MEMORIAM

TANTON - In ever-loving memory of a dear son and brother. Pte. Leonard George Tanton, of the 2nd Batt. Canadian Regt., who was killed somewhere in France, April 12th, 1917.

We pictured his face returning,
We longed to clasp his hand;
But God has postponed the meeting
Till we meet in a better land.
From his loving Mother, Sisters, and Brother.

The East Kent Gazette

SATURDAY, APRIL 16, 1921

IN MEMORIAM

TANTON - In loving memory of a dear son and brother, Leonard George Tanton, who was killed somewhere in France, April 12th, 1917.

Cherished memories of one so dear,
Often recalled by a silent tear;
'Tis only those who have loved and lost,
Who can realise war's bitter cost.
From his loving Mum, Sisters, and Br-other.

The East Kent Gazette dated 9th June 1917 reporting Leonard's death wrote that he was killed when he was hit by shrapnel in the head, as he left his dug-out. Leonard is remembered on Sittingbourne War Memorial, Sittingbourne Holy Trinity Church WW1 Memorial, and the Baptist Church Memorial.

His brother Lance Corporal Herbert, 4th Battalion, The Buffs, served from August 1915 to July 1919. Herbert spent his time in India and was shot in the chest and arm in February 1917 and survived the war.

TAYLOR, James Thomas Andrew

272070, Engine Room Artificer 2nd Class, Royal Navy, HMS Arethusa.

The Avenue tablet for J. Taylor records that he was a Private. The St Michael's WW1 Memorial Window list of names in the East Kent Gazette edition of 7th January 1922 records a "James Taylor, *HMS Arethusa* (killed in action)." It is probable that an error was made on the tablet.

James was born in Chatham on 4th December 1883 and baptised at St Paul's Church on 13th January 1884. He was the eldest of the seven children of James Nathaniel and Rosina (née Moir). His siblings were George William, Alfred Charles (1887-1888), Rosina Margaret (1889-1890), Florence Maria, Blanche Edith, and Margaret Rosina. In 1891 the family were living at 37 Church Street, Chatham, and James' father was a boiler maker. The family had also lived in Simonstown, South Africa, as the two youngest were born there in 1894 and 1896.

When James, aged 22, joined the Navy for 12 years, on 18th December 1905, he had brown hair, hazel eyes and was 5ft 6¼in tall. His first posting after training was to the store ship *HMS Tyne*, on which he served for three years. On 2nd April 1911, when the census was taken, his naval records show that he

---

[129] Library and Archives Canada (LAC); War Graves Registry: Commonwealth War Graves. RG150, 1992-1993/314, Box 127

was serving on *Pembroke II* at Chatham. His family were living at the Lord Raglan Public House, Hazel Road, Slade Green, Kent, where his father was the beer-housekeeper. James was at home with them, and his occupation was recorded as a coppersmith, the same as it had been when he enlisted.

James and Marjorie's Wedding
Credit: Andrew Taylor (Grandson)

James married 25-year-old Marjorie Emma Clabburn on 6th March 1915 at St Augustine's Church in Norwich, Norfolk, her hometown. At that time, he was serving on the submarine and repair ship *HMS Cyclops*, which was based at Scapa Flow. He remained on *Cyclops* until 5th September 1915, when he returned to *HMS Pembroke II* for training, after which he was posted to *HMS Arethusa* (pictured below) on 30th October 1915.

On 11th February 1916, James was on board the Chatham built light cruiser *Arethusa* when she struck a mine just off Felixstowe, Suffolk, which had been laid by the German submarine *UC-7* the previous evening. The explosion occurred under the machinery spaces, and she lost power. The destroyers *Lightfoot* and *Loyal* tried to take her in tow but on each occasion the tow rope parted, and *Arethusa* drifted on to the Cutler Shoal and broke in half.

Eleven men, including James, in the boiler room area, drowned. On the docks at Harwich his wife was waiting for him to tell him they were expecting their first child.

James and Marjorie's son, James Edwin Taylor, was born on 30th July 1916 in Norwich and baptised there on 3rd September that year. A few months later on 12th November 1916, James' mother Rosina died when she was living at the Ship Inn, 22 East Street, Sittingbourne.

James is commemorated on Chatham Naval Memorial, Sittingbourne War Memorial and St Michael's Church WW1 Memorial Window.

THACKER, John William

17364, Private, 5th Battalion, Northamptonshire Regiment.

John was born in Sittingbourne on 20th July 1892, to John William and Susan Mary (née Tucker). He had a younger sister, Rose Dorothy.

In 1911 the family were living at 32 The Wall, Sittingbourne, John was working as a labourer in the brickfields and his father as a labourer in the paper mill. His sister died in 1913 aged 18. The East Kent Gazette reported on her inquest in the 19th April 1913 edition. Rose was working as a domestic servant in Sittingbourne for the jeweller Mr. Young when she was found on the foreshore at Sheerness at 3.45am on 11th April 1913. It appeared that Rose had been washed ashore by the tide and the coroner returned a verdict of "Found Drowned".

John was working as a butcher when he joined the Royal Navy in December 1913. However, he only served for three weeks as a ship's steward on the cruiser *HMS Hermes*. His service record shows that he was paid off.

When he joined The Buffs on 23rd August 1914, he was 5ft 6in tall, and transferred to the Northamptonshire Regiment in February 1915. He arrived in France on 31st May 1915.

A month before John left for France, he married 23-year-old Laura Violet Lake, on 3rd April 1915 in St Mark's Church, South Farnborough, Surrey (pictured right). At the time John was based at the Tournay Barracks, North Camp, Farnborough. They had one daughter named Laura Violet, who was born on 5th February 1916.

At the start of May 1916, John's battalion was in billets in Lillers, 30km north-west of Lens. While they were there, John reported ill to a field medical unit on 4th May 1916 and two weeks later on the 14th he was moved to a hospital in Rouen. On 29th May he was transferred to No. 25 Stationary Hospital, Rouen, where he died from paratyphoid, contracted whilst on active service, on 3rd June 1916. He was buried in St Sever Cemetery in Rouen.

Locally, John is remembered on Sittingbourne War Memorial. His wife, Laura, received his personal effects of identity disc, 11 letters, Gospel, wallet, photos, cap badge, safety razor, metal brooch, and a linen bag. She also received his pay and gratuity, as well as his Victory and British War Medals. She remarried in June 1917 in Todmorden, Yorkshire, to Air Mechanic William Ward Duckworth, Royal Flying Corps, who had been serving since August 1915.

THOMAS, Alfred

182101, Able Seaman, (RFR/CH/B/5746). HMS Lancaster, Royal Navy.

Alfred was born in Stoke, Kent, on 2nd April 1879. He grew up with his mother Ellen and stepfather George Hutchings, an agricultural labourer, and half-siblings Emily, Clara Elizabeth, Edith Maud, Thomas George, Herbert, Mary Ann, Wilfred William, and Edward Charles.

On 22nd November 1894 Alfred joined the Royal Navy, and on completing a 12-year term transferred to the Royal Fleet Reserve.

At the beginning of 1914 Alfred married 29-year-old Clara Rosetta Austin, from Faversham. They lived at 11 Laburnum Place, Sittingbourne, and had four children, Clarice Ivy (born 1910), twins Reginald Alfred and Violet Emily (born 1914), and Leonard Wilfred (born 19th January 1916).

On 2nd August 1914, Alfred was recalled to the Navy and posted to the battleship *HMS Mars*, patrolling the Humber and Dover Straits. In January 1915 he was transferred for a year to the cruiser *HMS Royal Arthur*, acting as a guard ship at Scapa Flow, Scotland. For the first two months of 1916 he was based at *HMS Pembroke I*.

On 2nd March 1916 he joined the cruiser *HMS Lancaster* (pictured right), which, the following month, was transferred to the Pacific. On 19th February 1918, the ship was sailing from St Felix Island, near Haiti to Callao, Peru, when Alfred died of pneumonia, aged 39.

Credit: Naval-history.net)

The ship's log[130] records at 9am on 20th February, the following day, the ship was stopped, and a funeral service was held at 9.20am, and Alfred was 'buried at sea' [131] in the Caribbean off the west coast of Cuba.

Albert is remembered on the Chatham Naval Memorial (pictured below), Sittingbourne War Memorial, Sittingbourne Holy Trinity Church Memorial WW1, and Milton Regis War Memorial. He was awarded the 1914 Star, Victory, and British War Medals.

Alfred's 20-year-old half-brother Wilfred joined up on 20th October 1910, and served with the 2nd Battalion, The Buffs (East Kent Regiment). Wilfred served in India from January 1913 to November 1914, before going to France in January 1915. On 21st May 1915 he was killed in France and is commemorated on the Ypres Menin Gate Memorial to the Missing.

---

[130] Admiralty, and Ministry of Defence, Navy Department: Ship's Logs. H.M.S. Lancaster. Class: ADM 53; Piece: 46029; February 1918. The National Archives (UK), Kew, England.
[131] Admiralty: Naval Casualties, Indexes, War Grave Rolls and Statistics Book, First World War.; Class: ADM 242; Piece: 010; (1914-1919). The National Archives (UK), Kew, England.

THOMAS, George William Francis

33989, Private, 1st/7th Battalion, Duke of Wellington's (West Riding Regiment).

George was born in Sittingbourne in 1890, the son of William, a brickfield labourer, and Sarah Cassandra (née Jordan). He had a younger brother, William Francis. George is recorded on the CWGC database as W F Thomas (the initials of his brother) however, the service number on the database matches George's Attestation Paper.

George's father died at some point between 1892 and 1898, and his mother married Thomas George Hollis in 1898 in Milton Regis.

In 1911 George was living with his mother, brother and stepfather at 14 Arthur Street, Milton Regis, and all were working as general labourers. By 1919 his family had moved to 28 Frederick Street, Milton Regis.

George was called up for service on 11th August 1917, and joined the Yorkshire Regiment at Richmond, Yorkshire. He was 5ft 7½in tall and had been working as a quarryman. His military papers record a number of misconducts. From the 11th to 28th October, he went absent, and again two days later until he was apprehended in Nottingham on 24th November. He also 'lost, by neglect, his clothing, equipment and regimental necessities.' On 8th December he received 56 days detention. On 31st January 1918 he was struck off as a deserter.

However, on 3rd April 1918 he joined the army again and was sentenced to one month's imprisonment for misdemeanour. On 22nd May 1918 he was posted and two days later transferred to the Duke of Wellington Regiment. The battalion War Diary for September and October 1918 is transcribed here:

	WAR DIARY [132] or INTELLIGENCE SUMMARY. (Erase heading not required.)	Army Form C. 2118.
Instructions regarding War Diaries and Intelligence Summaries are contained in F.S. Regs., Part II, and the Staff Manual respectively. Title pages will be prepared in manuscript.		
Date	Summary of Events and Information	Remarks and References to Appendices
2-9-1918 to 13-9-1918	Stationed in VILLERS-AU-BOIS, near ARRAS. Training.	
14-9-1918 to 23-9-1918	Moved to ROCLINCOURT. Cleaning and baths. Training including German light and heavy machine guns.	
24-9-1918 to 6-10-1918	Moved to area of FEUCHY. Time spent training interceded with swimming competition in nearby lake for 10 men and battalion lost by a length and a quarter. Football and rugby competitions, and gymkhana.	
7-10-1918 to 8-10-1918	Moved to the BUISSY area, near ARRAS. Time spent improving and constructing shelters, cleaning the Lewis Guns, and salvaging.	
9-10-1918	Short notice to move to SAILLY area and set about improving the shelters there.	
10-10-1918	11pm - Battalion arrived at ESCAUDŒUVRES. Remained in the open awaiting orders.	

---

[132] War Diary: 1/7 Battalion Duke of Wellington's (West Riding Regiment). WO-95-2802-1. April 1915-May 1919. The National Archives (UK), Kew, England.

11-10-1918	*2am - Moved east to NAVES, arriving at 5am. Battalion advanced, through the Canadians who were holding the line, attacking with tank support on the road to within 3km west of VILLERS-EN-CAUCHIES.* *Held the enemy overnight. Moved to reserve.*
12-10-1918	*Battalion had reached the east of VILLERS-EN-CAUCHIES.*
13-10-1918	*Brigade reinforced by 19TH LANCASHIRE FUSILIERS and attacked to just east of LA SELLE RIVER.*
14-10-1918	*West of AVESNES-LE-SEC, brigade relieved by 14TH INFANTRY BRIGADE.*
15-10-1918	*Brigade cemetery formed at WELLINGTON CEMETERY.*

George was killed in action, on 11th October 1918, aged 28. He was buried in Wellington Cemetery, Rieux-En-Cambresis.

Credit: ww1cemeteries.com

The cemetery was created by the Duke of Wellington's Regiment after the capture of the village in October 1918 and is the final resting place for over 300 burials, of which over 80 are "Known unto God," 131 of the 225 identified burials are from the Duke of Wellington Regiment, and of those, 118 died on the same day as George. An additional 48 burials are from other regiments who also died on the same day. With the exception of ten burials, the remaining 48 died within the following month.

George is commemorated on the Sittingbourne War Memorial. His pay and gratuity were paid to his mother, who also received his Victory and British War Medals.

THOROGOOD, John

1195, Corporal, 5th (Kent) Battery, 4th (Home Counties) Howitzer Brigade, Royal Field Artillery.

John was born in Sittingbourne in September 1877, one of the fourteen children of John, a shoemaker, and Frances (née Chappell). In 1911 his parents and some of his siblings were living at 5 Station Place, Sittingbourne, sadly, by then six of his siblings had died. John had two half-sisters, Kate, and Clara Ann Jemima, from his mother's first marriage to William James Busbridge, who died in 1875, aged 25. His siblings were Maria Elizabeth, Florence (1881-1883), Alice Lydia, George Henry, Lily Victoria (1887-1890), Kathleen Frances, Clara Ellen, Albert William, Philip Miles and two unnamed infants. John's father died on 23rd August 1917.

John joined The Buffs (East Kent Regiment)[133] on 12th October 1895. He was 5ft 5¾in tall with light blue eyes and dark brown hair, and he had been working as a brickfield labourer. Just a month after joining he was

---

[133] UK, Royal Hospital Chelsea Pensioner Soldier Service Records. WO-97-6078. 1900-1913. The National Archives (UK), Kew, England.

promoted to Lance Corporal, on 21st November, though on 9th January 1896 he reverted to Private. He was promoted back to Lance Corporal in March 1902 and five months later to Corporal. He served a 12-year term and was discharged on 11th October 1907.

During this time John served in India (December 1898 – February 1901), Burma (February 1901 – March 1902) and South Africa (March 1902 – October 1902). For the latter he was awarded the Queen's South Africa Medal with the Transvaal Clasp.

John, on 2nd April 1904. at St Michael's Church, Sittingbourne (pictured left), married 25-year-old Lydia Sophia Pashby, from Whitstable. They lived at 21 Harold Road, Sittingbourne, with their children, John Henry George (born August 1904), Frances Lydia Kathleen (born May 1907), Mima Ellen (July 1909) and Harry (born August 1912).

John was recalled by the army on 8th March 1915 and sent to France a year later, on 10th March 1916, as a Corporal.

On 9th May 1916, John was taken ill, when he suddenly complained of a severe headache and at 10.30am he was admitted to 25 Field Ambulance, where he was completely unconscious. He died the following day, at 2.30am, on 10th May 1916, aged 38. The doctor who completed a post-mortem recorded that John died from 'an extensive cerebral haemorrhage on the whole of the left hemisphere of the brain', and that in his opinion 'the cause of death was cerebral haemorrhage, resulting from disease commencing subsequent to March 8th, 1915', the date being when he re-enlisted.

The War Diary for the 25 Field Ambulance[134] records that it had moved to Millencourt on 4th April 1916 and established itself in buildings vacated by 9th Field Ambulance, including the church (pictured right), a barn and several scattered small houses. The diary added "accommodation defective, water supply scant, all drinking water brought from the town of Albert."

John was buried in the Millencourt Communal Cemetery Extension where his headstone is inscribed with "DEATH DIVIDES BUT LOVING MEMORIES CLING".

370 — MILLENCOURT (Somme) - L'Eglise — The church.

AUSTRALIAN WAR MEMORIAL

Credit: Australian War Memorial

[134] War Diary: 25 Field Ambulance. WO-95-1703-2. November 1914-April 1919. The National Archives (UK), Kew, England.

The cemetery extension, which was designed by Sir Reginald Blomfield, was used by units and field ambulances and it is the final resting place for 340 burials and five German burials.

Locally, John is remembered on Sittingbourne War Memorial and St Michael's Church WW1 Memorial Window.

His personal effects, including a purse, ring, photo, cards, letter, a French-English vocabulary, and a handkerchief, were returned to his wife Lydia. She received his pay and gratuity as well as his Victory and British War Medals. Lydia did not remarry.

TOMKIN, William Stephen

G/13602, Private, 6th Battalion, The Buffs (East Kent Regiment).

William was born in 1897, in Sittingbourne, the second child of Frank Henry and Alice (née Glover). His siblings were Stuart Frank, Florence Lena, Irene Alma (1904-1905), Kate (1907-1907), and Doris May.

In 1911 the family were living at 49 Pembury Street, Sittingbourne, and his father is recorded as a coachman for a hotel. Unusually, William's father had listed his children who had died on the census that year, but their names were struck through.

William's brother, Stuart, joined the 4th Battalion, The Buffs, on 4th March 1913, arriving in France on 5th August 1915 and fought at the Somme. He survived the war and was awarded the 1915 Star, Victory, and British War Medals.

When William enlisted in Canterbury on 8th March 1915, he was 5ft 6in tall and had been working as a grocer's assistant. He arrived in France on 29th December 1916.

The War Diary for William's battalion during the period when he went missing in 1917 is as follows:

Instructions regarding War Diaries and Intelligence Summaries are contained in F.S. Regs., Part II, and the Staff Manual respectively. Title pages will be prepared in manuscript.	WAR DIARY [135] or INTELLIGENCE SUMMARY. (Erase heading not required.)	Army Form C. 2118.
Date	Summary of Events and Information	Remarks and References to Appendices
13-4-1917	ARRAS: Battalion rested in the Caves all day. (Under the city of Arras are a network of quarry tunnels, dating from at least the Middle Ages. At the end of 1916, led by the New Zealand Tunnelling Company, a team of 500 tunnellers, including British coal miners, were brought in to expand the mine tunnels. They had many uses, including as supply depots and a hospital.)	
14 to 15-4-1917	Marched to billets in MONTENESCOURT, then to billets in SAULTY.	
16 to 22-4-1917	Time spent reorganising, bathing, and firing practice.	
23 to 25-4-1917	Marched to billets at NOYELLETTE, then onto DUISANS and back to ARRAS.	

---

[135] War Diary: 6 Battalion Buffs (East Kent Regiment). WO-95-1860-3. September 1916-December 1917. The National Archives (UK), Kew, England.

26 to 28-4-1917	Inspections, musketry practice and lectures on open warfare.
The diary included a FIELD STATE report dated 26th April 1917, which recorded a Fighting Strength of 40 Officers, 949 Other Ranks, 11 Riding horses and 41 Draught and Pack horses and mules. The Ration Strength, however, was for 934 personnel and 52 horses.	
29-4-1917	Cleaning trenches from cemetery to old British front line. Amount of material collected was enormous.
30-4-1917	Battalion moved into front line at MONCHY-LE-PREUX relieving 7TH BATTALION NORFOLK REGIMENT.
1-5-1917	After dark 7TH BATTALION, EAST SURREY REGIMENT took over our trenches and we moved to positions in shell holes.
3-5-1917	3.45am - An intense barrage opened, and a creeping barrage opened at the rate of 100 yards per 3 minutes. Battalion advanced at same time. Due to darkness, snipers, and machine gun fire, it was difficult to obtain information on progress. Fairly quiet with exception of sudden bursts of artillery fire and continuous sniping. Dusk - Battalion ascertained it had suffered severe casualties.
4-5-1917	Morning - Battalion relieved by 6TH BATTALION, THE QUEENS. CASUALTIES 9 officers killed or missing, 3 wounded 360 Other Ranks (no breakdown noted in the diary for killed, wounded or missing.)

William was officially recorded as 'Missing presumed dead' on or since 3rd May 1917. He was 19 years old and is commemorated on the Arras Memorial to the Missing.

William is remembered on Sittingbourne War Memorial and Sittingbourne Holy Trinity Church WW1 Memorial, where he is inscribed in error as M. S. Tomkin. His father received his pay and gratuity, and his Victory and British War Medals.

An additional 126 men were recorded as missing from the 6th Battalion on the same day and they are also commemorated on the Arras Memorial. Seven men were buried locally. A further 122 Buffs from other regiments are also commemorated on the Arras Memorial who also fell on 3rd May 1917.

The 3rd and 4th May 1917 became known as the Third Battle of Scarpe, which resulted in the British Army suffering nearly 6,000 men killed with little gain. The battle also involved the Australian and Canadian forces.

Pictured right - the village of Monchy-le-Preux in April-May 1919.
Credit: Canada. Dept. of National Defence/Library and Archives Canada/PA-004367.

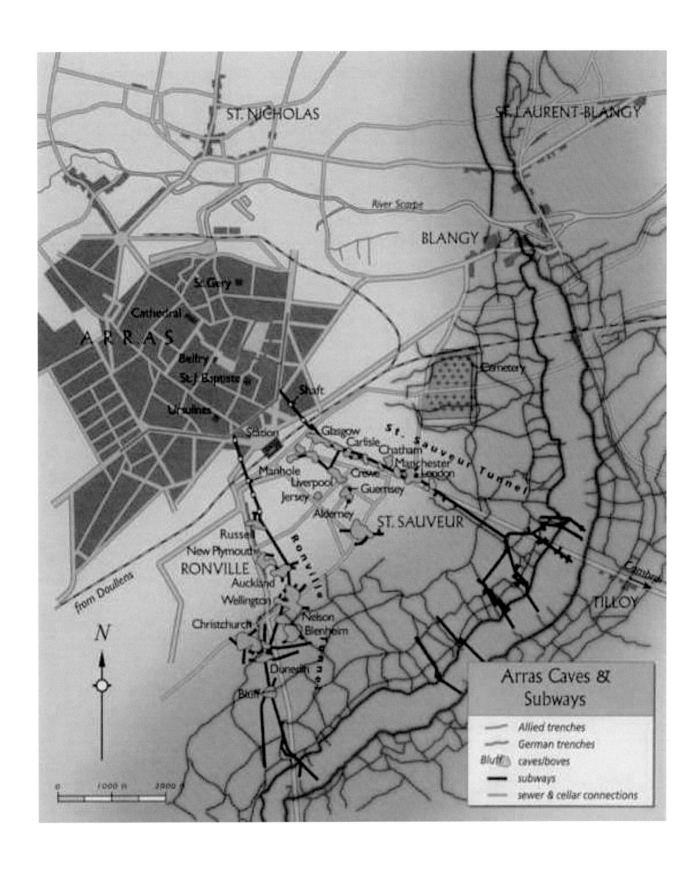

Map showing the caves under Arras and
the trench positions for both the allied forces and German forces.

TONG, William Harold

G/18877, Private, 10th Battalion, The Queen's (Royal West Surrey Regiment).

William was born in Sittingbourne in 1898, the second of the four children of Frederick William, a coachman, and Mary, a dressmaker. In 1911 the family were all living at 3 The Wall, Sittingbourne. William's siblings were Frederick Gordon, Florence Amelia Gladys, and Leonard Victor.

The East Kent Gazette of 24th May 1913 announced the appointment of William's father as a park keeper and gardener, at the Albany Road Recreation Ground (below).

William's brother Frederick served in the Suffolk Regiment from February 1916 and was posted to Mesopotamia the following September, then to India from July 1917 to February 1919. He was discharged the next month on the 21st March 1919.

William had attended St Michael's Boys School, and before enlisting he was employed in the brickfields, working for Messrs Wills & Packham Co. Ltd.

William was recorded as being killed in action on 22nd September 1917, aged 19. This is the date recorded by the CWGC. The regiment's War Diary entry for this period is as follows:

Instructions regarding War Diaries and Intelligence Summaries are contained in F.S. Regs., Part II, and the Staff Manual respectively. Title pages will be prepared in manuscript.	WAR DIARY [136] or INTELLIGENCE SUMMARY. (Erase heading not required.)	Army Form C. 2118.
Date	Summary of Events and Information	Remarks and References to Appendices
1-9-1917 to 15-9-1917	Battalion in billets and training at SAINT-MARTIN-AU-LAËRT. Divisional Commander was presenting medal ribbons. Training and practising attacks	
16-9-1917	Marched to SAINTE-MARIE-CAPPEL.	
17-9-1917	Moved to THIEUSHOUCK.	
18-9-1917	Battalion marched over border to RIDGE WOOD, near DICKEBUSCH.	
19-9-1917	Battalion kitted out with bombs, extra ammunition, and two days rations. Assembled ready to attack on the 20th.	
20-9-1917	Under the cover of darkness, using prepared taped path, Battalion assembled in line from HET PAPPOTJE FARM to SHREWSBURY FOREST. Objectives was JAVA TRENCH, then to push on to TOWER HAMLETS RIDGE. Area subjected to intense bombardment for several days.	

[136] War Diary: 10 Battalion Queen's (Royal West Surrey Regiment). WO-95-2643-1. May 1916-October 1917. The National Archives (UK), Kew, England.

20-9-1917 continued	5.40am - Battalion advanced in close formation, hoping to beat German barrage. Only moved 75 metres when German machine guns opened up, which did great havoc. Some men managed to work their way around the machine gun positions and successfully silenced them. 2pm - Battalion very disorganised but managed to reach its objectives. Dug in for the night. Intermittent shelling from the Germans.
21-9-1917	2pm to 7pm - Subjected to very heavy German shelling increasing in violence towards the end. 7pm - Germans attacked in strong numbers and repulsed by British artillery and rifle fire.
22-9-1917	Germans shelling. Men suffering from lack of sufficient water and food.
23-9-1917	Half the Battalion relieved by 1ST CAMBRIDGESHIRE'S. No rations or water arrived.
24-9-1917	1am - Remainder of Battalion were relieved by the 1ST HERTFORDSHIRE'S.

ROLL OF HONOUR.

KILLED BY A GERMAN SNIPER.

In our issue of October 13th we published particulars of the death of Private William Harold Tong, aged 19 years and seven months, of the Queen's (Royal West Surrey) Regt., the second son of Mr. and Mrs. F. W. Tong, 3, The Wall, Sittingbourne, who was killed in action in Flanders, in September. Mrs. Tong has since received the following letter giving details of how the gallant young fellow met his sad end :—

"October 14th, 1917.—Dear Mrs. Tong,—I regret to tell you that your son was killed on September 21st, about 5.30 a.m., when the Company attacked the enemy close by and south of Tower Hamlets. He was killed by a bullet through his head by an enemy sniper, and had no pain or suffering—and was buried close by where he fell. . . . I wish to express to you our deep regret at the loss of your son, and we all sympathize with you in your great loss.— Yours truly, REGINALD BOWDEN, Major."

The East Kent Gazette dated 13th October 1917 reported that William died on 20th September 1917, and his Pension Index Card records the date as 21st September 1917. Whichever is the correct date, William is remembered by those who loved and knew him.

An additional report was published in the 1st December 1917 edition of the East Kent Gazette (pictured left).

William is remembered on the Tyne Cot Memorial to the Missing, Sittingbourne War Memorial and Sittingbourne Holy Trinity Church WW1 Memorial. Seventy-two men from William's battalion were killed during the four days of fighting, with 57 of their names inscribed on Tyne Cot Memorial. William was awarded the Victory and British War Medals.

TOWN, Albert Charles

T/205308, Private, 8th Battalion, The Queen's (Royal West Surrey Regiment).

Albert was born in Maidstone and was baptised at Holy Trinity Church there on 5th February 1897. He was one of four children and sadly, the only one to survive infancy. His siblings were Kate Emily (1889-1890), Herbert Valentine (1892-1895), and Edward Arthur (1898-1902).

Albert's parents were Charles and Emily Jane (née Dorsett). In 1901, Albert's father was a plasterer, publican, and lodging housekeeper, and they were living at 72 Week Street, Maidstone. The 1891 Post Office Directory and Kelly's Directory 1903 lists this address as the "Windsor Castle". By 1911 they had moved to the George Hotel, High Street, Sittingbourne, and his father was a licensed victualler.

Albert enlisted in Canterbury joining the 2nd Battalion of the Royal West Surrey Regiment before being posted to the 8th Battalion.

At the start of July 1917, his battalion was resting and training in Coulomby, France, as recorded in its War Diary.[137] The first week of training included bombing, Lewis gunnery and rifle grenades, and the second week for an offense operation, using a to-scale flagged course. From the 18th to the 23rd, his battalion travelled 70km from Coulomby to a camp near Heuvelland, Belgium, via Renescure, Caëstre, Eecke and Reningelst, Belgium (route below). The battalion remained in camp until 29th July, when they moved to the trenches, just to the north of Klein Zillebeke.

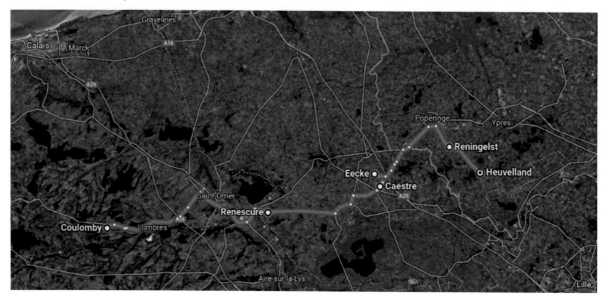

Map data ©2023 Google, Imaginary ©2023 Landsat / Copernicus, Data SIO, NOAA, U.S. Navy, NGA, GEBCO, Imaginary ©2023 TerraMetrics

On 30th July 1917, the day was spent resting and moving stores up to the front line. At 9pm, Albert's battalion moved forward to the assembly positions and completed this by 3.45am the next day. During this time the enemy laid down constant shell fire, 'which thickened as dawn approached.' At 3.50am the barrage commenced, to be immediately returned with 77mm and 4.2inch Howitzers, on to the front line. At 3.54am the leading companies advanced and charged their first objective, Jehovah Trench near Klein Zillebeke, and without opposition achieved their objective. This action resulted in 16 prisoners being taken. The companies proceeded 200 metres further east to take Jordan Trench, their second objective. The diary recorded the opposition was minimal, except for machine gun fire from nearby Bulgar and Culist Woods, together with accurate enemy barrage, causing many casualties. The rest of the day was spent consolidating their position and collecting the wounded, though the enemy fire was still accurate. Heavy rain stopped work in the evening as the ground became slippery and muddy.

Scene from the Somme

---

[137] War Diary: 8 Battalion Queen's (Royal West Surrey Regiment). WO-95-2214-4. July 1917-September 1917. The National Archives (UK), Kew, England.

The 1st August 1917 was another rainy day, making conditions worse and more enemy fire caused more casualties. Albert's battalion was relieved at 11.45pm by the 9th Battalion East Surrey Regiment.

Albert was initially reported "Missing in action" during the night of 31st July and 1st August 1917, and later was officially recorded as "Missing presumed Killed, on or since 1st August 1917". However, there is a Red Cross record[138] recording he was taken a Prisoner of War and died on 1st August 1917.

Albert is remembered on the Ypres Menin Gate Memorial to the Missing, Sittingbourne War Memorial and St Michael's Church WW1 Memorial Window. His father received his pay and gratuity, as well as his Victory and British War Medals.

TOWNSEND, Charles

342373, Armourer's Mate, HMS Cressy, Royal Navy.

Charles was born in Aston, Birmingham, Warwickshire, on 27th December 1876, and he was baptised at St James' Church in Handsworth, Staffordshire. He was one of eight children of Robert, a core maker in an iron foundry, and Elizabeth (née Simpson). Charles' siblings were Robert Arthur, Charles Edward (1869-1870), Nora Mary, Albert (1875-1875), Albert George, Benjamin Herbert, and two unnamed children who had died.

On 7th October 1898, Charles joined the Royal Navy and completed his 12-year term on 6th October 1910. In 1901 he was serving as an Armourer's Crew member, and was stationed aboard *HMS Wildfire*, which was docked at Sheerness and acting as a gunnery school.

On 11th February 1908, in West Bromwich, Staffordshire, he married 23-year-old Eleanor Maude Trice, from Lynsted, Kent. Their only child, Richard Charles Robert was born on 18th January 1911 in Smethwick, Staffordshire. By then Charles was employed at a small arms factory as a gun finisher and the family were living at 277 Oldknow Road, Birmingham.

Charles re-joined the Navy on 21st August 1911, serving until 10th October 1912. At the outbreak of war, he returned once again to the Navy on 2nd August 1914 and was posted to the cruiser *HMS Cressy* (pictured right), which was part of the patrols of the Broad Fourteens, the eastern end of the English Channel.

The *Cressy* was held in reserve for the first naval battle of the war, the Battle of Heligoland Bight, fought on 28th August 1914, which resulted in the British sinking three German light cruisers. The *Cressy* was tasked with transporting 156 German sailors back to England.

---

[138] Prisoners of the First World War, the International Committee of the Red Cross. Prisoners Of War 1715-1945. FindmyPast.co.uk

On the morning of 22nd September 1914, *Cressy* was on patrol with *Aboukir* and *Hogue*, off the western coast of the Netherlands, 70km north-west of Rotterdam. Their destroyer escorts had been forced to

remain in harbour due to bad weather. At 6.20am, the U-boat *SM U-9* (pictured left) hit the *Aboukir*, with a single torpedo, resulting in her sinking. Just over half an hour later at 6.55am, *Hogue* was struck and sunk by two torpedoes. The firing of the torpedoes lightened the weight of *U-9*, which caused her to broach the service. *Cressy* spotted the submarine and tried to ram her. She then resumed trying to rescue any survivors before being struck by a torpedo and capsizing at 7.55am. Dutch ships and British trawlers picked up 837 survivors. Records show that 1,464 crew were lost across the three ships, with 562 on *Cressy*, 528 on *Aboukir*, and 374 on *Hogue*.

Charles was one of those who died, aged 37. At that time his wife, Eleanor, was living at 151 East Street, Sittingbourne, where she was a fruiterer and greengrocer. Charles is remembered on the Chatham Naval Memorial to the Missing, Sittingbourne War Memorial and St Michael's Church WW1 Memorial Window.

For several years the East Kent Gazette published an "In Memoriam", from his wife and son, at the time of his anniversary. Each time the same poignant message was printed: "Never forgotten."

The three ships were part of 7th Cruiser Squadron, which also included *HMS Bacchante* and *HMS Euryalus*. The squadron had gained the nickname "The Live Bait Squadron" due to the ship's ages, all were about 14 years old, and had inexperienced crews. On 21st August 1914 Commodore Roger Keyes wrote to his superiors of this fact, which had reached the attention of First Lord of the Admiralty Winston Churchill. On 18th September 1914 he met with First Sea Lord Prince Louis of Battenburg, and they agreed that the cruisers were to be withdrawn, though due to the lack of replacements and the current building of new cruisers they would remain on station.

The loss of these three ships claimed the lives of 41 others from the district of Swale. Their names are:

HMS Cressy

Chief Armourer George John Blandford, 36, from Sheerness.

Chief Armourer Harry Nicholls, 40, from Sittingbourne.

Chief Stoker John William Scarfe, 41, from Sheerness.

Chief Stoker William Brattle, 39, from Sheerness.

Engine Room Artificer 1st Class Edmund James Piper, 49, from Sheppey.

Ordinary Signalman Ernest Irons, 20, from Minster.

Petty Officer 1st Class John Mason, 32, from Sheerness.

Royal Marine Light Infantry Colour Sergeant Horace Farmer, 40, from Sheerness.

Royal Marine Light Infantry Private Joseph Robert French, 31, from Rainham.

Royal Marine Light Infantry Private William James Cooley, 39, from Sheppey.

Sick Berth Steward Charles James Davies, 35, from Newington.

Signaller Willie George Collins (aka Chittenden), 49, from Faversham.

Stoker 1st Class Charles Edgar Arnold, 26, from Hernhill.

HMS Aboukir

Able Seaman Edward Charles Wigg 32, from Faversham.

Able Seaman Frederick Charles Hamilton, 35, from Murston.

Able Seaman Sidney Smith, 34, from Milton Regis.

Chief Armourer Frederick William Court, 40, from Sheerness.

Chief Stoker Henry William Barling, 38, from Sheerness.

Engine Room Artificer 1st Class Frederick Charles Dering, 37, from Sheerness.

Leading Carpenter's Crew Robert Allison, 48, from Sheerness.

Leading Stoker Harry Beanland, 31, from Lower Halstow.

Royal Marine Light Infantry Private Ernest George Carter, 25, from Upchurch.

Royal Marine Light Infantry Private Herbert Chown, 32, from Milton Regis.

Royal Marine Light Infantry Sergeant William Horace Mann, 30, from Sheerness.

Stoker 1st Class Charles Ambrose Lamkin, 27, from Milstead.

Stoker Petty Officer William Edward Harvey, 29, from Hernhill, near Faversham.

HMS Hogue

Armourer Robert Johnston, 40, from Sheerness.

Chief Armourer Thomas Robert Waters, 39, from Sheerness.

Chief Petty Officer Joseph Leonard Edmonds, 41, from Sheerness.

Chief Stoker Henry T Mason, 41, from Upchurch.

Chief Writer John Henry Howes, 34, from Sheerness.

Engine Room Artificer 1st Class Daniel Cottier Innes, 39, from Sheerness.

Petty Officer Gunnery Instructor John Edward Thurgood, 35, from Sheerness.

Petty Officer Stoker Henry T Allen, 42, from Milton Regis.

Petty Officer Tom Bellesby, 34, from Sheerness.

Plumbers Mate Maurice Justice, 29, from Sheerness.

Royal Marine Light Infantry Private John Edmund Fisher, 41, from Milton Regis.

Royal Marine Light Infantry Private Thomas John Taylor, 42, from Faversham.

Ship's Steward Reuben George Barnard, 32, from Sheerness.

Stoker 1st Class Edward James (Valentine) White, 38, from Sheerness.

Stoker 1st Class John Baker Thomas, 25, from Milton Regis.

With the exception of two men all are commemorated on Chatham Naval Memorial. The remaining two, Frederick Dering and Horace Farmer were recovered and buried in s-Gravenzande General Cemetery, Netherlands. This cemetery also contains 97 unidentified burials, many of which are from the three ships.

A memorial to all three ships stands in Chatham Historic Dockyard with the inscription:

First World War 100th Anniversary

To commemorate the loss of three Chatham Division Cruisers

His Majesty's Ships ABOUKIR, HOGUE and CRESSY

and 1,459 men on 22nd September 1914 as a result of enemy action in the North Sea

Unveiled by His Royal Highness The Duke of Kent KG

on 22nd September 2014

Credit: Susan Featherstone, IWM War Memorials Register

TROWELL, Alfred Edgar

23650, Private, 2nd Battalion, Royal Warwickshire Regiment.

Alfred was the eldest child of Alfred John and Mary Ann Lacey. He was born in 1879 in Sittingbourne, and his siblings were Laura Lilian, Rodney, Harry, and Frank. In 1911 his parents and brothers were living in Bobbing, Kent, where his father was a fruit grower and his brothers also worked on a fruit farm.

In the summer of 1909, Alfred had married Grace Elizabeth Webb, and in 1911 was living with her at 21 Burley Road, Sittingbourne, their son Claude Harcourt was born on 20th July 1911. Alfred was a carpenter and joiner when he enlisted in the Royal Engineers in Sittingbourne before he was transferred to the Warwickshire's.

Instructions regarding War Diaries and Intelligence Summaries are contained in F.S. Regs., Part II, and the Staff Manual respectively. Title pages will be prepared in manuscript.	WAR DIARY [139] or INTELLIGENCE SUMMARY. (Erase heading not required.)	Army Form C. 2118.
Date	Summary of Events and Information	Remarks and References to Appendices
15-9-1917 to 27-9-1917	*Battalion located at SETQUES.* *Time spent on Bullet and Bayonet courses, training on action to take in a Gas Shell attack, undertaking battle exercises and played football.*	
28-9-1917 to 29-9-1917	*Marched and entrained 65km east to HOOGE TUNNEL and on to dugouts just outside of YPRES.*	

[139] War Diary: 2 Battalion Royal Warwickshire. WO-95-1664-3. September 1914-November 1917. The National Archives (UK), Kew, England.

1-10-1917	Battalion moved to HOOGE CRATER (pictured above).
2-10-1917	Moved to ZILLEBEKE LAKE.
3-10-1917 to 4-10-1917	50 men working for 22ND MACHINE GUN CORPS for carrying purposes and 250 men tasked with moving trench boards from HOOGE CRATER to ZILLEBEKE LAKE.
5-10-1917 to 6-10-1917	50 men working as stretcher bearers at HOOGE CRATER. Battalion moved to a camp at HELLEBAST.
1-10-1917 to 6-10-1917	CASUALTIES 4 Killed, 32 Wounded, 14 Missing and 8 Shell Shock.
7-10-1917	Battalion into the line at POLYGON WOOD, near ZONNEBEKE.
8-10-1917	Holding the line.
9-10-1917	5am - Battalion attacked nearby BUTTES and JUDGE COPSE. By 7.30am - pushed through JUDGE COPSE and reached the Cemetery, met with machine gun fire. 9TH DEVON'S sent back to JUDGE COPSE to mop up.
10-10-1917	Battalion remained in position. 11pm = Relieved and returned to ZILLEBEKE LAKE.

Stretcher Bearers - IWM (Q 5935)

Alfred was officially declared "Missing presumed killed on or since 9th October 1917". He was 38 years old. He is remembered on the Tyne Cot Memorial to the Missing, Sittingbourne War Memorial and the Bobbing Church Memorial. He was awarded the Victory and British War Medals, and his wife received his pay and gratuity.

Alfred's youngest brother, 24-year-old Private Frank, 54th Coy, Machine Gun Corps (Infantry) was killed on 3rd May 1917 and is commemorated on the Arras Memorial to the Missing. Locally he is also remembered on Bobbing Church Memorial.

The East Kent Gazette edition dated 11th May 1918, under the headline "SOLDIER BROTHERS CAPTURED AND MISSING", reported on the fact that both Alfred and Frank were missing, stating Alfred 'had been gone since September' and Frank for 'twelve months.' The captured brother was Gunner Rodney of the Royal Field Artillery, who was reported as 'officially a prisoner of war'. The newspaper article stated he had been captured at St Quentin and that his wife, Maud, had received a postcard from him saying he was "well and not wounded". Rodney was repatriated following the Armistice.

TYLER, Benjamin

179307, Gunner, 464th Battery, 179th Brigade, Royal Field Artillery.

Benjamin was born in Sittingbourne in 1897, and he was baptised on 23rd January 1898 in St Michael's Church. He was the tenth of the twelve children of Arthur, a gas stoker, and Elizabeth Ann (née Waters). His siblings were Alfred Edward, Susanna Elizabeth, Arthur George, William Henry (1886-1912), Richard, Albert, John, twins Rosa May (1895-1895) and Elizabeth Ann, Robert (1900-1927) and Frederick George (1902-1924).

The Tyler family lost one of their twin daughters in infancy and four other sons, Arthur (aged 36) and William (aged 26) from illness, Robert (aged 27) drowned in the Turf Canal, Exeter, whilst serving on *SS Pegrix*, and Frederick (aged 22).

Robert's death was the subject of an inquest which was reported in the Western Times dated 16th December 1927. The coroner returned an "Accidental Death" verdict, as it appeared Robert had slipped and fallen into the canal.

Benjamin's older brother, Arthur, served as Private in The Buffs (East Kent Regiment). He served from March 1915 to October 1915 and spent three months in France. He was discharged, being declared "no longer physically fit". On 30th November 1920 he died at home from Pulmonary Tuberculosis and was buried in Sittingbourne Cemetery. As he served and died within the CWGC qualification period, his grave is marked with a CWGC headstone (pictured right). Arthur is not commemorated on the Avenue or the town's war memorial. As no records related to the decision process exist, it is assumed his short service, cause and date of death were a deciding factor.

Before Benjamin enlisted, he was employed by Smeed Dean and Co. Limited, as a mate on the barge *Russell*. He enlisted in Sittingbourne and served in France from February 1915, aged 17. The 6th April 1918 edition of the East Kent Gazette reported that during his time there, he had been gassed and suffered once from shell shock. The newspaper also reported that on 21st March 1918 he was hit by a machine gun bullet in his stomach. He died two days later, aged 21, on 23rd March 1918.

Benjamin's mother received a letter from the Chaplain, which contained Benjamin's dying message, "Give my very best love to my parents and family, and to all in Sittingbourne who know me."

Benjamin was buried in the Mont Huon Military Cemetery, Le Tréport.

Le Tréport (pictured below) was a major hospital centre, with four Canadian general hospitals, two American hospitals and Lady Murray's British Red Cross Hospital, together with No. 3 Convalescent Depot. Mont Huon Military Cemetery, designed by Sir Reginald Blomfield, is the final resting place for 2,128 Commonwealth and 200 German burials, together with seven from the Second World War.

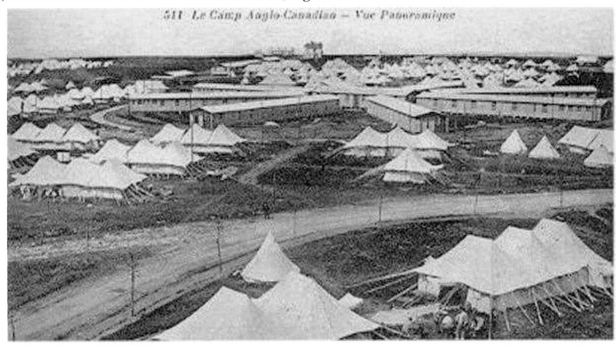

Benjamin is remembered on Sittingbourne War Memorial and St Michael's Church WW1 Memorial Window. His father received his pay and gratuity as well as his Victory and British War Medals.

TYLER, Gordon Herbert

GS/23593, Private, 17th Lancers (Duke of Cambridge's Own).

Gordon was born in Sittingbourne in 1896 and baptised in Milton Regis on 15th December 1896. He was the youngest son of Henry James, a house painter, and Margaret (née McGregor). Gordon's father died in 1899, at the age of 36, leaving Gordon with only his mother and his two brothers Reuben McGregor (born 1891) and Douglas Henry (born 1893). In 1901 they were living at 4 Rock Road, Sittingbourne, his mother was running a boarding house with there being four boarders at that time – as the house had only three bedrooms it would have been quite crowded.

By 1911, his brother Reuben, aged 19, had been employed as a grocer in several Co-operative stores, and his brother Douglas, aged 18, was an engineer at a cycle works which Gordon, aged 14, also worked at as an errand boy. They were all living with their housekeeper mother, at 113 High Street, Sittingbourne, the home of her employer Alfred King Burford Richard William Taylor, who was a surgeon and physician.

In 1915 Gordon enlisted at Canterbury and for 13 months he trained at Curragh Camp in County Kildare Ireland. He arrived in France in April 1916 with The Lancers.

299

The Lancers War Diary[140] records on 17th May 1917 the fighting troops marched to billets at a new area at Ennemain, arriving at 1pm. The next day the dismounted troops relieved the 176th Battalion in the front line.

The diary entries mainly noted the movement of officers to and from the trenches and an entry for 23rd May read "Billets – Hot and fine weather and no rain since 17th May." It also noted the regiment's strength as:

Officers	Other Ranks	Horses
33	605	553

The entry for 16th June 1917 read "Dismounted Coy relieved from trenches night of 16/17. Marched back to camp at HAMELET."

Gordon is recorded as dying of wounds, aged 20, on 16th June 1917. He was buried in the Tincourt New British Cemetery (pictured right). Records show that Gordon was originally buried, close to his final resting place, and his grave was marked by a cross. As Tincourt cemetery was not started until June 1917 it is probable that this was a temporary situation, as a number of other soldiers were buried close to Gordon.

Credit: ww1cemeteries.com

The 28th July 1917 edition of the East Kent Gazette reported on Gordon's death under the headline:

"SITTINGBOURNE SOLDIER
ACCIDENTALLY KILLED".

The article noted that when Gordon left school, he had become an apprentice in the grocery department of the Sittingbourne Co-operative Society. After five years he moved to the Abbey Wood, Kent, branch (pictured below).

The newspaper report added that on 15th June a nursing Sister at No. 36 Casualty Clearing Station, based at Tincourt, wrote to Gordon's mother informing her that 'Gordon, on the 13th had been accidentally thrown from his horse and brought to the station unconscious. Everything possible was done for him.'

Gordon is also remembered on Sittingbourne War Memorial, St Michael's Church WW1 Memorial Window, and the Baptist Church Memorial. His Victory and British War Medals, together with his pay and gratuity were granted to his mother.

140 War Diary: 17 (Duke of Cambridge's) Lancers. WO-95-1159-4. January 1917-February 1918. The National Archives (UK), Kew, England.

For several years his mother and brothers posted "In Memoriam" in the East Kent Gazette". Two emotional postings are included below.

<table>
<tr><td>

The East Kent Gazette

SATURDAY, JUNE 15, 1918

IN MEMORIAM

TYLER – In loving memory of my dear son, Gordon Herbert Tyler, of the 17th Lancers, killed in France, June 15th, 1917.

Jesus standeth on the shore

Of every woe!

The antidote and comforter

For all below!

Oh! Meet him, "in the midst," of all

That crusheth thee.

So wilt thou learn to live above

Life's misery!

From his loving Mother and Brothers.

</td><td>

The East Kent Gazette

SATURDAY, JUNE 19, 1920

IN MEMORIAM

TYLER – In loving memory of a dear son and brother, Gordon Herbert Tyler, 17th Lancers, killed in France, June 15th, 1917.

Gone is the one we loved so dear,

Silent the voice we loved to hear,

Too far away from sight and speech,

But not too far for our thoughts to reach.

From his loving Mother and Brothers.

</td></tr>
</table>

TYLER, Leslie Charles

M2/156669, Private, Royal Army Service Corps.

Leslie was born in Sittingbourne in 1896, the son of Valentine William, a baker and confectioner, and Jane (née Rowell). He was the seventh of eleven children, with his brothers and sisters being Valentine Vincent (1885-1886), Daisy, Georgina Violet, Ivy Jane, Archibald William, Annie May, Lilian, Nelson William, Eric Valentine, and Ralph. The family had lived at 5 East Street, Sittingbourne, from at least 1901.

Leslie's brother Archibald served the duration of the war as a shipwright and worked at Chatham dockyard from January 1914 to March 1916, before he moved to work at Rosyth dockyard, on the Firth of Forth.

In 1911 Leslie was living with his sister Daisy, and her husband Henry Rossiter, and was working as a winder boy at a wallpaper manufacturer in Greenhithe, where his brother-in-law Henry was also employed as a dryerman.

When Leslie enlisted on 11th February 1916 at Grove Park, Sittingbourne, he was 5ft 8½in tall. He arrived in France on 19th May 1916.

His Service Record includes a copy of a Court of Inquiry, which was held on 23rd June 1919, with regards to Leslie's Medical Report. The report recorded he had Pulmonary Tuberculosis since 1915 and had Pleurisy and Sanatorium treatment before he enlisted. The report added that he was admitted on 1st March 1919 to No. 41 Stationary Hospital, France, with sweating and weakness, and on 6th March 1919 he was moved to No. 1 South African General Hospital in Abbeville. Two days later he was evacuated to Bermondsey Military Hospital, England. On 21st June 1919 he was sent home by ambulance. The report concluded that he was suffering from Tuberculosis, in both lungs.

Just a month later on 17th July 1919, Leslie died from the disease at the age of 23. He was buried in Sittingbourne Cemetery, and is remembered on Sittingbourne War Memorial, St Michael's Church WW1 Memorial Window, and the Baptist Church Memorial.

Leslie was awarded the Victory and British War Medals, which were delivered to his father, who still lived in East Street.

VANDEPEER, Sidney Leonard

G/13746, Serjeant, 1st Battalion, The Buffs (East Kent Regiment).

Sidney, also known as Dick, was born in Sittingbourne in 1896 and baptised at St Michael's Church on 14th February 1897. He was the youngest of the thirteen children of Henry Austin and Dorcas (née Kingswood). His siblings were Selina Maria, Walter Henry Stephen, Ellen Jane, Alfred Henry, Edward William Bertie, Oliver Henry, (1882-1903), Lilian Alice Maud, Hedley Victor, Florence (1890-1890), May Jemima, Dorcas (1893-1893) and Bessie Rosina.

Sidney's father, Henry, died in 1929 and the East Kent Gazette dated 24th August 1929 noted that he had kept the Golden Eagle (pictured below) at 1 Station Street, Sittingbourne, the Ship Inn, East Street, Sittingbourne, and then the Castle public house in Queenborough. By 1911 he was employed as a marine store dealer and living at 50 Shakespeare Road, Sittingbourne. The newspaper also reported that Henry had been a renowned long-distance runner, winning several races over a mile and four miles, from 1874 to 1881. In 1879 he won a 24-hour race in Wolverhampton, covering 144 miles, and a 26-hour race at Lambeth, London, where he beat 25 of the best men in the country.

Sidney had attended Holy Trinity Day School, Sittingbourne, and Queenborough Council School, before he went to work for Messrs Hubbard and Son, as a warehouse man.

In 1915, Sidney's older brother Hedley crossed the Atlantic and landed in the USA. From there, he travelled to Ontario, in Canada.

When he enlisted in Sittingbourne on 31st May 1915, Sidney was 5ft 8½in tall and had been working as a grocer. Sidney was posted to 3/1 Battalion, Royal East Kent Mounted Rifles and gained promotion to Corporal just five months later. He was posted to the 1st Battalion on 6th January 1917, on the same day that he arrived in France. He was promoted to Serjeant on 4th May 1917.

The regimental War Diary of Sidney's last days has been reproduced here:

Army Form C. 2118.

	WAR DIARY [141] or INTELLIGENCE SUMMARY. (Erase heading not required.)	
Instructions regarding War Diaries and Intelligence Summaries are contained in F.S. Regs., Part II, and the Staff Manual respectively. Title pages will be prepared in manuscript.		
Date	Summary of Events and Information	Remarks and References to Appendices
1-6-1917 to 10-6-1917	Relieved 2ND YORK'S AND LANCASTER'S on the right of the front at the village of HULLUCH, near LENS. Each day's entry noted the number of casualties, which amounted to 24 wounded and 7 died.	
11-6-1917	Relieved by 2ND YORK'S AND LANCASTER'S. From the front the battalion split, with the A and B Companies marching to FOUQUIÈRES-LÈS-BÉTHUNE, and the C and D Companies to ALLOUAGNE.	
11-6-1917	FOUQUIÈRES - Horse show (Drive) in full swing. Battalion won first and second prizes for the Officer Charge, and first for the Light Draught (Stripped).	
12-6-1917 to 14-6-1917	No diary entries.	
15-6-1917	Tug of War. Officers v Sergeants. Officers won easily.	
18-6-1917	Horse show. Battalion won first prize for the Light Draught (Stripped), together with second.	
19-6-1917	A and B Companies and the Drums marched to MAZINGARBE.	
20-6-1917	Relieved the 2ND YORK'S AND LANCASTER'S in the trenches.	
23-6-1917	C and D Companies moved to trenches.	
24-6-1917	Battalion attacked, in three waves, the German lines in HULLUCH. Soon reached and took trenches, doing damage to a great extent. Captured 15 prisoners and two trench mortars. Some trouble was experienced to get the enemy out of his dug-outs, but those were overcome by gentle persuasion using tear bombs. Enemy unsettled, and their barrage very weak, against our splendid barrage. CASUALTIES - 14 killed, 76 wounded and 21 missing.	

Sidney was recorded as one of the missing and officially declared as killed in action on 24th June 1917, aged 20. He is remembered on the Loos Memorial to the Missing, Sittingbourne War Memorial and St Michael's Church WW1 Memorial Window. He was awarded the Victory and British War Medals.

On reporting his death under the headline "SITTINGBOURNE SOLDIER DIES FACING THE FOE", 7th July 1917 edition of the East Kent Gazette included a picture of Sidney in his sergeant's uniform, and printed a letter that his mother was sent, it read:

"June 27th, 1917. – Dear Madam, - it is with great regret that I have to inform you that your son, Sergt. S. Vandepeer, of this Battalion was killed in action about 9.30 p.m. on the 24th instant. We were making a raid on the enemy's trenches and had got as far as the Germans' second line, when your son was killed outright by a shell. He was a splendid fellow, and died

---

[141] War Diary: 1 Battalion The Buffs. WO-95-1608-3. 1917. The National Archives (UK), Kew, England.

like a hero. I had had a lot to do with him in the Company, and he had the making of a fine N.C.O. he need not have gone into action, as he had a bad arm at the time, but he refused to go sick until after the raid. So, you have every reason to be proud of him. All the officers and men of his Company join with me in offering our deepest sympathy to you in this trouble. It might interest you to know that the raid was a great success, thanks to such men as your son. 'With deepest sympathy, I am, yours sincerely, V. NEWTON Moss, Lieut. – P.S. Unfortunately, we could not recover his body, but all his personal effects were left behind so will be forwarded in due course.-V.W.M."

Sidney was remembered by his family, as shown by these emotive "In Memoriam" published in the East Kent Gazette in 1920.

The East Kent Gazette

SATURDAY, JUNE 26, 1920

IN MEMORIAM

VANDEPEER - In loving memory of our dear Son and Brother, Sergt. Sidney Leonard (Dick) Vandepeer, who was killed in action June 24th, 1917, aged 21 years.

A loving son, and one so kind,
No-one to fill his place we find;
Though in a foreign land he's sleeping.
We leave him safe in God's own keeping.
Never Forgotten by his Mother, Father, Sisters

The East Kent Gazette

SATURDAY, JUNE 26, 1920

IN MEMORIAM

VANDEPEER – In loving memory of our dear Brother, Sergt. Sidney Leonard (Dick), who was killed in France, June 24th, 1917.
We sometimes deem his pleasant smiles
Still on us sweetly fall;
His tones of love we faintly hear,
His toils are past; the victory won:
But our hearts are very desolate
When we think of our brother that's gone.
From D. and T.

WAKELEN, Frederick Norris

200855, Private, 1st/4th Battalion, The Buffs (East Kent Regiment).

Frederick's registered surname was spelt Wakelen. However, his military documents record his surname as Wakelin.

Frederick was born in Milton Regis and was baptised there at St Paul's Church on 1st February 1894, with only his mother, Fanny, named. She was the daughter of William George Botting, a brickfield labourer, and Emma (née Wakelen), and they adopted Frederick. This is reflected in the 1901 and 1911 census where he is recorded as their son, under the surname Botting.

Frederick attended Murston School and the Wesleyan Bible Class, winning several prizes. In 1911, he was living with his grandparents, who were also his adoptive parents, at 21 Murston Road, Sittingbourne, and was employed as a brickfield labourer by Smeed Dean and Co.

In 1898, Frederick's mother, Fanny, married George William Silk at Blean, Kent, and in 1911 Fanny was living in Whitstable with their children George William, Elizabeth Mary, Walter, Frank, Sidney, Percy, and Bertha, who were Frederick's half-siblings. Shortly after that census was taken, the family emigrated to Strathcona, Alberta, Canada. Fanny's husband, and her son George, both signed up in Edmonton to join the 51st (Edmonton) Battalion, which was part of the initial Canadian Expeditionary Force that was formed in 1914 and both went to fight in Europe in 1916.

Frederick enlisted in 1914 and went to India in 1916. He was admitted to hospital on 6th November 1917, but despite the care and attention of the medical authorities he died of emphysema in India, aged 23, on 2nd January 1918. Frederick was buried the next day in Bareilly Cemetery, India.

He is remembered on Sittingbourne War Memorial and St Michael's Church WW1 Memorial Window. His pay and gratuity were paid to his grandfather William George Botting, who also received his British War Medal.

Frederick's death was reported in the 6th April 1918 edition of the East Kent Gazette. The newspaper reported, incorrectly, that he was an orphan. Frederick's Commanding Officer, Lieutenant-Colonel Gosling wrote to his grandparents informing them of his death and time in hospital. He added:

> "During the time your grandson has served with the battalion, he always showed himself to be a well behaved and efficient soldier, and very popular with all who knew him. Please accept the sincere sympathy of myself, officers, warrant officers, N.C.O.'s, and men of this battalion at the heavy loss you have sustained."

Tragically, Frederick's mother, Fanny, lost both her husband, George, and their eldest son, George William Silk, on the same day, 7th September 1916. They were both serving with 15th Battalion, Canadian Infantry. Their deaths were reported in the Edmonton Journal on 16th September 1916 (pictured right).

Fanny's husband George was buried in the Australian Infantry Burial Ground, Flers, (pictured below left) and her 19-year-old son was buried in Bouzincourt Communal Cemetery Extension (pictured below right), where the two cemeteries lie 20km apart.

HUSBAND AND SON ARE BOTH KILLED

Mrs. George W. Silk Hears Sad News of Casualties in Somme Fighting

Mrs. George W. Silk, 9346 80th Ave. S.E., Edmonton South, has received a telegram announcing the death in action of her husband, George W. Silk, Sr., and her eldest son, George W. Silk, Jr., both of whom met death at the same time, September 9th.

Father and son were members of the 51st Overseas Battalion and were drafted into the 48th Highlanders of Toronto. They were members of Holy Trinity church, George W., Jr., being an active worker in the Sunday school. The deepest sympathy of a large circle of friends is extended to Mrs. Silk and family.

Credit: ww1cemeteries.com

WALKER, Frederick Henry

VR/3298, Ordinary Seaman, H.M. Trawler Goeland II Royal Naval Canadian Volunteer Reserve.

Frederick was born in Faversham on 2nd September 1882 and was baptised there at St Mary of Charity Church on 22nd December 1882. He was the youngest son, and the sixth of the seven children of James, an agricultural labourer, and Jane (née Peters). His six siblings were Emma Jane, James William, Alfred, George Edward, William Thomas, and Annie Maria. By 1890 the family had moved to 81, Shortlands Road, Sittingbourne.

In 1901, 18-year-old Frederick was a mariner for the Sittingbourne based firm Smeed, Dean and Co, and the census records him aboard the barge vessel *George*.

Four of Frederick's siblings emigrated to Niagara Falls, New York, USA: George in 1905; Emma and William in 1907; and Annie in 1925. Frederick himself arrived in New York, to join his brother George on 24th June 1906, aged 24, on the steamship *St Louis*. At the time of Frederick's death, he was living at 232 Emerald Street, Hamilton, Ontario, Canada.

Frederick joined the Canadian Navy on 5th January 1917 and was sent to England for his training. He was then posted to the trawler *Goeland II* (pictured right), which was on minesweeping duties. He died, aged 34, on 27th July 1917, after he fractured his skull, whilst the trawler was docked at Dover. A witness on the trawler reported seeing Frederick trip over a bollard.

The East Kent Gazette dated the 11th August 1917 reported on the inquest into Frederick's death. The inquest was held at the Esplanade Hotel, Dover.

The article reported that Frederick was living with his mother at 103 Shortlands Road, Sittingbourne. A surgeon told the inquest that when he arrived, life was extinct, and his skull was fractured in a manner that was consistent with a fall. With the deceased being a heavy man, that would be the likely cause. The jury returned a verdict of Accidental Death.

He was buried in Sittingbourne Cemetery, and is remembered on Sittingbourne War Memorial and St Michael's Church WW1 Memorial Window.

Harold was born in 1900 in Sittingbourne, the son of Edith May Kemp. Shortly after his birth his mother married Frederick Walker in Milton Regis. In 1901 they were living in Rodmersham Green, where Frederick was employed as a fruit farm labourer.

Harold is recorded on the censuses with the surname 'Walker' and is recognised as his mother's son. By 1911, the family had moved to 62 Murston Road. Harold had a sister and brother, Elsie May (born 1905) and Harold Frederick (born 1920).

Harold enlisted at Canterbury joining the 53rd (Graduated) Battalion, Duke of Cambridge's Own (Middlesex) Regiment. It is probable he took part in the Sinai and Palestine Campaign that occurred in and around Jerusalem before his death.

Harold died at Connaught Military Hospital, Farnborough, Hampshire (pictured right), on 25th October 1918 from 'Influenza and Broncho Pneumonia'.[142] He was buried in Sittingbourne Cemetery, and his grave is marked with a private memorial, which also records that he was buried with both of his parents.

Harold is also remembered on the Sittingbourne War Memorial and St Michael's Church WW1 Memorial Window.

His death was reported in the Roll of Honour in the East Kent Gazette on 9th November 1918, and 'In Memoriam' was printed for him over many years. Pictured left, one from 1919.

The East Kent Gazette

SATURDAY, OCTOBER 25, 1919

IN MEMORIAM

WALKER - in loving of Harold Hector Walker who died, October 25th, 1918, aged 18 years.

Oh, why was he taken, so young and so fair,

Taken from home and those who loved him dear;

Only those who have lost can ever tell.

The pain at our hearts at not saying "Farewell."

Deeply missed by his loving Mum, Dad, and Sister Elsie

---

[142] Death Certificate England and Wales. Registration District of Hartley Wintney. 25 October 1918. WALKER, Harold. Number 18.

WARNER, Joseph John

28898, Private, 8th Battalion, East Yorkshire Regiment.

Joseph was born on 16th March 1898 in the Sailor's Horn Inn, The Quay, Milton Regis, where his widowed maternal grandmother Olive was the publican. His birth certificate records he was a twin, as his time of birth 11.30pm is recorded. His twin brother Albert Edward sadly only lived for a short period as his death was registered between April and June, and he was baptised two days after his birth. Joseph was baptised in the parish church Holy Trinity on 3rd July 1898.

Joseph's parents were Joseph John, the publican of the Golden Fleece Inn in West Street, Sittingbourne, and Sarah Ann (née Bartlett). He also had a younger brother, Robert Thomas (1901-1918). His mother was widowed in 1901 and she continued as the publican at the Golden Fleece, with her brother, Edward George Bartlett, running the business.

Joseph attended Borden Grammar School and on leaving, worked as a motor mechanic and driver at Pullen Brothers, in Park Road, Sittingbourne (pictured right).

He enlisted at Herne Bay on 28th February 1916, a fortnight before his 18th birthday, and joined the Motor Transport Division of the Royal Army Service Corps but was transferred for training to the South Staffordshire Regiment. At the start of June 1917, he was drafted to France, where he transferred to the East Yorkshire Regiment.

An extract from Joseph's battalion War Diary is reproduced below:

	WAR DIARY [143] or INTELLIGENCE SUMMARY. *(Erase heading not required.)*	Army Form C. 2118.
Instructions regarding War Diaries and Intelligence Summaries are contained in F.S. Regs., Part II, and the Staff Manual respectively. Title pages will be prepared in manuscript.		
Date	Summary of Events and Information	Remarks and References to Appendices
30-6-1917	*Very dull, windy and wet. Battalion marched to LEBUCQUIÈRE. A miserable march on account not a house in the village is whole.*	
1-7-1917	*The day was spent quietly. Church parade cancelled on account of the rain.*	
2-7-1917	*Today is sunny and fresh. Enemy shelled our neighbourhood.*	
3-7-1917	*Moved to trenches at LOUVERAL. Relieved 1/8 WORCESTERS. Night quiet except for shelling of our guns.*	

---

[143] War Diary: 8 Battalion East Yorkshire Regiment. WO-95-1424-2. September 1915-February 1918. The National Archives (UK), Kew, England.

Bapaume Village - a short distance from Lebucquière

4-7-1917	Quiet and uneventful. Weather fine. Practically no shelling. Patrols being sent out.
5-7-1917	Nothing unusual on our front.
6-7-1917	Our artillery saw action during the night and early morning. Germans shelled LEBUCQUIÈRE at times.
7-7-1917 to 9-7-1917	Nothing in particular to report. Weather fine and warm.
10-7-1917	Quiet day. Relieved by ROYAL WELSH FUSILIERS and returned to billets at LEBUCQUIÈRE.
11-7-1917	Weather glorious. Day spent resting.
12-7-1917	Weather glorious. Training in morning and troops bathed at nearby BEUGNY.
13-7-1917	Still hot and sunny. Parades cancelled as battalion tasked with digging a communication trench.
14-7-1917	Much cooler and dull. Battalion at rest after night work.
15-7-1917	The men got very wet and so much that church parade was cancelled.
16-7-1917 to 17-7-1917	Men resting.
18-7-1917	sent back to the trenches at LOUVERAL

AUSTRALIAN WAR MEMORIAL   A02285

Credit: Australian War Memorial

Joseph died from wounds on 14th July 1917 at No. 3 Casualty Clearing Station, at Grévillers (pictured left), just 16km from where they were billeted. Joseph's death was reported in the East Kent Gazette edition of 21st July 1917, under the headline "AN OLD BORDEN BOY'S DEATH." The newspaper reported that a nursing Sister at the hospital wrote to say that "the young fellow was brought in on the 14th severely wounded in both legs. He died the same day, having been unconscious throughout." The Sister conveyed her great regret and sympathy, adding he would be buried at the station cemetery.

Joseph was aged 19 years when he died on 14th July 1917. He was buried in Grévillers British Cemetery. The cemetery was started by No. 3 Casualty Clearing Station and the final layout designed by Sir Edwin Lutyens. It is the final resting place for 1,923, of which 10% are KNOWN UNTO GOD.

He is remembered on the Sittingbourne War Memorial, as well as at Borden Grammar School and Sittingbourne's Holy Trinity Church. His mother received his pay and gratuity.

The unveiling of a memorial tablet to John at Sittingbourne's Holy Trinity Church (below) was

Credit: ww1cemeteries.com

reported in the East Kent Gazette on the 2nd February 1918. The brass tablet was dedicated on 26th January 1918, after which the prayers "For those who have died in the faith" were read.

The service was conducted by the Reverend J. C. Eyre Kidson, who had lost his own son, Charles on the 17th October 1918 (see page 198).

Tragedy hit the family again, as reported in the East Kent Gazette dated 23rd November 1918, under the morbid headline A HOUSE OF DEATH. It records that three people died within a week, at Joseph's home of the Golden

Fleece, from influenza. Firstly, on 17th November, Harriett Raycraft, who had been adopted by Sarah's mother, the next day was Sarah's brother Edward and three days later her son Robert. Sarah, herself, also contracted influenza, but survived. His mother Sarah was still the publican of the Golden Fleece until she died in 1942.

WATCHUS, Percy

G/5792, Private, 6th Battalion, The Buffs (East Kent Regiment).

Percy was born in Murston on 28th July 1886 and was baptised in the parish church of All Saints on the 10th October. He was the ninth of the fourteen children of Philip, a market gardener, and Louisa (née Kennett). His siblings were Louisa, Philip (1877-1879), Sydney (1878-1881), Edward (1879-1880), Albert, Ellen (1882-1883), Maud, Edith (1885-1885), Walter (1888-1914), Florence, Alfred, William, and Amy.

In 1901, Percy was working as a reeler's assistant at the paper mill, then on 10th February 1904, aged 18, he joined the Royal Navy. He was 5ft 7½in tall and served on the cruisers *HMS Terpsichore* and *HMS Barrosa*, before he was discharged on 30th March 1905. He was serving as a Domestic 3rd Class, whose duties included stewarding. The reason for his discharge, on his service record, is given as S.N.L.R. (Services no longer required). On 26th November 1906, Percy re-joined the Navy and was posted to the cruiser *HMS Natal* (pictured right). His service again was short, and he was discharged for a second time on 16th August 1907, the reason recorded was 'unsuitable'.

H.M.S. NATAL 1905-1915

By 1911 he was working as a fishmonger, and living with Annie Davis at 5 Cross Lane, Milton Regis, together with his stepson Herbert George Davis (born 1905) and his child Amy Rose (born 1907). Although living together as man and wife, they were not officially married until 1915. They had two further children, Annie Louisa (born 1911) and Percy Philip (born 1916). By the time their youngest child was born they had moved to 14 Hawthorn Road, Milton Regis.

Percy joined the services for a third time, in November 1915, on this occasion the Army.

Instructions regarding War Diaries and Intelligence Summaries are contained in F.S. Regs., Part II, and the Staff Manual respectively. Title pages will be prepared in manuscript.	WAR DIARY [144] or INTELLIGENCE SUMMARY. (Erase heading not required.)	Army Form C. 2118.
Date	Summary of Events and Information	Remarks and References to Appendices
1-6-1916 to 9-6-1916	Battalion at BURBURE. Time spent on parades, training and route marches.	
10-6-1916 to 26-7-1916	Entrained to NAOURS. Time spent on parades, training and route marches. Engaged in battle exercises.	
27-6-1916	Battalion marched in an arc via VILLERS-BOCAGE, to FRÉCHENCOURT. Drums led the way and arrived in billets at 10pm.	
28-6-1916	Poured with rain. Planned march east to BRESLE was postponed.	
29-6-1916	Route march in the morning.	

[144] War Diary: 6 Battalion Buffs (East Kent Regiment). January 1916-August 1916. WO-95-1860-2. The National Archives (UK), Kew, England.

30-6-1916	3,000 Mills grenades were issued and denotated, in the morning.
	(The entry does not include where or why they were denotated.)
	8.35pm - Battalion marched to billets at BRESLE, arriving at 11.45pm. Heavy shelling from our guns during the night.
1-7-1916	6.45am – Battalion left BRESLE and marched the short distance, through heavy traffic, to MILLENCOURT.
	Received orders to proceed to the intermediate line north of ALBERT. Whilst on the march, received orders to relieve 25TH BRIGADE at CRUCIFIX CORNER, (which was situated in the village of Bazentin le Grand.) Arrived at 2.45am.
2-7-1916	Battalion occupied PENDLE HILL, CONISTON STREET and CARTMELL STREET TRENCHES, on the southern edge of AUTHUILLE WOOD.
	Later in the afternoon enemy bombarded OVILLERS-LA-BOISSELLE (below).

3-7-1916	3.15am – Battalion advanced with 6TH QUEENS to the right, 6TH ROYAL WEST KENTS on the left and 7TH EAST SURREY in support.
	Both flanks subjected to machine gun fire. First wave of battalion suffered few casualties until they reached the German wire. Succeeding waves suffered heavily in No Man's Land.
	On reaching the trenches the men commenced bombing them and soon the communication trench was blocked, creating casualties inflicted by German bombs. Impossible to remain in German trenches, men were withdrawn back to British line.
	German artillery accurate in their heavy firing on our trenches.
	10.30am - Message sent that no further attacks to take place that day.
	1pm - 7TH EAST SURREY REGIMENT took over front line with THE BUFFS in support, in CONISTON STREET.
	During the night a number of wounded were brought in.
	CASUALTIES - 11 officers, 263 Other Ranks.
4-7-1916	Quiet day, some shelling in the afternoon. Rained heavily from 3pm.

Percy was 29 years old when he was killed by an enemy shell whilst moving forward to attack the German lines on 3rd July 1916.

He is commemorated on the Thiepval Memorial to the Missing, and locally on Sittingbourne War Memorial and Sittingbourne Holy Trinity Church WW1 Memorial. Milton Regis remembers him on their War Memorial and St Paul's Church Memorial. He was awarded the Victory and British War Medals. Percy's widow, Annie, received his pay and gratuity.

WATTS, George Thomas

Hired Skilled Labourer, HMS Princess Irene, H.M. Dockyard.

Credit: David Hughes

George was born on 14th February 1892 in Eastchurch on the Isle of Sheppey. He was the eldest of the ten children of George and Sarah Ann (née Batty). His siblings were Thomas Ransley, Ethel Mary, William John, Elizabeth Annie, Walter Charles, Lily, Ernest Edward, Rosalie (1908-1909), Mary Ann and Robert.

In 1911 his family were living at Breach Lane, Lower Halstow, with George, his father and brother Thomas all employed in the brickfields as labourers. In 1914 George married Lilian Annie Robinson at Milton Regis.

George was 23 years old in 1915, and, with his young wife Lilian, was living at 108 Shortlands Road, Sittingbourne. She was the eldest daughter of Mr E L Robinson formerly of Sittingbourne, who by then was living in Canada, and they had been married for fourteen months.

He had been working at the Dockyard (pictured above) for three months and he used to travel to and fro, by train every day.

George left home early, as usual, on the fateful day in May 1915. He woke that morning and took a cup of tea to his wife, as he usually did, and bade her goodbye. Downstairs he chatted with a relative, Samuel Thomas Booker, a young married man who lived at the same house.

They bade each other "Good morning" and George left the house, but returned the next minute for his handkerchief, which he had forgotten. A few more words were exchanged, and then, with the remark "Well I must be off or I shall lose my train".

George left home for the last time, and was one of the Sheerness Dockyard Labourers who were working on *HMS Princess Irene* in the Medway when the ship exploded that day.

When the sound of the explosion was heard Mrs Watts exclaimed "Oh, my George!" At that moment she did not know the cause of the terrific explosion, and it was strange that she connected her husband with it.

Later in the day the sad news of her young husband's death was broken to her. In March 1916 she moved to Ontario, Canada to join her parents.

George is remembered on Chatham Naval Memorial, and on Sittingbourne, Sheerness and Lower Halstow War Memorials, and St Michael's Church WW1 Memorial Window.

Princess Irene (pictured above) was an ocean liner that was requisitioned by the Royal Navy, from her owner Canadian Pacific Railway. She was converted to an auxiliary minesweeper, and was moored in Saltpan Reach, in the Medway Estuary, 4km west of Sheerness.

At 11.14am on 27th May 1915, whilst being loaded with mines, she exploded and disintegrated. It was reported that she emitted a 100m high column of flame. The death toll was 345, of which 76 were civilian dockyard workers. Only 32 bodies were recovered for burial.

It was reported that nine-year-old Hilda Johnson and 47-year-old farmhand George Bradley, on nearby Isle of Grain, were also killed. Wreckage was found at Detling, 17km (11 miles) away. There was one survivor, a Stoker David Wills, who suffered severe burns.

A Court of Inquiry ruled that a faulty primer was to blame, though evidence was given that the priming was being carried out by untrained personnel and in a hurried manner. The names of the civilian dockyard workers are listed on the Sheerness War Memorial and on a memorial board in Holy Trinity Church, Sheerness.

WILLIAMS, Bertie John

1422, Private, 4th Battalion, The Buffs (East Kent Regiment).

Bertie was born in Sittingbourne in 1896 and baptised at Holy Trinity Church, Sittingbourne, on 21st February 1897. Bertie was the second eldest child of John and Harriett (née Brooks). His siblings were Mabel (1895-1897), George, May Elizabeth, Sydney (1901-1901), Dorothy (1902-1903), John Edward, Eleanor Maud, and Horace Leslie. In 1911, this family were living at 7 Cockleshell Walk, Sittingbourne, with Bertie and his father employed as brickfield labourers. Before the war Bertie also worked at Millen and Chrisfield, Stonemasons, in Milton.

Bertie's Attestation Papers record he enlisted with the 4th Battalion, The Buffs, on 7th May 1912 at the age of 17 years and 6 months, he was 5ft 5in tall and had been working for Smeed Dean and Co. The 4th Battalion was a Territorial Unit and he was embodied into full service on 5th August 1914, aged 19, and posted to India on 29th October 1914.

On 6th July 1915, Bertie died of appendicitis in Mhow, India, after being admitted to hospital on 19th May 1915. Bertie was buried in Mhow New Cemetery and is remembered on Kirkee 1914-1918 Memorial, Mumbai, (pictured right) which was erected to commemorate over 1,800 service personnel buried in civil and cantonment cemeteries in India and Pakistan whose graves were considered to be unmaintainable after India gained its independence in 1947.

The East Kent Gazette edition dated 7th August 1915, with the headline "WITH THE 4th BUFFS AT MHOW. INTERESTING LETTER FROM A SITTINGBOURNE MAN" reproduced a letter from Regimental Quarter Master Sergeant Hutchens (see page 173) on the 6th and 7th July 1915. The letter wrote about the battalion's time at Mhow, which was spent training. It added that recreation was mainly around sports including cricket, football, hockey, and boxing. The letter concluded with news of Bertie's death, saying "a gloom had been cast over the battalion." It added that he had received an operation a few weeks previous, and despite the care of the doctors and nurses he failed to recover.

Bertie is also remembered on Sittingbourne War Memorial and Sittingbourne Holy Trinity Church WW1 Memorial, Milton Regis War Memorial, St Paul's Church Memorial and Old Boys Milton Council Schools Memorial. He was awarded the Territorial Force War Medal and British War Medal.

William's sister May signed up for Queen Mary's Army Auxiliary Corps on 14th July 1919 but was discharged on 19th September 1919 for being underage. May had declared she was a year older than her actual 19 years.

WOOD, William Charles

265305, Sapper, Inland Water Transport, Royal Engineers.

William was born on 6th August 1884 in Ash near Dover. He was from a large family of ten children and was the second youngest. His siblings were Eliza, Mary Ann, Harriet Elizabeth, Emma, John, Henry William, Charles (1880-1882), Annie, and George. His parents were William and Emma (née Ellen), who died when William was just seven years old. William's father worked on farms as a waggoner and stockman.

In 1901 William and his younger brother George were working as farm servants on Gore Farm in Upchurch. William's older brother John had joined the Royal Navy, aged 19, in 1895. John had progressed to Chief Stoker when his ship, the scout cruiser *HMS Pathfinder* was sunk by U-boat *SM U-21* in the North Sea on 5th September 1914, and he died at the age of 39. John is remembered on the Chatham Naval Memorial.

In addition, William's nephew, 19-year-old Private Stanley James Styles, served in the 19th Battalion, Machine Gun Corps and was declared as having died on 18th April 1918 after being posted as missing, though he was later found and buried in Messines Ridge British Cemetery. Stanley was the son of William's sister Harriett.

His brother George served as a Petty Officer in the Royal Navy from 7th May 1902 to 9th June 1922, a period of 20 years. He was recalled on 28th August 1939 and served to 12th June 1942 when his commander approved his discharge, aged 56.

William enlisted in Faversham and served with the Inland Water Division. He died, aged 32, on 26th May 1917, when his boat *W.D. Tug H.S. 69* (War Department, Tug, Harbour Service 69), hit a mine off the coast of St-Valery-en-Caux, 30km from Dieppe. She had sailed from Dover and stopped at Dieppe on her way to Le Havre. The mine struck under the engine room, causing her to sink within a minute. Of her thirteen crew, seven survived and were rescued.

An Inland Water Transport HS Tug

A Court of Inquiry[145] was held on 23rd August 1917 at Dover to investigate the loss. The crew were questioned and reported the tug had left Dieppe harbour at 6am, bound for Le Havre, when an explosion occurred at about 7.30am and caused the vessel to sink rapidly. She was estimated to be 2km north-west of Saint-Valery-en-Caux. Seven survivors, clinging to flotsam and lifebuoys, were rescued after 1½ hours in the water by the French armed trawler *Marie Rose*. Those who survived told the Court of Inquiry that they believed that the vessel had hit a mine. Five other crew members were lost:

- Lance Corporal William Robert Fox, 52, from Kingston-Upon-Hull, Yorkshire.
- Sapper George Paice, 40, from Portsmouth, Hampshire.
- Sapper John Joseph Townsend, 33, from Teddington, Middlesex.
- Sapper James Plunkett, from Vancouver, Canada
- Sapper Stanley Kingdom, 21, from Barnstaple, Devon.

Unexpectedly they are commemorated on the Basra Memorial, with the exception of Sapper Paice, who is buried in Janval Cemetery, Dieppe. In 1916 the work of the Inland Water Transported was extended to Mesopotamia, and therefore those who died are remembered on the Basra Memorial (pictured right).

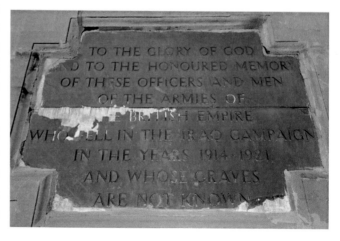

A copy of official records proving that William and his crew were lost off the coast of France was submitted to the Commonwealth War Graves Commission in 2022, and they agreed that their names would be inscribed on a new tablet on the Brookwood 1914-1918 Memorial in the UK.

145 Soldiers' Documents, First World War. WO 363. Paice, G. Service Number 232533. The National Archives (UK), Kew, England.

The Inland Water Transport Division was formed in December 1914 to supply and maintain communication and transportation of food, supplies, ammunition, and the evacuation of wounded. by barge and tug, along the canals of France and Belgium.

William is also remembered on Sittingbourne War Memorial and St Michael's Church WW1 Memorial Window. His pay and gratuity were split amongst his two brothers and four sisters. He was awarded the Victory and British War Medals.

William's pension index card, records he had a child named Kathleen Elizabeth Wood, born 9th May 1913 in Sittingbourne. Kathleen's mother was Ada Sophia Lockyer, and they lived in Harold Road, Sittingbourne.

WOODALL, T

A plaque on the Avenue bears the name of T WOODALL and the East Kent Gazette edition dated 27th December 1924 made a request for further information for some names, for the Sittingbourne War Memorial, and this included the name of T. Woodall.

Research to date has yet to identify this individual and is ongoing to enable his story to be told.

Though T. Woodall's story cannot be told at this time,

We remember him, as did those who knew him.

For the Fallen

With proud thanksgiving, a mother for her children,
England mourns for her dead across the sea.
Flesh of her flesh they were, spirit of her spirit,
Fallen in the cause of the free.

Solemn the drums thrill: Death august and royal
Sings sorrow up into immortal spheres.
There is music in the midst of desolation
And a glory that shines upon our tears.

They went with songs to the battle, they were young,
Straight of limb, true of eye, steady and aglow.
They were staunch to the end against odds uncounted,
They fell with their faces to the foe.

They shall grow not old, as we that are left grow old:
Age shall not weary them, nor the years condemn.
At the going down of the sun and in the morning
We will remember them.

They mingle not with their laughing comrades again;
They sit no more at familiar tables of home;
They have no lot in our labour of the day-time;
They sleep beyond England's foam.

But where our desires are and our hopes profound,
Felt as a well-spring that is hidden from sight,
To the innermost heart of their own land they are known
As the stars are known to the Night;

As the stars that shall be bright when we are dust,
Moving in marches upon the heavenly plain,
As the stars that are starry in the time of our darkness,
To the end, to the end, they remain.

Robert Laurence Binyon (1869-1943) wrote his poem at the beginning of the war. He was a museum curator and poet. He had served as a volunteer in 1915 for the French Red Cross as an ambulance driver and medical orderly. The fourth stanza is commonly spoken at Remembrance services.

Layout of the Avenue

The memorial tablets appear to have been installed in alphabetical order, in a clockwise direction, starting at the entrance to Albany Park and ending at the entrance to the cemetery on the opposite side of the road. This assumption is due to the fact a number of the original tablets on the section by the cemetery are in alphabetical order.

With all the changes and developments, most of the names follow the original pattern, though some tablets have been installed in different positions, others are missing, one name, G A Harrison, is duplicated and some men are remembered on a central plaque.

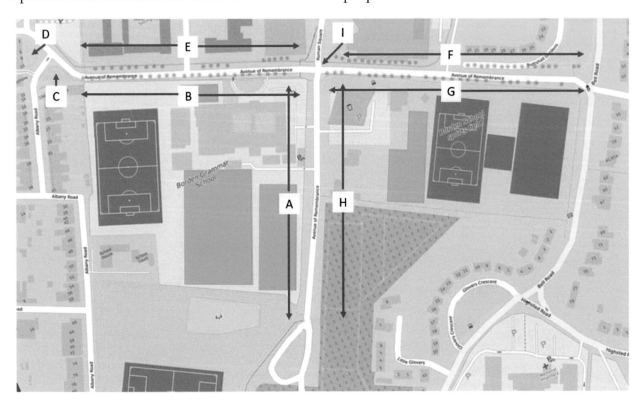

The names appear in the following order:

Section A Albany Park up to Roman Square Junction	Section H Roman Square Junction to Cemetery
Harry Thomas AKHURST	Leonard George TANTON
Ernest Alfred ALLEN	James Thomas TAYLOR
Leslie ANDERSON	John William THACKER
Charles John ARMOND	Alfred THOMAS
David ASHBY	George William Francis THOMAS
Thomas William ASHLEE	John THOROGOOD
Frank ASHWOOD	William Stephen TOMKIN
Bertie ATTWATER	William Harold TONG
Ernest ATTWATER	Albert Charles TOWN
Alfred John BAKER	Charles TOWNSEND

Section A Albany Park up to Roman Square Junction	Section H Roman Square Junction to Cemetery
Ernest BAKER	Alfred Edgar TROWELL
Harry John BAKER	Benjamin TYLER
Percy John BAKER	Gordon Herbert TYLER
William Thomas BAKER	Leslie Charles TYLER
Charles Frederick BALDOCK	Sidney Leonard VANDEPEER
Charles William BALDOCK	Frederick Norris WAKELEN
Charles William BARHAM	Frederick Henry WALKER
G BARHAM	Harold Hector WALKER
George BARNARD	Joseph John WARNER
William Alfred BARNES	Percy WATCHUS
Frederick Henry BARRETT	George Thomas WATTS
Albert John BARTLETT	Bertie John WILLIAMS
Thomas BATCHELOR	William WOOD
George BEECHAM	T WOODALL

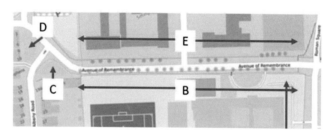

Section B Borden Grammar School to Albany Road	Section E Albany Road to Roman Square
George Henry BELSOM	Alfred GAMMON
Ralph Edgar BLACK	Cecil Edwin GRANT
Bert Percy BLACKMAN	Frederick Ernest GEE
Ernest Percy BODIAM	Archibald William GOATHAM
Albert John BOLTON	Charles Henry GOATHAM
Frank John BONNETT	James Walter GOATHAM
Herbert BOWER	Walter GOATHAM
Gordon Victor BRAY	Reginald Bertram GORELY
William BRENCHLY	Harry HIGGINS
George William BREWER	Cecil Aubrey HEUNER

Section B Borden Grammar School to Albany Road
Edward Thomas BROWN
Percival BROWN
Sydney John BROWN
William Robert BROWN
George BURDEN
Edward BURLEY
George Leslie BUTCHER
Stanley BUTLER
Clifton William John CARRIER
Frederick Frank CASTLE
Frederick CHAPMAN
Frederick Sherlock CLACKETT
Samuel Henry COOMBES
Robert COUCHMAN
William John COUCHMAN
Henry CRAYDEN

Section E Albany Road to Roman Square
Harry Josiah HENDERSON
George Alick HARRISON
Arthur Henry HARRIS
William John HOOK
Guy Steele HORSFORD
Sidney John HOLDSTOCK
Leonard Steele HORSFORD
George Frederick HORTON
Sydney Alderich HORTON

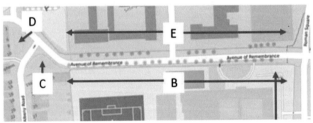

Section C Albany Road Triangle (South side)
Robert CROUCHER
Hubert Stanley CROW
George James DAVIS DCM
Harry DEVERSON
George Hambrook Dean DOUBLEDAY DSC
Percy Arthur Walter DOWNING
Henry Thomas ELEY
Ernest Archibald FREEBORN

Section D Albany Road Triangle (North side)
Frederick Thomas DORRELL
S STEERS
Arthur John STICKELLS
George Percy STORR
Charles SUTTON

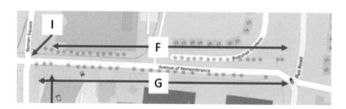

Section F Roman Square to Bell Road (North side)	Section G Bell Road to Roman Square (South side)
George Alick HARRISON	Frederick Thomas PASHBY
William George HUXTED	William Stephen PAYNE
William Thomas JARMAN	Frank PAYNE
Herbert Horace JARRETT	John Thomas Richard PETTETT
Rupert George JARRETT	George William PILBEAM
Edward John JARVIS	Harold James PHILPOTT
Samuel JENNER	Thomas QUAIFE
Edward George JULL	James Daniel RALPH
Roland John KEANE	Walter Frederick RANSOM
Arthur Harold KEMSLEY	William John REEVES
George KEMSLEY	John Martin RICHARDS
William Edward KEMSLEY	Percy Anthony RICHARDSON
Charles Wilfred KIDSON	William John RICKARD
Bertie John KNIGHT	George Henry ROCKLIFFE
William LUCKHURST	Henry ROSSITER
William Benjamin LUCIA	Alfred Warren RUSSELL
George MALNICK	Sidney SAGE
Frederick Charles MEAD	Herbert William SAWYER
Lawrence MEARS	Peter George SCOTT
Thomas MEARS	Frederick James SHAW
Henry Sidney George MILGATE	Charles Edward SHILLING
Wilfrid MILLEN	Edward Paul SHRUBSHALL
Ernest William Cornelius MILLS	Sham SHRUBSHALL
Frank Edward MILLS	Arthur James SIMMONS
Stephen John PAGE	Harry John SIMMONS
Edward Thomas Henry MOORE	Sydney SKINNER
Alfred George PAGE	Frank Alfred SMEED
Walter Henry NORRIDGE	Ernest Stephen SMITH

Section F Roman Square to Bell Road (North side)	Section G Bell Road to Roman Square (South side)
Frank PANKHURST	Henry John SMITH
Arthur Wallace PARKS	

Section I - Central Avenue Plaque	
William Edward Roger DRAKE	George William HADLER
John EDWARDS	Karl HADLOW
John Arthur EDWARDS	William Thomas HADLOW
Frank ELLIOTT	Percy Oak HANCOCK
William John FAGG	Ernest William HOOK
Sidney FISHER	Ernest Sydney ERVIN
Alfred FOSTER	

Names with no current tree, plaque or location	
George William HUTCHINS	Clarence Victor LUCKHURST
Thomas HUXTED	G W PELVIN
George Frederick William LONGFIELD	

Age Profile

This chart shows the age profile of the men commemorated on the Avenue. The average age is 26 years 11½ months. For comparison, the average age (where known) on the CWGC database is 26 years 6 months.

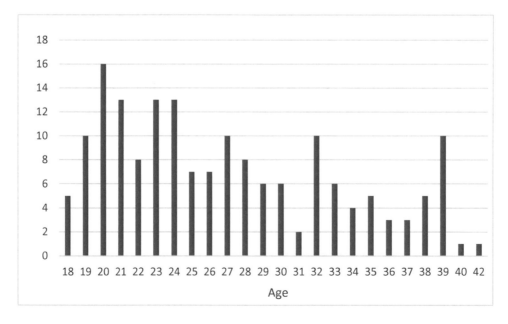

Where They Lived

The map below shows where the men lived, based on either available information at the time they lost their lives, or from the 1911 census. The map shows how close together they lived, with some roads suffering multiple losses.

The families would also have known each other from the occupation of the men's fathers, as a fifth of them worked in the brickfields and others worked in key community roles, including publicans, bakers, and grocers.

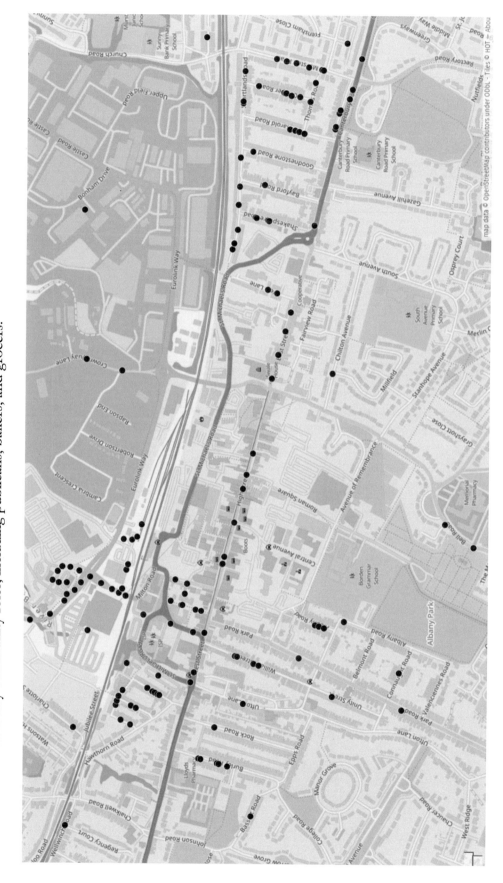

Where They Lost Their Lives

The following table and maps show where the men on the Avenue lost their lives:

Country	Number
France	89
Belgium	29
England	20
Iraq (Mesopotamia)	6
India	4
Turkey (including Gallipoli)	3
Egypt	2
Germany	2
Israel and Palestine (including Gaza)	2
Italy	1
Namibia	1
Tanzania	1

At Sea	Number
North Sea	4
Scapa Flow	3
English Channel	3
Thames Estuary	2
Irish Sea	1
Pacific Ocean	1
North Atlantic Ocean	1

Unknown	7

A study of the CWGC database, of over a million casualties, reflects a similar table to that shown above for the Avenue men, on where the fallen lost their lives. The table below shows that 93% of losses were restricted to just ten countries (in this instance the UK is being counted as a country).

Country	% of Total Losses
France	53%
Belgium	19%
United Kingdom	7%
Iraq (Mesopotamia)	4%
Turkey (including Gallipoli)	4%
Egypt	1%
Israel and Palestine (including Gaza)	1%
Greece	1%
India	1%
Germany	1%

The high number in the UK can be attributed to: the wounded who were brought home and later died; the influenza outbreak; and training accidents.

A further 3% of the losses, over 33,000, are commemorated in the UK on memorials to the Royal Navy and Merchant Navy, where they have no known grave. These memorials are primarily Tower Hill, Chatham, Plymouth and Portsmouth.

This map shows the global spread of where the men lost their lives, from the Pacific Ocean across to India and Iraq.

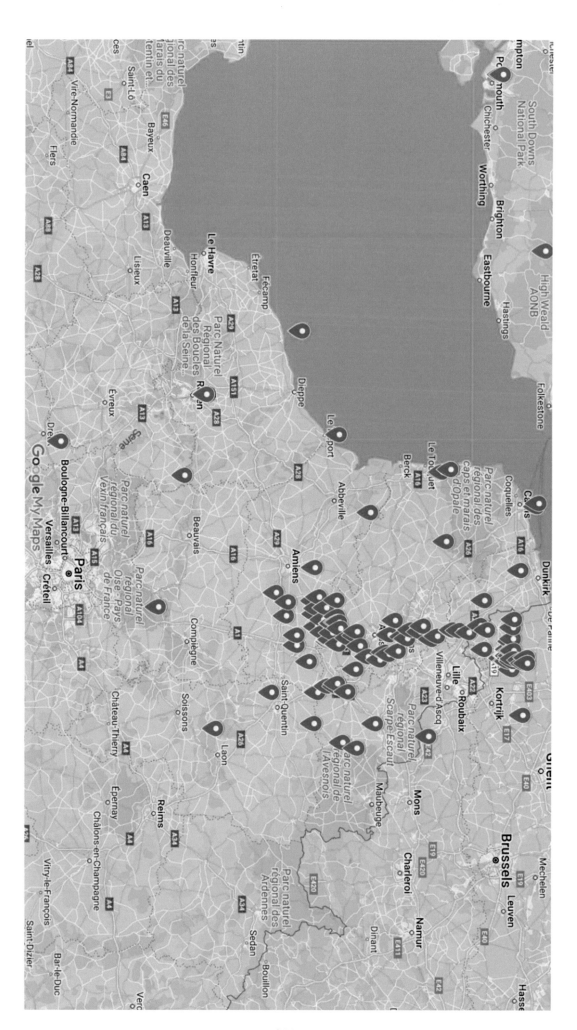

The majority of the men lost their lives in France and Belgium, where major battles had taken place.

Regimental Listing

The men identified in the Avenue served in 59 different regiments of the Army, the Royal Navy, the Air Force, and civilian services.

The table below shows the number of men who served in each service and regiment:

Regiment/Service	Number
Army	
The Buffs (East Kent Regiment)	41
Queen's Own (Royal West Kent Regiment)	11
Royal Fusiliers	8
Royal Field Artillery	7
Royal Engineers	5
The Queen's (Royal West Surrey Regiment)	5
Canadian Infantry	4
Australian Infantry A.I.F.	3
Machine Gun Corps (Infantry)	3
Royal Army Medical Corps	3
Royal Garrison Artillery	3
East Surrey Regiment	2
King's Royal Rifle Corps	2
London Regiment	2
London Regiment (Royal Fusiliers)	2
Middlesex Regiment	2
Northumberland Fusiliers	2
Oxford and Bucks Light Infantry	2
Royal Army Service Corps	2
Royal Warwickshire Regiment	2
Worcestershire Regiment	2

Regiment/Service	Number
Army	
East Yorkshire Regiment	1
Essex Regiment	1
Gloucestershire Regiment	1
Grenadier Guards	1
Hampshire Regiment	1
Honourable Artillery Company	1
Household Battalion	1
Household Cavalry	1
Kent Cyclist Battalion	1
King's Shropshire Light Infantry	1
Lancashire Fusiliers	1
London Regiment (County of London) London Irish Rifles	1
London Regiment (The Rangers)	1
Machine Gun Corps	1
Machine Gun Corps (Cavalry)	1
Natal Light Horse	1
North Staffordshire Regiment	1
Northamptonshire Regiment	1
Royal Dublin Fusiliers	1
Royal East Kent Yeomanry	1
Royal Munster Fusiliers	1

Regiment/Service	Number
Army	
(Duke of Cambridge's Own) Middlesex Regiment	1
10th (Prince of Wales's Own Royal) Hussars	1
17th Lancers (Duke of Cambridge's Own)	1
18th London Regiment (London Irish Rifles)	1
Bedfordshire Regiment	1
Cambridgeshire Regiment	1
Canadian Field Artillery	1
Canadian Pioneers	1
Duke of Wellingtons (West Riding Regiment)	1
East Lancashire Regiment	1

Regiment/Service	Number
Army	
Royal Scots Fusiliers	1
Royal Sussex Regiment	1
Royal West Kent Regiment	1
Sherwood Foresters (Notts and Derby Regiment)	1
Somerset Light Infantry	1
South African Medical Corps	1
South Staffordshire Regiment	1
South Wales Borderers	1
The King's (Liverpool Regiment)	1
Welsh Regiment	1

Navy	
Royal Navy	15
HM Dockyard Sheerness	2
Royal Naval Reserve	2
Royal Marine Light Infantry	1
Royal Naval Canadian Volunteer Reserve	1
Royal Navy Division	1

Air Force	
Royal Flying Corps	1
Royal Air Force	1

Unknown	
Unknown	4

Treatment of Casualties

Sixteen of the Avenue men died at Casualty Clearing Stations (CCS), which were also known as Clearing Hospital, until mid-1915.

© Queen's Printer for Ontario, 2022 L. Bruce Robertson fonds, F 1374, Archives of Ontario.

Field Marshal Douglas Haig had decided that more lives could be saved if soldiers were treated at the earliest opportunity, close to the front line. There was an organised chain of treatment stations between the front line and the Casualty Clearing Stations, which was the last stop before evacuation. The British CCSs were managed by the Royal Army Medical Corps (RAMC), and the Canadian and Australian armies.

The Casualty Clearing Stations were small villages in their own right, normally located by railways and waterways for easier and quicker transportation. They were also mobile, moving as the front line changed. A typical CCS catered for 50 beds and 150 stretchers, though later in the war this increased to about 1,500 beds. There were about 50 CCSs established. The CCS was normally led by a RAMC Lieutenant Colonel, with seven medical officers, 78 other ranks, dentist, pathologist, seven nurses from the QAIMNS (Queen Alexandra Imperial Military Nursing Service), and non-medical personnel.

The chain from the front line started with Regimental Aid Posts (RAP) (pictured right), located 200-300 yards behind the front line; often in shell holes, dug outs or ruined buildings.

Soldiers either walked or were carried in by stretcher bearers. The medical team treated the soldiers and they either returned to their duties, or were moved by stretcher bearers, often over muddy and shell-pocked ground, whilst under shell fire, to an Advanced Dressing Station (ADS).

Advanced Dressing Stations had more protection than RAPs, often being set up in bunkers or underground dug outs. They had more supplies and equipment than the RAPs, though still limited in the care they could provide. There was no capacity to hold casualties so, after treatment, soldiers returned to duty with their unit, or were moved along the chain by horse drawn or motor transport to a Main Dressing Station (MDS).

The Main Dressing Stations although not staffed usually with a surgeon, were normally equipped with a surgeon's roll of instruments and sterilisers, for life saving operations only. The next step was a Field Ambulance (FA), which were mobile medical units. The Field Ambulance was more akin to today's Minor Injuries Unit and comprised of stretcher bearers, an operating tent, tented wards, nursing orderlies, a cookhouse, washrooms, and a horse-drawn or motor ambulance. Later in the war they were equipped with surgical teams and by the autumn of 1915, some had trained nurses.

Field Ambulance outside a Dressing Station

The end of the chain before evacuation was the Casualty Clearing Station, located several miles behind the front line. Facilities included medical and surgical wards, operating theatres, dispensary, medical stores, kitchens, sanitation, incineration plant, mortuary, ablution blocks, and sleeping quarters for the nurses, officers, and soldiers of the unit.

Transportation to the CCSs was initially in horse-drawn ambulances, which was a painful journey, before motor vehicles and narrow-gauge railways were provided. Early on, the casualties were laid on the floor in rows, and by 1915 they were on trestles, with the British Red Cross providing comforts like sheets, pillows, and bed socks.

Big events challenged the CCSs with the first Battle of Ypres creating between 1,200 and 1,500 casualties in twenty-four hours and during the Battle of the Somme in July 1916, when between 16,000 and 20,000 casualties occurred on the first day of the offensive. Many soldiers died from infection and the seriousness of their wounds, resulting in cemeteries being created close to the stations. Due to the nature of these cemeteries, very few graves lie being marked as just 'Known unto God.' The cemeteries at two of the CCS's, Rouen and Étaples, are the resting place for 22,201 casualties, of which only 45 are marked as 'Known unto God.'

HM Hospital Ship *Britannic*

Casualties were evacuated from the Casualty Clearing Stations by ambulance trains, road convoys, or canal barges to the large base hospitals near the French coast, or to a hospital ship heading for England. Some of the base hospitals were run by voluntary organisations, notably the Red Cross and St John Ambulance as a combined organisation known as Voluntary Aid Detachment (VAD). In the areas such as Étaples, Boulogne, Rouen, Le Havre, and Paris the general hospitals operated as normal civilian hospitals. Soldiers could remain there until fit to be returned to their units, or were sent across the channel in Hospital Ships for specialist treatment, or discharge from the forces. The arrival in 1917 of the Americans, brought assistance in the provision of personnel, and they took over running six British General Hospitals.

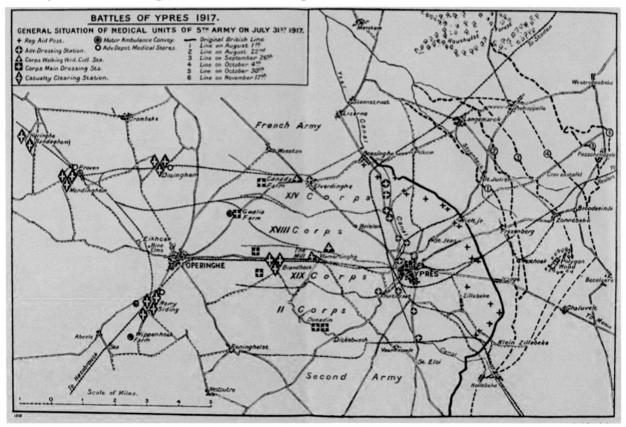

Local Memorials

There is a Sittingbourne War Memorial as well as a Milton War Memorial, as at the time of the First World War Sittingbourne and Milton were two separate towns, each with their own town council, which amalgamated later in 1929.

There are also many war memorials in local churches, as well as in Borden Grammar School and Sittingbourne Post Office. Some of the men resided in both Sittingbourne and Milton, so as a result may appear on both of their town's memorials, and some are also on other local village memorials.

This section provides information on the local memorials in Sittingbourne and the memorials in Milton Regis that are mentioned within the men's stories.

Sittingbourne War Memorial

The Sittingbourne War Memorial, in the form of a Cenotaph, meaning 'empty tomb', was unveiled on 22nd May 1921, in the Albany Recreation Ground. The Memorial was paid for by public subscription and designed by Messrs Palmer-Jones and T F W Grant FRIBA.

The original memorial stood 6 metres tall, was constructed of oolite stone and inscribed with 181 names. All the names are reflected in the Avenue of Remembrance.

A Memorial Committee was created and one of their tasks was to determine the list of names to be commemorated. The records of the committee no longer exist and research to date has been unable to identify how the names were chosen to be included on the memorial. The names and number of men to be remembered has also, over time, changed.

The Memorial was moved due to its state of disrepair and attacks of vandalism. It was dismantled and moved to nearby Central Avenue and rededicated on the 2nd September 1990. The site of the original memorial can still be seen as a semi-circular shape remains at the central entrance to the cemetery in Albany Park.

The memorial is a cenotaph and has a two-stepped base in a paved area surrounded on three sides by a raised flower bed supported by a stone wall incorporating integral stone seating. The front of the cenotaph has a tablet with the dedication. Above this is a low relief carving of an angel flanked by a soldier and a sailor. Above this is a carving of the Kent insignia within a laurel wreath. On the top of the cenotaph is an upright metal laurel wreath with poppies and ribbons, which was an addition to the original memorial. The WW1 names are on tablets placed on the sides and back of the cenotaph. A further seven WW2 names were also later added, see page 350.

Surrounding three sides of the cenotaph is a bench which has 78 Second World War names inscribed on inset brass plaques on the bench back. The insignia of each of the army, navy and air force is placed before the respective list of names. There is also a plaque for the Korean War. There are a further 15 Second World War names listed on trees in Central Avenue.

Behind the benches are plaques from the Men of Milton War Memorial, which stood in Holy Trinity Church, Milton Regis, until it was destroyed by a falling tree during a storm in 1987. The plaques were then relocated to this spot. A replacement War Memorial at Milton Church was dedicated in 2012.

Next to the cenotaph is a memorial garden with four Victoria Cross memorial tablets. The names of the four local Victoria Cross holders are:

- Private John Freeman VC (1833-1913), 9th Lancers, awarded 1858.
- Colonel Donald Dean VC OBE DL (1897-1985), Queen's Own Royal West Kent Regiment, awarded 1918.
- Lieutenant- General Sir Philip Neame VC KBE CB DSO (1888-1978), Corps of Royal Engineers, awarded 1915.
- Major James McCudden VC DSO & Bar MC & Bar MM (1895-1918), 56 Squadron Royal Flying Corps, awarded 1918.

St Michael's Church WW1 Memorial Window

Dedicated on 7th January 1922, the memorial window is adorned with 86 names of which 81 appear on the Avenue of Remembrance. The parish church documents do not record how the names were compiled and no reason has been identified why the additional six names on the window are not commemorated on the Avenue.

335

The window consists of 36 lights, with the names on the central light on the bottom row, depicting the figure of Christ. The remaining four lights of the bottom row represent the allied nations, with each depicted with a warrior figure, crowned with a laurel wreath, and holding the banner of their country. The five lights on the row above is praise to the allies for supporting Britain and based upon the song of the church, the Te Deum. The top 28 lights are a selection of the regimental and naval badges.

The central light also carries the following inscription:

"To God's infinite glory and to commemorate those of his servants who
at the call of king & country, left all that was dear to them, endured
hardships, faced dangers and passed out of the sight of men by the path of duty
and self-sacrifice giving up their own lives that others might live in freedom.
Let those who come after see to it that their names are not forgotten."

Holy Trinity Church, Sittingbourne

Holy Trinity church is situated at the west end of the town and commemorates 73 of its parishioners on a brass plaque, dedicated by the Bishop of Dover on 16th July 1919. The bishop also dedicated a locally made set of oak choir stalls, with poppy head finials. At a later date, a second plaque was installed with an additional six names.

Of the Avenue men, 65 are named on this memorial.

Milton Regis War Memorial

This memorial includes the names of 29 Avenue men.

On 26th October 1919 the Men of Milton Memorial Cross (pictured left), was erected outside the entrance door to Milton Regis's parish church of Holy Trinity. It was dedicated by the Lord Bishop of Dover and paid for by public subscription; the memorial's plaques list the names of 198 fallen.

The Portland Stone Ionic cross stood 16½ feet tall (4.2m), before it was damaged beyond repair in a great storm on the night of 15th October 1987. The original panels were then moved to be on stone plinths behind the benches around Sittingbourne's war memorial. A new Memorial Cross (pictured right) was installed on the original spot and dedicated on 12th October 2012 by Royal British Legion Chaplain Patricia Tatchell, with 16 additional names.

St Paul's Church, Milton Regis

At the time of the First World War, St Paul's church became the parish church for Milton Regis, because Holy Trinity was in a poor state of repair. A teak memorial, made from salvaged wood from the 121-gun sailing ship of the line, *HMS Britannia,* was unveiled on 2nd September 1917. The memorial listed 101 names and was unveiled by Colonel R Bryon DSO, Section Commander, Sittingbourne.

After the war ended, an additional 96 names were added to the memorial. The memorial was removed from the church in the late 1950's prior to its demolition in January and February 1957. It stayed forgotten in the vestry of Holy Trinity Church, Milton Regis, until 2011 when it was restored by local historian Terry Matson and unveiled in the same church, on 17th September 2011.

Of the 197 names, 23 are also commemorated on the Avenue.

Old Boys Milton Regis Council Schools

Fourteen of the Avenue men are commemorated on the Old Boys Milton Regis Council Schools memorial. The original oak memorial recorded 72 names of former pupils, with eight names being added later.

The unveiling of the memorial, on 30th May 1921, was carried out by Sir Mark Collett, Chairman of the Kent Education Committee in the quadrangle of the school, commonly known as The Butts.

The memorial was then installed in the boy's school, which is now called Milton Court Academy. The memorial was lost for many years, stored in a cupboard, then rescued and restored, organised by local historian Terry Matson, and then once restored the memorial was unveiled in October 2007.

Edward Lloyd WW1

Sittingbourne's paper mill, which was owned by Edward Lloyd, lists 54 names on their memorial, of which 14 names are also listed on the Avenue.

The mill's memorial was originally installed in Lloyd's club house on the Avenue (see page 16) until October 2018 when it was moved to Kemsley Paper Mill, following the club house changing from UK Paper Leisure Club to The Appleyard.

Baptist Church, Sittingbourne

The First World War memorial lists 12 of the Avenue men amongst its 34 names.

The unveiling on 3rd December 1919 was particularly poignant and emotive as the presiding minister, the Reverend John Doubleday's son George, (see page 116) was amongst the names listed. In addition, Mr George Kemsley had the honour of unveiling the memorial, which contained the names of his three sons (see page 192).

The church on 11th July 1948 unveiled a second memorial to commemorate six men who lost their lives in the Second World War. Sadly, this memorial also has the names of three Gransden brothers; Albert, Charles and Laurence. The latter two are buried in Sittingbourne Cemetery and Albert was buried in Italy.

Congregational Church, Sittingbourne

This church, in the High Street, is now known as the Covenant Love Chapel and was formally the United Reform Church. The memorial of 14 names in the church, commemorates seven of the Avenue men.

The memorial was unveiled on 4th January 1920 by a surviving member of the congregation Sergeant S Dungey MM, and brother of one of those named, Sergeant George Arthur Dungey, who served in The Buffs.

The inscription on the memorial reads; "To the Glory of God, and in sacred memory of the undermentioned members of this Church and Congregation who gave their lives in the cause of freedom, during the Great War, 1914-1919."

The church also holds a 'Roll of Honour' memorial to those that served.

St Mary's Church, Sittingbourne

Two of the Avenue men are also commemorated in St Mary's Church. This memorial was unveiled in April 1920 and commemorates 11 men in total.

An inscription reads "To God's glory and in honoured, grateful and undying memory of those worshippers in this church who gave their lives in the Great War 1914-1918."

A second inscription at the base of the tablet reads "Greater love hath no man than this, that a man lay down his life for his friends." St John XV.13.

Borden Grammar School

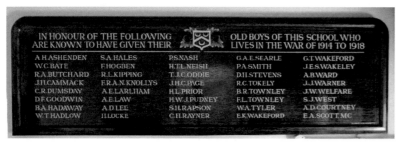

Two of the Avenue men attended Borden Grammar School, which at the time of the First World War was located at College Road, Borden.

The memorial lists 40 Old Bordenians who lost their lives.

The school in addition to the memorial, commemorates the school's fallen with; a sports pavilion; a clock (pictured right); and above each classroom door is a wooden plaque inscribed with one of the boy's names, their regiment and date they died.

The school also has memorials to commemorate the Second World War, Boer War (1901), Korean War (1951), and Northern Ireland (1974) conflicts, that claimed the lives of past pupils.

Wall of Reflection

The Historical Research Group of Sittingbourne (HRGS) in 2018 created a Wall of Reflection to commemorate the centenary of the end of the First World War. The wall remembers 1,149 names from Sittingbourne and Milton Regis, together with the surrounding local villages, which includes the 182 names commemorated on the Avenue.

The Wall of Reflection, measuring 6 metres by 2 metres, was unveiled in the atrium of The Forum, Sittingbourne, by HRGS's President, Deputy-Lieutenant of Kent, Paul Auston DL, on 4th November 2018, and was then relocated into HRGS's Heritage Hub in The Forum, where it remains today on display.

Other Local Memorials

There are over 240 memorials in Sittingbourne, and the wider district of Swale, that commemorate the fallen of the First and Second World Wars, and other conflicts. There is also a memorial in Bredgar churchyard for one man killed in the Anglo-Zulu War (1879).

Information about all of Swale's memorials is available from HRGS's Heritage Hub, The Forum, Sittingbourne ME10 3DL, and online at the Imperial War Museum War Memorial Register (iwm.org.uk/memorial) and War Memorials Online (warmemorialsonline.org.uk).

CWGC Memorials

Of the 182 names commemorated on the Avenue of Remembrance, 65 are listed as missing and as such are commemorated on one of the CWGC Memorials to the Missing in France, Belgium, England, and Iraq. Listed below are the main memorials on which 49 of the Avenue men are commemorated.

The CWGC website has descriptions of each memorial and cemetery, with its location, casualty names, and historical context of the memorial or cemetery. It should be noted that the number of names of the missing changes as the they are found and identified, and additional names are added as casualties are officially declared as missing and recognised as war casualties.

Thiepval Memorial

Seven of the Avenue men are commemorated on the Thiepval Memorial in France.

The Thiepval Memorial is known as the Memorial to the Missing Men on the Somme, which is the largest CWGC memorial. It commemorates 72,331 officers and men of the United Kingdom and South Africa who have no known grave. Over 90% of the names inscribed died over a five-month period from July to November 1916.

The memorial was designed by Sir Edwin Lutyens and was unveiled on 1st August 1932 by Edward, Prince of Wales, in the presence of the President of France.

It was constructed between 1928 and 1932, and in 2021-2022 a restoration and repair programme was completed, which included the name panels. Many of the panels were out of date with names requiring removal, as a result of their bodies being found and longer being missing, plus names added where research had identified names that were not known at the time of its construction.

Adjacent to the memorial is the Thiepval Anglo-French Cemetery, which is the final resting place of 600 soldiers, discovered in December 1931 to March 1932, on the Somme battlefields. The 600 burials are equally split between Commonwealth and French forces, and 492 of them are "Known unto God.'

Ypres (Menin Gate) Memorial

Eight of the men remembered in the Avenue are commemorated on the Ypres (Menin Gate) Memorial in Belgium.

This memorial is notable, as each evening at 8pm, the Last Post is sounded by buglers provided by the Ypres fire-brigade. This ceremony started on 2nd April 1928 and has been held every day since, except for the period from 20th May 1940 to 6th September 1944, during World War Two when Belgium was occupied by the Germans.

The memorial is CWGCs second largest and commemorates 54,585 names. The memorial, designed by Sir Reginald Blomfield with sculpture by Sir William Reid-Dick, which was unveiled by Lord Plumer on 24th July 1927.

Basra Memorial

Four of the Avenue men are commemorated on the Basra Memorial in Iraq, which was known as Mesopotamia during WW1.

Designed by Edward Warren and unveiled by Sir Gilbert Clayton on the 27th March 1929, the Basra Memorial is the third largest CWGC Memorial. This memorial commemorates 40,635 Commonwealth forces who died fighting in Mesopotamia from the Autumn of 1914 to the formal end of hostilities in August 1921.

The Memorial, until 1997, was in the naval dockyard at Maqil, until it was moved and re-erected in the middle of a major battlefield of the first Gulf War (1990-1991), 32km along the road to Nasiriyah.

Tyne Cot Memorial

Eight of the Avenue men are commemorated on the Tyne Cot Memorial in Belgium.

This memorial is the fourth largest with 34,982 inscribed names. It was unveiled by Sir Gilbert Dyett on the 20th June 1927 and designed by Sir Herbert Baker, with sculptures by Joseph Armitage and Ferdinand Blundstone. The memorial is one of four dedicated to the missing in an area known as the Ypres Salient in Belgian Flanders, which was formed in October and November 1914, during the First Battle of Ypres. The British Expeditionary Force wrestled and secured the town from the Germans, pushing them back to the ridge at Passchendaele.

The memorial is part of the boundary of Tyne Cot Cemetery, which is laid out around a captured German pillbox. The cemetery itself is the largest Commonwealth cemetery in the world by number of burials.

Arras Memorial

Five of the Avenue men are commemorated on the Arras Memorial in France.

The Arras Memorial is the fifth largest CWGC memorial. It was designed by Sir Edwin Lutyens, with the sculpture by Sir William Redo Dick. It was finally unveiled on the 31st July 1932 by Lord Trenchard, Marshal of the Royal Air Force.

The Memorial commemorates 34,800 servicemen from United Kingdom, New Zealand and South Africa, who died between the spring 1916 to August 1918, in the Arras sector.

Chatham Naval Memorial

Twelve of the Avenue men are commemorated on the Chatham Naval Memorial in Kent, England.

It is one of three identical CWGC memorials dedicated to sailors, aviators and marines of the Royal Navy. The Chatham Naval Memorial is situated in the Great Lines Heritage Park overlooking the town of Chatham, Kent. The other two memorials are in Plymouth and Portsmouth. The memorials were designed by Sir Robert Lorimer and Chatham's was unveiled on 26th April 1924 by Edward, Prince of Wales.

The Royal Navy Admiralty committee allocated personnel to a 'manning port' for administrative purposes, which were recommended as Plymouth, Chatham, and Portsmouth. A decision was made that each port should have an identical memorial bearing the names of their naval personnel with no known grave.

Chatham Naval Memorial commemorates 8,556 WW1 names and 10,098 WW2 names.

Books of Remembrance - Canada

Two of the Avenue men are commemorated in Canada's First World War Book of Remembrance.

Commemorating the loss of more than 120,000 service personnel, Canada has produced eight Books of Remembrance, covering all conflicts. They are housed in glass cabinets in the Memorial Chamber in the Peace Tower, which is within the Canadian parliamentary complex in Ottawa. Every morning a member of the House of Commons Protective Staff turns the pages of the books.

The First World War Book of Remembrance was conceived by a veteran, Colonel Archer Fortescue Duguid DSO. The altar, where the book rests, was unveiled on 3rd August 1927 by Edward, Prince of Wales. Dedicated on 11th November 1942, the book had originally been expected to take only five years to be completed.

This book is the largest of the eight books and has more than 66,000 names inscribed. The original book was ten inches thick and weighed sixty-eight pounds. In 1959 it was rebound and split into two volumes.

The names are available to search online at the Veterans Affairs Canada website, www.veterans.gc.ca/eng/remembrance/memorials/books/search.

The other seven Books of Remembrance commemorate:

- Second World War
- Newfoundland – commemorates Newfoundlanders lost in the First and Second World Wars
- South African / Nile Expedition – commemorates those who died during the South African War (1899-1902) and the Nile Expedition (1884-1885).
- Korean War – commemorates those lost in the Korean War (1950-1953)
- Merchant Navy – commemorates Merchant Mariners lost in the First and Second World Wars
- In the Service of Canada – commemorates service personnel lost since the Second World War
- War of 1812 – commemorates those lost whilst serving as a colony of Great Britain.

Gallantry and Distinguished Medals

The medals are listed in the order that they should be worn in the United Kingdom. The ORDER OF WEAR list was published in The London Gazette, 11 January 2019, Number 62529, Supplement No. 1. ORDER OF WEAR entitled CENTRAL CHANCERY OF THE ORDERS OF KNIGHTHOOD.

The general rule is that non-British insignia should be worn after the British orders, in the date they were awarded, with the first being orders, then decorations, and then medals. The exception is if the individual is attending an occasion connected with the awarding country because then pride of place would be given to that country's awards.

Victoria Cross

The Victoria Cross (VC) is the highest military award for gallantry in action. The medal was established by Queen Victoria on 29th January 1856 and originally made from a bronze cannon captured during the Crimean War (1854-1856). The majority of VCs after December 1914 were made from Chinese cannons, believed to be from the First Opium War (1839-1842).

None of the Avenue men were awarded the Victoria Cross, though there are four recipients from Swale that hold the VC (see page 335).

Distinguished Service Cross

Lieutenant George Hambrook Dean Doubleday was awarded the DSC (see page 116).

Established as the Conspicuous Service Cross for officers on the 28th June 1901 by King Edward VII to 'recognise meritorious or distinguished services before the enemy'. It was renamed the Distinguished Service Cross in October 1914, and in 1916 it was authorised that Bars could be awarded for further acts of gallantry.

The medal is a cross with a circular centre, which is the royal cypher of the reigning monarch, King George V during World War One. The reverse is simply the hallmark, as the medal is made of silver. The cross is hung from a ribbon of dark blue with vertical central white stripe.

Distinguished Conduct Medal

Regimental Serjeant Major George James Davis was awarded the DCM (see page 112).

The medal was instituted in 1854 by Queen Victoria during the Crimean War, to recognise acts of gallantry of warrant officers, non-commissioned officers and men. At this time it was the second highest gallantry award for all ranks below commissioned officers, second to the Victoria Cross, though the First World War prompted a change due to an expected overwhelming demand for the medal, which could devalue those already issued. From March 1916 the DCM was reserved for exceptional acts of bravery and the Military Medal was instituted as an alternative.

The 36mm silver medal was struck with the King's head, and on the reverse the inscription 'For Distinguished Conduct in the Field', with the rank, initials, surname, and unit of the recipient, engraved on it. The ribbon is crimson with a central vertical dark blue stripe.

Military Medal

Lance Corporal William Thomas Jarman (page 179) and Serjeant Frank Alfred Smeed (see page 269) were awarded the Military Medal.

The Military Medal was awarded to Other Ranks, being the equivalent of the Military Cross, awarded to commissioned officers. It was instituted on the 25th March 1916 and backdated to 1914. It was awarded for gallantry and devotion to duty whilst under fire during a battle on land. The medal could be awarded more than once, with a bar being added to the original medal's ribbon.

The London Gazette records that during the First World War, 115,589 were awarded, with 5,796 first bars, 180 second bars and one third bar.

The medal is 36mm in diameter, with the monarch on the front and the rear inscribed with 'FOR BRAVERY IN THE FIELD' below the Imperial Crown and royal cypher and surrounded by a laurel wreath. The ribbon is dark blue with five white and red stripes. The rim is impressed with the recipient's name and service details.

Australian stretcher bearer, Private Ernest Albert Cory (1891-1972) was the four times recipient of the Military Medal. He served from January 1916 to June 1919.

Mentioned in Despatches

Lieutenant George Hambrook Dean Doubleday was Mentioned in Despatches (see page 116).

Mentioned in Despatches was a recognition of a gallant or meritorious action taken in the face of the enemy, reported in an official account by a superior officer and sent to the War Office. The mention was published in The London Gazette, and was the only recognition received until 1919 where a certificate was introduced. In 1920 an emblem of a bronze oak leaves was issued retrospectively back to 4th August 1914. The emblem was worn on the Victory Medal, the British War Medal, or if no medals were issued, on the individual's tunic. The London Gazette recorded 141,082 Mentioned in Despatches between 1914 and 1920.

A newspaper article reports Serjeant Cecil Edwin De Gant (see page 134) was Mentioned in Dispatches, though no entry in The London Gazette was identified.

Campaign Medals and Stars

Medals were awarded to those who saw service in World War One and met the specified criteria. Five campaign medals were available, for men and women, with a maximum of three of these being issued, although exceptions to the rule did occur.

Medals were automatically issued to non-commissioned soldiers. However, officers, or their next of kin, had to apply for them. Medals were struck on the edge, usually with service number, rank, first name or initial, surname, and military unit (Regiment or Corps), except Stars, where the inscription was instead on the reverse of the medal. For those that had retired, through illness or wounds, or been honourably discharged, a Silver War Badge was awarded.

1914 Star

The Star, also known as 'Pip' or the 'Mons Star', was awarded to those who had served in France or Belgium between 5th August 1914 to midnight on 22nd November 1914 inclusive. This period was the first sixteen weeks of the Great War, and it included the battle of Mons, the retreat to the Seine, the battles of Le Cateau, the Marne, the Aisne, and the First Battle of Ypres.

A bronze clasp was added for those that had served under fire of the enemy, with the inscription '5th AUG. – 22nd NOV. 1914'. About 40% of medals issued included the clasp.

This bronze star was established in 1917 by King George V and available to members of the British and Indian Expeditionary Forces, Royal Navy, Royal Marines, Royal Navy Reserve, and the Royal Naval Volunteer Reserve. The latter was for those who served ashore with the Royal Naval Division in France or Belgium.

Recipients were also awarded a ribbon, which could be worn as part of a ribbon set. For those that had the clasp, a silver heraldic rose could be attached to the ribbon. Approximately 378,000 1914 Stars were issued.

1914-15 Star

This medal was established in December 1918. The 1914-15 Star was not awarded alone. The recipient had to have received the British War Medal and the Victory Medal.

The Star was awarded to British and Imperial officers and men, who had served in conflict, in 1914 and 1915, against the Central Powers of Germany, Austria-Hungary, Bulgaria and the Ottoman Empire. The reverse is plain with the recipient's service number, rank, name, and unit impressed on it.

This was also known as 'Pip', like the 1914 Star, as those recipients were not eligible for the 1914-15 Star.

An estimated 2.4 million of these Stars were issued.

British War Medal

The British War Medal, also known as 'Squeak', was established on the 26th July 1919. It was made of silver and awarded to those who had served between or on the 5th August 1914, the day after war was declared and 11th November 1918, Armistice Day. Though this was extended to include those who had served in mine-clearing and the intervention in the Russian Civil War of 1919 to 1920.

It was awarded to officers and men/women of the British and Imperial Forces who either entered a theatre of war or entered service overseas.

The front face had an effigy of King George V, with the words "GEORGIVS V BRITT: OMN: REX ET IND: IMP:.", translated as "George V, King of all the British Isles and Emperor of India."

The recipient's service number, rank, name, and unit were inscribed on the medal's rim.

Approximately 6.5 million British War Medals were issued. An additional 110,000, made of bronze, were issued to those who served in the Chinese, Maltese, and Indian Labour Corps.

Mercantile Marine War Medal

This bronze medal established in 1919 was awarded to Merchant Navy personnel who had served and made a voyage through a war danger zone.

The medal's front was the same as the British War Medal and the reverse has a laurel wreath around the rim with an image of a merchant ship on a stormy sea with an enemy submarine and an old sailing ship to the right of the merchant ship.

Inscribed on the rim are the words "FOR WAR SERVICE/MERCANTILE MARINE 1914-1918." The ribbon colours represent the starboard and port running lights of a ship with the white centre line representative of the masthead steaming light.

There were 133,135 Mercantile Marine War Medals awarded.

Victory Medal

The Allied Victory Medal was recommended by the inter-allied committee in March 1919 and was agreed that each of the 14 participating nations would design their own Victory Medal, though, the design had to incorporate the winged figure of victory and the coloured ribbon.

The British bronze medal was designed by W McMillan, with the front depicting a winged classical figure representing victory.

Approximately 5.7 million victory medals were issued. Interestingly, eligibility for this medal was more restrictive and not everyone who received the British War Medal ('Squeak') also received the Victory Medal ('Wilfred'). However, in general, all recipients of 'Wilfred' also received 'Squeak' and all recipients of 'Pip' also received both 'Squeak' and 'Wilfred'.

The recipient's service number, rank, name, and unit were impressed on the rim.

Territorial Force War Medal

Instituted on 26th April 1920.

Only members of the Territorial Force and Territorial Force Nursing Service were eligible for this medal. They had to have been a member of the Territorial Force on or before 30th September 1914 and to have served in an operational theatre of war outside the United Kingdom between 5th August 1914 and 11th November 1918. An individual who was eligible to receive the 1914 Star or 1914-15 Star could not receive the Territorial War Medal.

The obverse (front) of the medal shows an effigy of King George V with the words "GEORGIVS BRITT OMN: REX ET IND: IMP:" The words are abbreviated and in full are "Georgius V Britanniarum Omnium; Rex Et India; Imperator", which translates as "George V King of all Britain and Emperor of India."

The reverse of the medal has the words TERRITORIAL WAR MEDAL around the rim, with a laurel wreath and the words inside the wreath FOR VOLUNTARY SERVICE OVERSEAS 1914-1919.

Approximately 34,000 Territorial Force War Medals were issued.

Pip, Squeak and Wilfred

PIP, SQUEAK AND WILFRED

Pip, Squeak, and Wilfred are the affectionate names given to the three WW1 campaign medals: the 1914 Star or 1914-15 Star, British War Medal, and Victory Medal respectively. These medals were awarded to the British Expeditionary Force and other Commonwealth forces and by convention all three medals are worn together, and in the same order from left to right when viewed from the front. The set of three medals or at least the British War Medal and the Victory Medal are the most likely medals to be found among family heirlooms.

When the WW1 medals were issued in the 1920's it coincided with a popular comic strip published by the Daily Mirror newspaper. It was by Bertram J. Lamb (Uncle Dick) and drawn by the cartoonist Austin Bowen Payne (A.B. Payne).

Pip was the dog, Squeak the penguin, and Wilfred the young rabbit. It is believed that A. B. Payne's batman during the war had been nicknamed "Pip-squeak" and this is where the idea for the names of the dog and penguin came from.

For some reason the three names of the characters became associated with the three campaign medals being issued at that time to many thousands of returning servicemen, and they stuck.

Mutt and Jeff

When the British War Medal and Victory Medal are on display together, they are sometimes known as "Mutt and Jeff".

"Mutt and Jeff" are also cartoon characters, first appearing in 1908 in the San Francisco Chronicle. They were characterised as horse race gamblers and the cartoon became a daily inclusion on the sports pages.

World War Two Fallen

Sittingbourne's War Memorial was moved from Albany Park in 1990 to Central Avenue. The memorial was re-dedicated on Sunday, 2nd September 1990 by Reverend Mark Hayton, curate of St Michael's Church, Sittingbourne.

On 8th April 1992[146] fifteen trees were planted running from the Avenue of Remembrance along Central Avenue, together with memorial plaques for some of Sittingbourne's World War Two fallen. Two months later, on 19th July 1992[147], Canon Francis Turner, who was the vicar of St Michael's, dedicated an additional 78 names, inscribed on 40 memorial plaques, that are mounted in the seating surrounding the War Memorial. In addition, seven names were added to the First World War Memorial at some point after 2014. In total 100 plaques, which from research we believe represents 98 men, women and children listed here.

The names commemorated are:

Name	Service	Date Died	Age
Central Avenue Tree (shown below left)			
AUSTIN, Frederick Leonard	Special Air Service Regiment	16-Oct-44	24
BRICE, Charles Ernest	Oxford and Bucks Light Infantry	03-Oct-43	29
FLETCHER, Herbert Ernest	Royal Navy	16-Sep-43	36
FOORD, Clifford Ashley Vale	Queen's Own Royal West Kent Regiment	10-Apr-44	22
GOLDFINCH, Cyril Thomas	Queen's Own Royal West Kent Regiment	27-Nov-42	23
HADLOW, Charles Sidney	The Buffs (Royal East Kent Regiment)	23-Oct-43	28
HOPSON, David Joseph	Royal Air Force Volunteer Reserve	19-Feb-43	20
JARRETT, Ronald Herbert	Royal Artillery	01-Jul-42	22
JOHNSON, Harold Leslie	Royal Navy	29-May-41	21
JUDGES, Norman Filmer	Royal Navy	09-Mar-45	28
KING, George Alfred	Merchant Navy	16-Aug-44	18
LACKFORD, Ronald William H	The Buffs (Royal East Kent Regiment)	22-Nov-42	26
MANTLE, Herbert William	Royal Air Force Volunteer Reserve	20-Jan-42	21
PRENTICE, Montague Adair	Royal Air Force (Auxiliary Air Force)	09-Aug-40	21
RAINS, Frank	Queen's Own Royal West Kent Regiment	20-May-40	21

Seat mounted plaques (shown above right)

Name	Service	Date Died	Age
AUSTIN, Harry	Royal Artillery	26-Mar-42	35
BAKER, Leonard Percy	The King's Regiment (Liverpool)	16-Jul-44	30
BEACH, Norman Joseph James	Royal Army Service Corps	15-Oct-44	20

---

[146] *East Kent Gazette.* 8 April 1992. p. 10. Findmypast.co.uk.

[147] *East Kent Gazette.* 22 July 1992. p. 11. Findmypast.co.uk.

Name	Service	Date Died	Age
BOURNE, Maud Elizabeth	Civilian casualty	07-Jul-44	20
BRANCH, Ernest Harry	Royal Armoured Corps	06-Sep-44	29
BRISSENDEN, Arthur Albert	Royal Navy	18-Aug-40	22
BROOKS, Edward William	Hampshire Regiment	01-Nov-43	23
BUNYARD, Frank Edwin	Royal Marines	01-Dec-44	22
CHITTENDEN, John Albert	The Buffs (Royal East Kent Regiment)	20-Mar-42	29
CLAYTON, Leslie Malum	The Buffs (Royal East Kent Regiment)	16-Nov-43	32
CLEY, F	(See ELEY on next page)		
COLE, Sydney	Notts Yeomanry, Royal Armoured Corps	25-Oct-42	23
COLEMAN, Richard Sidney	Royal Marines	05-Jan-43	30
CRUTCHLEY, Gladys Rose	Civilian casualty	29-Sep-40	24
CRUTCHLEY, John Michael	Civilian casualty	29-Sep-40	2 months
DAVIES, Raymond Leonard	Queen's Own Royal West Kent Regiment	16-Dec-43	25
FIDLER, George	Queen's Own Royal West Kent Regiment	14-Apr-44	22
FORGAY, J	(Unidentified to date)		
FOSBREY, B	(Unidentified to date)		
FOWLER, Kate Elizabeth	Civilian casualty	29-Sep-40	59
GAMBELL, Nellie	Civilian casualty	29-Sep-40	67
GODFREY, Maurice Frederick	Royal Air Force Volunteer Reserve	20-Feb-44	21
GORE, Alfred	Royal Navy	01-Jun-40	43
GREEN, William Henry	Royal Air Force Volunteer Reserve	07-Nov-44	29
HALL, Robert Knowles	Royal Air Force Volunteer Reserve	22-Jul-44	22
HODGES, Percy Harold	Dorsetshire Regiment	26-Jul-43	34
HODGES, R	(Unidentified to date)		
HOUGHTON, Roy William L	Royal Air Force Volunteer Reserve	08-Aug-43	20
HUBBARD, Eric Ronald	Irish Guards	21-Feb-45	19
HUGHES, Robert Henry	Royal Air Force Volunteer Reserve	14-Oct-44	25
JEFFERY, Raymond Percy	Royal Inniskilling Fusiliers	18-Jan-43	29
JEFFERY, William George	Royal Air Force Volunteer Reserve	11-Aug-44	22
JEMMETT, Leslie Lloyd	The Buffs (Royal East Kent Regiment)	21-May-40	20
KEMP, Stephen Frank	Royal Navy	17-Dec-42	39
KINGSNORTH, Cyril Leslie	Royal Air Force Volunteer Reserve	24-Sep-43	21
KITNEY, M	(Unidentified to date)		
KITNEY, Ralph	Royal Air Force Volunteer Reserve	02-Apr-42	21
LUMBY, Walter Ernest	Hong Kong Dockyard Defence Corps	17-Jan-45	59
MACLAREN, Thomas Arthur	Royal Navy	02-Oct-42	39
MANN, Leonard	The Buffs (Royal East Kent Regiment)	07-Sep-44	28
MANUELL, Roy	Civilian casualty	30-Sep-40	7
MARTIN, George	Royal Armoured Corps	08-Aug-44	36
MILES, Patrick Christopher	Royal Navy	10-Jan-41	22
MOUNT, Albert George Edward	Royal Air Force Volunteer Reserve	08-Jun-44	19
MOUNT, John Luther	Seaforth Highlanders	01-May-45	24
MURTON, Edward George	Seaforth Highlanders	19-Apr-44	31
NEAVES, Eric John	Royal Army Service Corps	20-Jul-42	27
NEWNHAM, Alfred E	Royal Air Force Volunteer Reserve	14-Mar-44	24
NORRIS, Ronald William David	Royal Air Force Volunteer Reserve	23-Apr-44	21
PACK, Ernest Frederick John	Royal Navy	13-Mar-42	31
PACKHAM, John Albert	Middlesex Regiment	19-Jan-45	24
PALMER, Ivo	Royal Navy	19-Dec-41	27

Name	Service	Date Died	Age
POTTER, Roland Albert	Royal Fusiliers (City of London Regiment)	11-Feb-45	30
PUXTY, Ernest Frank Edward	Royal Army Service Corps	14-Jun-40	27
RAYFIELD, Albert Frederick V	Royal Engineers	04-Oct-44	29
RAYFIELD, Horace Charles	Royal Navy	16-Apr-43	25
REEVES, Ronald George R	Royal Navy	30-May-41	30
RICHARDSON, Cecil John	Royal Air Force Volunteer Reserve	08-Feb-42	32
RIDDEN, Charles Ernest	The Buffs (Royal East Kent Regiment)	21-May-40	20
ROGERS, Edward John	Queen's Royal (West Surrey) Regiment	29-Apr-43	22
SCALES, Edward George	Durham Light Infantry	17-Jul-44	31
SELLEN, James Alec	The Buffs (Royal East Kent Regiment)	17-Jun-40	24
SHILLING, Albert	Hampshire Regiment	26-Feb-43	20
SHOEBRIDGE, A A	(See SHOOBRIDGE)		
SHOOBRIDGE, Arthur George	Royal Navy	05-Apr-42	40
SHRUBSALL, Leonard Richard J	Royal Air Force Volunteer Reserve	29-Mar-43	29
SIMMONS, Ronald Charles	Royal Air Force Volunteer Reserve	05-Dec-42	21
SKINNER, Dennis James	Civilian casualty	29-Sep-40	17
SPICE, K	(Unidentified to date)		
STOKES, Sydney James	Royal Air Force Volunteer Reserve	15-Nov-41	29
TAYLOR, P C	(Unidentified to date)		
THOMPSON, Kenneth James W	Royal Hampshire Regiment	03-Oct-44	18
TURNER, William George	Royal Artillery	09-Nov-42	41
WHEELER, Douglas John	Royal Navy	09-Dec-42	23
WHEELER, Leslie Walter	Grenadier Guards	05-Nov-44	24
WHISKIN, Thomas Edward	Royal Army Service Corps	09-Apr-44	20
WILDISH, James Alfred David	Royal Air Force Volunteer Reserve	29-Oct-42	28
WRAIGHT, Sidney Albert G	Royal Air Force Volunteer Reserve	09-Feb-43	22

War Memorial (pictured below)

Name	Service	Date Died	Age
BARRY, Terence	Royal Ulster Rifles	05-Dec-43	22
BOURNE, Alexander Hamilton	Queen's Own Royal West Kent Regiment	05-Oct-45	26
BRICE, Leslie Ronald	Dorsetshire Regiment	06-Jun-44	23
ELEY, Frederick William James	Notts Yeomanry, Royal Armoured Corps	14-Aug-44	21
FOSBRAEY, John Edward (Jack)	The Buffs (Royal East Kent Regiment)	13-Nov-43	30
GREEN, Charles Frank	The Queens Own Royal West Kent (The Buffs)	30-Apr-43	25
WHITEHEAD, Raymond T	Royal Air Force Volunteer Reserve	28-Nov-43	21

Glossary of Abbreviations and Acronyms

2/Lt	Second Lieutenant – junior commissioned officer – subaltern/ensign
ADC	Aide-de-Camp, a military officer acting as a confidential assistant to a senior officer
ADS	Advanced Dressing Station
ARP	Air Raid Precaution - WW2 civil defence
BSc	Batchelor of Science, a degree focused on sciences, mathematics, or engineering
CB	Companions of the Order of the Bath
CCS	Casualty Clearing Station
CSM	Command Sergeant Major
DCM	Distinguished Conduct Medal
DD	Doctor of Divinity, the holder of an advanced academic degree in divinity
DSO	Distinguished Service Order
FRIBA	Fellow of the Royal Institute of British Architects
GCIE	Grand Knight Commander of the Most Eminent Order of the Indian Empire
GCSI	Grand Knight Commander of the Order of the Star of India
HAC	Honourable Artillery Company - Territorial Army unit
HMAT	His Majesty's Australian Transport
HMS	His Majesty's Ship
HMT	His Majesty's Transport Ship
IWGC	Imperial War Graves Commission
Lt	Lieutenant - junior commissioned officer – also referred to as a subaltern
MA	Master of Arts, a master's degree awarded by universities
MM	Military Medal
NCO	Non-Commissioned Officer, achieved the rank of officer by rising from the lower ranks rather than by receiving a commission
PLC	Public Limited Company
RFC	Royal Flying Corps
RMLI	Royal Marine Light Infantry
Sap	A military term – covered battlefield trench
SMS	Seiner Majestät Schiff, translates to His Majesty's Ship
SNLR	Services no longer required
SS	Steamship
TD	Territorial Decoration
TSS	Troop Transport Ship
VAD	Voluntary Aid Detachment – civilian support to military medical services
VC	Victoria Cross – The highest military decoration
Billets	Military term – accommodation for military personnel
Bombing	Military term – infantry offensive operations using hand-grenades
Cantonment	A permanent military station in British India
Lewis Gun	A machine gun
Mortar	Military Term – an artillery piece that fires a shell in a high arc
Platoon Sergt	Platoon Sergeant / Serjeant
Territorials	Territorial Army – reserve army units established for home defence but could support regular army on foreign operations
The Buffs	Infantry Regiment – The Buffs (Royal East Kent Regiment)
Vickers Gun	A machine gun

Army Hierarchy

Army Units

The table below shows the hierarchy and size of army units (men being a body of people).

Name of Army Unit	Strength of Unit
Section	10 - 14 men
Platoon	40 - 50 men
Company	160 - 200 men
Battalion / Regiment	800 - 1,000 men
Brigade	3,000 - 4,000 men
Division	10,000 - 12,000 men
Corps	20,000+ men
Army	40,000+ men

Non-Commissioned Ranks

The following lists the non-commissioned ranks within the army, in order of seniority, from the lowest rank up to the highest.

Private   An ordinary soldier. He may be appointed to Lance-Corporal.

Corporal   Typically the senior non-commissioned rank in charge of a Section in an infantry battalion, and may be appointed to Lance-Sergeant in a Guards Regiment.

Sergeant / Serjeant	Typically the senior non-commissioned rank in charge of a Platoon in an infantry battalion. Serjeant with a 'J' was used in the British Army up until 1914, though inter-changed. The 'J' spelling remained the official one into the 1930s, when it was finally displaced, however, some units retain the 'J' spelling as a tradition.
	The title of the rank of Corporal and Sergeant is sometimes seen modified by the specialist trade of the soldier, such as Corporal-Wheeler or Sergeant-Cook.
Colour-Sergeant	The rank from which a man may typically be appointed to Company Sergeant Major or Company Quartermaster Sergeant.
Warrant Officer Class II	Rank introduced by Army Order 70 of 1915, becoming that rank from which a man may typically be appointed to Company Sergeant Major or Regimental Quartermaster Sergeant. (The Colour-Sergeant could no longer be appointed as a Company Sergeant Major).
Warrant Officer Class I	The rank from which a man may typically be appointed to Regimental Sergeant Major.

Commissioned Ranks

Second-Lieutenant	Ensign in a Guards Regiment (Platoon)
Lieutenant	Which with Second Lieutenant referred to as a subaltern (Platoon)
Captain	Company Commander
Major	Officer of field rank - Battalion second in command
Lieutenant-Colonel	Officer of field rank - Command of a Battalion viz 4th Battalion the Buffs
Colonel	Officer of field rank - (a staff officer rank rather than for operational purposes)
Brigadier-General	Officer of field rank - Brigade Commander viz 1st Brigade
Major-General	Divisional Commander viz 1st Division
Lieutenant-General	Corps Commander viz 1st Corps
General	Commander of an Army viz 1st Army
Field-Marshal	Commander of a grouping of Armies. The highest rank in the British Army since 1736.

Royal Navy Rank Structure

Non-Commissioned Ratings

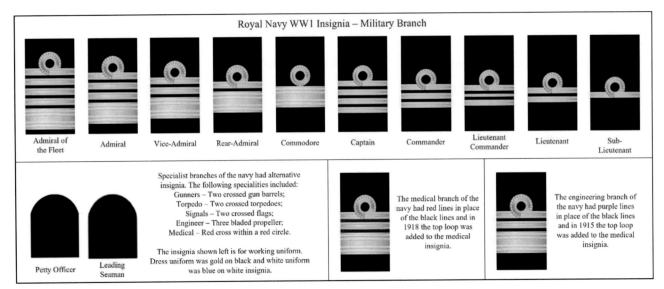

Royal Navy WW1 Insignia – Military Branch

Admiral of the Fleet | Admiral | Vice-Admiral | Rear-Admiral | Commodore | Captain | Commander | Lieutenant Commander | Lieutenant | Sub-Lieutenant

Petty Officer | Leading Seaman

Specialist branches of the navy had alternative insignia. The following specialities included:
Gunners – Two crossed gun barrels;
Torpedo – Two crossed torpedoes;
Signals – Two crossed flags;
Engineer – Three bladed propeller;
Medical – Red cross within a red circle.

The insignia shown left is for working uniform. Dress uniform was gold on black and white uniform was blue on white insignia.

The medical branch of the navy had red lines in place of the black lines and in 1918 the top loop was added to the medical insignia.

The engineering branch of the navy had purple lines in place of the black lines and in 1915 the top loop was added to the medical insignia.

Boy 1st and 2nd class	Junior rank aged between 15 and 16 years.
Ordinary Seaman	The rank at which all adult ratings started in the navy.
Able Seaman	Lowest rank for a navy rating and achieved on completion of training.
Leading Seaman	Responsibility for a group of Able Seamen.
Petty Officer	Responsibility for a section within a department.
Chief Petty Officer	Interface between officers and ratings.

Note: Ranks could reflect a particular trade or branch, viz – Chief Petty Officer's may be referred to as - Chief Stoker or Chief Yeoman of Signals.

Commissioned Officers

Midshipman	Starting rank for officers in the navy, since 1837.
Sub-Lieutenant	Automatic promotion from Midshipman after one year.
Lieutenant	Promotion gained after meeting expected standards.
Lieutenant Commander	Responsible for leading a department.
Commander	Commanded a ship or more senior position on shore.
Captain	Commanded a large ship or more senior position on shore.
Commodore	Senior officer for at least two naval vessels.
Rear-Admiral	Officer in charge of the rear section of a fleet and flies their flag on the ship.
Vice-Admiral	Commanded a fleet of warships and auxiliaries.
Admiral	Highest rank that a serving officer can be promoted to, and commanded a fleet or group of ships or held a naval post on shore.
Admiral of the Fleet	Highest rank of the Royal Navy since 1688.

Note: Ranks could reflect a particular branch, for example the Royal Naval Air Service – ranks reflected the flying aspect, viz - a Lieutenant Commander would be referred to as Squadron or a Commander as a Wing Commander.

Index

Other titles available by the Historical Research Group of Sittingbourne

THEIR NAME LIVETH
FOR EVERMORE

Sunshine Passes

Shadows Fall

But Love and Remembrance

Outlast All